CORREGIDOR

OASIS of HOPE

50th Anniversary
Bataan — Corregidor
By
ASBURY L. NIX, CWO, RET.

Library of Congress Catalog Card Number: 92-060804

ISBN: 0-942495-19-5

Distributed by Trade Winds Publications Co.
1541 Ellis St.
Stevens Point, WI 54481

Printed in the United States of America by
Palmer Publications, Inc.
Amherst, Wisconsin 54406

Dedication

In memory of those who made
the supreme sacrifice in the
defense of freedom

MANILA AMERICAN CEMETERY AND MEMORIAL
Fort Bonifacio, Republic of the Philippines
Courtesy of American Battle Monuments Commission and David Obey

Acknowledgements

The author wishes to express his sincere appreciation to the multitude of sources that made this book possible. The support and encouragement of my wife of 46 years, Hazel, and family during the past three years in development of the final manuscript.

Richard E. Francies and Clifford Keller, who furnished many of the rare photographs of the Philippines. Adrian Martin provided valuable information during his research for his book, *Brothers from Bataan, POWs 1942-1945.*

The authors who have published books on the same general subject. Parts of their experiences serve to illustrate the big picture of life as a prisoner of war and their fates during captivity. Every effort has been made to acknowledge their contribution to American history.

In Our Image, America's Empire in the Philippines by Stanley Karnow, is quoted for his very graphic description of the beautiful islands of the Philippine Archipelago. Mr. Karnow's brilliant work describes the colorful and exciting history of the Philippine society, cultures, economics, geographical, and political life spanning five centuries of Spanish and American domination of the Philippines. This work is deemed essential to historians in understanding the islands and its people.

Our Paradise, A GI's War Diary by Ernest O. Norquist, and *Brothers from Battan, POWs 1942-1945* by Adrian Martin are corroboration of the events beginning with the shipment to Japan in August, 1944 and the final year in Hanawa, Japan.

Bataan Diary by Dr. Paul Ashton; *The War Diaries of Weary Dunlop* by E.E. Dunlop are excellent accounts of the prisoner of war experience from a medical viewpoint. Dr. Ashton and Dr. Dunlop present in great detail the frustration of the Allied medical personnel in attempting to alleviate the sufferings of the prisoners with absolute minimum or non-existence of any reasonable facilities, equip-ment or medicinal supplies. Thousands died from sheer debilitation and disease that could have been prevented with proper medical attention. Dr. Ashton was an American doctor and served in the Philippines. Dr. Dunlop was an Australian in Java and the Burma-Thailand Railway. Their accounts parallel the problems of the medical profession in dealing with an oriental attitude toward the sufferings of prisoners of war in two different areas.

Captured on Corregidor, Diary of an American POW in World War II by John M. Wright Jr. Lt. Gen. Ret.

Surrender and Survival, The Experiences of American POWs by E. Bartlett Kerr.

Some Survived, An Epic Account of Japanese Captivity in World War II by Manny Lawton.

Blood Brothers, A Medic's Sketch Book by Eugene C. Jacobs. Col. Ret.

The above authors' gripping accounts of the fateful voyage of the Hell-Ships, *Oryoku Maru, Enoura Maru* and the *Brazil Maru* are indicative of the fate of prisoners of war subjected to incalculable dangers during transport in unmarked ships. Quotes from their stirring accounts are used in substantiation of the terrible treatment of hapless human beings in wartime. These accounts are the epitome of the total brutal disregard of all human rights of prisoners of war.

The Other Nuremberg, the Untold Story of The Tokyo War Crimes Trials by Arnold C. Brackman. The story of the war crimes perpetrated on Allied prisoners of war are described accurately and very eloquently by Mr. Brackman in his book. Over 90,000 documents and transcripts were reviewed in preparation. The International Military Tribunal's final complex judicial decisions and sentences were executed. Many of Japan's wartime leaders and lower level military were tried, convicted, executed, or imprisoned as a result of these lengthy trials. Each ex-prisoner of war and future generations of scholars and historians

Acknowledgements (continued)

should read this final chapter. It is important to understand and evaluate the overall causes and results of the mysteries of the oriental concept of moral values in World War II.

United States Submarine Operations in World War II by Theodore Roscoe. This excellent account of submarine patrol reports, maps and photos are quoted for purposes of illustrating the complex problem of identifying legitimate targets and the inevitable loss of prisoners of war traveling in unmarked armed enemy merchant vessels. The rescuing of stranded survivors by submarines is seldom possible under wartime conditions. The dramatic rescue account in Part Eight was an epic rescue to be remembered.

Other publications germane to this dark period are listed in the Bibliography for historical reference. Many are out of print and very rare.

Contents

Acknowledgements v
Prologue ix
Part One, The Dark Clouds of War 1
Part Two, The Fortunate, Not So Fortunate, Unfortunate 27
Part Three, The Fortunate 59
Part Four, The Japanese Prison System 71
Part Five, Cruise of the *Noto Maru* 91
Part Six, Mitsubishi Copper Mine 107
Part Seven, The Freedom Train 131
Part Eight, The Unfortunate 147
Epilogue 173
Appendix 1, Personnel Roster 179
Appendix 2, Order of Battle 181
Appendix 3, Main Armament 182
Appendix 4, Corregidor, POW Camp No. 9 183
Appendix 5, Hell Ships 187
Appendix 6, *Notu Maru* 189
Appendix 7, Work Details 203
List of Illustrations, Sketches & Maps 211
Index 212
Bibliography 214

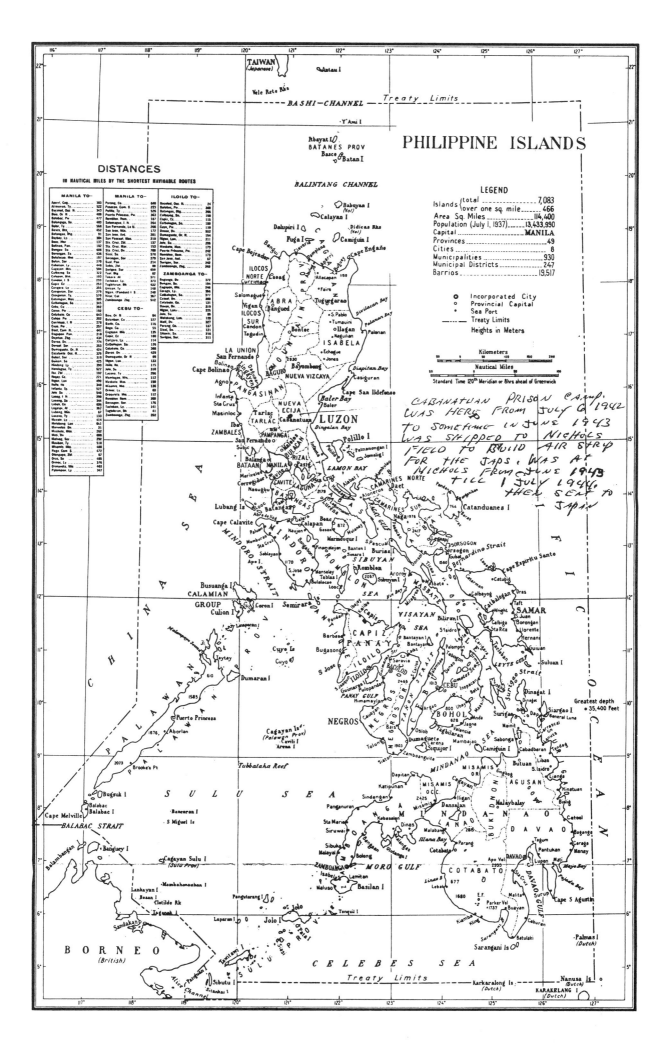

PHILIPPINE ISLANDS

DISTANCES
IN NAUTICAL MILES BY THE SHORTEST NAVIGABLE ROUTES

LEGEND

Islands total	7,083
Islands over one sq. mile	466
Area Sq. Miles	114,400
Population (July 1, 1937)	13,433,990
Capital	MANILA
Provinces	49
Cities	8
Municipalities	930
Municipal Districts	247
Barrios	19,517

○ Incorporated City
◦ Provincial Capital
▪ Sea Port
– – – Treaty Limits
–––– Heights in Meters

Kilometers
Nautical Miles
Standard Time 120th Meridian or 8hrs ahead of Greenwich

CORREGIDOR

OASIS OF HOPE

PROLOGUE

A PRISONER OF WAR
1942-1945

ASBURY L. NIX
CWO RET.

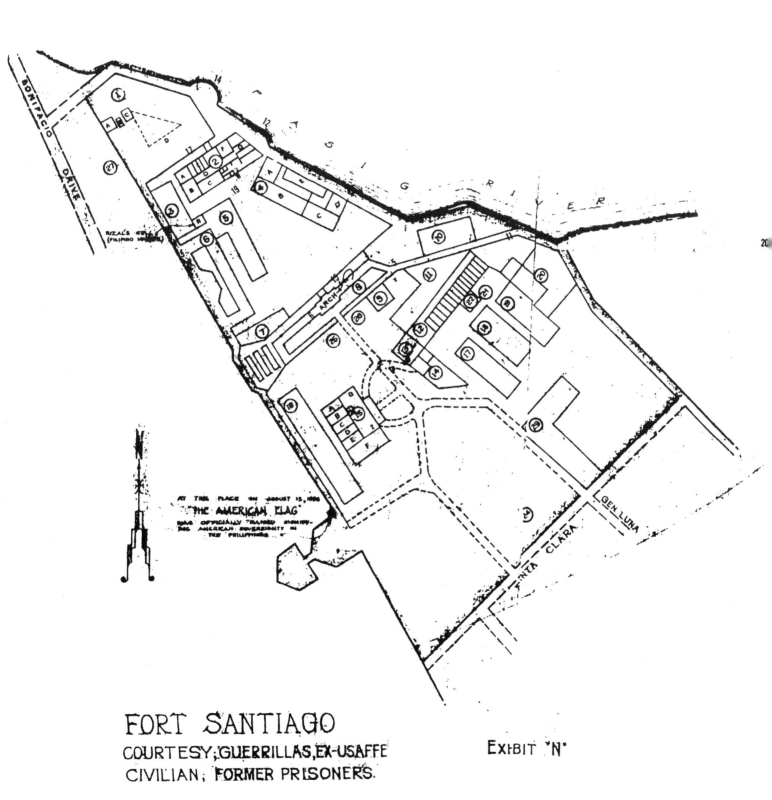

FORT SANTIAGO
COURTESY; GUERRILLAS, EX-USAFFE
CIVILIAN; FORMER PRISONERS.

EXHIBIT "N"

LEGEND
FORT SANTIAGO
MANILA P. I.

Fort Santiagi was used by the Japanese during the occupation of Manila as Kempetai Headquarters The map shows the location of the main part of the Fort.

1. Kempetai Headquarters, Manila Unit.

   a. Major Nishimura*s Office

   b. Adjutant's Office

   c. Underground cells

2. Torture rooms, Investigation and electric and water

   a. Detention Cells

   b. Interrogation room and torture chambers

   c. Japanese galley and mess hall

   d, Stairways

   e, f, g & ,h Detention cells

3. Garage

4. Quarters and Infirmary, cells below

   a. Detention cell

   b, Quarters

   c. Infirmary

   d. Doctors quarters

   e. Under ground cells and second floor certure
l   chambers, interrogation rooms

5. Officers Quarters

6. Jose Rizal's cell, Filipino patrriot, executed by the Spanish.

6. Kitchen

7. Lecture and Tagalog classroom

8. Arch- Inside were Jap Officers quarters

9. Garage

10. Bath house

11. Stable

12. Sixteen detention cells

13. Water cure detention cell

14. Men and womens bath house and torture

   Chambers

15. Administration Bldg. Col. Nagahama Office and

   Filipino informers., cells a,b,c,d   e were coccupied
by Americans.Coonelss .Straughn, Santos T

Noble, Nakarm Capt, Barker abd Gen. Grant and Martin Moses

   F, Quarters

   G. Office

   H. Toilet

   I. Guard room

16. Quarters

17. Tool Shed

18. Repair shop

19. &20 Shed

21.. Water Faucet for prisoners

22. Guardhouse

23. Barracks

24. Main Gate

24-27 Garden tended by prisoners for Japanese

Courtesy of Dr. Paul Ashton

Many prisoners never survived the hell of the old Fort Santiago, They were put to death or died in prison. Several survived to tell of the horrors, hellish torment for those unfortunate to fall into the hands of the dreadful Secret Police, (Kempetai).

Fort Santiago was used as the Headquarters for the United States Forces in the Philippines prior to the outbreak of the war. Fort Santiago was an integral part of the overall Intramuros (Walled City). Its history goes back to 1571 when wooden walls were built to repel or ward off early Chinese pirates. The massive walls were constructed 1n 1580 and were built from some of the heavy stones used as ballast for ships coming to the Islands in the 14th century. It was protected by a double moat with water from the Pasig River. The fort was planned and built by Miguel Lopez de Lagaspi.

Some of the cells below ground were subject to flooding and were a part of the torture of prisoners in the lower cells. The Intramuros was completely destroyed by Americans when the Japanese Navy and Marines holed up in the Walled City. The gates were blasted to allow tanks to enter.

The Philippine government has restored some of the old city and plans to repair the numerous gates that were damaged. This program was started by President and Mrs. Marcos.

Prologue

The Southern Pacific train rattled across the vast plains of the southwest in early June of 1939, bearing innocent army recruits bound for the Philippines. The recruits were oblivious to the future. They were leaving their homes for adventure and travel to far off places. They were the flotsam of the depression and would soon be cast upon the shores of America's Empire in the Pacific. Their names would forever be entered into the fabric of history as America's Foreign Legion. Destined to defeat, humiliation and death as prisoners of war of a country, they knew as a source of cheap souvenirs with the label, "Made in Japan." They would enjoy their short sojourn in the tropical paradise that would soon evolve into the horrors of war and the hell of prisoners of war. They were the first line of defense and expendable for America's complacency and lack of preparation for war.

American soldiers who have served in the beautiful islands of the Philippines, since Admiral Dewey sank the Spanish fleet, have either been impressed or disillusioned. The impact upon one's mind when first stepping ashore is one of excitement, exuberance and the thrill of being in a tropical paradise. An army band greets you with martial music and everyone is overjoyed. Everywhere there are a multitude of unfamiliar sights. Beautiful palm trees line the streets, hundreds of flowers bloom everywhere, the skies are an azure blue with soft shadows, the cool breezes blow in from the bay and everything seems like a picture from a travel brochure.

The first flush of excitement becomes one of realization of being so far from home and how are you going to cope with working and living in this strange land. Such a marvelous contrast to the hills of central Texas. Arrival at your assigned post gives you the impression that life here is not going to be bad at all. Beautiful clean barracks, spacious lawns and plenty of recreational facilities. Clark Field, Fort Stotensberg, Fort McKinley or Corregidor, with their outlying islands, are dream places for a soldier. Duty hours are 0600 to 1300 hours, five days a week. Filipino house boys clean the barracks, make the beds, shine shoes, take care of laundry, no working in the kitchen. Filipinos do all of the kitchen police (K.P.) duty. Hair cuts twice a month and a shave each day by a barber for four pesos ($2.00) a month. The only duty is maybe guard, charge of quarters and other military duties. Siesta time from 1400 to 1600 hours, mandatory quiet in the barracks. Not bad duty for $21.00 a month plus good food and clothing. Pass policies are generous. The life of the peacetime soldier in the Philippines was great for the professional soldier. Evenings there were the clubs on base, snack bar, theaters, interunit sports events and educational facilities.

The night life was fast and many choices were available in the cabarets, and many bars catering to the American soldiers with dance hall girls at a dime a dance. Dark skinned olive eyed beauties with black hair at every hand. Maybe a bicycle ride along the many picturesque boulevards or ride an English-style double decker bus along scenic Dewey-Boulevard for a few centavos. The first few months are truly an adventure. Soon the glamour begins to fade and some start to refer to the Filipinos as ignorant, dirty and primitive Gooks. These men soon fall into the clutches of alcoholic euphoria of San Midget Genebra (gin) at .35 or .40 centavos a fifth and are lost in the arms of John Barley corn. Some even fake insanity and seek a Section Eight discharge (convenience of the government). The opportunities for education, travel and sight-seeing are numerous.

The beautiful city of Baguio, the summer capitol, high in the mountains of northern Luzon makes one think of home. Tall pine trees, clean clear air and plenty of places to explore, cool nights and no mosquitoes make this reminiscent of home. A short bus trip from Baguio are the fabulous verdant green terraced rice paddies, climbing the mountains like giant steps into the mists above. Truly a stupendous irrigating project to utilize the tropical rainfall to the maximum for growing rice.

High school geography books touch only lightly with a brief description of economy, exports, culture and a very brief outline of a countries history. They fall short in describing the great beauty of this tropical paradise. The Philippines have a long history dating back to the earliest days of exploration by the seafaring men of Spain, Portugal and other maritime nations at the turn of the 14th Century.

Stanley Karnow's book, *In Our Image, America's Empire in the Philippines*, presents an interesting narrative picture of these fantastic islands. "The Spanish settlers and Americans who came centuries later were overwhelmed by the beauty of the Philippines. Their wonderment was not misplaced. The archipelago, one of natures glories, is indeed a brilliant tapestry of land, sea, sky, fields, mountains, wildlife and people. All so dazzling and diverse as to seem unreal.

Seven thousand islands spread for a thousand miles from north to south like pieces broken from the mainland of Asia. Only a thousand islands are inhabited and only a few larger than one square mile. Their topography is a quilt of contrasts. Lush green plains and verdant hills stretch out against a horizon of jungled clad peaks as high as 10,000 feet, some active volcanos. Placid lagoons encircled by coral reefs, bathe fine white sand and elsewhere the surf dashes against rugged cliffs, with a coast line longer than the United States.

Everywhere is near the sea, itself a study of extremes. Shallow channels separate the islands, while the ocean off Mindanao, plunges down six miles, the deepest spot on earth. Monsoon rains fall with biblical intensity bringing fertility and decay.

The Philippines are ablaze with flora and fauna. Rich forests of mahogany, rattan, bamboo and palms of a dozen varieties blanket its landscape. Tropical flowers and nearly a thousand varieties of orchids bloom everywhere. The forest abounds in animal life, monkeys, wild boar, savage buffalo (tamarao), and giant bats; and reptiles such as cobras, pythons and iguanas. Specialists have not yet fully classified its vast assortment of exotic birds and species of multico-

Map of Philippines and surrounding area. By Engineer Department, U.S. Army. Courtesy Clifford J. Keller.

lored butterflies. The smallest known fish, (pondoka pygemaea) inhabits its surrounding waters along with tuna, sharks, barracudas, lapa-lapa, porcupine fish, stingrays, giant green turtles, oysters the size of soup bowls, and clams as big as bathtubs. Its prized shells fetch fancy prices on world markets.

Dissimilarity also characterizes the Filipino people. They speak eight different languages and some seventy dialects and the linguistic jumble is only one clue to their variety. The Illacono's of northwest Luzon, a relatively arid area, austere and venturesome and make up many of the immigrants to Hawaii and California. The Tagalogs from the central area of Luzon are protypical Filipinos because of their political, professional and cultural preeminence. But Tagalogs differ among themselves according to region and all the people of Luzon consider themselves to be distinct from the Vasayans, who have spread out from their central islands to exploit Mindanao and the Sulu Archipelago—the terrain of Mindanao all most perpetually dissident Muslim called Moros.

Meanwhile aboriginal tribes like the Illfugos, Bontocs, Aetas and Illongots, former head-hunters roam the highland jungles as they have for millennia."

This was the Philippines in all of it's glory. One had only to be objective and look behind the scenes to appreciate it's beauty. Little did I realize that this was to be my home for over five years, when I first set foot on the shores of Luzon and the streets of Manila, the Pearl of the Orient.

I had left the cotton fields of Texas, seeking the good things of life. The depression and the slow recovery had unwittingly prepared me for what lay in the not too distant future. I had been used to a strict father, who mandated instant obedience without question. The army discipline was strict and I was prepared to make the most of any opportunities.

Two years of an idyllic atmosphere, euphoric pleasantries and avid interest in the history, culture, customs and the friendly nature of the people, cast a spell over my mind. This is the one and only place and the rest of the world fades into the distance.

In September 1939 on the opposite side of the world a small, evil, black cloud appeared on the distant horizon. The Nazi's under Adolph Hitler invaded Poland. More ominous clouds began to form as Britain and France tried appeasement while they rattled their sabers. The war clouds grew darker and more dangerous as the year 1940 rolled by. We read of these in newspapers and magazines and discussed them in the barracks and work place. I was due to rotate in May of 1941 for return to the states. I decided that I would extend to the following February. Soldiering was great in this fantastic land. I had interesting duty, knew my way around the town, was on friendly terms with the Filipinos in the shop and the civilians outside. I had attained a respectable rating of PVT. 1st Class Specialist which doubled my pay. I took a job in my spare time at Santa Ana Race Track on weekends. I was ready to ride this gravy train with biscuit wheels to the end of my enlistment.

My old stateside flame had married and I was too wrapped up in the pleasantries of life to read the handwriting on the wall. New equipment, airplanes, trucks and new troop units began flooding into the islands. Troop units like the New Mexico National Guard 200th CAC (AA), 192nd and 194th Tank Battalions, new bomber wings with modern B-17's, and modern P-40 fighters to replace the obsolete aircraft. The increased military activity sent no signals of alarm bells into my blinded mind. General MacArthur had been recalled to active duty and was now the Com-

mander of United States Forces in the Far East (USAF-FE). The British Battleships H.M.S. Repulse and Prince of Wales had dropped anchor in Manila Bay enroute to Singapore. We were able to meet some of the British sailors and talk about the war in Europe. Their reply to our questions were "No speak English."

The dark storm clouds of war were slowly creeping into the pacific beauty of the Philippines. Ignorance is bliss and the silver lining was passing into reality. The typhoon of war with its black clouds swept into the placid islands like the foul breath of nature. Never again would the islands recover their former glory. Only the survivors could remember Manila as the fabulous Pearl of the Orient.

The month of November 1941 had been an exciting and extremely busy one for the small detachment in the port area of Manila. Ships were coming in loaded with all types of new equipment and new troop units. Our work of inspection, servicing and distributing the multitude of new equipment afforded little time for reading the handwriting on the wall. December payday gave us a respite and we had a big steak fry at one of the men's houses off post with lots of White Horse Scotch and broiled steaks. The weekend of December 7 would see the end of paradise and the beginning of hell descend on our little bit of jungled islands.

Monday morning of December 8, 1941, I could not believe the Manila newspapers or the voice of Don Bell, the radio broadcaster. "PEARL HARBOR BOMBED BY THE JAPANESE, WAR IS DECLARED." Everyone was shocked, incredulous, unbelieving. Pandemonium broke out—draw weapons, ammunition, helmets, gas masks, roll field packs, expedite vehicle processing, dig trenches for air raids, fill fire buckets, everyone rushing pellmell on some assignment, false air raids and hordes of planes bombing Cavite Navy Base. Possible invasion by airborne paratroopers or land forces kept us nervous and scanning the skies, with ears to the radio listening for news from Hawaii and damages to the fleet. Our first day at war and not a sign of the enemy. Night brought more confusion, blackout, no passes, everyone tense and alert. Even the alcoholics were sober. Intense dis-

xviii

cussion of the probabilities of tomorrow, voices raised insisting that we would not be attacked. The Japanese would not be that foolish, they would be wiped out in two weeks. The Asiatic fleet had gone out to do battle. A myriad of rumors cast a cloud of doom on our utopia.

Our introduction into battle was yet to come and we were ready for the struggle. Our morale was high and our enthusiasm knew no bounds. Our hopes were high that Uncle Sam would be there when we needed him.

The Japanese did not see fit to bomb the port area warehouse area, but concentrated on hitting the airbases and the Navy facilities in Cavite, across the bay from Manila. The airfield at Iba, home of the 3rd Pursuit Squadron was wiped out. The dead were brought to the morgue in port area. Any doubts in our minds was erased by the sight of a truckload of mangled bodies and the bombing of Nichols field and Cavite. Many men emptied their weapons at the planes as they banked over Manila. Futile firing of a magazine from a 45 automatic or Springfield rifle released some of the tension and frustrations.

The civilian Filipinos who worked on the depot were bewildered, and could not comprehend the enormity of the situation. Air raid alarms were frequent. The Filipinos would scatter to the four winds. Hasty evacuation of the warehouse began and troops were dispatched to alternate locations. The motor transport detachment moved into the Santa Ana Race Track while a temporary shop was set up in the Santa Ana Cockpit. Incredible but the first night in our new quarters, I slept under one of the tables of the restaurant in the owners section of the grandstands. This seemed odd in that I had worked there two weeks before and had lunch in the same place that was now our quarters.

The city was in turmoil, the people were frightened and asking what was going to happen to them. The entire city was blacked out with many false air raid alarms. Each time the air raid alarm was sounded the people would dash into the streets looking for some shelter in drainage ditches or culverts. Many reports of saboteurs flashing lights or signals added to the confusion of the civil authorities and the military police. Filipino

drivers would turn on their headlights for a second and then off again, even though they were supposed to be blacked out. Military police had to break many headlights to prevent them from being used.

The strong Japanese landings in Lingayan

USAT Republic

USAT Grant

USAT Meigs

USAT U.S. Grant departing Manila
U.S. Navy Transport Chaumont *and* Henderson *served the*
Naval Forces in the Islands and China.

Gulf, Aparri and the east coast of Luzon forced a change in plans. General Wainwright was to delay the advance towards Manila. This would allow troops from the south to cross a key bridge at Calumpit and swing south into the Bataan Pennisula. General MacArthur decided to declare Manila an open city and ordered all troops out of the city. This decision reduced the possibility of bombing the city and the resultant casualties to the civilian populace. The military hastily collected military stores and loaded barges with food and supplies to be transported to Bataan and Corregidor. Large stocks of fuel stored in tank farms were demolished and a heavy black smoke poured over the city. General MacArthur had planned to defeat the enemy on the landing beaches. However, the situation was critical and he decided to revert to the

Orange Plan, a contingency option that envisioned all units to retreat into the Bataan Pennisula. The defense of Manila Bay from the fortified islands in the bay with the main force holding onto Bataan until relief could be sent from the states.

The order to move out came down and our detachment and the 34th Light Maintenance company (PS) left Manila on December 21, 1941, for Bataan. The road into Bataan after the turn at Calumpit Bridge was choked with military vehicles streaming south. The road was a two lane macadam top with gravel shoulders. The dust from the heavy vehicles rose high in the air. Surprisingly, the Japanese did not strafe or bomb the road. We were fortunate again and the Japanese would regret their inaction. The dark clouds of war had shattered our utopian tropical paradise.

Mount Mayan Volcano last erupted 6 June, 1935. Courtesy Clifford J. Keller.

A marvel of engineering by primitive farmers in mountains north of Baguio on Luzon. Courtesy Richard Francies.

Volcano crater within a volcano crater forming a lake within a lake.

Guadalupe Ruins—Relic of the old Spanish Empire. Founded about 1620.

Illacanos, Irefugos, Bontocs and Igorotes of northern Luzon, were very primitive and spoke different dialects. Courtesy Richard Francies.

Rice was the main staple for the natives. Maximum utilization of rain water in mountain terraces is essential. Courtesy Richard Francies.

This gate was severely damaged in 1944 by direct artillery fire. Courtesy Richard Francies.

Plaque at Fort Santiago. Courtesy Richard Francies.

Bamboo Organ, Las Piñas.

The Bamboo Organ

Father Diego Cera a member of the Agustino Recoletos Friars began the construction of the organ in 1818. The 950 bamboos were covered for six months with sand from the beach to preserve them from the attacks of bamboo bugs.

The work was finished in 1822. Twice the organ was badly damaged, in 1862 by an earthquake, and in 1882 by the rains as the church's roof was blown up. They repaired it partly. The organ has an electric blower since 1932.

In 1917 Father Faniel, a Belgian missionary, completed the repair of the organ with the help of the Las Pinas people. The bamboo organ is the only one of its kind in the world.

The famous Las Pinas Bamboo Organ, constructed in 1862.

Nipa palm house of natives in northern Luzon. Courtesy Richard Francies.

Rural scene.

Escolta shopping center.

Caraamato, near San Agustine Church.

Spanish sentry tower.

Tropical sunset, Manila, P.I.

Entry port, Walled City.

Dewey Blvd. traffic was opposite which made driving difficult with American-made autos (circa 1940). Courtesy Richard Francies.

A home away from home for many service men, YMCA building. Courtesy Richard Francies.

Pasig River with inter-island boats, Manila, P.I. (circa 1940). Courtesy of Richard Francies.

Army-Navy Club. Courtesy Clifford J. Keller.

Observation and photographic flights were the primary missions for the Douglas O-46 in the Philippines (circa 1940).

Pan American Terminal, Canacao Sea Plane Base P.I. (circa 1940). Courtesy Clifford J. Keller.

Army Depot Port Area, Fort Santiago and Pasig River Bridges. Courtesy of Clifford J. Keller.

Constructed by the Spanish in 1590-1593. A nine-hole golf course was built in the original moat around the outer walls. Right center is Quartel De Espana and Santa Lucia Barracks, home of Hqtrs. and 1st Bn. 31st Infantry Regiment.

Central Post Office, Fine Arts Theater, Jones St. and Quezon Bridges (circa 1940). Courtesy Richard Francies.

Manila Hotel. Courtesy Clifford J. Keller.

CORREGIDOR

OASIS OF HOPE

PART ONE

THE DARK CLOUDS OF WAR

Excursion to Togaytay

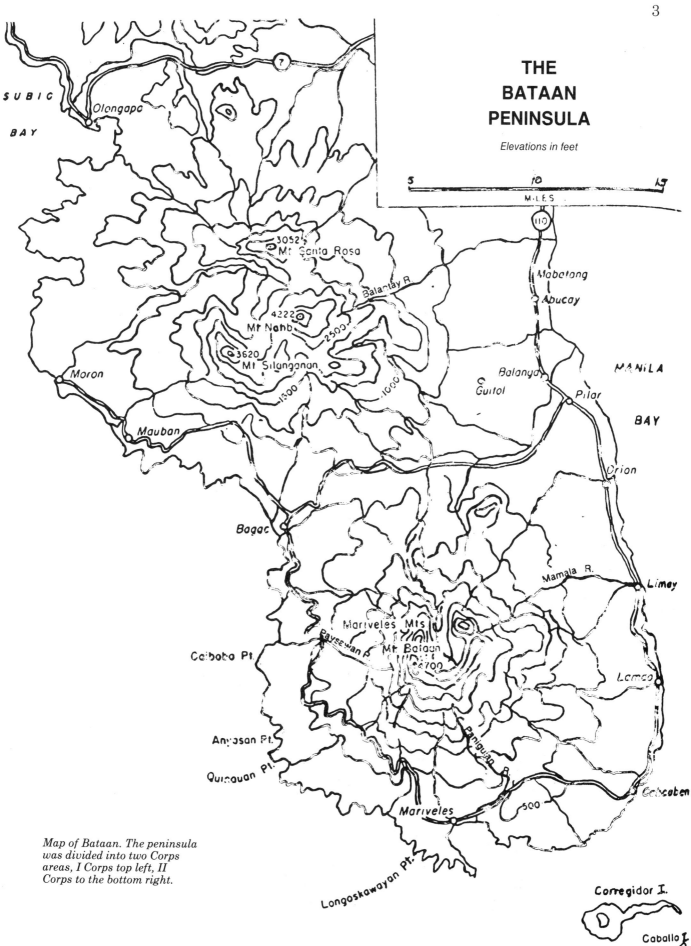

**THE
BATAAN
PENINSULA**

Elevations in feet

5   10   15

M·I·E·S

SUBIC
BAY

Olongapo

Mt Santa Rosa
3052

Balantay R.

4222
Mt Natib

2500

3620
Mt Silanganan

1500

1000

Moron

Mauban

Mabatang

Abucay

Balanga

Guitol

MANILA

Pilar

BAY

Orion

Bagac

Mariveles Mts.
Mt Bataan
4700

Bagac

Pantol

Cabcaben

Anyasan Pt.

Quinauan Pt.

Mariveles

500

Longoskawayan Pt.

Mamala R.

Limay

Lamao

Pantingan R.

Map of Bataan. The peninsula
was divided into two Corps
areas, I Corps top left, II
Corps to the bottom right.

Corregidor I.

Caballo I.

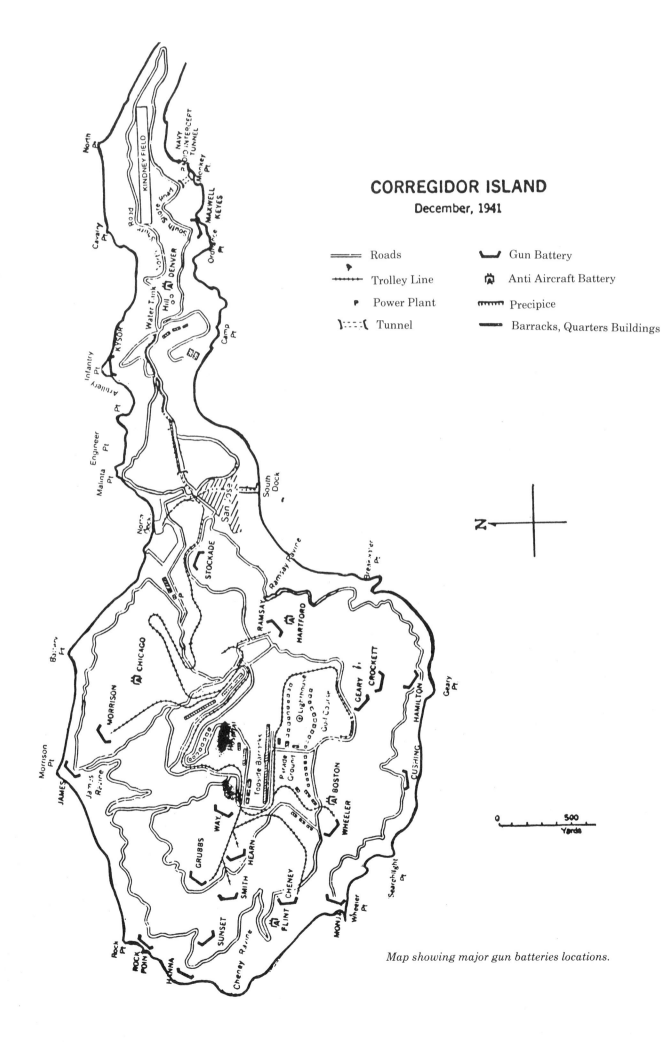

CORREGIDOR ISLAND
December, 1941

Roads		Gun Battery	
Trolley Line		Anti Aircraft Battery	
Power Plant		Precipice	
Tunnel		Barracks, Quarters Buildings	

Map showing major gun batteries locations.

Affectionately called Old Lady USNT Canopus *served as submarine tender. Scuttled April 1942 by crew near Mariveles (circa 1941).* National Archives 80-G-1014615.

Above: the 4th Marines arrived in early November 1941 at Olongapo in Subic Bay. National Archives 117-N-CDT-14312.

Left: elements of the 31st Infantry Regiment, American's Foreign Legion, march through a native village. The regiment saw service in Siberia and China and later in Korea.

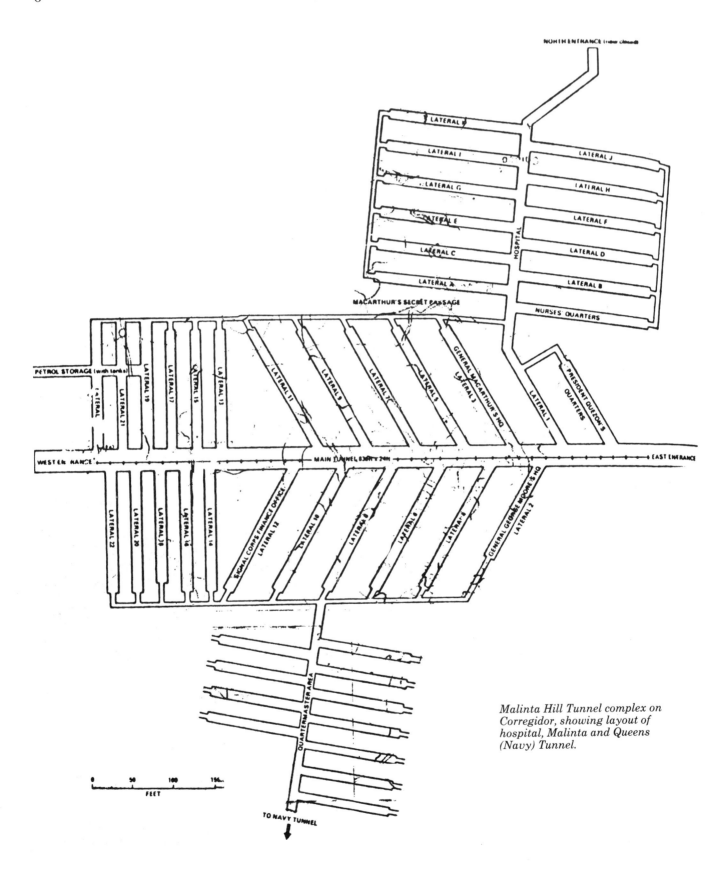

Malinta Hill Tunnel complex on Corregidor, showing layout of hospital, Malinta and Queens (Navy) Tunnel.

USAT Republic and Golden Gate Bridge.

Aerial view of Corregidor. Monkey Point in foreground. National Archives 111-SC-200883.

U.S. ARMY

These boats were used to transport personnel and supplies in the Manila Bay area.

The island was serviced by an electric powered rail system to all parts of the island for personnel and heavy freight.

Part One

The Dark Clouds of War

The tropic sun was slowly disappearing behind the Mariveles Mountains, silhouetted against the brilliant sunset colors of the fading day. The U.S. Army Mine Planter Harrison slowly eased out of the Mariveles Harbor, into Boca Chica Channel, (north channel). I turned and watched the colorful panorama of a tropical sunset. A sight that was ever changing in its beautiful display of colors of the rainbow. As the ship edged out into the channel off Corregidor, I turned to the north and watched the flashes of light and could hear the rumbling of the heavy gun fire of the artillery duel between the Japanese and American forces on the Abucay Line.

I thought of the many friends who were on the line in northern Bataan. The flashes of light grew brighter as darkness descended and the rumbling grew in intensity. The American-Filipino Army was locked in battle. The long struggle for Bataan had begun, with high hopes of American relief as their only source of strength. The undaunted American-Filipino Army was confident. A huge naval force was steaming up from the South China Sea and their struggle would be over. I was day dreaming as we made our way towards the dark mass of land ahead. My thoughts of the future were bright and full of hope and faith in our country and God.

The time was late January of 1942 and I was on my way to a new assignment on Fort Mills, Corregidor. I had just been promoted to staff sergeant and was filled with a renewed sense of duty and the challenges of the future. I had arrived on Bataan Christmas Eve with the 34th Light Maintenance Company (IS), commanded by Capt. Pasha Robbins. The drastic change from a peacetime heavy maintenance shop in Manila to a wartime field shop on Bataan was traumatic. We had to readjust our routine and were providing support to the

combat forces. Our location in the jungle off the road near Little Bagiou was ideal. The dense jungle growth and huge towering trees provided excellent cover.

The hectic change in operations had come suddenly with the outbreak of the war. The warehouses in the port area were prime targets. We had moved out of the port area and established a temporary shop in the Santa Ana Cockpit with quarters in the Santa Ana Race Track dining room. On the 23rd of December, we were ordered to move to Fort Stotsenberg and then were changed to Bataan. The logistic conditions on Bataan were compounded by the multitude of makes and models of vehicles that flooded into Bataan. Every conceivable vehicle had been pressed into service in the hectic evacuation of Manila and the falling back of the forces on Luzon. Native buses, civilian autos, trucks and military vehicles with hundreds of civilian Filipino drivers were organized for operational control.

Spare parts were non-existent. A system of cannibalizing was implemented. Items like hydraulic brake fluid, battery acid, and distilled water were acutely short. Substitutes had to be improvised. Glycerin was mixed with alcohol for brake fluid, sulfuric acid was extracted from chemical ammunition and a still was built to produce distilled water. The amazing ability of the American soldier to improvise was apparent at all levels and very important to the support mission. We had picked up several American civilians and an orphan maintenance detachment without tools and equipment that had just arrived the week before the war.

The outline of the Rock slowly materialized out of the dusk as the ship eased in towards the north dock. With a ringing of bells and the rumble of the engines being reversed, we eased alongside the pier and disembarked. My old friend and shop mate from Manila, Staff Sergeant Edward J. Larson was waiting to meet me. I piled my duffle bag into the truck, S/Sgt. Larson congratulated me on my promotion and assignment to the Rock. Soon we were on our way to our bivouac area. Little could be seen as we slowly climbed a grade, in total blackout. I could vaguely make out buildings as we passed. I had watched during the last days of December, when the Japanese used dive and high flying bombers in the first air attack on Corregidor. In the dark, I could see no evidence of damage except occasionally, we would slow down for bomb craters in the road.

This was my first time on the fabled Rock, an imposing fortress guarding Manila Bay. The chain of forts, Corregidor (Fort Mills), Caballo (Fort Hughes), El Friale (Fort Drum), and Carabao (Fort Frank), lie across the throat of Manila Bay like a necklace. On the trip out from San Francisco aboard the U.S.A.T. Meigs in July of 1939, I had been busy in the hold getting ready to off-load our cargo of 250 head of horses and mules. I had heard many stories of the Rock and its fortifications. Now, I would be able to see how formidable it would be in the days to come. We

Lt. Col. John N. Shanks T.C. was the officer in charge of the shop in Manila and Corregidor. Survived the hell-ship Oryoku Maru *(circa 1955). Courtesy of Charles Hilton.*

soon reached our destination and Sgt. Larson pulled the vehicle into a building. The officer in charge (OIC) Captain John N. Shanks, greeted me with a cheery hello.

I had known the captain since arriving in the islands and was assigned to the shop in the port area. At the time he was a master sergeant. I was welcomed by the other men, S/Sgt. Archie Golson, S/Sgt. Ralph Reynolds, Sgt. William Standridge, Cpl. Charles M. Hilton, Cpl. Ernest S. Haddox and others. After a few minutes chatting with the men, we made our way to the sleeping area with a caution to watch my head. We were in total blackout with only the faint light from the skies. Our sleeping area was under what seemed to be wooden bleachers. I soon had my cot up and gear stowed underneath. Captain Shanks said we would be up at first light.

As I lay on my bunk before falling asleep, I could hear the far off rumble of the artillery and see the brightening of the sky as the battle wore on in Bataan. I thought of the good times and the soft lilting laughter of the madonnas and the dalogas as they strolled along the Luneta and Dewey Boulevard in far off Manila. I had enjoyed the easy going life in the beautiful city. Now the people of Manila were behind the Bamboo Curtain. I wondered what fate held in store for the people of Manila. Were they being mistreated or was Japan treating them with respect and dignity?

I arose at dawn's early light and prepared for the day. I looked around and found we were in a sports arena at Middleside below the back side of the station hospital. The arena had been modified into a shop. Sleeping areas were under the bleachers on the north side. A portion of the bleachers on the west side had been removed as an entrance to the shop. The east end had about a 12-foot break and overlooked a ravine. The shop area was the playing court for basketball and a boxing ring. Though small in area compared to the shop in Manila, it sufficed for the purpose it was being used for. Several of the Filipino civilians, who had worked in Manila, had reached the Rock to augment the military personnel. They were specialist mechanics and would prove valuable to our mission. The sports arena lay in a low area behind the station hospital with a large open area towards the hospital. The preliminary survey gave me an idea of the area.

Just at the break of day, we arrived at the mess area at Bottomside. This was below the Quartermaster Tunnel to the north of the west entrance to Malinta Tunnel. This was also referred to as the Petrel Storage Tunnel. The field kitchen had been set up in a small break with a tent fly overhead, which served as the galley. I greeted several of the enlisted men and some of the officers of the Quartermaster.

Breakfast consisted of pancakes, syrup, bacon and scrambled eggs with real coffee. This was an improvement over the rations we had been receiving on Bataan. There were no mess tables and the men spread out and sat on whatever was available. Some sat in a dobie squat, (sitting upright with feet flat on the ground in a squatting position). Immediately after chow, we had a second canteen cup of coffee, washed our mess kits and headed back up the hill to the shop area.

As we wound our way back up the road, our driver took us around the Topside area. The officers' quarters and the golf course showed the damage of the air raids. The destruction of the mile long three story barracks of the 59th Coast Artillery Regiment was extensive. The damage to the officers' quarters and the barracks had rendered them unusable after the attack in late December of 1941. The troops had moved out to their respective position. Each gun battery position was of heavy reinforced concrete. The batteries were 12-inch disappearing guns, mortars and barbette type, with smaller caliber in some areas. Most guns were limited in degree of traverse. They were antiquated and designed to prevent ships from approaching from the south. The disappearing batteries were useless for firing into Bataan. Their primary purpose was against a naval threat from the South China Sea, through either the Boca Grande or the Boca Chica channels into Manila Bay.

The officers' quarters were severely damaged. The officers had moved out to prepared positions with their troops. The dependents had been evacuated to the United States in May 1941. The 59th CAC barracks on Topside had no roof and the windows were blown out. Extensive damage rendered them totally useless. This was rumored to be the longest barracks in the army and housed the regiment

and all of its ancillary elements. The post was beautiful with clubs, swimming pool, theater and other facilities for the peacetime army.

Lt. General Douglas MacArthur, his family, the High Commissioner Mr. Sayre and President Manual Quezon and his staff had occupied quarters at the east end of Malinta Tunnel near officers' beach. The bombing in late December had forced them to seek a safer location in Malinta Tunnel. However, we could see that the superficial building damage would not affect operations.

We arrived back at the sports arena and parked the truck under a shade tree on the northeast side. Each man returned to the sleeping area for morning toiletry functions. It was full daylight by this time, I wandered out to look the building over. It was a sheet metal roof mounted on 8" x 8" timbers with no side walls. The station hospital sat on higher ground overlooking Boca Chica Channel and Bataan. A low, flat area extended to the rear of the hospital for about 100 yards. The hospital staff and patients had been moved to the hospital laterals in Malinta Tunnel. The hospital suffered some damage to the roof and the shell shutters that were used during rainy season. The arena was in good repair and had only minor damage. The arena inside was well lighted by the tropical sun. The open sides allowed cool breezes to flow from any direction. Work tables were set up and some shop equipment was in place. It was apparent that we were limited in what could be accomplished. Parts supply and local purchase would not be available. Some items could be manufactured at a large machine shop at Bottomside.

The shop in Manila was a major base maintenance facility, capable of complete disassembly, overhaul and rebuild of motor vehicles. Most of the shop equipment was permanently installed and could not have been moved out in the time allowed. Our mission on Corregidor was to salvage major components and assemblies from war damaged vehicles to support the vehicles on the Rock and Bataan. Cannibalizing was the only source of parts. As I wondered around the shop area, I spotted a familiar vehicle, a long black Buick sedan. It was one of two limousines the Quartermaster had purchased for General MacArthur, when

12

he was called to active duty by President Franklin D. Roosevelt in July of the previous year. A Chrysler and a Buick limousine had been delivered to our shop for servicing. They were inspected and placed in service.

The Buick had been parked near the east entrance of Malinta Tunnel. During one of the air raids, a near miss had dumped the side of the hill down on the rear half, caving in the roof and breaking most of the glass. Sgt. Standridge, Cpl. Hilton and a Filipino sheet-metal worker were restoring the top and bringing it back to usable condition. It would never have its former beauty but could still serve as the General's automobile. With no windows or rear glass, it was truly "air-conditioned." We later recovered the Chrysler after it was hit by artillery fire. The radio from

it was pressed into service, it was capable of listening to Radio KGEI, San Francisco. This was our only source of news from outside. It was nice in the evening to hear the music and news from home. We would lay on our bunks and think of another world and hope that we could make it back to the Golden Gate. The shocking news of Pearl Harbor did not dim our hopes of seeing a strong Naval force coming to our rescue.

Capt. Shanks showed me around and explained the emergency shelter that we would use when needed. It was ingenious, a two-inch galvanized pipe had been anchored into a manhole leading to a storm sewer and secured to the bleachers at the top. The earth had been dug out around the manhole and cribbing erected in a four-foot square. During an air

Finance Lateral during the siege of Corregidor. Sgt. James W. Emanuel center foreground. National Archives #111-S249636C.

raid, one only had to step into the hole and slide down the pipe into a concrete storm sewer, about two-feet by four-feet high. Low benches had been constructed. Lights had been rigged along with emergency battery lights and a field telephone. There was about 12 feet of earth on top and a 150-foot long opening into the ravine to the east of the arena. It was to prove its worth in days to come. My first visit during an air raid came later and I was surprised to see a mural painted on the wall in charcoal. A beautiful woman in a kimono sitting upright on a couch. The artist, Cpl. Charles M. Hilton, was excellent and came up with some nice work. It also gave one something to think about, other than the sounds of war above. We named her Princess and would daydream during long enforced hours in the shelter about the girl we left behind.

Several fox holes had been dug around the perimeter of the shop providing additional security. On the south side of the shop, a concrete drainage ditch had been constructed to carry off the tropic rains from the roof. This ditch was about eighty-feet long and two-feet deep in a V shape. The only casualties we suffered were in this ditch. In February the Japanese had established artillery positions in Batangas Province, enabling them to fire on Fort Frank, Fort Drum and Corregidor. The guns could fire directly on the two nearest forts and at extreme range across Boca Grande Channel and harass Corregidor. The only sounds would be the shell screaming and an explosion.

Four Filipinos ran for the ditch during one of these actions. The second round hit the edge of the roof and showered them with shrapnel. Two were killed outright and the other two were not hurt. During one bombing raid a wooden barracks and spare ammunition to the northeast of our shop was set afire. We were given a rare display or pyrotechnics and a shower of shrapnel from the exploding ammunition.

Days became routine and we learned to adapt to the situation as we went along. Air raids by high altitude bombers were frequent. We had no planes to contest the air space. Air raids were not as dangerous as the intermittent artillery fire from Batangas. Corregidor

is shaped like a tadpole, an elongated island and a difficult target to bomb from high flying aircraft. Our best air raid alarm was Sgt. Standridge and a black dog we had adopted. When Sgt. Standridge turned off his acetylene torch and Blackie sat up and listened intently, one had better be alert, for there would soon be planes overhead. It was said that Stan could hear the planes when they left Clark Field north of Manila.

At the beginning of hostilities, the three-inch anti-aircraft (AA) batteries of the 60th CAC (AA) were equipped with powder train fuses. Maximum effective range was up to 20,000 feet. Battery Boston commanded by Captain Warren Star was located adjacent to Battery Wheeler. It was the only unit with mechanical fuses with a maximum range of 8000 yards.

Urgent requests for mechanical fuses from stateside were rushed in by submarine. The new mechanical fuses were allocated to Battery C. on Morrison Hill, commanded by Captain Godfrey R. Ames. The 60th CAC (AA) gunners were able to reach 8000 yards, much to the surprise of the Japanese. This range gave a very small firing window. In March of 1942, two bombers came in from the east and the gunners of the 60th CAC (AA) locked on target as they came into range over Boca Grande Channel. Fire! One plane went down on the east side and the second lost a wing and crashed in Boca Chica Channel to the north. Everyone in the open on the Rock watched and shouted with joy. Now those devils in the sky knew they had better beware of the Rock. The uplifting of morale was tremendous and the subject of conversation for days. The men of the 60th CAC (AA) established a very good record. Their positions were in the open but they stood to their weapons and gave a good account of themselves.

Early March of 1942, we went down for our early chow. The cooks had prepared "Spam" the night before and put it on steel trays. There were about 300 men eating from that mess. Shortly after returning to the shop, I was seized by severe stomach pains and intense vomiting. The air raid alarm sounded and bombers were overhead. I didn't care if they hit me. I was so sick, I would have appreciated the relief. Sgt. Larson piled me into the pickup and drove me to the hospital in Malinta Tunnel. They were jammed with men waiting to get into the hospital. At least half of the 300 men must have been affected. I was finally admitted and given a saline solution to drink, which promptly bounced back. The nurse insisted I drink more. I soon felt better, but stayed there overnight and returned to duty the next day. This was my first and last visit to Malinta. I was very impressed with the facilities and the mountain above gave a sense of security. I still preferred the fresh air out side and was glad to get back to the shop.

Some poor souls never wanted to get out and remained as long as possible. The only time they would venture outside was to smoke. Never more than a few feet so they could scuttle back in case of danger. They reminded me of prairie dogs on the western plains.

Uncontrolled fear becomes overpowering and pervasive. Even though our shop was in an exposed area, we could reach shelter in no time. Many of the men developed "Tunnelitis." This was incurable and no amount of persuasion could get them out. If they did leave, at the first opportunity they would sneak back.

One reserve lieutenant was unable to function as a transportation officer for one of the Philippine Army divisions on Bataan. He could not take the stress and was relieved, sent to Corregidor and assigned to our shop. He was commissioned direct from civilian life and had no military training. Major Shanks (promoted by this time) explained the situation and that we were to take it easy and not spook him. Sgt. Larson picked him up from dock side shortly after dark. He bedded down and soon was asking how far it was to the Tunnel? How do you get there? The next day was relatively quiet and he stuck around. It was not long before he disappeared. Major Shanks dug him out of the crowd in Malinta and returned him to the shop. We tried to show him that it was safe and that he should have no fear. Again, he bugged out and never returned. Many who were unable to take the strain would move to the tunnel. Evidently the headquarters left them alone, as long as they did not interfere with normal operations. This resulted in hundreds of tunnel rats huddling along the corridors, unattached and

Battery Crocket and other disappearing guns were not effective in counter battery fire. They were limited in degrees of travel and could only be fired towards the China Sea.

Close-up of 12-inch mortar. Courtesy Gwynn Faber, USN Res.

contributing nothing. The sudden transition from the good life into one fraught with danger was more than they could handle. They could have had serious charges filed against them.

Time was going fast for us. Up at the break of day, the trip to the mess area, back to a long day in the shop or scurrying into the bomb proof. By this time we were down to two meals and half rations. We would try and save a little for a snack at noon. We were able to maintain our weight and health. Energetic men can always come up with a little extra by scrounging, trading, or by knowing someone in the right places. Many of the mechanics from other units would stop in to get parts and were the source of rumors and information. One frequent visitor and one I would meet

Squad room showing troop accomodations.
Courtesy Clifford J. Keller.

Early warning system used by the 60th CAC anti-aircraft
batteries.

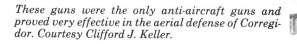

These guns were the only anti-aircraft guns and
proved very effective in the aerial defense of Corregidor. Courtesy Clifford J. Keller.

16

again was Ship Fitter, 2nd Class Elmer J. White USN. He was one of the many beached sailors and had been attached to the 4th Battalion of the 4th Marines. Another visitor was Captain Herman Haucks, a Battery Commander of the 59th CAC.

One battalion of men from various ships, Cavite Marines and grounded Air Force men made up the 4th Battalion of the 4th Marine Regiment. Most of the table of organization and equipment units (TO&E) had been at reduced strength prior to the war. As surplus men became available, they were assigned to under-strength units.

The Japanese pressure on Bataan increased and the Fil-American Forces were pushed back. The artillery range shortened and some of the big guns on Corregidor could be brought to bear on Bataan. Available with 12-inch rifles were Battery Smith and Battery Hearn. These batteries were barbette type and could be fired on a 360 degree circle. Battery Geary was a 12-inch mortar battery with two firing pits. A pit contained four 12-inch Model

1890 mortars, B Pit contained four Model 1908 12-inch mortars. These guns had been removed from east coast emplacements and shipped out to the islands in the early 1900's. The high angle of fire made them ideal for counter battery fire on Bataan. Fort Hughes' Battery Craighill had one battery of two pits with four guns each of 12-inch Model 1912 in each pit. These eight guns were the most modern. One battery with two 14-inch disappearing rifles also comprised the main armament on Fort Hughes. Fort Frank on the east side near Batangas had two batteries. Battery Kohler had two pits, each pit had four Model 1908 12-inch mortars. Battery Green had two 14-inch disappearing rifles pointed into the South China Sea. These two batteries were connected by a 670-foot tunnel. Fort Frank was commanded by Lt. Col. Napolean Boudreau.

Fort Drum, the concrete battleship, midway of the south channel, was equipped with two naval type twin 14-inch turreted guns. They were mounted on the top deck of the fort

Huge gun deck of the concrete battleship, Fort Drum, east of Corregidor.

Practice firing of upper twin 14-inch guns on Fort Drum in Boca Grande Channel.

on Topside. Battery John M. Wilson was the top turret and could swing 360 degrees. Battery William L. Marshal was the lower turret and could fire 230 degrees. Each projectile weighed 1660 pounds and required 430 pounds of powder. Maximum range was 19,200 yards due to limited elevation. During the hot weather the temperature in the interior would reach 100 degrees. This raised the explosive power of the powder and range exceeded 20,000 yards. The projectiles were armor piercing (AP). There were no high explosive projectiles (HE). This reduced the effectiveness on land-based targets. Other guns complementing the big guns were two batteries with two six-inch gun casemates in the east and west sides of the fort. The guns were mounted one above the other with primary mission of protection of the mine fields and engage destroyer type ships. These batteries were Benjamin K. Roberts and Tally B. McCrea with effective range of 10,000 yards. Later, Battery I 60th CAC (AA) manned a three-inch antiaircraft gun mounted on Topside along with 50 caliber machine guns manned by a detachment of Marines. The fort required about 200-230 men of E. Battery, 59th CAC Regiment commanded by Lt. Col. Lewis M. Kirkpatrick.

The concept of using a small rocky island of about one acre was conceived by a 1st Lt. John M. Kingman in 1908. His suggestion through channels was accepted and work began in 1909. Fort Drum was completed in 1917. It was a completely self-supporting unit with water distillation plant, air compressors and electric generating plant. It was connected to headquarters on Fort Mills by underwater cable. The walls of the fort were 14 feet of reinforced concrete with 14 inches of armor plating on the turrets.

Fort Drum and Fort Frank were primary targets of 240 mm artillery from Batangas. Fort Drum never suffered a single casualty. Life in this formidable fort was like living inside of a drum and was extremely hot when buttoned up.

One other four gun mortar battery, Battery Way, was not in operation in the early part of February and March. Our shop area was about 300 yards from Battery Way gun pit. The other batteries, Crocket, Wheeler, Cheney, Ramsey, James, Flint, Monja and Grubbs, were of no use in covering Bataan. During the battle of the points, on the south end of Bataan Peninsula, the Japanese attempted to land in force from the sea in the rear of American lines. This force was pinned down by counterattack by a provisional battalion of sailers and grounded airmen from the USS Canopus and Air Corps units.

The batteries from Fort Drum pounded away with their 14-inch guns. Battery Geary laid on with 12-inch mortars and Batteries Hearn and Smith with 12-inch rifles. The Navy used small craft with jury-rigged armaments attacked from the sea. The 57th Infantry (PS) was called on to help the Provisional Battalion. With this combination of fire and manpower, the Japanese were eliminated.

When Fort Drum fired over our heads, the sound of those 14-inch shells sounded like a

Troops training with 20 and 50 caliber machine guns.

Six-inch disappearing gun to cover channel and mine fields.

These weapons were primarily oriented towards the sea. They were useless in counter battery fire into Bataan.

freight train passing. Sometimes a rotating band would break loose and scream like a Comanche Indian. The mortar battery on Fort Hughes was manned by a group of sailers. The 92nd Coast Artillery Regiment (PS) was equipped with 19 guns in eight batteries of 1918 model Long Tom 155 mm rifles. Their assignment was roving gun batteries. They would move in, set up, fire several rounds and scoot for another position. The 91st Coast Artillery Regiment (PS) manned several fixed secondary batteries.

The sounds of battle on Bataan in late March were growing closer and the final struggle for that piece of jungle hell drew to a tragic close. We were starting to draw fire from some of the longer range big field pieces of the Japanese Army. Our counter battery fire was giving them tit for tat. Each time we fired, the Japanese were able to pinpoint our gun positions and their fire increased in accuracy. Also in March the firing from Batangas Province stopped as the guns were pulled out and sent to Bataan.

C Battery, 60th Coast Artillery (AA) on Morrison Hill was hit hard in March and suffered casualties from shelling. A call came in to render aid in transporting causalities to Malinta Hospital. S/Sgt. Larson made one trip and on his return, the Japanese laid an artillery round to the rear of his truck, killing one man and severely injuring S/Sgt. Larson. He suffered the loss of his right arm and severe wounds to the back. A vehicle moving during daylight hours made a dust trail that could be seen from Bataan and promptly drew fire. S/Sgt. Larson remained in the hospital until after the surrender.

The Japanese lost no time after the collapse of Bataan in moving into lower Bataan with all available artillery. The Japanese intended to make short work in the reduction of Corregidor. Much face had been lost because of the stubborn Fil-American forces. The Battling Bastards of Bataan, "No Momma, No Papa, No Uncle Sam," disappeared into the fires of Japanese hell on earth. Their gallant but hopeless stand inspired the world. The Death March followed and the exhausted and sick survivors disappeared into the prison camps. The March of Death was the epitome of human cruelty and set the pattern for the future.

The fall of Bataan brought a tremendous change to the Corregidor garrison. Casualties rose and movement during daylight was extremely hazardous to life. We would eat before daylight and again after dark. Blackout became a way of life. Normal activities practically ceased as far as any productive work was concerned. More time was spent in the area of our bombproof. We were soon living like the prairie dogs, ever alert to every noise and ready to take cover.

The Japanese concentration of heavy weapons were moved and set up before the survivors were moved out of Bataan. Howitzer batteries were set up near hospital No. 2 at Little Baguio and immediately opened fire. Counter battery fire was hampered by reluctance to fire due to the existence of the hospital, a definite advantage to the Japanese and little could be done about it. Soon, the fat was in the fire and Photo Joe was busy shooting pictures and plotting all of the gun positions. Spotters were posted on the heights of the Mariveles Mountains to provide data for Japanese artillery units.

Many men escaped from Bataan and were absorbed into the various units on beach defense. Primary beach defense fell to the 4th Marine Regiment. This fine organization had arrived in Olongapo only two weeks before the war started. Shortly after arrival they moved down into Bataan. They had been stationed in China and were excellent additions to the command. One platoon, under Lt. Mike Dobervich, was detached and assigned as security guards at General Jonathan Wainwright's Headquarters on Bataan. The balance of the unit went to Corregidor.

Lieutenant Lester J. Petersen, who served in the shop in Manila, had been commissioned in January, just before I had departed for Corregidor. His first duty station was to General Wainwright's Headquarters. He was an excellent technician and deserving of the promotion. He became good friends with Lieutenant Michael Dobervich of the 4th Marines. They survived the Death March together. I met Lt. Dobervich many years later. He told me of the long march and of the horrors and brutality along the 65 mile trek of death.

Also arriving from China were elements of the Yangtze River Patrol vessels. These small ships had been designed for inland waters. They were shallow draft, flat bottomed vessels with little freeboard and light armament. Their journey through the open waters of the China Sea, shadowed by Japanese naval forces was an epic in seamanship, determination and skill.

The fall of Bataan was a serious blow. The grand plan, WPO 5 (Orange Plan), for the defense of the Philippines was predicated on holding onto Bataan and Corregidor until the arrival of a large naval force to relieve the beleaguered forces. The serious losses at Pearl Harbor made this impossible and the result was inevitable. In ignorance of the true damages to the fleet, we never gave up hope that a miracle would happen and the great armada was on its way.

Efforts were made to bring in supplies and critical items. A supply line from the southern islands was established using small inter-island steamers. Without air cover or adequate naval ships, this system had some limited success. Other efforts included PBY patrol bombers that slipped in at night and brought some small amounts of medicines and took out critical personnel. Submarines were used and could bring in more supplies and carry out more passengers. Vital records, critical personnel and the Philippine Government's gold were also sent out. The arrival of the relief force was a facade and no one wanted to believe otherwise.

The fall of Bataan removed any hope of delaying the march of the Japanese Empire. Already they stood on the Malay Pennisula, Dutch East Indies, Hong Kong and French Indo-China. Their sweep towards Australia was rolling like a juggernaut. The paltry Allied Forces opposing them in the Philippines and the Dutch East Indies were only a minor obstacle. The unexpected delay in the Philippines was a serious loss of face to the Japanese Commander, General Homma. He was ready for the grand finale. Fresh reinforcements had been brought in. The stage was set for the Americans to be booted out of the Far East.

The defiant fortress of Corregidor and its outlying islands were ready as could be. Most of the main batteries were in action and the men stood to their posts. Among the troops

Lt. General Homma, commander of the Japanese Army, lands at Lingayen Gulf.

that returned to Corregidor from Bataan was Battery E of the 60th Coast Artillery. They had been operating searchlights on Bataan. This AA battery under the command of Captain William Massello was not one to twiddle their thumbs while there was a fight nearby. Captain Massello learned of the plans to activate Battery Way and volunteered for assignment to the 59th CAC and Battery Way. He asked for and received permission to man Battery Way.

Battery Way was another of the 12-inch mortar units. The four guns were Model 1890 and had not been manned up to this time. The men fell to work and soon had three of the four ancient guns in working order. Eric Morris in his book, "*Corregidor, The End Of The Line,*" gives an excellent description of the activation of Battery Way. "The battery had a very short supply of anti-personnel ammunition. Most was for armor piercing. Captain Massello and some of the ordinance artificers modified the projectiles to shorten the fuse."

An attempt was also made to modify the projectiles to permit firing at aircraft in the hopes a shell could be exploded in midair. The experiment did not work out as hoped.

The Japanese began to pound the Rock with their big 240 mm howitzers and smaller 105 and 155 mm howitzers, life grew indeed hectic and dangerous. As long as Battery Way did not fire, our shop was reasonably safe and we could move around and do some work.

Our battery chargers were gasoline engine operated and were set up on the lower level of the hospital. This kept down the noise but required frequent checking. A trip up the hill was made fast and sometimes one had to remain there during a barrage. A good shelter was the freezer locker. Located in the basement, with two floors above and well insulated with cork, it provided excellent haven.

The batteries that had been doing most of the firing now became prime targets. The Japanese established excellent observation posts high in the hills of Bataan and brought in an observation balloon. The air superiority allowed targets to be selected and precisely located. The barrage began in earnest and the damage mounted.

Casualties increased among the exposed anti-aircraft batteries of the 60th CAC and beach defenses on the low land to the east of Malinta Hill were brought under heavy fire. The Rock was being challenged. All that could be done to withstand the onslaught had been done. The Rock was prepared to meet the challenge. The troops and their guns were ready and eager to mix it up with the enemy.

Our detachment was attached to the newly activated Battery Way for rations. This was much better than the long dangerous ride to Bottomside, before daylight and after dark. We would scoot out of our drainage sewer, move along the ravine, across the road and we were fairly safe. We were able to observe the progress in getting the battery in action. Up until this time, no shots had been fired and the Japanese didn't realize it was being brought into action. Once it was ready, all hell broke loose with the first salvo.

The main thorn in the side of the Japanese had been Batteries Hearn, Geary, Craighill and the 14-inch guns on Fort Drum. These batteries were well located behind the bulk of the highest parts of the Island. Battery Geary was just below the golf course on the south side of Corregidor. Fort Drum with its heavy reinforced concrete construction could operate with impunity.

Early in May, Battery Geary came under concentrated heavy fire from the big 240 mm howitzers. The powder magazine lay in the center between A and B pits. The ammunition magazines lay to the west and east end of the double battery. The concentrated fire soon caused a fire in the powder magazine. The commander ordered an evacuation. About 11:00 hours, 2nd of May, the battery blew up with a tremendous explosion. The roof was four feet of reinforced concrete covered with about 12 feet of earth. The powder magazine literally disappeared. The explosion shook the Rock like a dice cup. The provisional battalion of the Fourth Marine Regiment was located around the southern periphery of the hill, just below Geary and extending from the south dock around to Battery Wheeler. The debris rained on them, most went over their heads into the China Sea. The two gun pits of the battery were completely demolished. The four 12-inch mortars in each pit were blasted from their mountings. One barrel from A Pit, weighing 13 tons was thrown a hundred yards, up onto the edge of the golf course. One 1890 gun in this pit remained on its mounts. The walls of the ammunition magazines were literally blown horizontally against the back wall of the ammunition magazine. The roof collapsed onto the debris of the walls. One of the gun tubes was charged at the time of the explosion. According to A.C. McGrew of San Diego California, the gun still has a round in the barrel. Al McGrew has made several trips to the Rock in the intervening years. B Pit to the east was also totally demolished. Two of the 1908 mortars were blown under the edge of the parapet of the magazine and the top partially caved in on top of walls and gun.

This was a major catastrophe and left only twelve mortars operative, the four 12-inch mortars in Battery Way and the eight in Fort Hughes' Battery Craighill that could bear on Bataan. Battery Craighill was manned by a group of beached sailors. Batteries Way, Craighill, Hearn, Smith, and the 155 mm guns of the 92nd CAC, (PS) along with Fort Drum's

14-inch turreted rifles constituted the only effective units that could bear on the assembly areas for Japanese landing barges near Cabcaban, on the shores of Bataan.

The Japanese had been slipping landing craft in at night under cover of heavy artillery barrages, in spite of the offshore patrolling by small craft operated by our naval units.

The final ten days, according to Colonel William Braly, Operations officer (G-3), in his book, *The Hard Way Home,* "The Japanese bombardment increased in tempo with an estimated 420 guns firing 200,000 rounds on two square miles of island." Approximately one round every four seconds. The defiant American forces returned fire and inflicted great damage on the assembly areas and the firing positions on Bataan. The Japanese bombardment really wreaked havoc on Corregidor. The tremendous amount of incoming rounds and the return fire created a noise like living in a boiler factory. Movement during daylight hours was extremely limited and was made in short dashes between rounds. The beach defenses near the 92nd CAC (PS) Garage and the small airstrip at Kinley Field took a terrific pounding. Fortunately, these positions were well dug in and casualties were kept to a minimum. We became nocturnal creatures and moved under cover of darkness or periods when the Japanese fire was slow.

The firing batteries of the 92nd were equipped with 155 mm Long Tom rifles and could be moved to different firing positions. These roving guns would set up, fired rapid fire for a few minutes and then moved to another location. The Filipino scouts were excellent soldiers with American officers. Some of the younger men were sons of scouts and were born on Corregidor, went to school there and followed in their fathers' footsteps. One of the battery officers was 2nd Lieutenant John M. Wright, Jr. (Lt. General Ret.), a West Point graduate whom I met later in prison camp.

The beach defenses had been strengthened with barbed wire aprons extending into the water. Trenches and machine gun revetments had been well placed and connected by trenches with supporting trenches to the trench mortar and machine gun pits. The con-

centrated fire in this low lying area, east of Malinta Tunnel, caused serious damage in holes being ripped in the barbed wire and destruction of machine gun and mortar positions rendering them untenable.

Battery Way continued active despite suffering great damage to the mortar pit. One by one, the three Model 1890 12-inch mortars fell silent. Captain William (Wild Bill) Massello's courage was inspiring. The critical point in serving the battery comes when the ammunition and powder magazines are opened to allow the guns to be recharged. Captain Massello would dash out and sweep the debris out of the path of the shot carts before each round.

Early in the evening of the fourth of May, we received a telephone call from Major Shanks that the telephone wires leading to Battery Way had been cut. He asked if we could check the lines in the ravine below our storm sewer outlet. A couple of us went out and located some broken wires and without test equipment, wired them back into the net. Evidently, we got the right wires connected as Battery Way continued to fire.

The night of the fifth of May 1942, the Japanese invasion forces under cover of heavy artillery barrage pushed off from their assembly areas near Cabcabin on Bataan. Murderous Japanese fire poured onto the beaches and exploding shells crawled into the defense positions beyond. A thunderous crescendo of noise reverberated over Corregidor. The dust and smoke stretched up and down the island. The defenders waited in silence, peering into the maelstrom for the first sight of the invaders.

Only two of Battery Way's mortars remained in action. The noise, the smoke and the increased intensity of the barrage and the scream of hurtling chunks of shrapnel sounded the approach of the invasion. Captain Massello, commander of Battery Way, sent his excess men to safer areas, leaving only enough to serve the remaining guns.

After a fast supper, we were ordered to work our way down the road that led to Middleside barracks and to hole up there. A tunnel about six feet high and eight feet wide had been bored into the hill just off the road. This was a timber trussed shaft. A group of civilians from Pacific Naval Air Base Contractors had been working to drive a shaft into the side of the hill. Many of these civilians performed yeoman work in construction of tunnels and enlarging the Queens Tunnel, adjacent to and connected with Malinta. Queens Tunnel was utilized as headquarters for the 16th Naval District and was also used for storage of critical naval supplies and equipment.

The Middleside tunnel was rigged with electric lights and was relatively safe from the heavy concentration of fire. Some of the men had come from excess personnel from Battery Way and other units not involved in operations. They were getting what little rest they could. Many had not slept and were dog tired. About 2000 hours, word was passed for us to be ready to serve as reserves if needed. The men fell to checking weapons and filled canteens from the lister bag set up near the tunnel entrance. Some lay down with their own thoughts and tried to get some rest. Our thoughts varied and many just sat silent or tried to read or chatted softly with their friends.

A Black Jack game soon started up as a way to keep one's mind occupied and to pass the time. Black Jack, as played by the troops, was a floating dealer game. If one got a Black Jack he may elect to be the dealer and banker. The game was wide open and the players were rather reckless and had a 'don't give a damn attitude'. They would not stand on 17, but call for a hit, and go busted. This soon eliminated some. Being of Scottish nature, I hung tight and played conservatively. I soon got the deal and continued to play on into the night. Somewhere around 0200, the game broke up.

I counted up my winnings and found that I had won 1700.00 pesos ($850.00). This was a lot of money and I did not want to lose it. It was fairly certain that the future was unpredictable. Some means of hanging onto such a windfall was important. It had to be on my person. Burying it was out of the question. I would probably never get back to Corregidor. I solved the problem by breaking it down into denominations, 100, 50 and 20 peso notes. I folded the larger bills, slit the waist band of my trousers and slid them around the waist. The 5 and 10 peso notes, I divided equally into two rolls and put them in my boots as arch supports. The one peso notes I put in my wallet. After taking these preparations, I settled down to wait. When I awoke, it was daylight.

After a quick breakfast of C rations, we patiently played the old army game of hurry up and wait. Word came down that we were to destroy our weapons by 1200 hours. General Wainwright had ordered the surrender of the fort. We were told that all resistance must cease. The deadline was imperative. The only item left was my rifle which I disassembled and threw the parts behind the retaining walls of the earth tunnel. The barrel and stock were smashed across the rail tracks. We were able to accomplish all the destruction before the deadline of 1200 hours.

We sat quietly in the tunnel. Some slept, some whispered, some were stunned and all were nervous and apprehensive. The strain of waiting for the unknown was heavy and ominous. An eerie quiet descended over the Rock. Intermittent shelling and bombing could be heard. The heavy bombardment slowed and soon all was quiet. Not a sound could be heard outside.

This was the first time in many months that we heard no shelling or the steady drone of bombers overhead. I sat and reflected on the past six months and thanked God that my friends and I had been spared. Our only detachment casualties had been the two Filipinos and Sgt. Larson. The time had gone by fast and everything had changed so dramatically from peacetime soldiering in the far off Philippine Islands. Easy times were gone. The American soldier had adapted to the Rudyard Kipling poem, "Only mad dogs and Englishmen go out in the noon day sun." The duty in the tropics had been good . . . the exciting night life . . . the reasonable price of food and drinks . . . the interesting trips into the interior . . . the horse races at Santa Ana. The Pearl of the Orient was now in the hands of the conqueror and we waited for the next shoe to drop.

What would our captors expect? Where would we be tomorrow? How would we be treated? Would the Japanese victors treat us in accordance with the Geneva Convention? What did the Geneva Convention say about treatment of prisoners of war? How long would we have to wait for the end of the war?

Fil-American Forces surrender in front of Malinta Tunnel, 6 May, 1942. Japanese photo, National Archives #111-SC-334292.

These and hundreds of other questions rushed through our minds with no answers.

We had heard nothing of the fate of the men on Bataan. Only later were we to learn of the horrible starvation, deprivation, degradation humiliation, brutal and harsh treatment of those gallant "battling bastards of Bataan" or the infamous horror trek to prison. Knowledge of this information would have sent cold chills up the spine of the men on Corregidor as we waited. Ignorance was bliss. The siege and the capture of Corregidor have been well chronicled by many good authors and well discussed by those who were there and those fortunate ones to survive. No attempt is made here to describe the tactics or strategy and conduct of the campaign.

The action on Corregidor marked the first time since the Civil War that the Coast Artillery's big guns had been fired in the defense of a major harbor. They never had fired at land forces coming in the back door. The British fortress at Singapore suffered the same defeat, invasion by land from the rear. Those gun batteries that could fire to the rear were tremendously effective. The Coast

Artillery was designed for employment against an invading fleet. The proud and glorious tradition of the Coast Artillery Corps and its long vigil of our sea coasts from the tip of Maine, along the Atlantic, Gulf and Pacific coast lines, the Panama Canal, Hawaii and the Philippines had become a casualty of time and technology. Many fine men had worn the dark red hat band and regimental crests of the Coast Artillery Corps. They served in many different posts at home and abroad. Here on fabled Corregidor, the Coast Artillery had gone down in honor and to the last minute had blasted their way into history.

The epitome of defiance to the invader can best be described in the last hours of Battery Way. Captain William (Wild Bill) Massello, gravely wounded and still directing his men of E Battery, had exemplified the corps' tradition. With intense sense of duty, antiquated weapons and green crew, they continued in action all night. Finally reduced to only one gun in action, they poured a devastating fire on the invading forces. In the early morning hours, they had fired 90 rounds of high explosives from one mortar. The barrel became so hot that the breech seized and the battery had to shut down. This is not to say that other batteries of the 59th, 60th, 91st and 92nd CAC were silent, they all contributed to the finale.

Even today, 50 years later, one gun of Battery Way stands with its muzzle pointed to the sky on that far off island known as Corregidor, "America's Gibraltar." This lone sentinel memorializes the Coast Artillery Corps' long line of service to our country from the War of Independence to the bitter end on Corregidor. Outmoded, obsolete, outgunned, and alone, the tradition of the Coast Artillery Corps preserves its place in military history.

The exalted traditions of service to our country and the thousands who once served in the Coast Artillery should never be forgotten. Major General Thomas H. Moore, Commander of Harbor Defenses, Subic and Manila Bay; Colonel Paul Bunker, Commander of the 59th CAC; Lt. Colonel Lewis Kirkpatrick, Commander of Fort Drum; Captain William Massello and Lt. John M. Wright Jr., 92nd CAC (PS); all graduates of the Military Academy at West Point. The thousands who were lost in the dreadful prison camps and those lost at sea on overcrowded filthy unmarked hell ships. They believed in their country and gave freely of themselves. They made the supreme sacrifice, in order that Americans are free under the Stars and Stripes, and the future defenders of freedom will not suffer the yoke of tyranny.

The debacle of the fall of the Philippines and the surrender of the largest force ever in American military history must be recognized as a memorial to the unprepared bureaucracy that was our government. The pleas from the sacrificed soldiers, sailors, airmen, and Filipinos can be heard in the evening: "Never again let America be UNPREPARED."

Battery Way. The two mortars to the right were knocked out by 5 May, 1942. The one in the left background was never in action. The mortar in the left foreground continued to fire until the very end (circa 1985). Courtesy of Gwynn Faber, USN Res.

CORREGIDOR

OASIS OF HOPE

PART TWO

THE FORTUNATE—NOT SO FORTUNATE—UNFORTUNATE

Station hospital, Fort Mills, Corregidor (circa 1987). Damage by Japanese bombing was not as severe as photo. Hospital was liveable 1942-1945. Right wing—American POWs; center rear—Japanese kitchen; left wing—Japanese quarters; lower right area—officers quarters 1942-1943; second door from right, lower level—my home 1943-44.

Part Two

The Fortunate, Not So Fortunate And The Unfortunate

The surrender of Corregidor and the imprisonment of the garrison's over 13,000 men in Japanese prison camps was the beginning of a long ordeal. The Bataan troops had been prisoners for a month. Some would be fortunate to survive, some would not be so fortunate and barely survive and some would be unfortunate and not survive. Some would be lucky and be shipped to good camps with fair treatment, fair food and fair medical treatment. Others would go to camps that were brutal, guards were more sadistic, as slave laborers with grossly inadequate food, medicines and shelter. Others would survive in spite of the terrible treatment, and would make it through the long years. The unfortunate would be sent to camps with severe hardships, starvation, no medical attention and many would die or be executed in the waning days. Others were subject to harsh treatment on overcrowded ships, only to die at sea at the hands of American forces. Such are the fortunes of war and Lady Luck smiles on some and others never see the smile.

The time had come for the valiant men of Corregidor to follow the battling bastards of Bataan into that never never land of hell on earth. Prisoner of war! Prisoners of war of a little understood oriental conqueror. A fate that was not of their making, beyond their control and certainly not of their choosing. A fate that could be blamed on the insensitivity and isolationist beliefs of those who swore to defend our system of life. Those who with the paucity of a miser, failed to act to prevent such a disaster. The foreign policy of our government was flawed. Those elected officials with a narrow viewpoint of the Far East and the approaching war clouds, failed in the trust placed on them by the people. They allowed such a debacle to occur. TOO LATE, TOO LITTLE, TOO LONG. A cynical penurious

effort was made to do what should have been done. The protection and defense of the Philippines should have been a matter of first priority before 1941. Now the young men of America and the unfortunate, poorly equipped and untrained Filipinos would pay the price of liberty with their lives. Not in combat, but in the horrible ordeal of prisoners of war. Never wavering in the hope, that Uncle Sam would return them to freedom. Undaunted, heads unbowed and with hopes high, they marched into an uncertain future.

We sat in the tunnel at Middleside, waiting our fate. We were resigned to the fact and trusting our conquerors to treat us in accordance with the terms of the Geneva Convention. The word came down on the morning of the 7th of May, 1942 to stand by to move out and form up on the road at the east end of the 60th CAC (AA) barracks. The time had come to face the conquerors. We slowly and carefully approached the exit. Deep in our guts was a sense of fear of the unknown. None had ever been face to face with an armed enemy under these conditions. There was no book to follow, no guide, and with only our trust in God and our own faith in mankind, we moved out into the bright morning sun.

A formation of double ranks was formed and we stood at ease. All eyes were on a platoon of Japanese soldiers standing on the road, hob nailed boots, wrap leggings, camouflaged uniforms, steel helmets with netting festooned with leaves and long rifles with fixed bayonets. A Japanese officer with a pistol and a long saber swinging from his belt, barked orders in Japanese. When all had cleared the tunnel, Japanese soldiers dashed into the tunnel to insure that all were out.

We stood ill at ease, apprehensive and nervous, as we watched. A foul taste of the bittersweet sense of defeat in our throats. They did not look to be as fearsome and menacing as we had feared. Shouts of "Bango, Bango" which no one understood. Our officers finally understood and gave the order to count off. A count was taken with much gesturing and shouting of commands in Japanese. Kora! Kora! Kora! None of us understood, but got the general idea of what they wanted. Open ranks was given and we stepped forward one pace and waited.

The Japanese enlisted men eased up and began to look each man over very carefully. By "Kora! Kora!" and gestures, they took watches, fountain pens, cigarette lighters, rings, and money. One soldier must have had ten watches on one arm. Slowly, one approached and took my watch and pen. He patted me on the hip and gestured that I was to take out my wallet. I slowly withdrew it from my pocket and he gestured and grunted for me to open it. His eyes lit up with greed, as I extracted the wad of single peso notes and a few five peso notes. He snatched it up and shoved it into his pockets. I was glad that he had not taken the billfold with pictures from home of some of my sisters.

Later I was to learn the reason for not taking the billfold. They had been instructed in their conduct that they would be punished if caught with personal items. I learned later that several of the men on Bataan had been so unfortunate as to have Japanese souvenirs on them when captured. They were executed without a trial. There were instances where an item would be returned by an officer or non-commissioned officer (NCO), and the Japanese soldier would get a dressing down with maybe a slap for emphasis. None of the personal items were worth the risk.

After stripping us of our few possessions, the Japanese soldiers formed us into a column and we started our journey into the long ordeal that lay ahead of us. Prisoners of war in a far off land, a fate that many would not survive. With a prayer that all would go well, we moved down the road towards Bottomside. The men were quiet and not a word was said as we walked along. Each man was looking around, gloomily aware of the omnipresence of our guards. We could see the terrible destruction of everything in sight. Buildings were blown to bits, all the trees and bushes were cut to about three feet high, craters blasted in the roads, debris littered the road. Huge craters gouged into the terrain could be seen. The devastating fire of the artillery bombardment had created a moon like landscape.

Saddened but with the knowledge that we had done our best, we trod on to we knew not where. We soon reached Bottomside to find all sorts of activity and coming and going of Japanese. A battered Plymouth came roaring along filled with jubilant Japanese soldiers, shouting and screaming as they tore past us. Long lines of Japanese troops fanning out on the roads to Topside, mopping up and collecting the men in the batteries on Topside. A long line of Americans and Filipinos flowed past. Our group fell in with them. We took the road that circled around the south side of Malinta Hill, past the road to Queens Tunnel and the barrio San Jose, around Malinta Hill to the water tower and Battery Denver. The road led through a greedy gauntlet of Japanese, scrounging anything of value that had been overlooked by previous greedy Japanese.

The carnage of battle was everywhere. The AA guns of Battery Denver, stood silent. We began to pass through the battle zone on the tail of Corregidor. Bodies of fallen marines, soldiers and sailors lay where they fell. Where were the Japanese casualties? Most of them had been moved by a POW detail. Our hearts were heavy and our feet were dragging, but we continued to move towards the 92nd CAC (PS) Garage area. I hoped that I would not be a part of the detail that would have to bury the dead. The sight and stench of the bloated bodies was horrible and overpowering. Our approach was on a slight rise and we could see a mass of humanity sitting on the ground.

The assembly area was packed and the long column filed into the area. Our escorts dropped off on the outer perimeter. We could see guard posts set up with machine guns pointing in our direction. We made our way into the mass of humanity and began to look for a place to settle down. Our group, Cpl. Haddox, Standridge, Hilton, S/Sgt. Golson and myself soon reached the area of the 92nd CAC Garage. There, with only a skeleton of the roof remaining, we settled down on the concrete floor.

Some of us had brought blankets, mosquito bars and some had a few clothes stuffed into a musette bag with personal gear. We were extremely naive and many had not brought important things like soap, tooth brushes, razors, mess gear, water containers or food. Many were without any headgear. Some had only the clothes on their back. How dumb we were! How unprepared for survival! No one was prepared for such an ordeal. A few men were moving about, looking for shelter, food, water or lost comrades. Shelter from the blazing sun during the day was nonexistent. Improvised shelters were constructed with anything the men could find. Work details were dragging in anything that could be put to use. The Filipinos were separated into a separate group. The first day was tolerable but grew worse as time went on. Water and food was the worst problem. Billions of black flies swarmed in clouds in the blazing sun. The only relief from the swarms of flies and filth was to get on a work detail. These details were varied and the men were not prohibited from bringing back any items that could be used for survival. The Japanese guards were not overly severe and scrounging in the area of work provided many items that were sorely needed. The survival under these conditions dictated group association. Small groups of friends banded together for the good of the group.

The water situation became desperate. The hot tropical sun overhead bore down and thirst became paramount. We could see no semblance of authority or signs that our officers were trying to bring order out of our chaos. The mass of men were without any form of organization and it was not evident that the Japanese were interested at that time in organizing a quasi military set-up for control. A single faucet dribbled a small amount of water to serve approximately 13,000 men. A line soon formed near the south side in hopes of getting water. Containers were extremely scarce. Some of the men had gathered up canteens from buddies with hopes of returning with filled canteens. This was not near enough to slake the thirst and they would then rotate and another would begin the long wait.

I had searched around the 92nd garage area for something to augment the canteens. I found a long leather range finder case about four feet long and six inches in diameter. The bottom had a grommet inserted in the center and a leather cap for the opposite end. I whittled out a wooden plug for the bottom. It had a carrying strap which would make it easier to carry. I got in the water line and after about four hours reached the lone spigot that served the estimated 13,000 or more men concentrated in the area. The water spigot only dribbled slowly. After filling the leather container and the canteens, I refilled the leather case. The leather was so dry that it soaked up about half of the water. I started back and arrived with about half of what I started with. It helped somewhat but tasted like an old shoe. It was appreciated by our group.

Another hazard of the water trip, was a gauntlet of guards. They would walk along the line looking for loot. They would tap on the hip pocket and motion for you to show your billfold. We soon learned what was expected and would show them our empty billfold. They would then say, "Tokay. Tokay?" This we learned, meant watch. Then they would ask for pens. Most of the men had already been stripped, but once in a while they would find something.

The third or fourth day, the situation had began to deteriorate. The hastily constructed slit trenches became overflowing. The lack of tools to dig more was acute, the absence of any water, sanitation, food and breakdown of discipline contributed to an increased rate of diarrhea and dysentery. The total lack of any hygienic facilities for washing hands, bodies or mess gear only increased the problem. The ground around the slit trenches became fouled and spread in other areas by feet tracking through the filth. Millions of black flies swarmed over everything. They would crawl into any body opening or on exposed heads, arms and legs. The huge green blow flies added their eggs to the slit trenches. Soon the slit trenches became infested with maggots. The only relief from the flies, misery, stench and filth was to try and fan them away, or completely cover with a blanket, shelter half or mosquito bar as long as you could stand the heat. Night brought welcomed relief from the merciless sun and the sticky flies. Another way to get out of the maelstrom of humanity, stench and flies was to catch a work detail. This had additional benefits. Each man was on the lookout for anything in the way of food, soap, clothing, hats of any kind, sheet metal or anything else that could be useful or traded. These details were put to work on the dock loading out the booty of war. The cold storage plant was cleaned out and the food was sent to Manila. This was a good detail to be on as the opportunity to strafe food items were many. The Japanese did not care for canned tomatoes or corned beef. None of the stores went to feed the mass of men except what could be strafed. No field kitchens were set up and there was no organized procedure to feed the men. Existence was catch as catch can. Survival was by individual initiative or group pooling of strafed items.

Japanese rations for their troops did not envision a central field kitchen and each individual drew dry rations and cooked his rice in their mess buckets. The POWs used whatever came to hand and scrounged for anything edible when they were on a work detail. This was brought back and shared with their group. Excess was either sold or traded for needed items. My cache of pesos came in handy for some items that were needed.

One of the men I had known in Manila, PFC LeRoy Becraft, had escaped from Bataan and wound up on the beach defense. He had previously served in the infantry and requested assignment to the 31st Infantry on Bataan with the hopes that promotions would come faster. He drifted into our area and told of being caught on a detail, recovering dead Japanese soldiers from the waters on the north side of Monkey Point. The Japanese approach to removal of casualties was rather brutal, but efficient in some ways. They simply piled the bodies on a funeral pyre and cremated them. The bodies that were killed in the landing barges and on the beaches were dragged up and an extremity such as an arm was hacked off and put on the funeral pyre. After the fire had died down they take a small white box and scoop some of the ashes into it. This accounts for one soldier and is marked with a name and returned to Japan. PFC Becraft was sickened by this gruesome attitude and hoped to never again go through such an experience. The fifth or sixth day, the men were so dirty and the stench had became so unbearable, whoever was running the show, persuaded the Japanese to allow the men to go swimming in the bay to the south of our assembly area. It was a wonderful feeling to slip into the cool waters and scrub down with soap, if you had any, or sand and get some of the filth off. We divided our group into two groups, one to watch the pitiful few belongings, while the other group bathed and vice versa. This was the first time we had been able to wash and it was enjoyed by all. However, it had adverse effects. Most men had been unable to shave and had grown beards. The bathing in the saltwater with no way to rinse, and the oppressive heat caused Guam (water) blisters to break out in the areas where hair grew. Then to try and shave in a little cold water was sheer torture. The filth of the living conditions and the swarms of flies made life miserable as the days slowly passed. Many men had no shelter from the blazing sun. Anything that could be used for shade was pressed into service.

M/Sgt. John Kunich of Service Company, 31st Infantry, found his way into our area. He had managed to escape from Bataan. John had been on detached service in our shop before the war. We were glad to see him and invited him to join our group.

Major John N. Shanks, our detachment officer, came to our group about eight days after the surrender. He had been with the senior officers and knew some of the things that were going on in trying to bring better conditions for the men. He told us that a detail was being made up to remain on the Rock and that he had put our names on the list. He thought it would be a good deal for us. Little did we realize our good fortune to be among the fortunate ones to remain on Corregidor.

The following day, about 300 men formed up near the road leading to the dock area. We had gathered up the few possessions we owned and were ready. The group moved along the road and soon came to San Jose barrio. This small barrio (village) had been the home of the Filipino dependents of the married scouts and the families of the civilian Filipinos who worked on the post. Most of the bahais (houses) had been demolished. We moved into the old slaughter shed or what was left of it.

Shortly after settling in, a group was called out for a work detail.

The Japanese moved us near the west entrance of Malinta Tunnel. The Japanese officer, through an interpreter, explained what we were to do. We were to spread out in a long line in Malinta Tunnel and remove all the weapons, gas masks, helmets, radios and other personal gear and bring it out and put it into piles near the entrance. This was the first time I had been in Malinta since early February when I was in the hospital overnight. The tunnel was about 30 feet wide, 30 feet high and 830 feet long. The entire width of the tunnel was piled high with the discarded clothing, paper from the files, file cabinets, desks, chairs, bedding and every other conceivable flotsam from the headquarters staff and the hundreds of tunnel rats. A bulldozer would have been better. The headquarters personnel had demolished everything possible. One of the cooks from our mess told me about his demolishing the First Sergeant's desk. He said, "I have always wanted to smash up a First Sergeant's desk". He took the drawers out one by one, tipped everything out. Then he kicked the bottom out and busted the sides apart. After busting the drawers, he kicked the panels out, broke the legs and left the top piled on the debris. "I always wanted to do that" he said.

We lined up along the narrow passage winding through from the west to the east portal and began to collect an armload of junk to carry out. A young lieutenant, about 10 men away from me, stepped up to the pile of debris and attempted to pull a weapon out. He grabbed it by the muzzle and pulled. The weapon discharged and shot him in the stomach. We rushed him to the hospital lateral, but he died before much could be done for him. A sad mistake for one who should have known better and to have survived thus far, to die in such a way. Equally sad that the former owner had so stupidly discarded his weapon without taking it apart and scattering the pieces.

The work continued with a lot more caution. We worked all day and late into the afternoon, then returned to the barrio. A more formal organization had began to form. Cooking gear had been scrounged, and the first hot meal of rice and C rations was served. Most of the men had obtained some mess gear or used their canteen cups. We sat around and shared smokes with those who had none and chatted about our situation and what lay ahead. There was no effort made to sort out the officers or noncommissioned officers. All were treated the same and the work details did not have an officer in charge. The rules of POW treatment do not require officers and non-commissioned officers to work unless they volunteer for work parties. The Japanese at this time considered us as hostages, pending the surrender of the southern islands, and therefore not prisoners of war. All were ordered to work irrespective of rank.

The burden of high command is heavy and awesome on a man charged with the responsibility of making decisions effecting thousands of lives. Such was the position of General Jonathan M. Wainwright as the Commander of the United States Forces in the Philippines. In his book, *General Wainwright's Story*, the general was faced with many adverse conditions. Beach defenses were pulverized, artillery was out of action, rations were running low, the enemy had landed tanks on the Rock and relief was impossible. The only alternative left open was capitulation or to continue the hopeless struggle. Uppermost was his responsibilities, concern for valiant men, the nearly 1,000 casualties and the nurses of the hospital. If the struggle continued, the possibility of a tank getting into the tunnel would be disastrous. There are some who would criticize the general for the decision to surrender. General Wainwright remarked to a member of his staff, "Now I know how General Robert E. Lee felt at Appamatox Court House."

The work of cleaning up after the battle went on for a few days when we noticed several small freighters lying off shore from the south dock. Soon, a long line of men began to appear from around Malinta Hill. Small landing barges began to shuttle men out to the ships, the prisoners were being removed to the mainland. Hopefully to a better place than they had been confined for the past three weeks in the hot sun and with very little shelter, water or food. We were unable to watch the entire loading process as our work

34

detail was called out.

The end of an era and the beginning of a new era for battered Corregidor began. Each day, work groups of 20 or more men were assigned work in clearing up the debris and junk. All material was collected, sorted and loaded out for shipment to Manila, some of the men were put to clearing up the gun batteries and magazines. We were still in the learning process and trying to understand the Japanese guards and their instructions. Most of them did not speak English and we did not speak Japanese. Things became rather hairy at times. Once, on a detail on Skipper Hill at Battery Sunset, we were told to remove a range finder. It was installed on a pedestal mounted in the center of a dugout. The roof had been constructed of timbers with about two feet of earth on top. The supporting timbers were nailed to the roof structure. The Japanese guard gestured for us to tip the roof over so the range finder could be removed. It was readily apparent that it would have to be disassembled. We tried to explain this to the guard. He threw rocks at us and gestured again. We laughed and shook our heads. He got mad and came around the cover and slapped me hard across the face. I realized that he meant for us to do as he said regardless of its impossibility. We lined up on one side and heaved and grunted to no avail. The guard came over and put his back into the struggle with no results. He then said to take it apart. A very simple lesson was learned from this experience and would serve as an example as time went on. Simply put, the old army adage, "Do as I say, don't ask questions."

This is very important in dealing with orientals. Face! Saving face! We learned not to put them in a position that would cause them to lose face or embarrass them and to obey orders without question.

We were to learn many more lessons of how to avoid trouble. Our education into the Japanese language began immediately. One of the first words was the shouted "Kora, Kora." When a guard screamed, "Kora, Kora." We never knew who was singled out, but halted whatever we were doing. The word literally means "Hey you!" Another word was "shigoto" translated means work. Takuson means a lot, thus "takuson shigoto" became a lot of

work. "Yasame" means rest or break. We had to learn to count off in Japanese for "tenko," meaning roll call, twice a day or when on detail. We would form up in two ranks and the corporal of the guard would give the command "bango," which meant to count off. Ichi, ni, san, shi, go, roku, nana or schichi, hotchi, kui, jui; which is one through ten. If the rear rank was even, the last man in the rear rank gave mon (even), kets (odd). Woe unto the one who could not remember Japanese numbers. He would get a lecture on the proper way to count off in the Japanese Army. We soon learned to put the same men in the front ranks and in the same numerical sequence. Thus he only had to know one word. The same for the man in the rear rank. Leave it to a GI, he will take advantage of the situation. During tenko, the man who happened to be seven (schichi), would butcher the Emperor's Japanese by giving the word "shits," The next man, eight, would give "hockey" (hotchi). The guard would give a hard look at the man, but didn't know whether he mispronounced the word or if he was smarting off. Another word was the command for count off, "bango." The word for toilet is "benjo," a slurring of the e, g and j in the words gave the men a sense of beating them at their own game. We had to be careful and know which guards spoke English or if the interpreter was near by. For all formations, we had to learn words like kio-suke—attention, kashira migi—eyes right, and tsai-kei-rei—salute or bow. These words were used in all formations and when officers or guard NCOs held formations. The commands were similar in usage as our commands. As long as we understood the meaning, and acted accordingly everything was okay. If not, the formations were longer while we learned basic Japanese commands.

In early July, a contingent of 76 men returned from Cabanatuan. They were held at Middleside for several days for interrogation. Later they joined us for work details. Most of them were technicians field grade or company grade officers. The senior officer was Lt. Col. Lewis Kirkpatrick. He had been the commanding officer of Fort Drum. The men from Fort Drum were taken to Ternate Batangas on the east shore of Manila Bay. Several were kept on Fort Drum to operate the power plant and water system. The covenants of the Geneva Convention were ignored as far as officers and noncoms working. All were treated the same in the early days. Another welcome asset to our group was Capt. Thomas H. Hewlett, Medical Corps. He was an excellent doctor and surgeon. Others included Capt. John J. Coughlin, Ordinance; Lt. George B. Sense, Artillery; Capt. Herman Haucks, CAC; Capt. Robert G. Cooper, Lt. John M. Wright Jr. and many others. Another man we had picked up while at the 92nd Garage, M/Sgt. John Kunich, Service Company, 31st Infantry, who had escaped from Bataan and had now joined our group. He had been detached service with the base maintenance shop in port area before the war.

This was the first time we learned about the Death March and the horrible death rate at Camp O'Donnell. Camp O'Donnell was the destination of the battling bastards of Bataan. The end of the death march and the armpit of hell for those unfortunate men. The horrible conditions described there made the hair stand up on our necks. There was not much we could do about it, but hope that we never went there.

The group had been sent to Cabanatuan and then returned to Corregidor. The hospital staff and the seriously wounded patients who were in the hospital in Malinta Tunnel at the time of surrender were kept there until July. The hospital staff were allowed to care for the American and Japanese casualties until they were able to travel. The Japanese had posted guards in the lateral leading to the hospital area. Japanese officers gave strict orders to their men to leave the nurses and staff alone. Among the patients were several Japanese who had been wounded during the invasion. There was a lot of leering and ogling but the nurses were not bothered. In July, after the patients had become well enough to be moved, the entire staff and patients were shipped to Bilibid Prison in Manila. The nurses were sent to the Santa Tomas internment camp where they were useful to the hundreds of women, children and men.

The group from Cabanatuan joined us about the first of July. We were moved from the San Jose barrio to Middleside, into the station hospital. This was a welcome change from the slaughter house. Triple deck bunks with mattress and mattress covers were set up in the lower level on the back side. It was rather crowded but beat sleeping on the cement floor of the slaughter house and the 92nd Garage. A cook shack was constructed on the south end of the hospital. Details scrounged up cook stoves, pots, pans, and a refrigerator was brought in from some of the officers quarters. The officers and some men occupied the first floor of the south wing. The Japanese took over the hospital kitchen and the north end of the hospital.

Later we were moved to the second and third floors. A barrier was constructed in the area near the stairs going to the upper level to separate the two areas. We moved out of the poorly ventilated basement into the second floor. The second floor had tall sliding shutters on three sides and overlooked Boca Chica Channel. Americans called it North Channel, and the Mariveles Mountains. The ward had a large veranda around the outside and had once had sliding panels with shell inserts for protection from the tropical rains and sun. The steel double decker bunks with mattresses gave the feeling of peacetime. We were not as crowded for space as in the basement. The improved living conditions with running water and electric lights were a great boost to morale. The ready availability of electricity for lights and hot plates gave us the feeling of living high on the hog. These luxuries of modern life are accepted as a matter of fact and were sorely missed when not available. The central power plant and water system were put back into operation by the Japanese Navy with American personnel from the Post Engineers staff. A sick bay was set up on the first floor. Work details scrounged medical equipment and some medical supplies. Furniture, footlockers, tables and some chairs. Hundreds of books were salvaged from the post library and were traded around. The sewer system was partly serviceable. A total lack of toilet tissue prevented use of the toilets, but allowed use of urinals and wash basins. The waste paper salvaged from the headquarters in Malinta was mimeographed special orders and other material.

Once when visiting the benjo uchi (toilet), I was browsing through the special orders and

R E S T R I C T E D

HEADQUARTERS PHILIPPINE DEPARTMENT
In the Field.

SPECIAL ORDERS)
NO.........23)   E X T R A C T   24 January, 1942.
            X   X   X

8. By direction of the President, _nder authority contained
in Public Law 18, 76th Congress, approv_ _, 1939, as amended,
OWEN WALLACE ROMAINE, having been dis_ _ flying cadet on
5 December, 1941, his entry on e_t_ _ _ as a Second Lieutenant, Air-Reserve (Serial No. _ _8th Materiel
Squadron effective 6 December, _ _ urgency of
the service having prevented _ _ce. Lieutenant ROMAINE will rank f_ _ _ess: 9
Taylor Avenue, Fort Thor_ _

9. By direc_ _ _ _ Law
252, 77th Congress, a_ _ _ _ad-
quarters USAFFE, file _ _ _ subject:
"Temporary Commissions i_ _ PAUL MONICO,
(O-890210), formerly Sgt., _ _ointed and
accepted commission as a Sec_ _ in the Army of
the United States, effective t_ _ to the Commanding
General, I Philippine Corps for _ _h Division (PA).

10. By direction of the Comma_ _eral, USAFFE, under the
provisions of letter USAFFE, Subject: _ndards of Efficiency for
Field Service", dated January 26, 194_, the following named officers,
now at Headquarters Philippine Army, are relieved from duty with the
organizations indicated and are attached to the 2d Regular Philippine Division:

Special Orders No. 23, Par. 12, HPD, 24 January, 1942, continued:

TO BE TECHNICAL SERGEANT (TEMPORARY)
Staff Sgt. JOHN T. OCEDEK, 6215008
TO BE STAFF SERGEANTS (TEMPORARY)
Sgt. RALPH E. REYNOLDS, 6731598
Pvt., Spec. 1cl ASBURY L. NIX, 6295289
TO BE SERGEANTS (TEMPORARY)
Pvt 1cl Spec 4cl MYRON A. MILLIKEN, 6974706
Pvt 1cl Spec 4cl HERSHEL B. COX, 6655073
Pvt 1cl Spec 6cl WILLIAM LILLEY, 6890943
Pvt. Spec 2cl WILLIAM STANDRIDGE, 6365438
Pvt. ERNEST A. DUFRANE, 6461836

COINCIDENCE
Special Orders 25, dated 24 January, 1942 were recovered under peculiar circumstances. I knew that I had been promoted to Staff Sergeant, I did not have a copy of the orders.
In 1943, while a POW on Corregidor we had gathered up a stack of paper from Malinta Tunnel for use as toilet paper. I had gone to the latrine and was idly browsing through the stack of paper, when I suddenly came to the order promoting me and several other men to Staff Sergeant.
Needless to say this piece of paper did not wind up in the pit.
These orders were carried through the POW camps and are original and well preserved for 46 years.

Special Orders #23, 24 January, 1942. Promotion orders signed by Allen C. McBride, Chief of Staff by order of Gen. MacArthur.

found Special Orders No. 25, dated 24 January, 1942. My promotion to staff sergeant was listed. I knew that I had been promoted, but did not have a copy of the orders. Needless to say, that piece of paper did not wind up in the benjo. I managed to carry it for the duration and made it page one of my new 201 File on return to the United States. Slit trenches were dug away from the building and were maintained to prevent flies and odor.

The galley was equipped with adequate facilities for washing mess kits and quaning gear. Food was provided from captured stores. Large quantities of cracked wheat were brought in along with bags of rice. The cracked wheat had been shipped to Japan for earthquake relief in 1925. Whether it had never been shipped to Japan or stored in bodegas in the Philippines, we didn't know. It was moldy and full of weevils and worms. The cooks cooked it into a gruel and served it with whatever they could lay their hands on. When served, the worms and weevils served as protein, but it was difficult to get down. The best way was to make for the bunk area in the darkest part of the basement and get it down without seeing all the proteins.

The change in a person's attitude about food occurs under severe shortages. Each man was acutely aware that survival of the strongest was the rule of the game. Amazingly, hungry men will constantly watch the other person as they go through the chow line. The mess officer had to stand at the serving line to insure equal portions of chow.

At first, a standard mess kit or canteen cup was used to measure the ration. Soon someone figured out a way to try and beat the game. A craftsman would take a standard aluminum mess kit and place it in a bed of sand. Careful pounding with a small hammer, the metal could be stretched to a greater depth. This resulted in a deeper mess kit and would hold more. The craftsman would charge for this service. Usually it would be a share of a ration of rice or whistle weed soup. A skilled and shrewd craftsman could accumulate a larger meal. This was known as jawboning, a form of commodity credit. The jawbone could be a specified share at a stated date or time or subject to call at the discretion of the craftsman.

A standard measure was used regardless of the depth of the man's mess kit. A lot of arguments broke out over the standard ration. Our education in the finer points of survival progressed by experience or from observation. We soon learned that there were two things one should have at all times, a standard GI (government issued) spoon and a P-40 can opener. The P-40 can opener was a component of the C rations. A man with these essential items would be in the position of being able to share any scrounged goodies. If it was canned, he had the opener and the spoon to eat his share.

S/Sgt. Larson, after recovering from his wounds, was shipped to the Davao detail on Minadanao Island shortly after he left Corregidor. Later, in July 1944, I was to meet him again in Bilibid Prison and he told me a humorous story. He asked a cook to open a can of corned beef. Sgt. Larson had only one arm, which he had lost just before the surrender and could not open a can of corned beef. The cook refused on the grounds that Sgt. Larson would have to share with him for the service. Sgt. Larson bided his time until the cook started to quan his corned beef. "The quan was on the stove, smelling awfully good." When the cook's attention was diverted, Sgt. Larson set his can on the edge of the stove and make off with the cook's quanned meal. Sgt. Larson was known as the "one-armed bandit" thereafter.

The Japanese allowed the men to cook up whatever they could find during the day on detail. This was usually shared with one's own group of buddies. Some was traded, or through a cooperative effort of finding someone with the items you needed, a man might find some flour and needed fat, cooking oil, yeast or sugar to concoct a batch of pancakes. At times this almost caused a fight. One of the fellows came up with what was assumed to be flour. He located some sugar, yeast and cooking oil and they agreed to share. The batter was mixed and ready for cooking when the call came for tenko (roll call). When they returned, they headed for a fire with a piece of boiler plate over it for a griddle. Lo and behold the batter had set up hard. The flour had turned out to be plaster of Paris. The poor fellow got a hard time about that.

The practice of cooking up a mixture, coined

38

a new word. Quanning, ingredients for quanning. Quan bucket—cooking utensil. Quan is derived from the Filipino word, "quan." Anything a Filipino could not name in English became "quan." It could be a carburetor, a fuel pump, or most any item that the Filipino couldn't name. Quanning was permitted by the Japanese as long as the fires were away from the building and were controlled. They had a real phobia about fire.

Smoking was permitted in the quarters provided an ashtray was in hand. A novel method of alerting anyone engaged in something not permitted or had valuables out, was to call "air raid" when a snoopy guard appeared. Immediate action was taken to prevent the guard from catching someone in a prohibited act.

The American soldier is an ingenious individual. When deprived of an item, he will come up with an alternate. Coffee was missed by all and a suitable substitute was charred rice, scorched until it was black. This was run through a grinder and produced a dark, course powder which was widely used as a substitute for coffee. It was drinkable and with a good imagination, passed for the real thing. One enterprising soldier of Swedish ancestors, would walk around with a quan bucket of water. In a slow Swedish drawl, he would say, "I vas ooust going out to make some coffee. I have the vater if you have the coffee."

Another sorely missed item was matches. They were impossible to find and usually were water-soaked and useless. Elements from an electric cookstove were salvaged and rigged on a piece of Formica. A switch was inserted in the line. When one wanted to light a cigarette, he flipped the switch and the coil would light up. Although very simple, it was an item kept secret from the Japanese. Zippo lighters and flints were much sought after. The lighter could be dipped in a gas tank as substitute for lighter fluid. They were valuable items and highly prized by the Japanese.

The rations provided from Japanese stores were rice, barley, mango beans, kelp, mitso paste (sour soybean paste), camotes (native sweet potatoes), some kind of greens (whistle weed, it was called), and cracked wheat. Tomatoes were also furnished in limited amounts. Polished rice was preferred by the

Nips. Unpolished rice was preferred by the Americans as it contained more nutrients. Fish were also provided. The rations of fish would lie on the dock in Manila and on the boat coming out without refrigeration and would be spoiled by the time they reached the galley. These were small silver fish, which we called Silver Dollar fish and were served in the soup—hair, hide, tail and all.

There were other sources of food supplies. The waters around Corregidor were a good source of fresh fish. Infrequently the Japanese would load beer bottles with dynamite and a short fuse. These would be tossed into the south bay and stunned fish would rise to the surface. Good swimmers would go out and bring them in. At times, this would provide a bonanza. Wicker baskets were used to collect the catch and would be loaded into a truck. While this was being done, one of the POWs would snatch a nice big one and throw it through the back window opening of the truck. The driver would tip the seat forward and the fish would slide under the seat. The Japanese never caught on as they were on the dock watching the excitement.

When the truck arrived at the Japanese galley, a line of POWs would form to carry baskets of fish upstairs. The POWs would set the basket down, grab a big fish, make for the stairs leading to the American side and throw it over the fence. Again the Nips would be watching the other end, excited about the good dinner they would have with such nice fish. A hazard of this type of fishing was sharks. They would come searching the area when they heard the explosions. They had learned from the bombing and shelling that fish were available without hunting.

Fruits of many varieties grew profusely in the tropics. They grew amazingly fast in the warm humid climate. One fruit, papaya, grew wild on the Rock and was one of the most productive trees. The problem was the men would not wait for the fruit to ripen. They would pick them green before they reached maturity and full size. Green papayas were edible when sliced and deep-fried. Another plant was a type of vine that grew on rocky hillsides. The tuber or root would wind down through cracks in the rock, swell out in hollow spots and squeeze through more cracks in the rocks. It would reach a length of four or five feet. The labor involved was strenuous and with care, using an old-fashioned army entrenching pick, a good amount could be dug out. It would then be grated and would form a dough that could be baked like bread. Other items were mangos, guavas, papayas and coconuts.

Generally scrounging was done with the permission of the guard or on Sunday under supervision. Camotes, Whistle Weed, rotten fish, and occasionally meat, made up the ingredients of the soup of the day. Camotes, were furnished in season, they were not as large as the sweet potato grown at home, but were a welcome sight.

The Japanese started to furnish a ration of four cigarettes a day. They were a welcome addition and served as trading material, and they had a psychological purpose. A good smoke after working all day in the sun and a meager supper, we could relax, dream, and enjoy one of the few nice things left to the POWs. Those who did not smoke would trade them for other commodities in lieu of money. Many men would receive their ration and very carefully cut each cigarette into four pieces. A holder was used to smoke each segment. Some would joke that their buddy could smoke a cigarette until the ashes fell behind his teeth to be used for tooth powder. Also available, through trading with the Filipinos on the scrap iron barges that came out from Manila, were native grown tobacco leaves. This was not cured, dried leaf tobacco and required some preparation. The leaves would be wrapped into a damp towel until the leaves were pliable. The stems and membranes would be removed and the leaves rolled into the shape of a cigar. This was used as a cigar or crimp cut for cigarettes or pipe tobacco. One of these cigars lit up would raise the hair on your head. Some would mix it with sugar and cure it to reduce it's potency.

Once, I contacted the Filipino crane operator on the scrap iron barge and asked him to bring back a plug of American chewing tobacco. The next trip out he brought me a plug of Brown Mule Chewing Tobacco. It was still wrapped in the original paper. I opened it up and sliced off a chew. It was full of tobacco worms. Even with the added protein, I couldn't chew it.

Black market items could be obtained through the Filipinos who came out with the barge. Their contacts in Manila were the Chinese merchants. However, the prices were high and the possible compromising of the Filipinos was possible. Some of the Japanese guards going on pass to Manila would bring some items back for trading. Filipino pesos were in great demand. However, this had to be on black market as the Japanese had issued invasion script. The funny money was the legal currency. Later under an agreement the Filipinos were granted semi-quasi government and printed an occupation peso as legal tender.

The Japanese started a small store at Middleside with some articles for sale. A Coca Cola was one black market dollar. Japanese cigarettes were just as expensive. Staple goods like sugar, salt, bulk mango beans, tea and fruit were more practical. The sugar was not refined and was coarse. The salt was mined from the sedimentation beds of salt-water in Manila Bay and was not cleaned. However, they were most sought after and served the purpose. A system of payment for labor was started in September of 1942. We were paid in Japanese script. The pay scale was based on rank. Privates received the smallest amount and officers the most. The payment was only 10 percent of the total and the balance was allegedly deposited in a bank. A pooling of money was set up and an officer would go to the store and buy the items the men specified. An account was kept for each man. This was voluntary and some men participated. The few yen we received would not buy much.

The general health of the men remained good. A moderate loss of weight by all was to be expected. Some of the men who had been on Bataan had reoccurrence of malaria and dengue fever, and were in worse shape than those who had been fortunate enough to be on Corregidor. Dr. Hewlett had some medicines and was able to control most cases. Several men turned up with appendicitis and surgery was required. An excellent group of medical corps personnel assisted and all recovered without complications. Late in 1942, the effects of malnutrition, beri-beri, edema and

40

pellagra, due to lack of certain vitamins, began to appear. Some with loss of vision due to optical atrophy and other indications of vitamin deficiencies became evident. Most were told to lay off reading and any straining of the eyes. The Japanese did at one time give us shots for tetanus and cholera. They insisted that the shots be given in the chest muscles.

The men who came back from the main camps in early June gave the first indication of the horrible conditions at Camp O'Donnell and Cabanatuan. We were appalled to hear of the terrible Death March from Bataan, the wanton disregard for human dignity, starvation diet, water shortages, lack of medical supplies, degradation and inhumane treatment. Listening to these stories made us realize how fortunate it was to have remained on the Rock. The men who returned were very pleased that they had been sent back.

Lt. Col. Lewis S. Kirkpatrick, as senior American officer (SAO), was able to get the Japanese to agree to a quasi-military structure of command. The men were organized into working details of about 25 men with an officer assigned as supervisor. Each officer reported to the SAO. Each group was assigned specific work assignments. Lt. Leonard E. Goldsmith was made OIC of the motor pool and maintenance. Myself, Sgt. Haddox, M/Sgt. Kunich and S/Sgt. Golson were assigned to this group. We used the same shop and tools that we had used prior to the surrender. A motley collection of trucks was rounded up and used for transporting men to work areas, hauling of scrap iron, and towing of wrecked vehicles to Bottomside for cutting into scrap iron. Lt. John M. Wright Jr. was assigned as mess officer and later as the executive officer to Lt. Col. Kirkpatrick. Captain Hewlett ran the sickbay and held sick call each day. This arrangement was better and order was established. The Japanese would assign certain guards to each working group and instructions for accomplishment of assigned work. There was less hassle and abuse of the men. The officers served as advocates for their men.

The Japanese told us early on that we were not prisoners of war but, we were guests of the Japanese emperor. Later, we were told that

now we were prisoners of war (horiyo). In other words we were to work at whatever and go wherever they so chose. The general attitude on Corregidor of the Japanese was one of moderate treatment, consistent with the accomplishment of the work to their satisfaction. Lt. Tokashige the senior Japanese officer in Camp No. 9, along with Japanese NCOs, received his orders from Manila. Occasionally an inspecting officer would show up and look things over. Another very important rule was bowing. Whenever one passed the Japanese guard house, it was mandatory to stop, face the guard and bow. This was to acknowledge the authority of the emperor and the Imperial Japanese Army. Bowing was to be done in a prescribed manner. One must halt, pull arms in tight against the sides and bow from the hips and hold it until the guard acknowledged it. One who did not do it right or forgot, received at the least a tongue lashing or a slap across the cheek or stand at attention for a time. The guard house was always a veranda or a porch with an open front. The corporal of the guard would sit at a desk or a table with four guards sitting in chairs lined up in front.

There have been numerous stories about American turncoats or traitors, who openly cooperated, collaborated and turned on Americans by some act or word. One individual of some notoriety was an American Army Sergeant, John David Provoo. He allegedly met the Japanese at the time of surrender dressed in a Buddhist monk's robe, shaved head, speaking fluent Japanese and volunteered his services. Provoo had lived in Japan and spoke the language very well. He and one other redheaded man (name forgotten), were assigned to work in the Japanese kitchen. At times, Provoo would act as interpreter. Allegedly, he reported an American major to the Japanese while at the hospital. The major reportedly asked for extra food, was denied, and allegedly insulted him and degraded the Japanese. The major was taken to Kindley Field and executed. Provoo was moved to our detail when the hospital moved to Manila and was a dog robber for the Japanese. He would appear on the third floor portico on the west side of the hospital in the evening and conduct a Buddhist ritual to the sun. Weird incantations and howling of unintelligible sounds could be heard. Provoo and the other man never associated with the POWs or came into the quarters of the Americans. *Note: When we were processed through Yokohoma in September of 1945 for debriefing, one of the questions asked was, "Do you know John David Provoo?"*

In 1951 at Governors Island N.Y., Sgt. Provoo was discharged from service. He was immediately arrested by the Federal Bureau of Investigation, and charged with the crime of treason. A lengthy trial was held in New York City. He was found guilty and sentenced to a life term in prison. The verdict was overturned on appeal to a higher court on jurisdiction grounds. He was later released as being deprived of a speedy trial. Treason requires two eye witnesses to the same incident. Capital crimes require only one eye witness for conviction. Witnesses were called from several countries to testify.

The demise of the colorful Coast Artillery Corps was not alone in its passage into history. Another element of the old army was the final days of the old dashing, slashing and spirited Horse Cavalry. Drawn from the fabric of time, the cavalry was a part of the colorful past of the old military history. The fall of Bataan was the final battle for this grand old horse mounted army corps. The 26th Cavalry Regiment (PS) went down to glory in the debacle of unpreparedness that was Bataan and Corregidor. Their horses were ordered slaughtered and fed to the starving troops on Bataan.

In June of 1939, as a recruit fresh off the farm in the hill country of Texas, I was sent to Fort McDowell, California, for shipment to the islands. A notice was posted on the bulletin board asking for volunteers to ride herd on horses and mules aboard the U.S. Army Transport Meigs. I volunteered to nurse maid 250 horses and mules. Fort McDowell was used as an assembly point for departure and return of troops. I had decided that I did not want to ride a troopship with hundreds of men who had never been to sea. Forty men were selected and sent to the Presidio of San Francisco. We lived in squad tents and waited for shipments from the remount stations. The incoming stock was penned at Fort Winfield Scott at the foot of the south tower of the Golden Gate Bridge. Once a day we would

march to Fort Scott and throw out bales of hay for the stock. On June 30, 1939, we embarked horses, mules and men at Fort Mason. We stopped in Honolulu and 30 days later arrived in Manila.

A detachment of the 26th Cavalry were at Pier One and the animals were loaded into antiquated chain drive FWD trucks for transport to Fort Stotensberg. There were several private mounts for some of the officers. During the voyage out, one becomes attached to their charges and certain animals become favorites. One particular mule, a fine specimen about 14 hands high, never appreciated being stuffed into the hold of a ship. Each time he was brought from his stall for grooming on the hatch cover, he would raise up on his rear legs and try to reach the top of the hatch. Others were regular pests, when they were hosed down they would nip you on the arm when you moved to the next animal. The thought never occurred to me that I would some day be eating one of these animals.

Late in July of 1942 we were returning to our billet area. We had come up around by Battery Geary and were moving along by the golf course. There grazing along was one government issued mule. He appeared to be the same animal that wanted freedom during the trip out to the Philippines. The Japanese guard stopped the truck and said, "Ichi ban (No. 1) messy messy (chow)." He stood up and shot that beautiful animal dead. We continued on to camp and returned with a couple of cooks and butchered it out. It was served to the POWs. I could hardly eat my chow. It was almost like eating a friend. I do not know where this animal spent the time on Corregidor. The terrific bombardment and shelling killed everything that was not covered and surely a mule would have been exposed. Thus the last of these wonderful animals passed into history as food for the hungry POWs. Most of the animals of the 26th Cavalry (PS) met the same fate on Bataan.

The new arrangement of American officers as buffers and advocates for the prisoners of war brought about a welcome change. We were allowed to move into the 2nd and 3rd floors of the hospital from the overcrowded basement. More room was allowed between bunks and there was no crowding. The partial roof of the building kept most of the men dry in rainy season. We experienced a severe typhoon in August. Shelter halves had to be rigged on the mosquito net cross bars as protection from the leaking roof. No work was ordered for two days. The wind sent pieces of sheet metal and debris slicing through the air. It was not safe to venture out unless nature forced one to make for the benjo uchi (latrine). Torrents of water cascaded off the buildings, almost horizontal with the force of the wind. The wind was gale force and the cook shack was blown away and wrapped around a tree. The men's clothing and bedding were soaked. After the storm abated the cook shack was rebuilt and work details were formed to clean up and restore a semblance of order.

The work details cleared all the laterals in Malinta Tunnel and the other tunnels. Other details collected, cleaned and performed preventive cleaning of ammunition. The scrap details collected all of the cars, trucks, vehicles and anything that was made of metal. Most of the trolley tracks were torn out and cut into scrap. One detail was assigned to collect all the sheet metal that had been blasted from roofs and tie it into bundles. It made no difference how rusted or beat up it was, straighten it out and tie it into bundles for shipment. Acetylene torches were brought in and all that was too big for one man to carry was cut into smaller pieces. An artillery prime mover, an International Harvester tractor, Model TD 18 with a front mounted winch, was used to drag vehicles and other large pieces to the cutting area at Bottomside. Another item—a crane, wheel-mounted, with hard tires, and a boom that would handle about 6,000 pounds, was also pressed into service for lifting. This machine had lost its steering gear and Master Sergeant Kunich and Petty Officer White, rigged a steering lever on the side and attached it to the drag link. It was made of a piece of steel about four inches wide and one-half inch thick. It was an arm buster. If the operator was not alert when one of the front wheels hit something, the machine would veer to the right or left. The operator had to release his hold on the bar or it would have broken his arm.

It was a shame that the Japanese did not realize or did not know that a lot of the equipment could have been useful. Perhaps they wanted to utilize the POWs as slave laborers. A good example was Company A, 803rd Engineer Battalion a Pennsylvania National Guard unit, that had been sent to the Rock to do some work on Kindley Field. Part of their equipment was a Caterpillar D8 bulldozer with a 12-yard LeTourneau towed scraper. The tractor/scraper unit could have been put into service, but the Nips said cut it into pieces. Having worked with this type of equipment, I was dismayed to see good equipment chopped into pieces. A unit such as this, at Nichols and Nielson Fields in Manila, could have moved more earth in one day than all those poor unfortunate POWs did in a month. There were other similar units on Bataan that could have been used. The oriental conception that manpower could do the job contributed to much suffering by those poor unfortunate souls serving like slave laborers in the repair of the airfields and construction of new roads in Tayabas.

One of the nicest automobiles to be chopped into small pieces was a beautiful Packard Clipper limousine. It was equipped with air-conditioning and had a bar in the rear seat. It belonged to Major Gen. Southerland, Chief of Staff to Lt. Gen. MacArthur. Many other staff cars and private autos suffered the same fate. The Japanese guard would stand around and watch the calculated destruction. Many of the men operating the torches did not have cutting goggles. They would watch until the metal became hot enough to cut, then apply oxygen and look away to avoid eye damage.

As the operator of the TD 18 tractor, the idea was to crush the vehicle down for easier cutting. I would approach a vehicle and ride up on top and crunch the body down. The usual procedure was to run in about second or third gear low range, ride up on the center of the vehicle and then lock one track and spin around. The TD 18 tractor had a speed of about 12 miles per hour in high gear high range and was equipped with steel pads over the grouser shoes. These were loose from wear and at full speed on a hard surface road made a clatter like a boiler factory. Occasionally the Japanese guard would signal to stop and let him ride. When this happened, a slight movement of the arm would slip into high range. After the guard was seated with rifle in hand, I would shift into 3rd gear, push the throttle wide open and head for a vehicle, ride the left track up onto the vehicle and then lock the left track and spin the tractor in a 360-degree turn. The guard would be clutching his weapon with no hand holds for him to grab. He could have been sent flying into space. Watching him out of the corner of my eye, I would let up on the steering clutch enough to keep him on the machine. One trip was enough for him. He would dismount and mutter something to the effect, "baka baka," which means "nutty or crazy." This was dangerous business. If the guard had been thrown off, I felt certain that he would have been extremely mad and would and could have gotten away with shooting me on the spot.

Another example of the Japanese ignorance of equipment capabilities was in the large marine machine shop at Bottomside. This shop was equipped with all the equipment needed for heavy support of the big guns, lathes, milling machines, drill presses and shapers. One lathe was capable of handling the tube from the 12-inch rifles of Battery Hearn and Smith. The bed bolts would be removed and a winch line attached to the top of a machine. The tractor would be put into reverse and the machine would be jerked from its base, usually on its face, smashing all the controls. It would then be skidded down a concrete road to the north dock. No attempt was made to recover anything in a usable way. Scrap iron was the objective. The POWs joked about the scrap iron helping to send ships to the bottom when attacked by our navy.

Lt. Goldsmith was our officer in the shop and motor pool area. The Japanese honcho was a typical example of most of the guards, short on brains and long on ignorance of mechanics. The only mechanical experience he had was riding a motorcycle in Japan. He would come up with the zaniest ideas on what could be done to a vehicle. The Americans would encourage him in his impractical ideas. We had several trucks and one beat up Plymouth sedan with no glass except the windshield. One of these trucks was a British combat truck, designed for use in the desert. It was equipped with high-flotation tires and a small cargo space. Its height made it difficult to load. A disabled GMC 2½-ton truck was also available. The honcho decided that the two trucks could be modified. The frames were cut just behind the cab and by welding the rear half of the GMC to the front half of the British truck a longer chassis could be made. No sooner said than done. M/Sgt. Kunich and Cpl. Haddox had the torches out and were cutting away. With the able supervision of our honcho, the two sections were welded together and a GMC truck body was mounted. The front axle was thrown out of alignment. This halfbreed could be driven up to about five mph and all was well. Above that speed it would start to shimmy and almost take the steering wheel out of your hand. The trick was to drive it just fast enough to shimmy hard but not to lose control. This put severe stress on the steering gear and it soon shook its self to pieces. Off to the scrap heap.

Another instance of the mechanical expertise of our mechanical genius was the replacement of a GMC engine. Lt. Tokashige and the Japanese NCO took M/Sgt. Kunich to Bataan to recover a GMC engine from a truck. They returned with the engine. The honcho, with encouragement from the American mechanics, decided it had to be stripped down, inspected, and reassembled. Forgetting there were no new gaskets or parts, it was taken apart. The honcho wanted to do the refitting. M/Sgt. Kunich acted as his assistant and handed him wrenches and tools. When the crankshaft was fitted into place there was no torque wrench, a long flex handled socket was used. Nicely snugged down without rotating the crankshaft to see if it was free. The connecting rods were tightened the same way. On completion of the job the engine was installed in one of the GMCs. The starter motor couldn't budge it. Bring on the TD 18 tractor and pull it. Every time the clutch was released to turn the engine over all the wheels would lock up. After some dragging around, it too joined the junk heap. M/Sgt. Kunich had worked in the engine repair section in Manila for two years before the war. He urged the honcho along knowing that the engine would be useless. Another truck the Japanese liked was a 2½-ton search light truck with a double cab. It had been designed for transporting a search light and generator. It was equipped with a long body and could haul more cargo than the conventional GMC. The Japanese idea was more and more scrap without consideration of the capacity or weight limitations. It would be loaded with five to eight tons. Fortunately for the Japanese, the trips were generally short. The guards liked it because they could ride in the double cab.

A tribute should be made to the manufacturers of U.S. Army vehicles. Severely overloaded, a minimum of maintenance, and lack of proper lubricants, they held up remarkably well. The TD 18 tractor was a good example. It was operated on ship's bunker fuel. Diesel fuel was not available. This fuel was low in viscosity and thick like tar. The fuel filters would clog up and had to be removed and the deposits scrapped off with a stick down to the filter, washed in gasoline and back into service. The track rollers were not greased, nor was the oil changed, just added more when it was low. The unit was a marvel of American engineering. Keeping it running was to the advantage of the POWs and saved them a lot of backbreaking work. The Japanese are fond of using a bamboo pole with a sling to move any heavy items. Without the trucks all of the scrap would have been handled by Yo-Ho poles and a sling. We were to learn more about Yo-Ho poles later.

Another idea our budding Japanese engineer came up with was a real Rube Goldberg marvel. The heavy shelling and bombing had annihilated the rail system. This was an electric standard gauge track system that ran to all the major batteries, housing area, troop billets, theater, cold storage plant, power house, machine shop and through Malinta Tunnel to a row of houses near the officers beach. The aerial electric system was gone and most of the traction units were demolished or converted into scrap. There were several flat cars about forty-feet long. Someone decided to manufacture an engine that could haul one flatcar loaded from the dock up to Malinta. The Japanese were shipping ammunition to Corregidor for storage in the tunnel. M/Sgt. Kunich and Cpl. Haddox, ever the ones to try anything that appeared possible but not practical, worked out a Rube Gold-

berg system for the job. A 40-foot flatcar was used as the basic vehicle. A utility diesel, model UD 18, 60 kw generator was brought in and the generator removed, and a clutch and housing were installed. A heavy-duty transmission and transfer case were connected to the output shaft with drive shafts going forward and aft. This resulted in extremely long drive shafts forward and aft with no pillow locks. Worm drive differential gears were fitted onto the car axles and a torque bar to offset the torque of the drive shafts. A 12 cfm air compressor was rigged with a belt-drive pulley behind the clutch housing and connected to the air storage tanks on the car. This marvel of Rube Goldberg engineering took about three months of trial and error. Finally the day for road test was set. The unit was on the flat ground at Bottomside. With M/Sgt. Kunich as engineer and the beaming honcho aboard, the engine was fired up and air pressure brought up to 100 psi. M/Sgt. Kunich eased the clutch in and the contraption moved along at about five mph. The Benjo Special was declared operational. All of the Japanese were happy. Now the movement of ammo could be moved along faster than by trucks.

The taisho (officer) in Manila would be very happy. The following day the Benjo Special pushed a flatcar over to the north dock for loading. Everything looked "ichi ban" (No.1). The flatcar was loaded about three tiers high with 105 mm ammo. Engineer Kunich had aired up and eased the clutch in and moved along about four mph. The long propeller shafts held up with very little whip. As the Benjo Special moved away from the dock area, it traversed a slight grade increase and the anti-torque rods from the differential began to bend, with the possibility of twisting the propeller shaft from the differential. Cpl. Haddox was walking along the side watching the drive train as it began to vibrate and whip. M/Sgt. Kunich eased up on the throttle and applied the brakes, shifted into reverse and eased back down on the flat area.

The Benjo Express was uncoupled and moved away from the loaded flatcar. Everyone came over to see what the problem was. The explanation of the trouble was translated by the interpreter, Superior Private Danjo to Lt. Tokashige. M/Sgt. Kunich, by sign language and pigeon Japanese, explained the problem to the Japanese. With many "Aso" (I see), they ordered more work on the Benjo Special. The welder was brought up and a jury rigged repair and beefing up of the torque rod was done. Welding of a piece of steel at right angles to the torque rod, the job was finished the next day. The major problem was the area where the torque rod was bolted to the differential housings, being only about two inches wide. The four-inch bar had to be cut to fit the curvature of the gear housing and created a weak spot in the anti-torque rods. The additional vertical reinforcement appeared to be what the doctor ordered and everything looked "ichi ban." The following morning everyone was ready for the Benjo Special to go to work. The unit was coupled to the flatcar and towed the car up the slight grade to a switch. The switch man, Cpl. Haddox, threw the switch and the ammo car was now at the front. The Benjo Special eased onto the tracks leading to Malinta Tunnel. The grade from the switch was slight, but increased the farther the rig went. About 100 yards from the tunnel the drive shafts began to whip violently. M/Sgt. Kunich applied the air, but had not built up the air pressure after stopping for the switching. The rpm on the shaft were not fast enough for the compressor to build up pressure rapidly. The Benjo Special came back down the grade faster than going up. It came to a stop near the switch. The Japanese held a conference and came to the conclusion that the Benjo Special was too dangerous to operate and relegated the Benjo Special to the cutting torches. The failure of the project was never in doubt by the Americans. The unloading and storage of ammunition in Malinta Tunnel continued at a slower pace.

One might ask why Americans would do this kind of work for the Japanese? There are two answers: the Japanese were interested in prolonging the work and anxious to avoid being sent south to the war zone. They apparently didn't want the work to be finished. They had it made on the Rock. They were living better than ever. They slept in hospital beds with clean sheets and inner spring mattresses, had good food, a roof over their heads, were not exposed to malaria and the duty was great for them. The American POWs knew this kind of work took up a lot of time and material, and hoped to remain on the Island as long as possible without incurring the wrath or suspicion of the Japanese. They knew also, that conditions on Corregidor were much better than the main camps.

The Japanese had developed a new approach to the Filipino prisoners at Camp O'Donnell. They assumed that the Filipinos would readily join in making the Philippines a part of the grand plan. Yankee imperialists would have been run out of Asia. They released the Filipinos from the prison camps. They were to join with Japan in the new "Greater East Asia Co-Prosperity Sphere." A Filipino puppet government was formed and the Filipinos were told they were now a part of "The Greater East Asia Co-Prosperity Sphere." Some of the released Filipinos were put into labor groups to perform jobs assigned in the interest of the Prosperity Sphere. This was a mistake as the Filipinos did not share the same view.

A group of about 50 Filipino (ex-prisoners of war) were sent to Corregidor. The work force, approximately 316 POWs, was reduced by the shipment of 65 men, most of them company grade officers, to the mainland and on to other camps in the islands as well as Japan. The work program was the same, cleanup and collection of scrap and stockpiling ammo in Malinta Tunnel and preservation of the big guns. The Filipinos were treated the same as the American POW's and shared the same billets in the old hospital. Their chow was the same. Living conditions were much better than they had at Camp O'Donnell with improved health care. The Filipinos had the highest death rate at Camp O'Donnell. They were told by the Japanese that it was for the glory of the Philippines and Japan. The Filipinos did not buy that crock of crap. They called it "The Greater East Asia Co-Poverty Sphere." They wanted to go home. Most of them were Philippine Army draftees from the southern islands and were very young and unhappy with the enforced separation from their families. Two of them were selected for a special detail.

They were assigned the job of fishermen for the Japanese kitchen. They were equipped with a diving glass and a manufactured spear gun. The spear gun was made from the bus bars from the generator switchboards. A point was hammered out and a barb was cut in the tip. A clay insulator, for passing electric wire through a wall, was secured to rubber bands cut from inner tubes. The spear would be put into the insulator and cocked or loaded by drawing back on the shaft of the spear, very similar to launching an arrow. The Filipios are natural swimmers. They would swim about the shores of the Rock and spear octopus, fish, eels and any other type of edible seafood. One item the Japanese like was Porcupine fish. They are poisonous unless one knows how to prepare them. When on the defensive they inflate and become very large with quills similar to a porcupine. The Japanese, as well as Filipinos, main staple is fish and rice with a small quantity of vegetables. The Filipino fishermen knew what was edible and came in each day with a good catch for the Japanese mess.

Skin diving can be dangerous. One of the Filipinos speared a good size sting ray. The ensuing struggle to overcome the sting ray, resulted in the Filipino losing the battle. The sting ray has a bony serrated spear that is normally sheathed in the long tail. During the struggle, the sting ray stabbed the fisherman in the chest. The bony spear lodged between the ribs very near the heart and broke off. His companions managed to get him ashore and he was taken to the hospital. Dr. Hewlitt tried to extricate the object, but found it would be difficult with the simple surgical tools available. The Japanese ordered him evacuated to Manila. We heard later that he had died.

The Filipinos were treated the same as the Americans in most cases. When they made mistakes or didn't understand they were treated a little harsher than the Americans. They appeared to be healthy enough, but did have some problems. Shortly after they arrived, Dr. Thomas Hewlett had four of them in a room in sick bay. One of them was seriously ill. The other three were not as serious and could be expected to recover and be discharged. The first Filipino died one day. The following day another, the third day another and the fourth died on the fourth day. This was a surprise to Dr. Hewlett and he could give no reason for three deaths, except

that they simply didn't want to live and gave up. This attitude was probably the reason so many died in the early days of imprisonment. The Filipinos did not have the stamina, determination and will to survive and were very depressed when out of their native environment.

The Filipinos are a very simple people with a latent talent that needs to be developed. They are easy going people, not aggressive and extremely poor. They are excellent craftsmen and artisans. Late in 1942 we received the first shipment of Red Cross supplies, there were many staple food items. This was like Christmas and the men enjoyed tasting food that was from home, even though it was also from Australia. Among the items received were sporting equipment, basketballs, baseballs, bats, even musical instruments, (guitars and violins).

There seemed to be few men among the Americans who had any talent for music. The musical instruments were given to the Filipinos. Very quickly some of them became fairly good musicians. They built a bass violin and some other musical items and played concerts. It was very entertaining and illustrated how emotionally starved for music the POW's were. The body needs more than just food.

The Filipinos were excellent soldiers when properly trained and led. Under some conditions of stress, they lose hope and have no faith in themselves to survive.

One Sunday, I had been getting a little sack time and on awaking, I headed for the latrine. I was a little groggy and did not pay attention to a Filipino standing at the urinal near me. I was intent on what I came for when I heard a low moaning or gurgling sound. I turned and could see the Filipino had his hands up to his throat and blood was running down his arm. I screamed for the medics and pulled him back from the urinal. He squatted down in a dobie squat and held his hands out. He was clutching a standard table knife. The poor man was standing at the urinal cutting his own throat with a dull knife. He did not want to mess up the floor, and was deliberately committing suicide standing up. The medics came and rushed him into the sick bay. Dr. Thomas Hewlett managed to staunch the blood flow. The Japanese ordered a boat and late that evening, I was one of the men carrying the stretcher up the gang plank. The Filipino looked up at me and said, "Joe, I do not want to live. Why do you try to save me?" The Filipinos were soon shipped back to the mainland of Luzon.

A group of men were shipped over to Fort Frank, near the Batangas shore. Carabao Island (Fort Frank) is a small island in the necklace of islands across the throat of Manila Bay. It lies about a 1000 yards from the Batangas shore. It rises about 200 feet above the water. The lowest spot is the dock area on the west side. A system of rail tracks rose from the dock up to a relatively level spot on top. It is a beautiful spot and was the home of two batteries of big guns, a 14-inch disappearing rifle and one battery of four 12-inch mortars. Each battery had its own back up power plant. The generators in these sites were antiquated Fairbanks Morse gasoline engines. Each of the four cylinders was separate with primer cups for starting. They were relics of the early 1900's but were operable. Fort Frank was commanded by Lt. Colonel Napoleon Beaudreau. It had been the nearest battery to Batangas and was effective in returning fire on the Japanese artillery positions that battered Fort Frank and harassed Fort Drum and Corregidor in the early stages. However, due to inadequate spotters it was difficult to spot the Japanese guns precisely. A team of men under one officer were sent in to Batangas and were able to locate the Japanese positions. The Japanese decided to pull the power plants out and ship them as more scrap.

The POWs had developed a rash on the crotch area. It was extremely painful and uncomfortable. The medics had been trying to develop a cure, but found it difficult to bring under control. We called it jungle rot. The medics finally settled on formaldehyde (embalming fluid), the cure being worse than the rash. A team of medics came over from Corregidor to give us the cure. The men were lined up on the parapet of the battery with little or no clothing. The cure consisted of a swab dipped in the fluid which was rubbed on the affected privates and crotch. A control agent to reduce the burning was immediately applied. I was one of the more fortunate and did not have a severe case of the rash. Some of

the other men were raw and in great discomfort. We were all for anything that would give relief from the malady. We formed up in a line with no pants or underwear and stepped forward for the cure. Needless to say, the burning sensation when the solution was applied was horrible. The second medic applied the counter agent immediately. This cut down the burning to a bearable point. One of the men ahead of me, Floyd Nicely, had a severe case and was amenable to anything that would cure him. He stepped in front of the medic, legs spread apart and received the treatment. The pain was so intense that he took off like a rocket around the parapet, screaming and cursing like a commando. The medics gave chase with the antidote and had to tackle him to apply the antidote. The cure though unorthodox, was a success and the rash soon disappeared.

The Japanese had a small garrison of about eight or ten men as a guard force permanently stationed on Fort Frank. Their primary purpose was to keep the Filipinos from raiding the island. There were four Americans who operated the power plant and water system. Their work was easy and they were extremely fortunate in that food was not a problem and they could catch fresh fish. They were allowed to stand on the high point on the north side and shoot sharks swimming close to the shore. They also had a clandestine radio and could listen to broadcasts from the west coast. The senior American was a navy petty officer. The group consisted of him and three army men.

Man's best friend, as relates to the canine family, were never more true than on Corregidor. There were several dogs that survived and were adopted by some of the men. One in particular, a small terrier named Jeff had adopted Lt. Goldsmith and would follow him about during the day. Jeff was in the sports arena one day and jumped a stray cat. The cat was on the upper bleacher on the south side. Jeff attacked and the scrawny cat stood his ground. It appeared to be a stalemate, the cat facing Jeff, and Jeff facing the cat. There was no room for flanking movements by Jeff. They stood there eye to eye about two feet apart. Neither one moved. Slowly and carefully the cat lifted one leg and then the other very alert and eased backward. Jeff, at each step backward by the cat, took one step forward. This appreciation of each other went on for several minutes. Slowly the cat eased back and was almost to the end of the bleacher. Something had to give. Finally the cat could see a vertical timber supporting the roof. Like a flash, he jumped for the post and escaped into the overhead timbers. Poor Jeff, he sat at the base and watched the cat and then reluctantly turned to something else.

Jeff was very congenial and everyone tried to save a little food for him. Roll call came each morning at 6:30. Jeff would spend the night on the lower floor where Lt. Goldsmith lived. Every morning Jeff would come up to where my bunk was located. If I was not out of the sack, he would stand up on his hind legs and scratch me on the back, as if to tell me to make tracks for tenko. I would get up and pull the shelter half up over my bed. Jeff would jump up on the bunk and curl up for a nap. Jeff was a real friend and went to Cabanatuan with Lt. Goldsmith in May of 1943. Somehow, he avoided the clutches of some of the scavengers who would have had him in a quan bucket. Most of the dogs at Cabanatuan suffered this fate. There were two that were fortunate to have made it through the camp, Jeff and a dog named Suchow, the 4th Marines' mascot. He had come down from China with the regiment.

One saving grace that is a part of America and a great morale factor was humor. Though living a simple monastic, isolated life without any females, liquor, movies, music, mail, or family, inadequate food and limited freedom, humor was still present. Part of the prisoner personnel was a group of American civilians. These men had been sent to the Philippines to construct air bases for the navy. The bases were being constructed by a consortium of large construction companies known as Pacific Navy Air Base Contractors. (PNABC) They were on Wake Island, Guam and the Philippines. All suffered the same fate. The men in the Philippines wound up on Corregidor and were put to work digging and enlarging the tunnel complexes. They were a swell group and worked and shared food at their mess table. The prisoners would band together into small groups in mutual support. They slept in the southwest corner of the ward on the

second floor. All of the shutters had been damaged and in the evening before lights-out they would talk about the jobs they had worked on in various parts of the world. Frank Rose, an employee of the Army Engineer, slept on an upper bunk. Charles Wiedlich, a Hawaiian dredging civilian employee, slept in an upper bunk at the end of Rose's bunk. Their area was silhouetted by the moonlight. After lights-out one moonlit night, Wiedlich fastened a dark thread to Rose's blanket. Several of us were in on the fun. Frank settled down to sleep. Charles pulled on the thread and the blanket would slowly creep down Frank's chest. Rose would pull the blanket back upon his chest. Charles waited patiently until Frank relaxed and slowly start pulling on the thread again. Frank would slowly raise his head up and try to see if someone was pulling the blanket. Silhouetted against the moonlight, those in the know were struggling to keep from laughing out loud. Frank would get out of bed and go to the foot of his bunk, trying to catch someone, then back into bed. Charles finally tired of the fun and everyone settled down. The next day at evening chow Frank told his companions that he thought he was going crazy. He recited the experience of the night before. The other fellows listened and sympathized with him but never told him the truth.

Frank Rose and his brother Robert (Bob) ate chow with the other civilians. They would finish chow and enjoy a smoke and bull session. They would fiddle around and wait until Frank started to gather up his mess gear. Absentmindedly, he would gather up more than his fair share and wash them. The fellows took advantage and got their gear washed. Frank was a little absentminded, but I suppose that was to his advantage under the circumstances.

The evenings were spent reading, studying, playing cards and reminiscing about home and dreaming about the time when we would be home and all the good things we would do. Many played cribbage and some just sat and told tall tales about their exploits. Visiting among the various groups and discussing the current rumor and its impact on us or the Japanese. Storytelling was a favorite. Once visiting with the civilians, Burl B. (Blacky) Kinder was telling of the time he was in Saudi

Arabia. Blacky had gone there as an equipment operator. The Arabs are notorious for their thievery. They also considered the Americans as hard drinking woman chasers and not immune to their stealing. Blacky was operating a crane one day and had shut down for lunch. He saw an Arab slip into the crane and steal a large crescent wrench and hide it in the sand nearby. Blacky didn't let on that he saw him, and soon returned to work. He swung the crane around a couple of times and shut it down and went to the tool box to get a wrench. He missed the crescent wrench and started to cuss everything Arab. He climbed down and looked around to be sure the Arabs were watching. He unzipped his pants and took out his penis, and holding it like a searching wand, moved around searching. When he reached the place where the wrench was hidden, he urinated and then kicked the sand away. Picking up the wrench, he returned to the crane, made a slight adjustment and went on with the work. He said, "I had no more trouble with the Arabs stealing from me." This story was a sample of the trivia that went on those long evenings.

A clandestine radio was in the hospital, cleverly concealed, and only a very few knew of its existence. The news that came over the radio on the progress of the war was spread among the men as a rumor. It might be attributed to a Japanese, or from the Filipinos who came to the Island or just plain latrine rumors. Some men took the rumors as gospel and pinned high hopes on a fantasy. When the fantasy did not come true they were depressed and despaired of any hope for their release. One greatly discussed rumor was that we would be repatriated soon. This never happened and was impractical from the start. The Japanese had demonstrated in China how they looked at those unfortunate captives who were put into slavery. They were not about to release their captives when they could use them as a labor force.

Many men would set a specific date in the future and were disappointed when it did not happen. This form of wishful thinking was detrimental to those who tried it. The best reply when someone asked, "When are we going home?" was "Another six months". Six months was repeated at any time and not changed. Eventually of course it came true. Psychologically this was easier on the mind.

The Philippine Government moved its stock of gold and silver pesos to Corregidor when Manila was declared an open city. The gold was shipped out on submarines. General Wainwright, in his book, tells of how the paper money was disposed of. "The command had about 140 million pesos, (70 million dollars). The serial numbers were recorded and transmitted to Washington. The finance officer was directed to dispose of the paper money by shredding and burning." About 17 million silver pesos were stored in Government Ravine. The steadily deteriorating situation dictated something would have to be done to dispose of the silver pesos. Late one night in March the boxes of silver pesos were loaded onto a vessel and then taken out into Boca Grande Channel and dumped overboard. The location was evidently discovered and the Japanese were anxious to recover it.

A group of American Navy men were dispatched to Corregidor to work at this task. These men had diving experience and were well equipped to safely dive in the waters off Corregidor. An air compressor was rigged on a small barge, which served as a diving platform and living quarters, when they were in port. The barge was tied up at North Dock and would be towed out each day. An experienced diver would suit up and a diver attendant would monitor the compressor and air lines while the diver was down. The objective was to recover the boxed silver pesos. Elmer White, a navy man, became acquainted with them and received permission to visit them when they were at the dock. White was one of the men in our mess group and would tell us of his visit. Several times he brought back a side of mutton. The navy divers were well fed and treated fair. They rigged a bucket from the side opposite to which the Japanese were working to haul up whatever silver they recovered. The diver on the floor of the bay would break open boxes and gather up loose silver and put it in the Japanese hoist bucket. While they were busy he would scoop up more and filled their bucket on the opposite side. The divers reported to the Japanese that all of the boxes had been broken open and the silver pesos were scattered on the sea bed. The silver that was filched by the divers was traded to the POWs on Corregidor. The divers would cash any government check for face value and would take checks from trustworthy men for cashing when they returned to the states. One chief petty officer (CPO) accumulated a sizable amount of checks. Lt. General John M. Wright in his book *Captured On Corregidor, Diary of a Prisoner of War*, refers to this incident. The silver pesos were blackened by their immersion in the salt water. Our group acquired some of these pesos through SF/2nd Elmer J. White. He would get prermission to visit the men on the barge on a Sunday and would bring back a side of mutton. With the extra mutton and the fresh stock of pesos to augment the pesos I had won, our group lived comfortable. Many of the other men also were fortunate enough to get silver pesos and were able to add to their food ration by trading the pesos to the Filipinos for funny money for purchasing from the Japanese store. Caution was essential as evidence of these pesos being in the hands of Americans could have endangered the divers. The navy divers were soon sent back to Manila after about two months. The divers reported to the Japanese that the silver was so scattered that it was difficult to recover. According to Elmer White and his conversations with the divers, most of the silver was intact and they had to break open the boxes in order to send some token of their work under water. Why the Japanese did not send their own divers down is a mystery and only serves as an example of the opportunities they missed by having POWs do the work.

A green house in Government Ravine had not suffered much damage during the reduction of Corregidor. Late in 1942 it was used as a bordello for the Japanese. Three dalagas (Filipina girls) were brought to the Rock from Manila. They set up shop in the small green house in Government Ravine. Some of the drivers of the trucks and the one staff car would be dispatched to the dock when the dalagas were allowed to return to Manila or returned from Manila. The driver was usually chaperoned by a Japanese. The girls were very friendly to the Americans and would talk during the short drive up to the green house. They would sneak a V sign with their hands and say they were doing their part. Evidently

they were, as most of the Japanese soon had venereal disease. This was a common practice with the Japanese Army. Wherever they were they would either ask for volunteers or forcibly persuade Chinese, Koreans or Filipino women to serve as prostitutes for the soldiers. However, they did not have adequate medical treatment and or prophylactic and very little if any preventive training. The quality of the Japanese guards was mediocre and not of the highest education level. They were the rejects and marginally inferior to the combat soldiers that originally captured Corregidor. The Japanese scheduled visits to the bordello by rank, privates in the morning, noncoms in the afternoon and officers in the evening.

The Americans were like Rip Van Winkle in regards to sexual activities and had no interest or contact with the residents of the green house, except the occasional call for transportation. The sexual desires had been stunted by the inadequacy of the food and the knowledge that it was not safe either from a physical point or a medical problem afterwards. Most of the prisoners had far more interest in food, rescue or survival to be bothered with the green house. The Filipinas were sent back to Manila after about two months.

The prime concern of the prisoners at all times was scrounging or strafing as it was called. This was the best method to acquire items that were needed. All had GI cots to sleep on, but most did not want sheets and pillow cases even though they were available. This eliminated the laundry problem. Most had a mattress cover as a sheet with shelter halves to protect the bedding. The art of successful scrounging depended on where one was at the time. Many men would scrounge during rest periods, ease out of the sight of the guards and sneak into an area for a quick look. The guards were lenient and in some cases aided or abedded in the practice.

One Sunday, Cpl. Haddox and I received permission to go to Battery Geary on a scrounging expedition. We figured that perhaps we could come up with something. This battery was so severely damaged in the explosion early in May that no one had paid much attention to it. We walked over the hill from the hospital and passed through the officers housing area. We searched one house and found some papers in a closet. Scanning over them we were amazed to find they were personal records of Colonel Paul Bunker, Commanding Officer of the 59th CAC. The colonel kept a running account of all the money he had received and spent for years. I was stirring around and found a pair of beautiful English riding boots, but one of them had a hole burned in the calf. They were my size and I took them along with the papers. We continued on over to Battery Geary and searched around. We noticed that the ammunition magazine on the east side had a slight clearance under the collapsed roof. We squirmed our way into the magazine toward the rear wall with a flashlight and got into a larger space. We were alert for any snakes that might have moved in. We looked around and could see some foot lockers that were not covered by chunks of concrete. We pried a couple open and found things just like the soldier had left them. The tray had some toilet articles, soap, tooth powder, writing material, brushes, comb, razor blades, playing cards and nice clean clothing. One of the items was a Wally Frank pipe. All of these items were a real bonanza. We gathered up our find and bundled it into some civilian clothes and khaki shirts and made our way out. It had been a good day, The Wally Frank pipe I kept and smoked it the rest of the time I was a POW. The upper tops of the boots were cut off and the leather used for wooden clogs. The foot parts were used as long as we were on the Rock.

We were aware that at anytime we could be shipped out and made plans to be prepared. Each of us had a new pair of shoes, clean pre-war starched summer uniforms, clean underclothes and socks. A cache of non-perishable food, and other essentials were carefully hoarded. Each man had a musette bag, blankets and a shelter half. The old army packs were not suitable as a pack. We latched onto some navy canvas hammocks and made up a pack to suit our needs. We used the shoulder harness and straps from the old style packs. Thread for sewing the straps and harness was made by stripping the thread from the navy hammocks. This gave us a piece about seven-feet long. With the aid of a shoe-

maker's awl and some bees wax, a usable pack could be made. We were prepared to move. We had learned our lesson on what to expect from Japanese in the way of needed supplies and equipment. We never knew how far and under what conditions we would travel. The packs were made up to carry the maximum possible for a long march.

As the year slowly passed the work continued at a reasonable pace. The men were not harassed as long as they appeared to be working. A few instances of punishment were meted out. The Japanese believed in group punishment. If something occurred on a detail the group was punished. A favorite tactic was to stand an individual at attention in front of the guard house. Sometimes, a miscreant was made to hold his arms out straight for long periods of time, usually without head gear. Lt. John M. Wright and my friend Sgt. Golson were recipients of this type of punishment. Lt. Wright and Sgt. Golson were ordered to carry two 155 mm projectiles to the Japanese quarters. In his book, *Captured on Corregidor; A Diary of An American POW in World War II*, Lt. Wright tells of this incident. "Sgt. Golson and I delivered the projectiles and in the process noticed two cans of cocoa. Sgt. Golson, with the nodded approval of Lt. Wright slipped one can under his shirt and left the Japanese area without detection. Later that day, the Japanese officer missed the cocoa and sent for the only two men who had been in the area. They both denied taking the cocoa and suggested perhaps one of the guards did it. The officer was not convinced and ordered Sgt. Golson to stand at attention in front of the guard house and excused Lt. Wright. After a couple of hours, Lt. Wright was called back and put at attention also. They were released after about three hours more and sent back to their quarters." Sgt. Golson was in my buddy group and I had known him from Manila days. The cocoa had been hidden in the truck that Sgt. Golson was driving that day. Later he shared with the rest of our group. We gave him a bad time about filching things. We reminded him of how angry his mother would be if she knew her favorite son was naughty and took things from the nice Japanese.

The fall of 1942 the Japanese started to pay the POWs in occupation script. A noncommissioned officer received about 20 Sen, 80 Sen were allegedly deposited in a bank for the future. This was supposed to be for our work per day. Lt. Wright in his book makes reference to this matter. "The scrip could be deposited with the SAO and he would make the purchases from the small store the Japanese operated at Middleside." Our particular group did not have any financial problems at that time. We still had silver pesos and the gambling winnings. There was not much to purchase except unrefined sugar and salt, tea, garlic, onions, corned beef and a few canned items. It was common to see one of us light a cigarette from a piece of scrip and joke about it. The Filipinos resisted taking script. They would rather have their pre-war pesos or something that could be sold for good money.

Japanese rations deteriorated in the fall of 1942 and the scrounging dried up except for papayas and there were not enough of them. The Japanese Navy maintained a detail at Bottomside to operate the power plant and water system. They also maintained a lookout post on Topside, near the lighthouse. On a scrounging trip one day near the lighthouse we came across a large papaya tree. It was loaded with large nearly ripe fruit. Attached to the tree was a sign in Japanese. We looked at the sign and shook our head. Cpl. Haddox pretended to translate the message. He said, "The sign reads that any American prisoner of war is welcome to take some of the fruit." Of course this was probably exactly opposite to what it said. We took a couple of nice large ripe ones and made tracks away from there.

The drying up of scrounging and the rotten fish and vegetables that were sent out from Manila made things a little on the rough side but not near as bad as our comrades in the other camps.

The head count had been declining with the completion of gathering scrap iron. We were in for a big surprise in late December, we received the best Christmas present possible. This would be our second Christmas without the customary turkey and all the trimmings. We were looking forward to a bleak Christmas. My thoughts turned back to the last Christmas, 1941. The 34th Light Maintenance Company (PS), which I was attached, arrived in Bataan on Christmas Eve. Our

mobile kitchen did not arrive until the 27th of December. Our Christmas meal that year was pears and pork and beans for lunch, and pork and beans and pears for the evening meal. Would we have less than that for the Christmas of 1942? We would have settled for the same menu at this time.

Lt. John M. Wright (Lt. Gen. Ret.) in his book gives a graphic description of the surprise arrival of a large shipment of Red Cross supplies. "On the 21st of December, 1942, a large shipment of Red Cross supplies consigned to British and Australian prisoners of war arrived on Corregidor. They were placed in the Japanese store room." The camp strength was 191 men. The supplies were bulk type and included sugar, corned beef, caramel, dried apricots, raisins, mixed dried fruits and cans of meat and vegetable rations. Also there were various items of clothing including some wool sweaters and a few hats. The following day we were given Canadian individual packages. They were divided among the men as there was not enough for each man.

Things were looking up and we had a respectable meal with **meat** that was not rotten. The cooks were really happy with good rations to serve instead of rotten fish and whistle weed soups with rice that had become standard fare. Rice was still the bulk food and eagerly sought after. The quan buckets got a workout as some desired to improve on the issued ration. issued ration.

S/F 2nd White managed to gather a batch of raisins and sugar and made up a batch of Raisin Jack. The raisins and sugar were put into a large glass jug and cached to await fermentation. This takes a little time and White would check it in the evening. The fermenting didn't seem right as it never got to full strength. One of the other men had found the cache and would siphon off the brew and replace it with water. Our group was pretty hot about it but we couldn't prove anything. We had planned to have a drink of Raisin Jack to celebrate the New Year.

Just as things began to improve and everyone was enjoying the Red Cross boxes from Canada, we received another surprise. In early January the Japanese received an American Red Cross shipment. This shipment was given to the Americans. Each man received an individual box plus a part of another. In addition there was clothing and bulk items of food. This was a real bonanza, each man was like a kid in a candy store figuring what he would eat first, how long he could make it last, or what he could trade for something he wanted most. Some gorged themselves with no thought of tomorrow. The items contained in the American Red Cross package included canned butter, a one-pound can of powdered milk, cocoa, chocolate candy, soluble coffee, jam, raisins, canned meat, cigarettes, a one-pound can of Half and Half pipe tobacco with cigarette papers and a rolling machine. We were in hog heaven and our world seemed much brighter. It was interesting to listen to the conversations as each man dug into his priceless box of good things from the land of the big PX.

Bartering began immediately as the men sorted out their goods. Some started trading for cigarettes, American Chesterfields, Camels and Raleighs. I was interested in the pipe tobacco and traded my share of cigarettes. The tobacco did not make good cigarettes even with the cigarette papers. With my hoard of pipe tobacco I was in good shape. Rationing of the tobacco and controlling the number of times per day made it go a long way. One of the real pleasures which I enjoyed was to light up my pipe after evening chow and just before going to bed. This was the time to reflect on our good fortune and plan for better times when we would be free again.

A lot has been said and printed about smoking being bad for your health. This is no doubt true when done to excess. Pipe smoking generally is not inhaled like cigarettes and was good for ones morale and peace of mind.

The quan pots were boiling every evening. One item that everyone enjoyed was a small can of Nescafe. We had been drinking burnt rice coffee so long and now had the real thing even though it was soluble coffee. How to make it last longer? Some of the men would dip a dry spoon in the powder and then into a cup of water. It was weak but the taste was there. The men were so starved for American type food that they had dreamed about it, and here on this lonely island far from home, their dreams came true and morale soared.

The theft of cached goods was fortunately at a minimum as a lot of the individual groups had footlockers that could be locked while out on work detail.

Many of the men appreciated the efforts of the International Red Cross organizations on their behalf. Certainly, I for one was, and have always contributed to the American Red Cross at every opportunity.

The work that most of the men had been engaged in for the past year began to slow down. It was the intention of the Japanese to ship some of the men to other camps and to Japan. They had hoped that the Filipinos would be eager to join in the Prosperity Sphere and that the prisoners could be shipped to Japan for labor groups, which were sorely needed. By the year of 1943 the war had begun to turn. The demand for soldiers in the many islands to the south and the loss of thousands of men in their plunge towards Australia and Southeast Asia, began to put a strain on manpower. However, the occupied countries did not cotton to working for the Japanese. The Philippines was not interested and the natives did little to cooperate.

Late in April we suffered a serious loss of the Senior American Officer, Lt. Colonel Lewis S. Kirkpatrick. Lt. Wright describes this tragic loss in his book very vividly. "Colonel Kirkpatrick had taken a shower and sat on the porch enjoying the cool breezes. He developed bronchitis that developed into pneumonia. Dr. Hewlett tried to save his life but was unable to do so with the limited medicine available. The Japanese wanted to cremate the remains and the American officers wanted to bury him in the cemetery at Bottomside. The Japanese prevailed and the officers prepared Col. Kirkpatrick for cremation. An American Flag was wrapped around the body and then a blanket to cover the flag. To the consternation of the Japanese the fire consumed the blanket revealing the American Flag." Fortunately there were no repercussions.

The American flag was hauled down when Corregidor fell and the old flagpole was bare. This particular flagpole had been a part of the history of the islands. It had been removed from the flagship of the Spanish fleet sunk in Manila Bay by Admiral Dewey in 1898. Each time we passed the old flagpole on Topside we were reminded of what was America and that the national colors once flew there. Each man deeply longed for the day when the flag would once again be flown proudly over the island. Many times at retreat formations tribute had been paid each day by a formal ceremony. The regiment would stand at attention, the regimental band would play the National Anthem and the flag would be slowly lowered to the waiting arms of the corporal of the guard. The long line of troops would be at attention, all others would stop and face the colors and salute. Even the children in the nearby officers quarters knew what they were required to do. My thoughts as I passed the empty flagpole would bring back the impressive and colorful ceremonies that was retreat. The troops would be dismissed and the beautiful sound of chow call would sound across the island. Day was done and each soldier could enjoy the cool of the tropical evening. The beer bar would call and the old soldiers would make for the beer hall. No hard drinks were served or allowed on the island, except in the noncommissioned and officer clubs. One more day of a two year hitch was finished. Many of the men had hidden small flags and took great care to protect and hide them from discovery, even at the risk of serious punishment and loss of that revered symbol of freedom. It is a sad day when our people, who have never witnessed such humiliation, have never felt the loss of freedom, or suffered the degradation and maltreatment under a conqueror, would seek to desecrate, deface or insult the flag and the republic it represents. The hundreds of thousands who have made the supreme sacrifice must turn in their graves at the mere thought of an ungrateful American, who would desecrate our symbol of freedom represented by the flag. That symbol has been the mecca for millions who have at great risks sought freedom under the red, white and blue flag of our country.

The work on Corregidor by the American prisoners was slowly coming to an end. Small groups of men had been shipped out to Manila. A last effort was made to remove some of the parts of the batteries that were severely damaged and useless as weapons. A detail was assigned the task of removing the

lead counterweights in Battery Crocket. The counterweights equaled the weight of the gun and its supporting mechanism. The counter weight absorbed the recoil after each firing and locked the gun in loading position. Each ingot of lead weighed about 7000 pounds. Each counterweight had about eight ingots stacked and attached to the retraction arms. These huge chunks of lead were hoisted out and hauled to Bottomside for shipment.

Captain Coughlin, Ordinance, inspected the powder magazines and assured the Japanese that some of the powder was old, unstable and should be destroyed. The Japanese had the men haul the powder to the south beach at Bottomside and spread it out in a long windrow and set it on fire. All of the disappearing guns were demolished at the time of the surrender. The Japanese made some attempts to repair them by replacement of some parts and only moderate care and preservation was done. They were useless as defense weapons both to the Americans and to the Japanese. The Japanese at this time had made no efforts to fortify the island. No new weapons were introduced and no trenches or other forms of fortifications had been constructed. The Japanese strength was probably about 200 or less including the Japanese Navy group at Bottomside.

Colonel William C. Braly in his book "*Hard Way Home*," quoted a Japanese officer before the men were moved from Corregidor, in June of 1942. "In 10 years this will be a beautiful park. Many Japanese will come here on vacation." There were other Americans on Corregidor. Certainly our group who were drivers would have observed some unless they were kept separate from us. There was a detail at Bottomside to operate the main generators and the water system. Major Robert Lathrop, engineer at Fort Mills, was the Senior Officer at Engineer Tunnel adjacent to Power Plant Ravine and a Captain Ronald O. Pigg, CE. Colonel Henry Stickney, USAFFE Engineer, was taken to Formosa with the senior officers and is listed in Col. Braly's book as being in Manchuria at the end of the war.

We had these modern conveniences at the hospital area when we moved to the station hospital. Lt. General E.M. Flanagan in his book, "*Corregidor, The Rock Force Assault*", mentioned that there was a detachment of 16 men under a Major Robert Lathrop, the former Post Engineer, Fort Mills. During the aerial assault and return to Corregidor, the Americans found no trace of this group. Perhaps and this is purely conjecture, this group could have suffered a similar fate as the men in Palawan. They were under the Japanese Navy and were trapped in shelters and burned to death. This brings up many unanswered questions. Were there American POWs at Bottomside? If so why didn't our group come across them at some time in the first or second year? What did happen to the group? General Flanagan referred to the fact that the Japanese Navy disagreed with the army on the defense of the islands. General Yamashita, the commander of the Japanese Army, did not want to defend Manila but opted to defend the northern part of Luzon. The Japanese Navy didn't agree and decided to defend Manila in a very tenacious manner resulting in the destruction of a large part of the city and over 100,000 civilian casualties. It would be logical to assume they were also responsible for the Manila Bay area. General Flanagan's book refers to the Japanese Navy and Marines as the opposing force in the recapture of Corregidor and Manila.

The cleaning out of Malinta Tunnel had been accomplished and the Japanese had shipped in ammunition for storage. The details working in Malinta were not closely supervised and the men would slip into the inner recesses looking for loot. The guards said nothing as long as the men got the trucks unloaded when they came up from the north dock. Somehow, and it is still a mystery, a large safe in the Chaplain's lateral of the hospital complex had remained untouched. M/Sgt. Kunich was one of the drivers who were assigned to haul the men down to Malinta. Kunich spotted this safe with the outer doors open and persuaded the not so smart Japanese guard to allow him to try and open the inner door of the safe. After several attempts, Kunich and another soldier succeeded in prying the door open. All the men crowded around to screen off the guard. When the door was pried open it revealed several cigar boxes and jars stuffed with jewelry, rings, necklaces, bracelets, gold dust in small

packets, watches, rings and a bunch of Spanish jeweled decorations presented to prominent Filipino families during the Spanish rule. The Japanese guard tried to see what was in the safe but the POW's squeezed him out. Grabbing a couple of the boxes and containers, Kunich stepped back and eased into the shadows and cached his treasure under the seat of the truck. The other men cleaned out the compartment and the guard never saw any of the loot.

That night after the detail returned to camp, Cpl. Haddox, Sgt. Golson and I met Kunich when he came into the sports arena where the trucks were parked. Kunich showed us the loot and immediately cached it in a secure hiding place. He also gave the guard several small trinkets to satisfy his curiosity. Sgt. Kunich and others sold some of the loot to the officers and some was sent to his wife in Manila. Our group benefited from this haul.

Lt. General John M. Wright refers to this incident in his book, *Captured on Corregidor, A Diary of a Prisoner of War*. Kunich was able to swap or sell small items as long as he remained on the Rock.

Early in the spring of 1943, the Japanese were scraping the bottom of the barrel to find enough scrap iron to justify their retention of the prisoners on Corregidor. They had stripped the island of everything except the big guns. Each time we came up the back road near the golf course, we passed one of the 12-inch mortar barrels from Battery Geary. It lay on the edge of the course just off the road about thirty feet. Lt. Tokashige or someone decided that this would be a good item to ship as scrap. The barrel weighed 13 tons and was about 18-feet long with a diameter at the breech of about 35 inches and about 18 inches at the muzzle. A detail was assigned to get it to Bottomside. We had no equipment to pick it up and haul such tonnage. Using the winch on the front of the TD 18 tractor, we were able to roll it onto the roadway. Two tractors were used to skid it down the asphalt pavement, leaving a long scar in the roadway. After getting onto a cement roadway it was finally skidded to the dock area.

The scrap iron barge had a P&H twenty ton crawler mounted crane on board. The crane had to remain in the center of the barge to

Photo of a 12-inch mortar barrel from Battery Geary, Corregidor on the banks of the Pasig River, 29 February 1944.

prevent the barge from tipping during loading operations. The junk that was loaded previously was lighter and the Filipino operator could move back and forth and stack junk around it. However, it was unable to pick up 13 tons with the boom out. In order to pick up the 13 tons, the operator would need to have the boom almost vertical from the center of the crane and the center of the barge. The edge of the dock was too far away from the center of the barge. The Japanese had two large 24-inch I-beams that were used to off-load the crane from the barge. The gun barrel was finally loaded by getting the mortar barrel onto the I-beam. A cable was attached to the crane hook and under the muzzle. By lifting slightly and swinging, the crane operator managed to slide it along the I-beam to a point at which the I-beam would tilt down to the

deck of the barge. The dock was about 15 feet above the deck of the barge. A line was fastened to the trunnions and secured to the tractor which served as a brake. As the gun barrel started to slide down the I-beam, one could almost sense the hope that something would slip and the 13 tons would smash through the barge, and the whole shebang would sink. No such luck and the Filipino operator breathed a sigh of relief that the job was finished.

Colonel William C. Braly in his book, *Hard Way Home*, quotes a story by a S/Sgt. Larry C. Wozniak, QMC, who had been on Corregidor for the first year, 1942-1943.

"Our work party at first consisted of about 500 men. Then in June of 1942, 45 officers (actual count was 90 men), headed by Lt. Colonel Lewis S. Kirkpatrick arrived from Cabanatuan. Thereafter the work party was reduced until only a handful remained. Many Japanese visitors, especially sailors came to Corregidor on sightseeing trips, starting in July 1942. Battery Geary or what had been Battery Geary, was a special object of their curiosity. You remember sir, when that battery blew up, one of its eight 12-inch mortars landed about a hundred yards away on the edge of the golf course. As a part of their metal salvaging operation, the Japanese took two tractors and a detail of POWs, and after two days of arduous work had finally dragged it down to the dock for shipment."

"During the loading-out process, when the crane had the big cannon in midair, something suddenly snapped and down went the old mortar to a watery grave. The Japanese were so astonished they were speechless, then gave way to a sickly smile. The Americans smiled too, but not so sickly."

This incident is recited here to illustrate the variance in stories by different people. Time Life Publishing Inc.'s book, *The Pictorial History of World War II*, illustrates the last known location of the mortar on the banks of the Pasig River near Fort Santiago. Evidently the Japanese could not load it or move it to the main piers for shipment.

Summer was on us and the weather was beautiful at least on Corregidor with the cool breezes from the China Sea. The prisoners had been extremely fortunate to have spent the first year on the Rock. They had not been abused or maltreated, but had a healthy environment and were in relatively good health. The major health problem had been the lack of some critical vitamins, which contributed to loss of vision.

The refugees from Bataan, who had been exposed to malaria had been able to control the recurrence of the fever. This group was in good physical shape and morale was high.

Persistent rumors of an impending move continued to spread. The guards would let slip small tidbits of information and the information from the clandestine radio was good. The Japanese had suffered a serious setback in the Battle of Midway and the battles in the South Pacific. All signs indicated something was in the wind.

Roll call on the evening of June 26, 1943, confirmed our worst fears, that our paradise was coming to an end. The Japanese announced that ahsata, (tomorrow) ike masta Manila, (you go to Manila). Everyone was to be ready at morning tenko formation. That evening and into the night men were packing their musette bags and packs with clothing, shoes, blankets, shelter halves, mosquito bars and personal effects. A lot of trading of food stuffs for their emergency ration needs and to reduce the weight of their gear. The quan pots were in heavy use. Many of the men quanned up their food stuffs and a feast was held by various groups. To hell with tomorrow, let us live today was the attitude of many. No one knew where, how or how far their next trip might be. The guards had been hinting at scoshi mati, anato ekee mas Nippon (which meant a small time, you go to Japan). A flurry of activity went on into the night. Curious Japanese soldiers who were not on duty would wander through the POW quarters idly looking at the packing. Some of them looked sad and worried. Their gravy train with the biscuit wheels would also be derailed. They could expect to be sent to the battle zones. Life on Corregidor had been good to them. They enjoyed hospital beds with inner spring mattresses, sheets, easy duty, minor harassment by Japanese officers, and an environment that was better than many had at home.

Roll call came too soon, many had not slept and had spent the night talking, trading, visiting and worrying. At roll call the men were ordered to lay out their gear for inspection in the street. Inspection was not new to these men, just that they had not stood inspection since the war began. Lt. Takashige accompanied by the sergeant of the guard slowly walked along and checked each man's gear. Occasionally, he would take something or say something to the man standing by his gear. Valuable items had been hidden on the body, tied in socks, rolled into the cuffs of trousers or concealed in some ingenious manner. The men were not shook down with body pats or made to remove their clothing. All men had good serviceable clothing and shoes with a complete mess kit, canteen, head cover and emergency supplies of food. They had learned their lesson well from their first trip to the 92nd Garage in May of 1942. They had marched into prison with little but the clothes

58

on their backs, now they were better prepared.

Now, most of the fortunate became the not so fortunate and the unfortunate. After the inspection was completed, 14 names were called to fall out to one side.

The fortunate men were: Captain John J. Coughlin, M/Sgt. John Kunich, Cpl. Earnest Haddox, S/Sgt. Asbury L. Nix; civilians: Lester Schwab, Richard (Lorin) Buttner, Kenneth Dunlop, Charles Wiedlich, Jack Davis, Frank Rose, Robert Rose, Sergio Olferioff, Blacky Kinder, and James Piland. We were ordered to put our gear back in the quarters and speedo speedo Judoso (quickly bring trucks).

Ninety-one men were hauled to the north dock and boarded a Japanese trawler-type boat. Hurried good-byes were exchanged with our friends of the past year. S/Sgt. Archie Golson and SF/2nd Elmer (Ed) J. White, from our buddy group, were among the departing men. As the boat slowly pulled away from the dock and disappeared around Malinta Point we waved to the men. Where were they going? Would we ever see them again? Were they being shipped to Japan or some other camps on Luzon? Why did they keep only 14 men on the Rock? These and other questions came to mind as we drove back up the hill to the station hospital that had been our home for a year. We drove the trucks back under the sports arena and returned to our quarters. A new era had begun. At least we were on familiar ground.

Colonel W.C. Braly in his book, *Hard Way Home*, gives an extract from a narrative article by Sir Winston Churchill, which was printed in *Readers Digest*, about his experiences as a prisoner of war during the Boer War in South Africa. It was appropriate for Colonel Braly's group and is illustrative of all prisoners of war;

Prisoner of War
Sir Winston Churchill

"It is a melancholy state. You are in the power of the enemy. You owe your life to his humanity, your daily bread to his compassion. You must obey his orders, await his pleasure and possess your soul in patience. The days are very long and hours crawl by like paralytic centipedes. Moreover, the whole atmosphere of prison is odious. Companions quarrel about trifles and get the least enjoyment from each others society. You feel a constant humiliation in being fenced in by railings and wire, watched by armed guards and webbed in by a tangle of regulations and restrictions."

The sentiments of Sir Winston Churchill were the sentiments of the prisoners of war of Japan. The Japanese conception of humanity was that we were the lowest creatures and thus were unworthy of humane treatment. We were the slaves of the Emperor through his military and would serve to near exhaustion and death. There was no accountability for such flotsam from the tides of war.

CORREGIDOR

OASIS OF HOPE

PART THREE

THE FORTUNATE

Mile long Army barracks, home of the 59th CAC Regiment after the invasion in 1944 by 503rd Regimental Combat Team, 11th Airborne Division.

Part Three

The Fortunate Few

The wheel of fortune spun again and the fortunate few selected to remain on Corregidor were pawns in the game of life. Prisoners of war of an oriental country are at the mercy of their captors. The fate of those so unfortunate, was to be in the right place at the wrong time. They were considered as unworthy, dishonored and therefore expendable. The Japanese samurai warrior code does not recognize defeat or surrender. The samurai warrior must never surrender or accept defeat, but commit hari-kari as the only honorable option. A small detail like the present could be eliminated in short order if the fickle finger of fate so decreed. What was our destiny, here on this small island that few even knew of before the war. The sands of time would tell. But for the present accept our good fortune and hope for the best. Six months more and it would be Golden Gate here we come.

The Japanese guards told us to settle down and clean the quarters up. The departing men had left a lot of junk and cast off bits of clothing. The Japanese had us move to the lower floor where the officers had been quartered. In this area there were four small rooms off a porch. Each room had four doors, one in each wall. One room at the south end had been walled in with a small wood burning cookstove, refrigerator, two small tables and some shelving. We took over the hospital beds that had been in use by the officers. Four men occupied a room with a bed in each corner. This allowed for good air circulation and passage to the other rooms and the porch. A fence was erected across the end of the hall adjacent to the stairs. The hallway was used for storage of excess hospital furniture. We soon had things in order and had disposed of the litter. Some items that were from the second floor, such as small tables and chairs, were used to make our quarters comfortable and convenient. A mess table was set up on the veranda. The next chore was to round up the supplies left in the galley and inventory what was available. Cooking utensils were gathered up and some were used for the small galley, which would serve the small group. Robert (Snuffy) Rose volunteered to serve as the chief cook. Snuffy had been a civilian in Manila and had volunteered to serve with the Army as a civilian.

When everything had been arranged, we gathered around the Captain to see what the big picture was all about. Captain Coughlin had been summoned to the Japanese quarters and Lieutenant Tokashige, through Superior Private Danjo as interpreter, explained what was to be the work of this small group. The men would be assigned to do preservation and repair to some of the big guns. The enlisted men were to be judosa utensha (truck drivers) and mechanics. The civilians would be the work detail under the supervision of the senior American officer as directed by the Japanese.

American civilians who were captured with the army received the same treatment as the military. There was no recognition of their status. Most of the civilians had signed contracts with their parent companies when they were shipped to the orient.

Two of the civilians, Snuffy Rose and Sergio Olferioff, were not under contract to the Pacific Naval Air Base Contractors (PNABC). Olferioff was a beached merchant marine seaman. His ship (President Grant) had pulled out of Manila at the outbreak of war, leaving several men ashore. Snuffy was employed by a civilian firm in Manila. His brother Frank Rose was an employee of the Engineer Department, USAFFE. The balance were PNABC employees. They were not worried about pay for the time of imprisonment as their contracts stipulated that they were employed by PNABC until their return to the states. Snuffy and Olferioff were not so sure of their status. The whole group had declined payment by the military as that would void their contracts. Captain Coughlin was an experienced ordnance officer and did have some health problems. He had only one kidney, but otherwise he was in good health. The health of the 14 men was excellent and could be attributed to their good luck to have remained on Corregidor for the first year. Most of the civilians were in their forties.

The men started work on the project that would consume considerable time. The Japanese had surveyed the main armament and decided that Battery Hearn could be repaired. The destruction by the Americans was readily evident. It appeared that they had shoved a sand bag into the muzzle, charged it with powder and a 1000-pound projectile, and drained the recoil cylinders before firing for the last time. About four or five feet of the barrel had sailed into the China Sea. The Battery did not have any fire control equipment as this had been demolished also.

A spare barrel was on the edge of the parapet about 75 feet from the gun emplacement and repair parts were available for the recoil mechanism. The spare barrel weighed 60 tons. Work began to remove the damaged barrel. This was a very slow process.

The damaged barrel was brought down to a level position. The carriage was then rotated roughly parallel to the spare barrel. The civilians were experienced in handling heavy items with the right type of equipment. Here there was nothing to lift, pull or move the two barrels. The first major part of the job was to round up the tools, rollers, cribbing and heavy duty hydraulic jacks that would be needed to accomplish this task. Wooden rollers were cut from telephone poles and cut on a lathe to about eight inches in diameter. The second most important was adequate heavy timbers for cribbing under each end of the damaged barrel. The first order of business was the easiest part.

The island was searched and the necessary heavy-duty wrenches were brought up to the Battery. Most of the heavy tools came from the ordinance machine shop or the marine shop at Bottomside. Some of the wrenches had to be made by cutting from steel plates with an acetylene torch. The cap screws on the recoil mechanism were about four inches across. Work progressed slowly and the detail was not harassed. The guards knew nothing about what was being done from a mechanical standpoint. As long as the men kept busy and seemed to make some progress everything was ichi ban. (No.1). Lt. Tokashige was a better class of soldier and must have been well educated, but not in engineering. He would

Battery Hearn, 59th CAC, Fort Mills P.I. This is one of two guns on the island that could be fired 369 degrees. Firing a projectile about 20 miles weighing 1250 pounds. The open pit invited counter battery fire and was used to fire into Bataan.

come around and Superior Private Danjo would ask questions as directed and give an answer from the Americans. Much time was spent explaining each detail and why it was taking so long with little noticeable progress.

The leveling of the barrel and the disconnecting of the carriage to allow slipping the barrel backwards and clear of carriage was slow and extremely critical. Cribbing was placed under the barrel for support and the heavy breech end was jacked up and cribbed. There was only one heavy-duty jack for this purpose, so it was lift a little and move the jack to the other end and lift some more until it was level and off the supporting carriage.

The recoil cylinder shafts were then disconnected from the main barrel and the movement out of the carriage could begin. Rollers had to be placed under the cribbing and aligned to permit the entire barrel to be moved. Movement was by inches, requiring much replacement of rollers and insuring complete alignment to avoid any side movement on either end. A work day was eight hours with a short break for midday lunch. Yasame (rest) breaks were allowed in the morning and afternoon. Saturdays were spent in cleaning up after the weeks work moving stocks of cribbing and rollers for the following week.

Evenings were pleasant and we always looked forward to what Snuffy had managed to quan up for the evening meal. The main dish was rice with corned beef, vegetables if the boat came in from Manila. Fish and vegetables were shipped every third day. If we were lucky it was tolerably fresh. The bulk Red Cross supplies were used to augment the issued ration from the Japanese. After the supper hour some would shower and change into shorts and a short sleeved shirt with wooden shower shoes. Kenneth Dunlop and I often had a session of cribbage. We would play five games each evening, put the cards away, and join some of the others in one of our favorite times of the day, sunset over the Mariveles Mountains.

Directly in front of our quarters, a Spanish muzzle loading cannon had been set up on a cement pedestal, pointing out over the Boca Chica Channel or the North Channel, as it was also known by the Americans. Boca Chica was the Spanish name and was the channel used by Admiral Dewey when he sailed into Manila Bay. Boca Chica means small mouth. Boca Grande (big or large mouth) or South Channel, lies between Fort Drum and Corregidor. A couple of park benches were placed on each side of the old cannon. This was a favorite spot in the evening to watch the beautiful tropical sunsets. Each day there was a kaleidoscope of colors, none like any before. Bull sessions went on until lights-out at nine p.m.

Antique Spanish cannon.

A wide spectrum of discussion went on each evening, from the current rumor to the latest news about the progress of the war. Many heated discussions were brought up and thoroughly threshed around. To settle many arguments we had a copy of the *1940 World's Almanac.* M/Sgt. Kunich would take the adversary role. The cry would go out for the almanac before the argument got too hot. An arbiter would look for the specific answer if possible. If the answer could be determined from the almanac and Kunich was wrong, his retort was always, "The book is wrong, tear the page out." Many tall tales were spun and avidly listened to about the many places the civilians had worked before joining PNABC.

Some had been in Saudi Arabia developing the oil fields, others had worked in the oil fields of Venezuela and the states. Some had worked on the Hoover Dam, Fort Peck Dam and other big projects. One of the stories told by these wonderful men was how a bunch of the PNABC men went to meet Lester Schwab at Cavite when the Pan American Clipper arrived. They figured that Lester had been giving out that he was a big shot and a limousine would be there to meet him. Jack Davis and Lorin Buttner arranged for a mangy bag of horse bones and the most dilapidated caratella in all of Cavite to be at the dock when Lester came in. Lorin and Jack were there to escort Lester to his chariot. As they walked along Lester kept trying to get in each limousine or car they passed. Upon reaching the end of the line they presented the ridiculous rig and driver and started to load his gear aboard. This all in front of the beautiful women and men who had been fellow passengers on the Clipper. Lester swore that he would get even with them at some future date. Sergio Olferioff, a naturalized American from Russia, told stories of his adventures as a quartermaster and seaman in the merchant marine.

Evenings were enjoyed immensely as the soft breezes moved in and the heat dropped to a comfortable 65 to 70 degrees. Near the old Spanish cannon were several gardenia bushes which flowered and gave off a delightful fragrance. The men would sit and softly chat about home, their families, their hopes and dreams. The Japanese guards would wander around in idle curiosity and say a few words in Japanese. The first man to spot a Japanese guard approaching would call out loudly for all to hear, "air raid." The men would cease whatever they might be doing which they did not want the Japanese to know about. Most enjoyable at lights out was to stoke up my Wally Frank pipe for a night cap and meditate about the future.

We were periodically allowed to write a Japanese-provided postcard to home. Only 25 words were allowed in the body of the card. It was always a difficult message to write. Obviously, they would be censored by Superior Private Danjo or someone along the line. Usually we wrote that we were well and not to worry with perhaps a reference to the hope that we would receive a letter from home. Once the Japanese came to us to ask us to write a letter to the International Red Cross, attesting to our good treatment by the Imperial Japanese Army. Many of the men did not want to write such a letter, even though we were in relatively good shape and had most everything except our freedom with a desire to be home. As it was to be a group

letter, a compromise was settled on. Richard Lorin Buttner was to write the letter. A rough draft was drawn up and was subjected to revision using a large dictionary. Key words were sought that would have double meanings and could be interpreted two ways. Pvt. Danjo would check on the progress and be assured that it was being written. Finally, Lorin typed the revised copy and it was submitted to the Japanese. We never heard any more about writing another letter. The censor, whoever he might be, would have had to have a college education with at least a masters degree in English. The letter was certainly over Pvt. Danjo's comprehension.

The Japanese had a different viewpoint when it came to bathing. The normal method as practiced by most Japanese at home is to use a hot tub of water to soak in after bathing. They will go to the public bath house in their G-string (underwear) and have a small hand towel and a wooden bucket. First order of business is to sit by the hot tub and wash thoroughly and rinse off outside of the tub. Then wash out the G-string and the hand towel and then climb into the hot tub for soaking. They never wash in the tub as we do in our bathtubs. The hot tub is for use by many people and would soon be filthy, if not done properly.

The Japanese had been using a standard shower without the luxury of a hot tub. Lt. Tokashige cut off the top of a 55 gallon drum. Pvt. Kisi, his orderly, scrubbed the drum out and set it on some rocks, filled it almost full and then built a fire under it. A wooden box had been placed beside the barrel on some shower boards. Lt. Tokashige appeared for the great day in his G-string and wooden slippers. A small hand towel was wrapped around his head and beaming with anticipation of relaxing in a hot tub. He was dreaming of his far away home in the Land of the Rising Sun. After scrubbing down and rinsing, the lieutenant was ready for the hot tub. Gingerly he tested the water and stepped in. He shot out of the water like a porpoise, screaming Japanese epithets. His poor orderly took the brunt of the verbal abuse. Kisi brought more cold water and the lieutenant was able to complete his Japanese-type bath. It reminded me of the days on the farm at butchering time in the fall. Back home on the farm, a barrel of hot water was used to scald a hog before scrapping off the bristles. The Americans got a great kick out of this incident with remarks about pigs and hogs.

The Japanese have a sense of humor and were interested in American humor at times. One had to be careful in telling a joke or a story so as not to insult them or cause them to lose face. They also were very interested in family pictures and whether we were married and had any children. I had been able to keep my billfold with several pictures and a couple of cards that I had obtained in Manila. The best one was a card with six bulls standing with rears to the viewer. A guard might ask how old I was. Most of us could not give numbers above 10 in Japanese. The six bull card would come out and one could point out one of the bulls with his tail hanging down, partly or standing straight up. Each bull represented 20 through 60 years with the tail at degrees of erection. The Japanese would understand that the card reflected sexual capabilities. This would leave them laughing. Ah so! You 60, me 20.

HOW OLD ARE YOU ?

Another card was a picture of a frazzled headed, cross-eyed mustached man that had the caption, "Boy, am I tired." To impress the Japanese how tired or overworked we were, when asked, "Como nichi wa?" (How are you?) the answer would be, "takuson shigoto, schoshe yssume, scochi messy messy" (lot of work, little rest, little food). The card would be shown and he would laugh and reply, " Sanso number ten, Roosevelt number ten, Roosevelt pati, Japan ichi ban, schochi matte, anato ike nasta America," (war no good, Roosevelt no

Boy-Am I Tired!

good, Roosevelt die, Japan number one, small time you go America). In their blissful ignorance, they thought the war was a personal affair between Roosevelt and Tojo. If one of them were to die the war would be over and all could then go home. Their viewpoint was rather unrealistic and indicative of the propaganda of the government and their limited knowledge of why they were in a war.

The work of removing the damaged barrel from Battery Hearn continued on into the rainy season. Once the barrel was cribbed and on rollers, extreme caution had to be exercised in the lateral movement backwards. Each inch of movement required precise pressure without getting out of alignment with the carriage. One slip and the 60-ton barrel could fall off of the cribbing or the rollers. The men had to be very careful not to be crushed by something giving away.

However, all was not work as we did have Sundays off. The thought of so much water around the Rock, there had to be some way to catch some fish. Lester Schwab decided to manufacture a hand line for fishing from the dock. Several of us pitched in to help make the line. We stripped threads from a canvas hammock, tied them together and made three strands about 100 feet long. The ends were tied to a post and a small breast drill was attached to the other end. By twisting the handle of the drill, the three strands were twisted into one line. Frequent pulling of the drill kept the line from twisting into knots. Tree bark was boiled in a pot and applied to keep the line wet. It was twisted and stretched again. After the line was finished a hook was made of steel bus bars from an electric switch board. Using an acetylene torch, it was shaped and a barb cut into the hook and tempered. The line could be coiled like a piece of rope, and thrown quite a distance. Lester was finally satisfied and received permission to go fishing on Sunday. He scrounged a fish head from the Japanese galley and headed for the north dock. Carefully coiling the line with a small weight near the hook with the fish head. He gave a healthy swing and let the line run out. The line sailed true and plunked into the water out 50 or 60 feet and settled to the bottom. Les secured the line to a cleat on the dock and sat back and relaxed to test his fishing skills. Suddenly, the line tightened. Les grabbed the line to set the hook. He attempted to hold the line but the fish was headed for the deep water. Les tried to hold back and turn the fish towards the dock. When the line ran out, the fish hit the end of the line and busted the line. The story of the big one that got away was told and retold at the gun club. Les reasoned that a stingray had simply taken hook, line and sinker with him. All the labor of making the line had gone for nothing.

Christmas of 1943 soon arrived and we were issued two Red Cross boxes each. We sat around Christmas Day and dreamed of the traditional Christmas dinner, turkey and all the trimmings with hot mince meat pie. We satisfied our stomachs with what was available. Snuffy Rose outdid himself by coming up with Rose's Christmas pudding. It was made with C ration biscuits, raisins, powdered milk and sugar. The main course was soup de jour with camotes, corned beef and plenty of rice. Nescafe coffee was served as a beverage.

A sober but thoughtful day, everyone wanted to talk about Christmas at home. Would the families save our gifts 'till we came home? This was our second Christmas as prisoners of war. Would the war be over in six months? Perhaps 1944 would be the year? The news was good and the allies were making progress in the south. Would General MacArthur make good on his promise, "I shall return!" Why had we not seen or heard some of those planes from the Navy and Air Force? These and other questions were asked sitting by the old cannon. With misty eyes and a faraway look, we scanned the skies to no avail. We still had hope and faith that the next year would be the year. Oh well, six months more.

The work was slowly going on at Battery Hearn, slow enough for the Americans and fast enough to satisfy the Japanese. The barrel had been pulled back enough to clear the carriage and was being moved to the edge of the parapet. January was a dry season with no rain to slow the work. Early February the replacement barrel had been cribbed and rollers were in place. The task of moving it into position was underway. As spring approached all were busy, even the Japanese guards. Spring is the time of year for planting gardens and looking forward to fresh vegetable and fruit. The papaya trees and the coconut palms were growing fast and added to our diet. The rations from the Japanese had not improved but, foraging and conserving of the Red Cross supplies, we were able to set a reasonably good table. We also had learned what native plants were edible and would look for these in the fast growing jungle. Our health was good, and we had no serious illnesses. However, some signs of malnutrition and beriberi were apparent. The fortunate few that had remained on Corregidor were blessed by Lady Luck.

The arrival of spring stirred the interest of Lt. Tokashige in the planting of a garden. With some seeds he had obtained in Manila, his orderly was put to work on a small plot of ground for his garden. Beans, onions, squash and watermelons were planted. The garden flourished with the warm tropical weather and rain. However, the insects were as voracious as the POWs and soon made their appearance. There were no insecticides available and the lieutenant was in a quandary, He solved the problem by turning out five POWs to eliminate the pests. At early light the guards turned the men out for the dawn bug patrol. Superior Private Danjo explained to the horiyos, they were to crawl along the row, remove and crush the insects in the ground. The men were assigned a row and crawled along looking for bugs. The leaves were badly eaten by the many bugs. Jack Davis looked at a poor bug crawling and trying to make his breakfast on the stems of a leaf. Jack turned to Les Schwab and said, "Look at this dumb bug, he doesn't know there are better leaves. Let's put him on a good leaf, where he can eat all he wants," The bug men chuckled and started transferring bugs to good leaves. Lt. Tokashige soon discontinued this early morning detail. The plants flourished and began to produce. The watermelons did the best. As soon as small melons began to appear, Lt. Tokashige had his orderly paint a number on each melon. Each morning the melons stood early tenko (roll call) and were counted off in Japanese.

We had been allowed to write several postcards to our families. We never knew whether they arrived. At least they would allay the families anxiety and fears. Our group did receive some mail. Reading the letters was great for our morale. Of course they were censored on the other end and by the Japanese. I received a package from my mother. She had no idea what our needs were, but the dried fruit mixed with the cookie crumbs were appreciated. I had written in my cards a sentence, "Does dad still smoke Prince Albert?" I had hoped to imply that Prince Albert Pipe tobacco would be nice to have. Mom did not understand. I did not smoke before so the message did not register. Whatever we received was appreciated whether it was written or edible.

The replacement barrel was slowly being positioned for entry into the carriage. Progress was slower as the large part of the barrel entered the carriage. Vertical, horizontal and lateral movement at both ends had to be precise to avoid binding. The breach area of the barrel was coated with heavy grease to reduce friction.

The news from our small radio was heartening and our hopes raised. Soon we could expect to see some evidence that the Americans were close. Our morale was high and the gun club was going full blast on conjectures and theories. Most of the stories had had been told and retold to a point of being ridiculous. The other listeners would start to taunt or jeer and start repeating the story. Our closed society with no outside contact with the other world narrowed our viewpoints, and shortened tempers sometimes flared. Overall the 14 men got along well and were a very good group to be with. The men came from widely different parts of the country and had a wide variety of experiences and opinions. Ken Dunlop was from Walnut Creek, California; Les Schwab, Lorin Buttner and Chester (Jack) Davis were from the San Francisco area; The Rose brothers were from Los Angeles; Piland was from Virginia; Kunich was from the Pennsylvania coal fields; Haddox was from New Mexico; Olferioff was from the Bay area and I was from Texas. Each drew on the strengths of the others and enjoyed discussing politics, philosophy, religion, books, sports and a large variety of other topics. We learned from each other and broadened our outlook on life.

There was a lot of time to reflect on our past lives, to analyze our weaknesses and strong points, and plan for a new life after the war was over and we were back in God's country. I resolved that some of the things I had done in the past were stupid and self-serving and should not be repeated. One resolution I made was that drinking to stupefaction was senseless and of no benefit. Alcoholism in the islands was a deadly disease that if not controlled could end in disaster. All forms of distilled spirits were inexpensive and plentiful. A fifth of San Miguel Genebra (gin) was only 60 centavos or 30 cents. The most popular with the old soldiers was gin.

In pre-war days a regular army soldier would serve a two-year hitch and be a confirmed alcoholic, make no grade promotions and return to the states as a private. He would get dried out or hit the port wine circuit. Generally, he never made any progress except trying to stay out of trouble and do his duty, until he was either discharged or reenlisted. Immediately after reenlistment, he would apply for overseas duty. On arriving in the islands, some were quarantined for two or three weeks and would be drunk the entire time. Some were returned to duty and some would be returned to the states as Section 8 (undesirable). The soldier who liked his liquor could make out on $21 a month. Generally in the islands, the duty was excellent and the duty hours reasonable. Off duty time could be spent in the bars or with a visit to the Chinese store for a bottle of gin and some sasparilla, then back to the barracks for the long evening.

Alcoholics were the worst off when the war started and their sources were cut off. The men on Corregidor satisfied themselves with beer as they were not allowed to bring hard liquor on to the Rock. Their craving for sugar was so great, they would seek anything as a substitute. Vanilla extract, bay rum or raw sugar was eaten to satisfy their craving for alcohol. When these sources ended, they soon dried out, probably for the first time in years.

Our rice mill was still in operation and we could grind rice into a flour. Snuffy Rose would mix up a batch of batter and serve rice pancakes with sugar syrup. Lt. Tokashige learned of this and sometimes in the evening, he would send his orderly, 2nd Class Private Kisi over to order a batch of pancakes. This usually happened after Snuffy Rose had put out his fires and cleaned up the galley. A request like this could hardly be denied. Snuffy Rose would start to make up the batter, all the time fuming and fussing about the ancestry of the Japanese in general and the lieutenant in particular. Kunich would volunteer to help and between those two one never knew what was in the batter. The profanity alone would have cooked the batter if it could have been concentrated on the grill. The orderly would take the pancakes to the lieutenant and return with a verbal comment about how much the lieutenant liked the pancakes (Very good, ichi ban. Aere gotto maska).

Second Class Private Kisi or Superior Private First Class Danjo would always come and make requests for transportation. At times, the lieutenant would visit the Navy officer at Bottomside. As the driver of the beat up old Plymouth sedan, on one occasion, Kisi went along for the ride and to insure that the car returned promptly. When they arrived at Bottomside, Kisi would tell the driver (Golson) to wait. Once he came out with a beer bottle full of brandy and gave the driver the bottle on returning to the hospital.

I had a peculiar experience with Private Kisi. We had delivered the lieutenant and the Navy officer back to Bottomside after a sake drinking session in the lieutenant's quarters. I parked the car below the Japanese galley to await the call for a return trip. Pvt. Kisi invited me to the Japanese quarters for a drink of sake and some messy messy. What the heck, nothing can come of having a swig of sake and some chow. I went up to the second floor with Kisi saying, "Quiet, Japanese haiti sleep." The table was set with several dishes of food with small dishes of soy sauce to dip the raw fish in. I proceeded to scarf up the goodies. Kisi had taken the small pot of sake and had a small candle burning under it to keep it warm. He kept insisting I drink the sake. Each time I would take a sip, he would fill the small cup again. Then he started to suggest that maybe I would like to sleep in the lieutenant's bed. The alarm signals went off in my mind, "This son-of-a-bitch is trying to get me drunk." We had always believed he was a little queer. He used to come around at shower time and ogle the nude bathers. Japanese customs of hospitality encourages the guest to drink heartily. They will take hold of the pitcher of sake and urge one to drink up. I said to myself, "Hold it buster, if anyone is going to get drunk, it is going to be you." At the first opportunity, I latched onto the pitcher and started to urge him to drink. In no time, he was feeling his sake. I had eaten most of the chow and had him drunk, so best I get the hell out of there. I started back to our side of the building by way of the central stairs and climbed over the fence. There was a lot of junk there to avoid running into. The drunken Nip followed me over the fence and fell with a crash and din of furniture. The layout of our quarters with four exits in each room made it easy to avoid Kisi. He was trying to catch me and I would ease around through each door. Kisi stumbled into the room where Lorin Buttner and Olferioff slept. He stumbled and fell into Buttner's bed. He grabbed Lorin in a very sensitive spot. Buttner came up and socked him hard on the jaw and jumped out of bed with an Indian blanket around his shoulders. Buttner started the same evasive tactics once he realized what was happening. I was watching them and almost died laughing at the spectacle. Buttner, in his birthday suit, striped blanket around his shoulders, and the drunken Japanese behind him. I nearly split with laughter. I realized this could get out of hand and slipped around the building and called for the guard. They came and escorted Kisi back to his quarters. Kisi didn't show his face for several days. When he did show up, it looked like he had been banged up by the lieutenant. Discipline in the Japanese Army can be rough on any lower grades. There were no repercussions and everything went along without ever hearing anymore about it. One thing for sure, I did not want another experience like that.

Progress in replacement of the barrel was nearing completion with insertion of the barrel into the carriage. The work of bolting things back together began. Odd jobs would come up at times and some of the men would be assigned to them. More deteriorated powder was removed from the magazines and burned on the beach.

Captain Coughlin once said, "If and when the Nips ever decide to fire Battery Hearn, I do not want to be on the island." There were ample opportunities to do shoddy or incorrect repairs or adjustments during the months of working on the battery. It is highly possible that some repairs were not according to the book. Photographs of the gun taken after the return of the Americans in 1944 are indicative of the condition of the battery after replacement of the barrel. The damaged barrel does not appear in any of the photos taken after the recapture of the Rock.

The Filipinos in the intervening years have pillaged the island and cut up as many of the various batteries as possible. This had to be done at night and without any equipment except acetylene torches. They have cut and peeled some of the guns into man size pieces and hauled them away in small bancas (outrigger canoes) equipped with a sail. The collection and selling of scrap iron was one of the ways the Filipinos existed during the occupation. The Japanese were desperately anxious to ship it to the home islands.

The Filipino government has not tried to prevent this and the results are noticeable in most of the batteries. Nature has taken over and many of the batteries are no longer accessible because of jungle growth.

We had been on Corregidor for two years and the work was practically finished. Ammunition had been stored in Malinta Tunnel. Most of the available scrap had been removed with the exceptions of the main armament. The war was going in our favor. The time grew near when the Japanese could expect that their time was limited. Our second anniversary of the fall of Corregidor had passed. The Japanese guards and the interpreter Danjo were hinting that we were to be moved.

In early June of 1944, one of the guards looked worried and said that four Americans on Fort Frank had escaped. We had known the Americans and had been on the island a couple of times. They evidently made contact with Filipinos on nearly Batangas Shore at Ternate and arranged for a banca to be hidden in one of the coves of Carabao Island. The radio broadcasts indicated that the Americans were getting near. About June 11, 1944, the four men slipped off and were long gone. We never heard of them again.

Lt. General E.M. Flanagan in his book, *Corregidor, The Rock Force Assault*, refers to an incident that clears the air in regards to these men. He states, "Four men who had escaped from Fort Frank in 1944 were questioned by intelligence officers, during the planning for the airborne landing on Corregidor in February. The G-2 section was interested in the strength of the Japanese forces on Corregidor. They reported about 600 Nips at that time." This was the first information, I had ever heard as to what happened to those four men who had been among the fortunate few, to have remained on Fort Frank for two years. My best estimate of the Nip strength would be about 200 at the time we departed in June of 1944.

This information made our group uneasy and wary of what repercussions we might expect from the Japanese. We had heard of the group punishment meted out to those who tried to escape at Camp O'Donnell and Cabanatuan.

Two weeks later, at evening tenko, we were told that we would move from Corregidor the next day, 27 June, 1944. We were to be ready the following morning. The evening was spent in checking our packs, eliminating any excess that could not be carried for a long hike. Snuffy Rose cooked up some of the food into a feast and everyone ate as much as possible and packed some away for traveling rations. This along with the hoarded Red cross food would tide us through a few days if no food was issued.

Lorin Buttner typed up a report on the latest news from our radio. I removed the heel from one of my boots and Cpl. Haddox stuffed the single sheet into the recess in the rubber heel and replaced the heel. Everyone had plenty of clothes suitable for the tropics, a good pair of shoes or boots, mosquito bars, shelter half, woolen blanket, underwear and socks. Most of it was like new as we had saved good clothes for this very day. The last session at the gun club was a sad time. Everyone was wondering what would happen, where would we go and would we be sent to Japan or some other camp.

The conjecture and postulating did not produce answers and all were nervous about the move. There was little we could do. We had two years on this Rock and no one really wanted to leave. Life had been good to us. We were in reasonably good health, none had lost much weight and the environment was excellent considering the circumstances. The only thing left was to sweat it out and play the hand that fate dealt. So far it had been a good game, now the deal was changing. We were back into the hands of Lady Luck, the Japanese had the controlling deal. Would we continue to be among the fortunate few or would we be among the not so fortunate or one of the unfortunate ones.

Morning came quick and most had not slept much but were ready to face our uncertain future. Six months more and we would be free men again. Early daylight the Japanese called us out and held inspection of our packs and musette bags. Nothing was taken and soon we were on our way. Each man was dressed in clean, pre-war starched khaki uniforms, polished shoes with a variety of headgear. As we marched down to the north dock we looked like a bunch of soldiers going on pass except for the heavy packs.

A Japanese trawler was waiting at the dock. We embarked and the lines were cast off. As the boat pulled away every eye was on Corregidor. Our thoughts went back to the past two years, the soft sea breezes, the smell of the frangipani, hibiscus, bouganvillea and gardenias ever present. The many hours of discussion around the old Spanish cannon, the many games of cribbage and so many friends who had gone on before us to we knew not where. Each man was silent and finally turned away from our memories of the fabulous Rock and faced the sea breezes for a sight of the Manila shoreline.

As our boat moved along with its single cylinder engine chugging, I looked the boat over and watched the engineer in the engine room as he tended the wheezing old diesel engine. So this was what they used for traveling throughout the Pacific. The entire boat was of wood, well constructed with a flaring bow. It appeared to be seaworthy and had probably been in the fishing fleet before it was pressed into service for the Imperial Japanese Army. The trip into Manila was about two and a half hours. We landed at pier five on the Manila waterfront. A truck was waiting to haul us away.

CORREGIDOR

OASIS OF HOPE

PART FOUR

THE JAPANESE PRISON SYSTEM

'You know where I want to go right after the war? To Hirohito's funeral.'

Part Four

The Japanese Prison System

The fortunate 14 men were about to follow in the footsteps of the not so fortunate and the unfortunate souls that had been in the camps on Luzon. Our introduction to some of these poor unfortunate men was shocking and showed how lucky the 400 men of the original detail on Corregidor had been.

Our truck sped along the familiar streets of Manila, all eyes were on the scene around us. Our impression of the plight of the Filipinos, under occupation for the past two years, did not reveal the true picture as we passed along the streets. There was very little visible damage from bombing. The declaration of Manila as an open city in December of 1941 was a blessing to the people and the city. There were not as many auto calesas dashing around picking up passengers. The auto calesa is a small motor vehicle built on a small auto chassis like the English Austin or similar chassis. They are equipped with two small seats on each side of the vehicle with entrance from the rear. They will carry about five or six Filipinos and deliver them to wherever they want to go for a few centavos. The rationing and or no available gasoline cut down this mode of transportation. The horse drawn caratella that carries as many as 10 persons along with pigs, chickens or vegetables and fruit were in evidence. The horse drawn caromata and caratela are similar but the difference is: a caromata is designed as a passenger vehicle with one seat behind the driver; the caratella is a cargo vehicle with seats along the sides for more passengers and cargo. The quaint horse drawn vehicles are pulled by a small pony and are driven at a fast trot. The clicking of the iron shoes of the animals is the music of Manila.

The auto calesa, horse drawn caromata and caratela are gaily decorated and painted. There was also a public transit, auto buses and electric street cars which ran on regular routes. All of these were hustling passengers and were loaded with Filipinos hanging on the outside and filled inside. At least they had public transportation. The usual street vendors could be seen in the shade of palm trees, their goods spread on a piece of cloth. The familiar call, of an old lady, "baluts, baluts," could be heard. Balutes are duck eggs that have been hatched until just before the duckling feathers appear, then they are boiled and sold to the natives. The natives break open the end and suck the small duckling out. A highly desired delicacy to the Filipinos. I have never heard of a GI who was drunk enough to try a balute.

Our trip through the city was like taking a country boy to town on Saturday, so many things to see, hear and smell. The smell of the Manila streets at first introduction reeks of horse urine, manure, open sewers and the many cooking odors mingled with the frarance of the many flowers and blooming bushes along the way. This mixed with the fumes from the cars, trucks and buses, the smell of the Pasig River (an open sewer) and the salt breezes, touches one nostrils with a lasting impact one never forgets. The calesas and caromata carry a basket hanging from the rear of the vehicle and the drivers are supposed to sweep up any droppings from their horses. Generally they do not stop when they are moving so the droppings remain on the street. Our passage through the streets reminded us there was another world and how we had missed it for the past two and a half years.

Manila, the Pearl of the Orient, had changed from the beautiful city with wide avenues, shady walkways with waving palms trees, and people who enjoyed life, into a drab and dreary place. There appeared to be less people

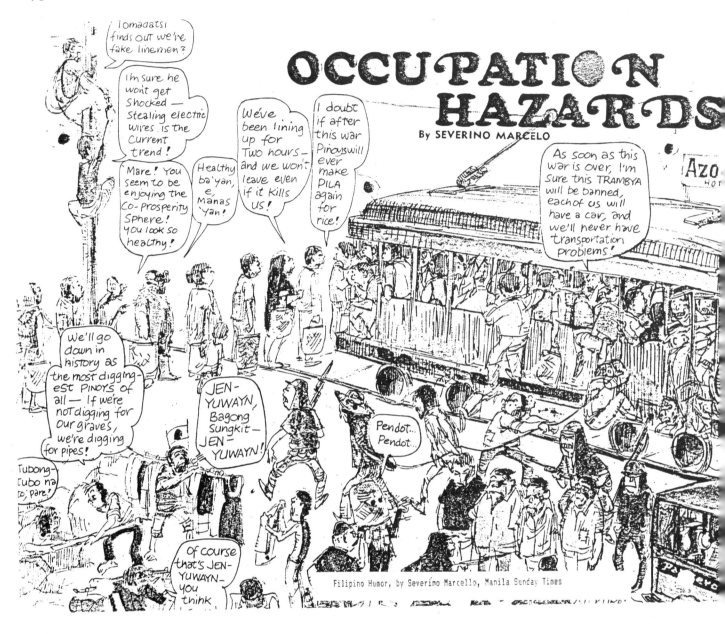

Filipino Humor, by Severino Marcello, Manila Sunday Times

and not near as much traffic.

One vehicle that caught our eye and was indicative of the shortage of fuel was a bus that had a stove-like apparatus on the back that gave off a trail of smoke. The vehicle had been converted to operate on charcoal which generated methane gas for the modified engine. How efficient and economical it was, we had no idea. At least the Filipino's were making the best of The Greater East Asia Co-Prosperity (poverty) Sphere public transportation.

Kunich, Golson, Haddox and I had worked in the port area, near pier one, for two years before the war. The familiar streets brought back many pleasant memories. The port area did not appear to have suffered any serious damage. There was no visible damage from bombing by the Japanese of the port area after the declaration of the city as an open city. Deterioration from lack of maintenance was apparent.

The declaration of Manila as an open city in December of 1941 was a blessing to the people and the city. The warehouses in the Quartermaster depot were opened to the public. The Filipinos must have had a field day with what the Americans could not move to Bataan.

Our truck pulled up in front of a massive stone building with high steel gates. The words inscribed across its front, BILIBID PRISON, brought us back to reality. The

gates opened and the truck pulled into the compound and stopped. Japanese guards hustled us out and formed us into ranks for roll call. When they were satisfied that we were all present according to their count, we were marched to an area with another gate through a wall. Once through this gate, we met our first Americans. An officer took charge and told us we were now in Bilibid Prison hospital. He assigned us to billets at the far end of the compound. Captain Coughlin was sent to the officers area.

M/Sgt. Kunich as the senior noncommissioned officer called for attention and the group marched to the assigned billets. Each man held his head high and stepped out smartly as though on parade. Starched khakis, polished boots, with packs, we moved through the compound. Many of the prisoners gave us a curious glance as we passed but most were hollow eyed, listless, gaunt and grotesque skeletons of their former selves.

So this was the infamous Bilibid Prison, the crossroads of the hell that was the Japanese prison system. Bilibid was used as a staging point for prisoners being shipped to other camps, Nielson Field, Nichols Field, Tayabas, Davao, Korea, Manchuria and Japan. It was also used as a hospital for those evacuated from the camps who were too sick to work. The senior American medical officer was Navy Commander Thomas Hayes, with Army and

76

Native transportation (circa 1940). Courtesy Richard Francies.

Ancient mode of transportation.

Common sight on streets of Manila (circa 1940). Courtesy Clifford J. Keller.

Delivery service, yo-ho pole and two baskets.

Crowded streetcars (Trambya) Avenida Rizal 1943, Manila during occupation, Manila Sunday Times.

Navy medics and doctors. The various wards were the old jail cells of the Philippine government penitentiary. Those who were excess and waiting transfer or shipment were quartered in some of the barrack type buildings or camped in the open compound.

After settling down and getting the feel of the place, I began to wonder to whom I would give the letter to that I had hidden in my boot heel. I had not had an opportunity to really case the place and see if I knew anyone. I did not know if there was any stool pigeons or whom I could trust. We had heard of the KempiTai (Secret Police).

I asked around and implied that I had some information and wanted to talk to the senior American officer or his adjutant. I was directed to a small masonry building in the rear of the compound. I was escorted inside. There were three men sitting at a table. I asked if they were in charge and they indicated they were. I felt I could trust them and took off my boot and handed it to the spokesman and indicated to remove the heel. A man was called and he took the heel off and replaced it. The spokesman took the typed onion skin paper and read it. He thanked me and dismissed me without further comment. At least I had brought them the latest news as we knew it before we left Corregidor.

At the time I did not know anything about the setup at Bilibid. I was to learn many years later from a book, *Bilibid Diary, The Secret Papers of Cmdr. Thomas Hayes, POW, Philip-*

Massive front gate and walls of old Bilibid Prison. Served as a prison hospital and staging area for movement of prisoners to other camps and Japan. Courtesy Dr. Paul Ashton.

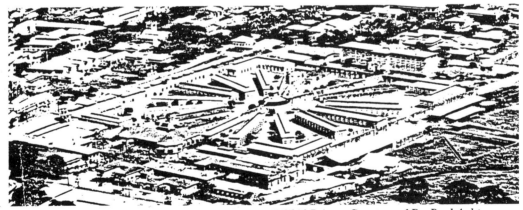

View of interior walls and guard control center Bilibid Prison. Courtesy of Dr. Paul Ashton.

Aerial view of layout of grounds and buildings in Bilibid Prison. Courtesy of Dr. Paul Ashton.

pines, 1942-45, by A. B. Fetter. The book gives an excellent account of the American incarceration in Bilibid from July 1942 to October 1944. The coming and going of the thousands who passed through this crossroads to hell, either going or coming from details in the islands and finally their last journey to Japan.

Bilibid was the purgatory between a living hell and the redemption from death that were the ghastly slave camps of the Japanese system. This grindstone separated the weak, sick and the disabled wretches from the stronger, more resilient ones; into grist for slave labor and feed for the satellite camps in the islands and Japan. The chaff from this grindstone of human misery, the weak, sick or disabled into a life of despair, endlessly awaiting misery at the threshold of death from those who were stronger. Like the flotsam of war, they drifted into the back waters of the prison system—the walking, living ghosts of Bataan and Corregidor. This was Bilibid Prison and the Japanese idea of humane treatment of prisoners of war.

Bilibid Prison is located in the heart of Manila in the Santa Cruz District on Calle Azcarraga Ave. The prison was built in 1865 by the Spanish for criminals. It had been used by the Spanish, Filipino and American governments until about 1940, when a new prison had been constructed.

I had visited this prison in 1940 when it was still an active prison. Little did I realize, that I would pay a return visit under vastly different conditions. The prison is roughly square in shape, each wall about 600-feet long with a dividing wall bisecting the square. In the center of this wall is a guard tower that overlooks the entire prison. Ten masonry barrack-type buildings with iron bars and external shutters radiate from the guard tower like spokes in a wheel, five on each side of the wall. The hospital was in one compound with the holding area for transients. The other side was used by the Kempei Tai. The outside walls were about 12-feet high with barbed wire and electrical charge. Broken pieces of glass were imbedded in the cement. It also had an electrocution chamber in a small building in the rear. Truly an awesome and grim repository for the human flotsam of war.

We started to visit around and look for friends from better days. One of the first ones I came across, was our good friend and former member of the shop in port area, Staff Sergeant Edward J. Larson (Swede). The last time I had seen him was in the hospital on Corregidor in March of 1942. He had lost an arm at that time and was evacuated to Manila with the hospital in July of 1942. Later he was sent to Cabanatuan and then on a work detail to Davao, Mindanaa, the southern most island of the archipelago. There were about 1300 men there. They had been shipped back to Luzon only a few days before we arrived.

We had a long visit and discussion about our experiences in the past two years. He was fortunate that he did not have to do the hard work in the fields. With only one arm, he could not swing the heavy hoes that were used in the fields. He said he had been assigned to work in the camp galley. Swede also attained some notoriety among the prisoners. It was customary for one to share anything he had if he could not open it. Swede told me of the time he had asked one of the cooks to open a can of corned beef for him. The cook replied that he would have to share with him. This ticked Swede off and he bided his time until the cook had quanned up a mess of corned beef with some onions and green peppers. When the cook was not watching, Swede sat his can of corned beef on the stove and made off with the cooks quan. Swede was known as the "one armed bandit" there after.

Davao was a harsh camp and several men had escaped. One of the escapees was Lt. Mike Dobervich, of the 4th Marines. Mike had been on the guard detail at General King's headquarters on Bataan. He made the Death March with my friend Lt. Lester Petersen. Many years later, Mike was able to tell me of how Lt. Petersen had been executed at Camp O'Donnell along with several others. "They had been searched by the Japanese and were found to have items of a Japanese nature, souvenir yen, pictures or other items of a personal nature." The possession of these items was automatic execution. The separated group was seen in an area under guard and were marched away and executed. This answered the question of why the Japanese soldiers did not take billfolds and other personal property when they rounded us up on Corregidor.

A day or so after our arrival in Bilibid, a large detail came into camp. It was the port area detail. They had been in one of the better details for most of the two years. Commander G.G. Harrison USN was the SAO. They were in reasonably good shape and had lived fairly well. They had become adept in the fine art of stealing staple goods from the cargos being shipped out of Manila, or sabotaging cargo. Among them were more of my friends, S/Sgt. Archie Golson and SF.2nd Elmer J. White. Both of them had been on the Rock for one year. Golson had been lucky and was the camp barber. One of the men was a navy man, B.M. 1st/Cl. R.C. Sheats, who had been one of the divers in the detail recovering the silver from Manila Bay. Sgt. Golson told me of the time the stevedores had snatched a box of chocolate candy. The candy was for pilots and acted as a no-doze. The men had a hard time getting to sleep.

Something must be happening, why were the Nips starting to pull in these large groups? Were the Allied forces closer than we thought? Where, How? What were they going to do with all these men? The Bilibid compound was crammed full, many men were having to sleep on the cement compound outside of the buildings.

The American Military system of accounting for personnel in a given area is unique to many other countries. The Americans who were charged with the administration of the various prison camps relied on the time proven method of accountability. Each man was physically accounted for by name, rank, serial number and duty status.

The Japanese had several Americans assigned on the SAO staff to monitor all shipments to Japan. A roster of those on a specific shipment was made. On arrival in Japan, the Japanese would notify the International Red Cross of the arrival in Japan by name. Any deaths that might have occurred during the voyage were omitted. This procedure appears in an extract from the files of the National Archives, microfilm No. 16, in a report of an investigation after the war.

During the time we were prisoners, many of us did not realize or know that once the Japanese had established camps with senior American officers (SAO) in charge with limited staff, they immediately reverted to our system of accountability.

For example, when a group was processed for shipment, a shipping roster was prepared for the group. Those on quarters or sick in the hospital were listed on a separate roster. When anyone was declared fit for duty, he was removed from the sick list and listed as available for duty. These transactions at Bilibid were very comprehensive. They were typed on paper, signed by a medical officer and made a part of the files of the hospital. A man coming in from another detail was carried as sick until an examination of the group was completed by the doctors at Bilibid. If they were found fit for duty within the parameters set by the Japanese, they were transferred to duty status and subject to shipment to the main camp at Cabanatuan. Our group of 14 men was held at Bilibid for 30 days. Some of the other transient groups were shipped out. A few of the men were shipped with details bound for Japan through Bilibid.

The records of the system at Bilibid and the accounting for all the men who passed through there, survived the war and is available to anyone. The National Archives in Washington, D.C. has many thousands of raw files on microfilm. I found copies of the admission of our group to the hospital at Bilibid, dated 4 July, 1944. Medical entry listed optic neuritis and beri-beri, assigned to non-duty status. Later transferred to duty status and became eligible for shipment to Cabanatuan.

Our stay at Bilibid gave us an opportunity to observe some of the grotesque examples of the abuse, malnutrition, and maltreatment in the pitiful skeletons of the men returned from Nichols Field and Las Pinas camps. One man, whom I had known before the war, returned from the Nichols Field detail. He weighed about 90 pounds with pipe stem legs, scrawny arms, hollow eyes and a distended stomach. A very pitiful sight. It always made me think, "It could be me except for the grace of God and Lady Luck's benevolence." We heard stories of men who would break another man's arm for a ration of rice so the victim would not have to work. The Japanese had a remedy for suspected malingering and riding the sick

JŪL 8 1944   (July 8, 1944)   DISCHARGED   S.Q.

MICHELS, Jean H.	Ph3c, USN	MALARIA	To Sick in Hospital
BEACH, Amos (O)	Pvt., USA	INTRACRANIAL INJURY	To Sick In Quarters
BURKE, Joe C.	Pvt., USA	INJURY ?? OF FACE	do
BROWN, Howard	Pfc., USA	ANKYLOSIS, rt. knee	do
HARRELL, Thomas	Pfc., USA	ANKYLOSIS, lft knee	do
BOYD, Donald L.	Cpl.,	MALARIA	To Standby Group
COKER, Lawrence L.	Sgt., USA	ARTHRITIS, chronic	do
DUNLAP, Kenneth A	Civilian	??	do
HOWARD, T.	S/Sgt. USA	MALARIA	do
JACQUES, Ralph J.	Cpl., USA	ARTHRITIS, chronic	do
WIX, Asbury L.	S/Sgt. USA	BERIBERI (Beri beri)	do
SCHWAB, Lester L	Civilian	CARIES, teeth	do
WALKER, Mack W.	S/Sgt. USA	MALARIA	do
BARR, Donald P.	Civilian	?? acute 7b	To Army Air Detail
BURRELL, William (O)	1st Lt USA	?? 7b	do
CRAWFORD, Jessie M.	Cpl., USA	?? right foot 7b	do
ROXWORTH, Durward L.	Pfc., USA	?? rt foot 7b	do
REYNOLDS, ?? Jr. Cox.USN		?? right leg	do
ROCH, Paul ?.	Pvt., USA	??	do
WILLIAMS, John ?.	Pfc., ??	??	do
GASPA, Louei J.	Ph2c, USN	?? acute	To Medical Staff.

THE BILIBID HOSPITAL, MANILA, P.I.

WIX, Ashbury T.   Sgt., U.S. Army
Admitted: 7-2-44   Diagnosis: Neuritis, Optic #543

Admitted from Corregidor with the above diagnosis, complaining of headaches, blurring of vision for past few months. Since he requests change of status to duty, patient is returned to duty this date.
7-3-44: To duty.

                    P. BUESS, Major, M.C., U.S. Army

Photostatic copy of a typical admission order to Bilibid hospital and subsequent disposition. Microfilm files, National Archives records. Courtesy Adrian Martin.

book. They would be put on short rations as long as they were sick or not working. This quandary made men desperate to get out of work at any cost and hopefully off the detail by going back to Bilibid Hospital. Many men were brought in that looked like living skeletons. The challenge to the skills of the medical staff with little or no medicine was enormous. Some miraculous recoveries made it worthwhile to keep trying to save as many as possible. One of the most frustrating problems for the medical personnel was the Japanese medical men. The doctors had to have the approval of the senior Japanese medical man for any decision on treatment. All of the American doctors were graduates of American medical school and were highly qualified in their fields. The total ineptness, lack of medical training and total disregard of the American expertise, by the Japanese, was exasperating and an insult to these gallant men. Skilled surgeons like Dr. Thomas H. Hewlett, Dr.

Paul Ashton, Cmdr. Thomas Hayes, Dr. Dan Golenturnik, and many others had to work under severe handicaps. In spite of totally inadequate facilities, lack of proper medications, adverse environment and no laboratories or X-ray equipment, they carried on in the best traditions of their profession. Thousands of patients with all types of medical problems owe their survival to these wizards of the medical world. Never have so few been asked to do so much for his fellow man.

The permanently disabled or crippled passed their time on rumors, spreading anything that appeared to be the current news. Others such as administrative, supply and cooks were fortunate to be busy enough that they were not bored. The 30 days our group spent in Bilibid were boring and time dragged slowly. We were not complaining as long as the food didn't get any worse than it was. We used some of the food stuffs that we had brought with us very sparingly. The standard fare was soup de jour with traces of pork or fish with some tops of carrots, radishes or whistle weed with a ration of rice. The morning rice was cooked into a gruel and called **lugao**. Sometimes there were mongo beans in the soup. They were excellent for nutrients. The rations were in better shape when received in Bilibid than some of the rations we received from Manila while on the Rock. There was no opportunity to scrounge or scavenge anything extra to eat. There was a small store where one could buy sugar, salt, onions, other native vegetables and fruit for quanning. This was limited by amount and availability of money. The staff did receive some medicines and supplies from outside of the prison. The Japanese did not like the idea of the Americans receiving supplies from outside sources. They felt it reflected on them and was frowned on most of the time.

In my rambling around, I came across an older civilian that I had known on Bataan, Max Blouse. He was about 60 years old. He had been the president of the Pampango Bus Company which served a large area of Luzon with civilian bus transportation. His superintendent, Bill Meese, had also been in the shop on Bataan as a civilian. The Pampango Bus Company had turned over all of their buses to the army to transport Philippine army troops. Most, if not all, of his vehicles wound up in Bataan with their Filipino drivers.

After the fall of Bataan, the American and Filipino civilians were treated the same as the military. Mr. Blouse, due to his age, wound up in Bilibid Prison. He was a wealthy man and stood to recover most of his losses at the end of the war. He could not get around very well, so he hired an air force man who had lost one leg to be his orderly at a stipulated price for the duration. A just and fair arrangement for both, if they lived to that day of freedom. (Max and Bill both died on the *Arisan Maru* in October 1944.)

When our 30 days were almost up, rumors of a shipment began to circulate. No one knew the destination or size of the group. We had all been returned to duty status and subject to any draft. About July 25 our Corregidor group was among a sizeable draft. The men from Port Area, Davao and some of the other camps (about a thousand or more men) were also available. Early in the morning we were rustled out and formed into columns of fours, counted and recounted amidst much hustle and bustle by the Japanese and Americans, insuring that all that were able to work were accounted for. With packs loaded with all our worldly possessions, we marched to the Manila railroad station and boarded box cars for our trip.

We were packed 50 men to a car. There was room to squat and sit on your gear but not much more. The side door pullman cars were narrow gauge and rather decrepit. My first thought was the Forty and Eight box cars of World War I, forty men or eight horses. Each man had been given the standard traveling ration, a ball of steamed rice. There we were in the pipeline, headed for Cabanatuan. Hopefully it would not be as bad as we had heard from so many who had been there.

After about four hours of train huffing and puffing, we finally pulled into a station and stopped. The Japanese guards who had occupied the doorway started to shout commands and hustle us into ranks for tenko. Fortunately there had been no escapes and the count was verified to their satisfaction. Soon the order to move out came and we shouldered our packs and started marching down a dusty road. The Filipinos were lined up along the streets, not daring to approach any of the Americans. Their facial features, the sly smiles and the slight movement of the hands gave us the impression that they were sympathetic to us, but hesitant to provoke the Japanese guards. They had seen this coming and going of prisoners for the past two years. About ten miles of marching brought us to a barbed wire enclosure on both sides of the road. We turned into the gate with Japanese guards lined up on each side. We had not been harassed or pushed too hard during the march with a short break about midway. We were glad that we had made our packs up to be carried easily. Though they were heavy, they rode nicely, high up on our backs and shoulders.

Line up for tenko, count off, then stand fast as the guards checked and re-checked the count. At last they turned us over to the Americans for assignment of quarters. We could see a long line of thatch covered buildings along a street. We were broken down into smaller groups and shown to the thatch-covered huts we would occupy. Fortunately, Kunich, Haddox, Golson and I were in the same hut. The civilians were in another grass covered hut nearby. We gladly eased our packs off and inspected our area. The huts were about 30 feet long and 13 feet wide. The roofs were thatched with nipa palm and the walls were of nipa palm on bamboo supports.

The nipa huts were divided in the center with dirt floors and two parallel planks for walkways. The sides had two levels with split bamboo spaced about an inch apart to form a sleeping platform. The lower deck was about 18 inches from the ground and the upper level was about four feet above. The normal capacity for Philippines Army was 28 men per hut or hootch as we called them. Each man stowed his gear at the head of his assigned space and spread his blanket or shelter half over the split bamboo. If he was lucky, he might have a straw banig (tagalog for sleeping mat). Quanning was not permitted in the hootches. An area was set aside outside for fires. Water was from a central water point. Crude makeshift showers were made from five-gallon cans hung on a pole. The usual slit trench with bamboo for seats served as a latrine. It was located near the outer fence. The compound was fenced with double barbed wire all around with guard towers at each corner. Across the center another fence bisected the compound, separating the main camp from the hospital area. The men were allowed to grow small vegetable gardens along the inner fence, slightly set back away from the inside fence.

We settled in and got our gear stowed and sleeping area squared away. Each man had enough space to sleep, about 20 inches between men. All slept head to toe alternately. After we settled down we talked to some of the men that were there. We wanted the scoop on how the camp was run, when and where the mess lines were and how often. The main thought was of food and what to expect in the way the Japanese ran things. We had to learn all the important rules to avoid trouble. Just after 5:00 p.m. the work details came in. They were formed up and tenko was taken. Each man was checked for smuggled contraband and then released to go to the bath house to clean up. Supper hour was 6:00 p.m. We joined the rush and were appalled at the condition of the men. It was a re-run of Bilibid. All were horribly underweight, just skin and bones. Many had ulcerated legs and arms, many showed the effects of wet beriberi. Some had been out on other details and returned to Cabanatuan as unable to work. Some had terribly distended abdomens. "It could be me," I thought as I waited for my turn for chow. Here were the not so fortunate Battling Bastards of Bataan. The men who had lived through the hell, that was Camp O'Donnell, Cabanatuan One and Two. This hell hole was known as Camp No. 3.

A standard ration of rice, soup de jour and a canteen cup of hot water for tea or coffee, if you had tea or coffee. The soup was good with a few pieces of vegetables and a whiff of carabao meat. A row of cans with hot scalding water for washing of mess gear was available. The men had learned the importance of keeping mess gear clean. We returned to our hootch and sat on the edge of the bunk and listened to the men around us as they cleaned up their chow.

Some of the men came around wanting to trade a portion of his food for tobacco, or something he wanted. A few would actually trade for tobacco. It seemed that it should be just the opposite. Deprivation works in different ways and each man has different values and priorities.

The men around us had been returned from various details and were generally too weak to work. Under normal conditions they would have been hospitalized. The Japanese system was to work them until they fell and then stand them up to work again. Only after a man was no longer able to work was he put on quarters or in the hospital. His rations were then cut until he returned to work. This was our second introduction to the main stream of forgotten and forlorn humanity. We wondered if we would be among the living if we had not been so fortunate to have been in a good camp.

Thousands had been shipped to Japan by the middle of 1944. Some had been shipped as early as 1942. Where were these unfortunate souls? What condition were they in comparison to these at Cabanatuan? No one knew and we could only say, "There but for the grace of God there goeth I." Thank God for our health and our lives after two years of captivity. We and those from Port Area had been extremely lucky for two years.

Two days after we arrived at Cabanatuan we were put on work detail. The men had told us of the many work details that were sent out daily from camp. There was no loafing here. Some of the permanent details were supply, woodcutters, carabao drivers and herders, and farmers. We found out soon enough as we were formed into groups and counted off as we passed through the gate bound for work. Talking to some of the fellows we learned that we were in a construction group and would be working building revetments for airplanes. We walked several miles and came to an area with a couple of shacks. We stopped and were checked again for proper count. One of the guards opened the door of a shack and began to pass out long handled shovels, wheel barrows and picks. We then moved over to an area where some mounds could be seen above the flat ground. We were split into groups of three. A wheel barrow had been brought along, and we were shown what was to be done by some of the Americans. Each group of three was assigned to a revetment site and the movement of dirt to form an embankment in a circular shape with an entrance for an airplane.

Much to our surprise, the workers were not harassed as long as they appeared busy. The system as worked out by the more experienced men was unique. One man would loosen the earth with the pick; one man would then shovel it into the wheelbarrow. The Irish buggy driver would then push the barrow to the point where the dirt was wanted and then spread. Every 30 minutes we would change: the picker became the shovel operator, the barrow driver became the pick operator. We could see that someone had convinced the Japanese that only "mad dogs and Englishman go out in the hot sun," or at least that these men would not be worked until they dropped.

This was a real eye-opener, something that could be done without fear of repercussions. It appeared that here we had run into the same delaying tactics by the Japanese, allowing the work to continue at such a leisurely pace. The Japanese were riding the gravy train with the biscuit wheels for all it was worth. As long as the Americans made visible progress, everything was okay. When a Japanese officer appeared, everyone appeared busy. These men had learned how to manipulate the Japanese guards and keep them off their backs. In the Americans favor was the fact they had not been shipped to Japan. Here they knew what to expect—don't rock the boat and avoid shipment as long as possible. The tropics were a heck of a lot better place to be than the northern climate of Japan. Besides it was a lot closer to the oncoming allied forces. Please hurry up, get us out of this living hell before we get shipped. So many had died and more will die soon, unless a miracle happens.

The noon-time break was another revelation on what happens to men that have reached the depths of hunger and will eat anything. Noon lunch was brought out from the kitchen and along with the rice was a nice roasting ear of corn. It had been a long time since we had anything like this delicacy. After I had finished eating the corn down to the cob, I started to throw the cob away. One of the men spoke up and said he wanted it. To our utter amazement he proceeded to eat the cob. Horses, pigs and cows will not eat corn cobs.

Back in Texas we either burned them as fuel or put them in the outdoor privy. The sight of an individual eating a corn cob that was so indigestible and tasteless was beyond us.

Another rude awakening was how many of the men at Cabanatuan had distended stomachs. The sight of a walking skeleton with a protruding stomach was sad indeed. It seems that some of the men would hang around the kitchen and sweat out anything that was thrown out as garbage. Rotten vegetable leaves, peelings or anything that looked edible, was salvaged by these scavengers. One item that would not cook up in the soup was fish bones. Some of the men would eat fish bones. If they got past the throat the bones would pass through the stomach and stick into the lining of the colon. The doctors had to remove these bones from the colon. It would seem that one trip for this surgery would have made a believer out of the scavengers.

This incident reminded me of the depression days on a ranch in Hill County Texas. The dust storms and severe dry weather had wreaked havoc on the grazing land and the cattle were starving to death. Some of the cattle would eat the Prickly Pear (cactus) that were not affected by the drought. The needle-like thorns would lodge in the throats of the cattle and block anything they tried to swallow. Many had to be caught and have the thorns removed. Man and beast are similar when they are starving.

The largest detail at Cabanatuan was the farm detail, with hundreds put to work in raising garden type crops to supposedly feed the prisoners. Others were put to work as animal caretakers with a few pigs, chickens and carabaos. Others had been put into the rice paddies to work. This combination should have provided ample food to feed the thousands of POWs. This was not to be, as the Japanese used most of it to feed their own troops. The Americans got only what the Nips did not want, carrot tops, camote tops, and bones from butchered animals and other waste residue. Even the entrails of the animals were used as part of the soup de jour. The same thing happened at other camps. Colonel Braly in his book, *The Hard Way Home*, refers to the harassment of the senior officers in the Formosa camps who had re-

fused to volunteer to work the farms because the Nips took everything and left the scraps for the Americans. Gen. Wainwright had to herd goats.

Rumors began to circulate about another shipment for the Land of the Rising Sun. Thousands had already been shipped there and no one knew where or what they were doing. No one wanted to go, but the Nip administrative staff and their medical novices were after the Americans to come up with names that could be shipped as laborers. We had been at Cabanatuan about three weeks when the Japanese began to squeeze again. Many of the labor groups from Davao, Port Area and other camps had swollen the camp population and strained the food supply system. The economic situation in the islands was a disaster. The natives were not producing enough food for themselves, much less the occupation army. The Co-Prosperity Sphere was aptly called the Co-Poverty Sphere.

The pressure for another list of men to go to Japan was increasing and the Americans began to screen men in accordance to the guide lines set by the Japanese. The list was posted on the bulletin board and everyone was sweating out whether they would be on the list. I went over and read through the list of names and found that all my military friends from Corregidor and Manila were on the list. Captain Coughlin and the P.N.A.B.C. civilians were not listed. We were asked at the time of screening if we had any serious illnesses or conditions. Captain Coughlin had only one kidney. I had said I could not see very well due to "optical atrophy, beriberi and malnutrition." I was in a quandry as to what would happen if we stayed there or if we went to Japan. A heated discussion was held with my friends on the pros and cons of the alternatives. I decided that I would volunteer to go with my friends rather than stay at Cabanatuan.

I went to the officer who had been making up the list and asked to be included in the sailing list. He was glad to do so, as some of the men were in worst shape than I was at that time.

The Japanese always held an inspection of men being shipped. This was a large detail, 1,000 men and a 35-man medical detachment, and took considerable time. The prisoners took advantage of the time to hide critical items. They had been through these inspections and, like all soldiers, had figured a way to beat the inspection. As the inspector passed along the file, the second file would pass over to the inspected file anything they did not want to have taken away from them. Once inspected, the Japanese inspector did not notice the activity behind him. The men had to be sure that some of the guards were not watching as the change was made.

Many men had ingenious ways of concealing contraband. We had been issued Japanese G-string (underwear). These G-strings are about 28 inches long by about six inches wide with a tie string for a belt. When wearing a G-string, it is tied about the waist and then brought up between the legs and tucked under the tie string in front. They are simple and easy to wash, as well as comfortable.

The men in the detail at Port Area, under Cmdr. G.G. Harrison, SAO, were known as "The Four Hundred Thieves." The detail was housed in the Marsman Building across from the docks and was one of the better details. They developed strafing to an art. When working in the holds of the ships, they were not supervised closely. They wore G-strings most of the time working on the docks or carried an extra G-string for looting purposes. The trick was to sew two G-strings together along the sides, making a long pouch. Down in the hold of the ship they would rip open sugar bags and fill the pouch with about two pounds of sugar. This would be cached until just before quitting time. They would tie the G-string on and pass through shakedown inspection with out detection.

Many of our men used the same trick with some of their hoarded supplies. One ingenious officer, Lt. George B. Sense, Artillery, placed two large bars of soap in a pair of socks and tied them together. He dropped them down his baggy pants so they hung on the crotch of the pants. The Japanese pants were extra large and did not show any revealing bulges.

The inspection took most of the morning. No one was allowed to return to the barracks and those remaining could not approach anyone on the shipment. We were allowed to answer the call of Mother Nature under close supervision. The standard traveling ration was issued; one rice ball about the size of a baseball. Inspection completed, we started our march out the main gate and waved good-bye to the remaining POWs. We thought they were fortunate to be remaining there. We were the fortunate ones, as time was to tell, and most of them became the unfortunate.

We arrived at the rail station about noon and immediately started to board the side-door pullmans (box cars). We were packed in tightly with hardly room to move. Soon the train began moving, much to our relief. At least the agony of crowding would be shorter the sooner we got to Manila. We arrived at the Manila station late in the afternoon. After a head count we started the short march to Bilibid Prison. Back to where we started three weeks before. Tenko, more counting and we were released into the compound. We were informed there was no room in the buildings and we would have to bed down in the open. Another night on the concrete. A couple of nights would not be so bad, we had done it before. The galley served a thin soup and ration of rice. Our little group shared a can of corned beef and brewed up a cup of coffee from our hoarded supply of Nescafe. Over a pipe of tobacco, we settled down for the night. It was the dry season and the tropical skies were filled with stars as we sat around and talked about tomorrow before turning in for the night. Each group of 200 had been told to remain together. The only ones moving around were a few late quanners. All fires had to be extinguished by 2100 hours.

The questions uppermost in our minds were: what type of ship, would we have plenty of room, what were our chances of attack by aircraft or submarine, how long would the voyage be, how far was it to Japan?

Some of the rumors floating around were interesting: we were to be repatriated, we were being shipped to a neutral country for the duration, we were going to Japan and the trip would take only ten days, we were to be issued a Red Cross box. We placed no credence in such fantastic fairy tales. They were only the dreams of men who had not lost hope. Our group had been extremely fortunate up to now. We were ready for the next phase of being a **horiyo**. We would take whatever came our way. We were anxious, hopeful, tired, fearful, and sleep came quickly.

We were awakened early and passed through the chow line for our **lugao** and warm water for tea. The usual rice ball was issued for traveling rations. Surprisingly, we were allowed seconds on rice. Word was passed to be ready to move out and that all canteens should be filled. It was the 26 of August 1944. None of us knew how the Japanese loaded prisoners of war or their own troops on transports. The reports of those who had been taken off of Corregidor in May of 1942 were indicative of what we could expect. They had been overcrowded, were pushed off of the ships into about eight feet of water, and forced to wade ashore onto Dewey Boulevard. The miserable men were then marched to Bilibid. The reports of the men who had been shipped to Davao and back to Manila were more ominous. They spoke of the cramming into one hold of the ship. Were these reports indicative of what we could expect? If they were true, it was going to be rough. Our shipment in the freight cars was also a measure of the insensitivity to human beings, especially horiyos. The ex-stevedores from Port Area had witnessed some of the shipments being loaded into crowded holds. We had been lucky so far, maybe our luck would hold for six more months.

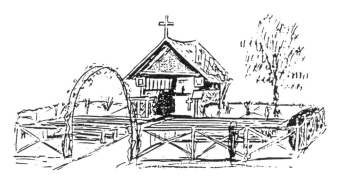

Thatched roof chapel in the dysentery ward area at Cabanatuan. Courtesy Eugene C. Jacobs.

The word was passed to form up our groups and prepare to march. We passed through the grim portals of Bilibid with an escort of Japanese soldiers. Columns of four, 200 to a company, 1035 men, the remnants of the once proud American forces in the Philippines.

Now two and a half years later, we were grimy, gaunt, hollow eyed, ragged specters of men.

We had a little time to observe the Filipinos as we passed through the streets. There were many bicycles, some with three passengers. Probably an ex-taxi driver or calesa driver serving the people. A few cars passed with Japanese officers. Horse drawn calesa and carometas, their horses at a full trot working for the Co-Prosperity Sphere. There were many people riding the electric trollies, jammed inside with people clinging to the sides like flies. How in the world did the conductor ever collect fares? How would the operator know when to stop to allow passengers to get out of the mass inside? Horse drawn calesa and carometas were apparently the major conveyance for most Filipinos. The Filipinos would stop and watch as we pass. Some wave and smile as if to say, "Hello Joe" as they give the V-sign surreptitiously. When the guards are not watching they throw bananas.

The Filipinos were still our friends and would have liked to give us food, but they had learned the harsh treatment when they were caught. The Japanese beat those who were unfortunate enough to get caught trying to help us.

Ben D. Waldron and Emily Birneson in their book, *Corregidor, Paradise to Hell* graphically describe the treatment of horiyo's and Filipinos. "The men from Corregidor were kicked out of landing barges and struggled ashore. They were formed into hundred-man groups and started marching along Dewey Boulevard. Wet, bedraggled, dirty, half sick, and thirsty with a blazing sun beating down, they straggled along. This was a show calculated to humiliate the Americans and show the Filipinos that the hated Yankees had been defeated by the Imperial Japanese Army. The Filipinos were supposed to be happy. Dewey Boulevard was lined with thousands of Filipinos with sad faces and openly crying. They were tossing food, candies, fruit and waving instead of cheering. The parade of vanquished Americans backfired into a fiasco. The Japanese became infuriated and began to beat men, women and children with rifle butts. It was no wonder that the Filipinos were reluctant to express their true feelings."

We reached the broad avenue near the main

piers of the Manila water front and halted in the hot sun. We could see ship's masts above the roofs of the piers. We were glad for the break and a chance to set our gear down and relax a bit. Shortly the Japanese officer came to the group leaders and said we were to return to Bilibid Prison. We started our march over the same route. I began to look for familiar landmarks. I could see P. Bonifacio Street leading to the Quartermaster Depot near Pier One, which had been my home for two years. Overlooking the Pasig River was the imposing Spanish fortress, Fort Santiago, with its guard posts jutting from the walls. We knew it by the name Intramuros (Walled City). The old moat surrounding the fortress had long since been filled in and the officer's golf course had been constructed parallel to the walls. Nearby was Jones Street Bridge across the Pasig River into the business district.

Inside the Walled City, the southeast corner was Quartel De Espana, the home of the 31st Infantry Regiment. In the southwest corner was the headquarters for United States Forces, Far East. To the northwest corner was the 31st Infantry, Third Battalion's home, Estada Major and Sternberg Hospital. Looking to the east as we passed along, we saw the Philippine government buildings flanked by wide beautiful streets with towering palm trees and flowering shrubbery. Rizal Stadium and the Jai Alai Arena were beyond.

Manila was a beautiful tropical jewel with many memories for me. A city in the Spanish tradition, with afternoon siestas, impressive schools and churches, and a culture all its own. Yet a city of filth, poverty, slums and unemployment. A city surrounded by intense farming, along with jungles, mountains and marshy areas. A land where the capataz system flourished; you purchased a job and kept it by paying off the honcho. The people were friendly and kind. Memories flashed through my mind: Santa Anna Race Track, where I once worked a part time job on weekends as a bartender in the owner's pavilion; the Santa Ana Cabaret, the largest in the world, with two bands playing popular music; fox trot, waltz or jitterbug; the taxi dancers for ten centavos a dance, wore colorful native costumes or maybe a dress from Sears with wooden slippers decorated with bright beads or brightly colored leather; Santa Ana Cockpit to watch the chicken fights. The native handlers with their favorite roosters staked out on short leashes, encouraged by their owners to ruffle up his feathers and excite them to fight. The voices murmured, placing bets. Their cheering for their favorite and moaned when one rooster killed the other and they had to pay their bets.

I recalled the religious Holy Days processions winding through the crowded narrow streets. The beautiful cathedral Santa Augustina, rose above the walls of Intramuros. Yet the southern islands were mostly Mohammedan. There were many dialects in the islands, each with unusual customs and traditions, such as the death wake in the home of the deceased, complete with a feast and a brass band to lead the funeral procession. Alas, how much I had enjoyed the many sights and sounds of this fabled and ancient city and now I was about to leave. One more night in the tropical paradise that was the Philippines, before the clouds of war had stormed over them. It would never be the same and the change would be for the better or the worse depending on the outcome of the war.

All these thoughts in the fleeting moments of reflection passed and soon we were passing through the austere portals of Bilibid Prison. Tenko was repeated again and then dismissal with instructions that tomorrow we would be leaving the Philippines.

We settled down and staked out our concrete banig (sleeping space) near one of the buildings and waited for chow call. It had been a nice day and we enjoyed the scenery as we walked the familiar streets. Supper time came with the usual soup with a little fish and vegetables with steamed rice and warm water for tea or coffee. Kunich brewed up a good quan bucket of coffee, and we settled down for the evening. Some of our friends came around to talk of the aborted shipment and the feeling that tomorrow we would be on our way again. The evening passed and faded into night. Unless we missed our guess, we would be awakened about 3:00 a.m.

Morning came quickly and we were glad to get off the hard concrete beds. Every protruding bone was sore and there was no position that was comfortable for very long. Breakfast was **lugao**, with a little brown sugar from our stock. Hot tea and a little grated cocoanut for topping. Word was passed to get mess kits washed, fill canteens, and draw traveling rations—a rice ball and a cocoanut. At first light of dawn we moved out for the long walk to the port area. We moved along in silence, each in his own thoughts as we retraced the route to the port area.

Our long column filed into the huge dock at Pier 5 and halted. The loading process begins at once. Waiting our turn to climb the long gang plank, we looked over our ship as we slowly advanced. The Japanese freighter, *Noto Maru*, of about 10,000 ton, looks relatively modern, seaworthy and in good shape. At least we did not get one of the old tramp steamers. This ship looks like it could make 15-20 knots easily. This was important and would perhaps insure our safe passage through the perilous submarine infested waters. Finally our turn comes and we moved up the gang plank onto the main deck. Scanning the deck area, we see modern steam winches for handling cargo. The deck appears cluttered with loading gear. We sneak a look towards the bridge area and see the ship's officers looking over their human cargo.

CORREGIDOR

OASIS OF HOPE

PART FIVE

CRUISE OF THE NOTO MARU

The Cruise of the *Noto Maru*

We make our way to the number two hold and look down. Men are being lined up from the port to starboard side along the forward bulkhead. Japanese guards are on the hatch covering, directing the men into ranks. The men are shoved and pushed into tight ranks but are not allowed on the covers. The long line winds down into the hold until we slowly fill the entire space. Our group winds up about midway between the port side and the edge of the hatch. All files are left standing until the entire 1,035 men are loaded. The long gang plank is removed and we are told to sit down. Sit down? Where? Every square foot of space is standing room only. The hold is only about 40 x 60 feet with about 20 feet of overhead clearance. There are no tiered bunks. Everything is on one level—the **deck**!

Each group of 200 has an American officer, a lieutenant and a senior noncommissioned officer assigned as group leaders. I am in the second group. Our OIC is a Lt. Peter Perkins and M/SGT. John Kunich is the NCO. Each man is assigned a number. My shipping number is 219. Most of the men are strangers to each other. There is also a medical group with doctors and medics. They have some medicines packed in a foot locker.

The men are shouting, cursing, pushing and shoving, trying to find enough space to sit. Slowly each squirms into a sitting position with their gear under them. The situation grows tense as each man tries to carve out enough space. The officers and NCO attempt to maintain some semblance of order in the chaos, noise and near panic as 1,035 men become sardines in the oven-hot hold. Finally, we settled into some order and try to make the best of the situation. The air is becoming foul and hot. The men strip down to a minimum of clothing.

The ship's bells and running feet on the decks can be heard as the ship begins to slip its moorings and ease away from the pier into the harbor. The movement of the ship brings in some fresh air and the men are quiet for a bit. We are on our way, we hope. The rumor is that it will be a seven to ten day journey. How can we make it for seven days in this sweat box? We are all twisted and squeezed into a seething mass of miserable humanity. How in the world are we going to get water, food or even take care of bodily functions? We had noticed there were about five benjos on each side of the ship. Primitive and scary to use with your rear hanging out over the side of the ship. They appear totally inadequate for a thousand men. Many have dysentery, malaria, dengue fever and all are suffering from the long ordeal. Crowding like this is only going to magnify the problem. We will need the patience of Job to get through this traveling ordeal on a Japanese cruise ship.

The ship's screw begins to turn, we can feel the vibrations and the welcome flow of fresh air through the open hatch. Are we on our way? Each man is still trying to adjust to the overcrowding and oppressive humidity and heat. Suddenly the sound of the anchor chain rattling down, comes to us from above. How long are we going to be anchored out here in the bay? Will they let us up on deck? Some men are beginning to clamor for water. They have not conserved water and they are hurting as the heat increases and the day drags. The clamor becomes louder. The Japanese guards watch from above, impassive and insensitive to the misery below. The officers pass the word to stay calm and quiet. Who are they kidding? The noise becomes louder. The Jap gunzo, (sergeant) yells in Japanese for quiet. He announces through the interpreter, that we must be quiet or the hatches will be closed.

This shocks the crowded hold into silent prayer that they don't close the hatch. Soon the noise increases and men are near panic as they scream for water and air. The Japanese follow through with their threat and start to close the hatch cover. This brings the howling screaming maelstrom of humanity to their senses. The officers try to calm the men by getting them to conserve on energy and stop crying and screaming. They point out that to continue to disobey the Japanese will only make matters worse. The Japanese leave a small opening of about 8 x 20 feet. The men calm down and start praying that the fiends don't close it all the way.

Five gallon cans of water are passed down and the shoving and pushing begins as men try to get to the water. The officers are clustered near the foot of the ladder. The officers scream and the NCOs shout for order. The noise ceases and the officers explain that the water will be distributed evenly. A method of distribution is worked out and again the men settle down and patiently watch as the precious water is distributed. The water cans are sent up and refilled. Soon everyone has received a canteen cup full. The men relax and wait for the food to be issued. Most have eaten their rice ball and some are digging into their emergency stocks.

The heat slowly eases as the tropic sun sinks into the west and the deck above begins to cool the miserable sweating mass. Innovative and ingenious ways of alleviating the crowded deck begin to appear. Some have fastened ropes to some pipe and fashioned a hammock from their shelter halves or blankets. This is ideal for them, while the rest struggle for squatting room. Five men are allowed to go on deck and visit the benjo. Just about the time one gets settled, one of the surrounding men has to go to the benjo. There is no passage way to the hatch cover and one has to step in between the men to move towards the hatch cover near the ladder. This is repeated in reverse when he returns and tries to squirm and wiggle into the massed human carpet.

An emergency benjo bucket has been set up on the hatch near the ladder. It is a wooden mitso bucket about 20 inches in diameter and 30 inches high. This is only for those who can not wait their turn on deck. Many men have dysentery and kidney problems and cannot wait. In some cases, for the men next to the sides of the ship, it is too late. They soil themselves and their clothes with no way to wash up. More screaming and cursing at the poor miscreant. Soon the men around him are fouled and the shouting and cursing begins again. I say to Cpl. Haddox and F/Sgt. Adrian Martin, "This is going to be one hell of a mess by the time we get out of this hold. God! I hope I don't get the runs and have to use that stinking bucket."

The only way out of this stinky hold is the single steel ladder in the corner of the hatch opening. Armed guards are posted on deck and only five men at a time are allowed on deck. The Japanese know that 1,035 desperate men could rush the guards and take the ship. That idea is quickly put to rest. There are machine guns mounted on the bridge covering the deck and hatch. It would be nigh on to impossible to get enough men on top side to overpower the guards. The devilish monsters have figured all the angles. What would happen if we were attacked by submarine or by dive bombers? The ship is not marked with Red Cross signs. No one wants to think of that horrible thought.

The *Noto Maru* had pulled out in Manila Bay, waiting for the convoy to assemble. The heat began to decrease as the sun sank in the west. This was off set by the lack of movement of the ship. It was very hot and the humidity was extremely high. The men were sweating profusely and trying to remain still. The passing of the water helped tremendously, and took their minds off the situation. We all began to think of how we were going to survive this hell hole.

Our first meal on the *Noto Maru* was served about 6:00 p.m.—steamed rice, soup and warm watered tea. The food was fairly good. It was sent down in large buckets. The officers insured that everyone received a fair ration. This was a horrible exercise in futility. There was no room for the men to line up and pass by the food servers. A final solution was worked out. Starting at the forward bulkhead, men moved slightly to allow the men to pass along the file from port to starboard. Each file would then shift forward until all the files had been fed. The food was greatly appreciated and took the men's minds off of the situation.

The men were so crowded that the only way to get down to deck level was to sit in the crotch of the man behind you and on across the ship. Only the devil himself could have thought of a more beastly and uncomfortable position to remain for any length of time. Each man had to adjust to the one in back and in front. Patience with each other was a virtue. There was no room for claustrophobia.

The washing of mess gear was an impossibility and could lead to more sickness. My friends around me worked out a solution to this problem. We would eat everything from the mess kit and use the warm water (tea) and rinse the mess kit and then drink the watered tea/rice mixture. This could be repeated until the tea was gone. If we had any water to spare, a little bit was used. A clean cloth (if available) was used to dry the gear. We had learned the hard way of the importance of keeping aluminum mess gear clean.

The most serious problem during the day was dehydration. The total lack of air circulation compounded the problem. Many began to pass out, especially those on the west side of the ship where the sun blasted the side of the ship. By sunset these unfortunate souls were near suffocation. Men who passed out were brought out to the hatch cover in the center of the ship to recover.

The senior American officer was Captain Charles Samson. Other officers were Captain E. Pearce Fleming, Lt. Peter Perkins, Lt. George B. Sense and Lt. Richard Pullen. The medical group consisted of six doctors and 29 medics. Among the doctors were Dr. Calvin Jackson, Dr. Dan Golenturnik and Dr. John Lamy. These officers faced a difficult, almost impossible, situation. They had learned to improvise and make do with what little medicine they had. The officers were able to establish some liaison with the Japanese and persuaded them to open the hatch for better air circulation.

The Japanese agreed to open the hatches on condition the horiyo's refrain from any further disturbances. The food and water had reduced some of the tension and fears, and the men were quiet. Our first night on the ship was uneventful with no lights except the bright star light for those with a desperately urgent mission getting to the benjo bucket. They woke many as they stepped on them. The return was worse because they were going into the stygian blackness beyond the hatch opening. Being stepped on was more preferable to being on the receiving end of an urge from someone who didn't make it.

Early in the morning it began to rain. Those close to the hatch took advantage and got a good shower. Those who had fouled themselves were able to rinse their clothing. Others set shelter halves to catch water and fill canteens. The rain cooled the hatch down and those who were unfortunate enough to be near the hatch were drenched and cold.

The miserable mass was awakened at dawn by preparations on deck to sail. At least we would not have to sit in a sweltering hold. The movement of the ship would generate some air movement. The beginning of the end or was it the end of the beginning. At any rate let's get this Maru moving.

Breakfast was served about 8:00 a.m. Several men were sent to the ships galley to bring the buckets of rice and soup to the hold. The debacle of trying to distribute food to 1,035 men in equal shares of rice, soup and water was repeated. The officers and the NCOs had convinced the men to cooperate and make room for the serving of the food. The process went along much better. The reports coming from those going to benjo were good. The fresh smell of salt water refreshed us after a miserable night. We were out of Manila Bay in a convoy of seven ships moving along the coast of Luzon. We were escorted by two Japanese destroyers. The medics had set up an area on topside near the hatch ladder and those who were sick could go up for condolences and maybe an aspirin.

During sick call several of the men near the ladder were called on to muscle the benjo bucket up the ladder. I watched as they slowly worked it up and was glad that I was not anywhere in that area. One slip and the whole stinking mess would spill on to the men below. The bucket had no cover and must have been 20 gallons of liquid fetid human waste. There must be a better way to run a railroad. Fortunately for them and their comrade below, the task was accomplished with no mishap. This was a daily chore and luckily there were no accidents.

The ship's engines began to slow and the word came down from above that we were in Subic Bay near Olongapo. There were about 20 other ships of all types. Must be a rendezvous for forming up large convoys. The first day at sea had been uneventful and the men seemed to be glad they were moving towards somewhere. We had no idea what our ultimate destination was.

The man sitting in front of me was First Sergeant Adrian Martin from De Pere, Wisconsin. He had been going to college in Madison and entered the army through the National Guard. He was assigned to the 200th Anti-Aircraft Battalion. The unit arrived in the Philippines two weeks before the war. Their unit had been deployed to the field immediately and fell back to Bataan with other units. He had made the infamous Bataan Death March. He survived the hell that was Camp O'Donnell and went on detail to Las Pinas. (Sgt. Martin was to play an important part in my future. Forty years later I was to meet his nephew, Adrian Martin of New London, Wisconsin, and work with him on an autobiography of his uncle.)

The men were so tightly packed around me that we seemed to be one. Close familiarity breeds comtempt and can also bring understanding and compassion. We became closer acquainted with those around us. They were a varied lot and came from different parts of the country. We had plenty of time to get acquainted and talk of our experiences in the prison camps. Some had been unfortunate and had been at Tayabas on a road project through the jungle or had been at Nichols or Nielson Fields, Davao, and some had spent the entire time at O'Donnell and Cabanatuan. There were sailors, marines, air corps, army and a few civilians. Listening to them tell stories about the Japanese prison system—how they had been brutally exploited and grossly mistreated—was almost unbelievable. It made the hair on the back of my neck stand up. Kunich, Golson, Haddox and I thanked God, our lucky stars and Major Shanks for our being able to remain on the

Rock for two years. Except for some signs of malnutrition and beriberi, we were in good shape. Perhaps we could make it home in six months. Looking at some of the skeletons around us, the thought flashed through my mind, "How many of these men will not make it?" Winter was only a few months away and most had been in the tropics for two years or more. The few clothes we had would be inadequate in a temperate climate such as Japan. Would the Japanese issue winter clothing? Surely they must have captured a ton of winter clothes somewhere. Or had they? Most of the captured countries were tropical.

The second night was broken by a disturbance on the starboard side of the hold. One individual in Lt. Sense's group had evidently gone berserk. Pandemonium and confusion broke out in the darkness. Lt. George Sense was a big man—about six-foot three-inches tall. He had been on Corregidor the first year. He was the officer who had put up a sign in the latrine warning the men not to wash their mess kits in the sinks, or you will find a number 12 shoe in your backsides. Very effective and to the point, he was one who faced a problem head on. Characteristically, this problem was promptly resolved by a discreet application of soap. Lt. Sense had tied a couple of bars of soft soap in a sock. He simply slugged the man without seriously hurting him. The dangerous situation was nipped in the bud and the men went back to sleep. There were no more problems.

One might censor the lieutenant for this type of action so unacceptable to the American way. However, one must bear in mind the horrible conditions in the blackness of the hold. Crowded, sweat drenched, suffocating humidity, dehydrated, sick, despairing and desperate men, clinging to life in one huge carpet of human bodies was a potential powder keg. This dangerous condition was defused and the hold returned to normal. The lieutenant should be commended for his prompt action rather than being censored. Lieutenant Sense was an exemplary leader, which we the people depended on and trusted to lead our young soldiers. He was my kind of a leader, men would follow and if necessary fall facing forward.

Dawn comes and the throbbing of the ships propeller is a comfort. At least we are moving and the sea breezes will help the air circulate and give some relief from the heat. The day passes like an arthritic caterpillar. The monotony is overwhelming and pervasive. Each individual is almost in a dormant state, until he is disturbed by someone answering mother nature. The grumbling rolls across the carpet of humanity.

Barley is served instead of rice and the soup had a taste of fish. There are more nutrients in the barley, but it has a deleterious effect for some. Everyone is adjusting to the crowded conditions, showing some consideration and patience by standing while others sleep. This situation could go on forever. The day passes and we have more rain showers. They are refreshing and some stand on the hatch cover just to get wet and others catch rain water to fill canteens. This is better than the heat. The night is a welcomed relief from the bedlam of day. A chance to sleep away eight or nine hours of the unmitigated hell. If one could only sleep and wake at the end of the voyage.

Sleeping is extremely difficult, no room to stretch out legs or turn over. I thought concrete was hard, but the steel deck is no better. The men are locked into a tangle of arms and legs. There are many complaints when one tries to move or stretch in their sleep. Complaining is of no use. We try to realize that it is necessary to adapt to an impossible situation, have patience and to slump into a trance like sleep.

During the night, I am overcome by intense intestinal pains and cramps. I hurriedly dash across the human carpet to the emergency benjo bucket. I feel a revulsion and almost vomit as I sit on the stinking bucket. Have I just diarrhea or is it dysentery? I hope the doctors have something to control my bowels. I never want to come back to this malodorous repulsive bucket. The lights from the stars dimly light the interior of the hatch. How in the hell am I going to find my little spot in this tangled mass of humanity in the dark. The men grumble as I pick my way back and finally find my spot of hell.

The thought occurred to me that I had not wanted to sail on the troop transport USS Grant for this very reason. I did not want to contend with the crowded conditions with a bunch of sea sick men. That would have been an idyllic cruise compared to this trip on the Noto Maru. I had volunteered to nurse maid 250 horses and mules on the USAT Meigs with only 40 men aboard. I preferred to shovel a little horse manure than to be with a bunch of men who had never been to sea. Here on this nauseating filthy ship, I feel like a canned sardine, only a sardine is not living. Am I living? Yes, but how long will we be living? We wouldn't have a chance of a snowball in hell if the ship is attacked. Pray that the US Navy doesn't catch this convoy.

Dawn came with no repeat trips to the bucket. After the morning meal and water was passed, sick call was announced. I stumbled out of my spot of hell and stood at the bottom of the ladder waiting my turn to go up. Sick call was held on the deck of the ship near the hatch opening. Finally I climbed up and spoke to Doctor Golenturnik. "I have a severe case of diarrhea," I explained. He took my temperature and said he had some medicine that might help. He measured out a heaping tablespoon of sulphadiazene powder and poured it into my G.I. spoon. I moved away and finally managed to get it down with very little water. I stayed as long as possible on deck. The convoy was under way on a northerly course not far off of the coast of Luzon. I looked around and could see the guards wearing life jackets. They seemed to be scanning the sky as well as the sea. There were about 20 ships in the convoy escorted by destroyers. So far we had no alarms, but we were out in open water and fair game for any patrolling submarine or airplane. Some of the sailors thought they heard pinging from submarines. The Noto Maru had no Red Cross markings, just a nice big target for any alert submarine.

I made my way down the ladder and reached my spot on the deck. I squatted in a dobie squat, like the natives. It was a position I had developed in the shop when working on brakes of trucks. It was much more comfortable than sitting on a steel deck or trying to lay down.

The ship was making good time and that was all right with us. The sooner we get to wherever we are going the better it would be for all of us. Traveling at the speed the convoy was making cut down the chance of interception by a metallic fish. None of us wanted to think of the eventuality, but certainly it was uppermost in our minds. Surely the American subs were seeking targets and ranging this far north. An unmarked ship was fair game.

Three miserably nights and days have passed. The rumors are rampant that we will be in Formosa tomorrow. Morale perks up and everyone is guessing and hoping this will be the end of the journey. Better to be in Formosa than Japan. The climate would not be as severe as Japan. All things considered, it has not been as bad as it appeared to be at the start. Everyone settled into a routine and tried to make the most of a bad situation. The food has been somewhat better than average. The extras that some have brought along alleviated the hunger pains. It was good to see the men share and control their impatience with each other.

We can feel the ship slowing as we approach the harbor. Word from top side is that it is Takao, Formosa. Thank God, we have made it thus far. Rumors are that there were explosions and some of the men had seen ships afire. Most of us were unaware of the attack and slept through it. Ignorance is bliss, someone once said. A few medics were permitted to remain on deck and pass the word down of what they could see. Conversation centered around what would be the result of a torpedo attack. We hoped a torpedo would hit aft or amidship so we would have a chance. A hit in the forward section and it would be Katy-Bar-the-Door for us. Lady Luck was still with us for here we are in Takao without mishap.
The *Noto Maru* had pulled into a dock and began to unload some passengers and cargo. The ship pulled away from the dock after loading other cargo. Our officers persuaded the Japanese troop commander to allow us to come on deck and be hosed down with salt water. Groups of 100 were allowed on deck wearing only G-strings or shorts. The ship's fire hose was used to flush the men down. It was fantastic to feel the cool water and scrub off some of the crud. Just to get out of the crowded hold to stretch legs, backs and arms with the soothing water was a terrific boost to morale and attitude. I could appreciate what that grey army mule was trying to tell me on the *Meigs* when he tried to nip me so he would get more salt water. I could sympathize with the mule that tried to climb out of the hold

when he was being groomed. They weren't so dumb.

One leg of the journey was complete. Manila to Takao is about 600 miles. The second phase would be about 800 miles to the main islands of Japan. Manila to Tokyo is about 1800 miles as the crow flies. Several of the sailors had made port calls to Takao with the Asiatic Fleet. They reported it to be a nice place with moderate climate. We hoped that some or all of us would be unloaded there—at least it would make more room for those left on board.

Late in the afternoon, we pulled away from the dock and sat in the harbor until dark. Shortly afterwards the ship began to vibrate and we were under way. Our course was northerly on the East China Sea. Japan was our destination. The showers on deck and the clean feeling had improved our morale. The evening meal was served along with hot tea while the convoy picked up speed. There were now seven large vessels escorted by destroyers. We relaxed into the ship board routine with a lot less grumbling. One rumor from top side was that we were being covered by a large Naval Patrol Bomber. The ships were pouring on the coal making good speed. This was fine with us and we languished into a sound sleep. The weather was somewhat cooler and a blanket felt good. Where were we going to land—in Japan, Korea, or possibly Manchuria? The consensus was that our destination would be Japan. Where in Japan? None of us knew much about the geography of Nippon. I was hoping we would remain in the southern part. Perhaps the winter would not be as severe. Whatever our destination, we hoped and prayed that it would be for a short time. Surely the war would be over in six months.

Boy, would a plate of eggs, hot biscuits, and sausage gravy be great now. Here I am thinking of food again. Is it better to dream about something you want or to worry about the future? Neither are possible in the near future. Why fret and anguish over something beyond your control. Settle back and accept the good as well as the bad. Facing reality makes good sense. What is to be will be!

A long sea voyage gives one time to think about the past as well as the future. This form of mind control allows a body to ignore the terrible conditions around him. Some find consolation in reading their Bible, if they have one. Some never loose their sense of humor, and others lapse into a trance almost to the point of hibernation. Others slip into mental seclusion or fantasize and become disillusioned with life. The power of positive thinking, whether one realizes it or not, can be a source of strength. One must have faith in God, himself, and his country, to overcome the power of fear, stress, negativism and things beyond his control.

The area which the *Noto Maru* had passed between northern Luzon and Formosa was a prime patrol area for American submarines. The western and eastern approaches to Japan were the main maritime routes of shipping of raw materials for the Greater East Asia Co-Prosperity Sphere. We had safely passed through that danger zone and now we are in another prime danger area between Formosa and Japan. We are relieved by the sounds of the propellers and the steady beat of the ships engines. The ships have the bits in their teeth and are headed for the land of the rising sun. It is home to the crews and they are as eager as we to make landfall. We, the poor sweating slaves in the hold, are resigned to our situation and pray that very soon we can get out of this sardine can. Under these conditions time is like an arthritic caterpillar slowly and laboriously making its way. Checkers, cards, reading, fantasizing and talking to our neighbors are the only way to ease the passage of time. Squirming into a space to stretch or relieve aching bones, we have become used to someone else's arms, legs or body bumping into us and try not to lose our patience.

Praise be to God, they gave us another salt water bath on deck. Strange what a little fresh air and water will do for one's morale. Whoever is in charge of this shipment is lenient and listens to the pleas of our officers. (SAO) Captain Charles Samson, Captain E. Pearce Fleming and the others are to be complemented on their accomplishment of making it as comfortable as possible for the men. I for one, and my friends, can appreciate their efforts.

The medical officers, Captain Dan Golenturnik, Major Calvin Jackson, Major Ralph Artman, Captain Max Bernstien, Lt. John Lamy and others have provided as much care as possible and have been able to help those poor creatures who are the worst off. None have died and morale and spirits have been good. There are a total of twenty-nine medical personnel on this shipment. One of the men is Ernest Norquist from Beaver Dam, Wisconsin, whom I came to know many years later. (Norquist kept a diary of his time as a prisoner of war. His book, *Our Paradise, A GI's War Diary* was published in 1989 and gives a graphic description of the trip on the *Noto Maru*.)

Four days of travel and the word is out that we are close to the end of the journey. The guards are beginning to look relieved and we can hear seamen rigging for unloading of cargo. The steam winches swing the booms out on the starboard side. The big day has arrived; the prisoners begin to come alive with anticipation of getting out of the crowded, stinking hold and feeling Mother Earth under our feet, even if it is Japan.

The fifth of September 1944, the *Noto Maru* pulls into a busy port. The men are allowed to go to the benjo-uchi on deck and by dallying along, they are able to see the harbor around them. There are many factories and the green mountains can be seen in the background. We heard through the grapevine that we are now in the city of Moji, on the northern part of the island of Kyushu. All prisoners are busy making preparations for debarkation. Everyone is packing up and collecting on jawbone debts. Conversation is animated and all are impatient to get off the ship. They are like a bunch of sailors after a long cruise, anticipating shore leave. We remain in the harbor all day and late into the evening. The Japanese medics line us up for the glass rod treatment for detection of dysentery. Rumors are rife with speculation on our ultimate destination and that the 1,035 men will be broken into smaller groups for various camps.

Later that night we felt the ship moving and the noises of preparations for docking could be heard as we spent our last night on the *Noto Maru*. Sometime during the night I was rudely awakened by a huge rat running across the mass of men. It passed over my chest. What a weird and eerie feeling of revulsion. It made me cringe and feel fouled. I suppose the rat was as scared as I was and could not find any deck to run on.

At dawn we received our last meal of barley and soup with tea. A second ration of barley was issued for later in the day. The gang plank was lowered into the hold and secured on deck shortly afterwards. The men were eager to get moving and seemingly in good spirits. The journey was true to rumor and we had arrived safely in ten days without losing any men or a serious threat to the ship, at least as far as we know. I am thankful that I volunteered for this shipment. I am still with many of my friends from pre-war days and we are safe in Japan. Our only wish is that we can stick together for the balance of the war and are not split up.

Slowly the long line of men start marching up the gang plank. Our legs are stiff and there is much stretching and twisting as we shoulder our packs and move out by groups of 200 men. When we reach the deck and start to look around, we can see that there is much debris left in the hold, as we take our last look at our purgatory of the past ten days.

No one is sorry to leave and all are eager to get ashore. The air is fresh, the sun is shining and the temperature is about 65 degrees. The guards are hustling us along and want to get us off the ship quickly. When we feel the solid dock under our feet, we breathe a sigh of relief for our good fortune. We have it "made in the shade" as the old saying goes. Let us get on with the roll call.

As the men came off the ship they were run through a delousing shower and formed into groups. After everyone was off the ship we were moved to a large open area near by and ordered to prepare for an inspection. I suppose this was equal to a customs inspection, as we had nothing to declare except our miserable bones. Everything had to be laid out and the game of out-witting the Japanese was repeated. We were anxious to know where we might be shoved into the labor needs of the Empire.

The inspecting officer and a gunzo (sergeant) moved along the rows of men and slowly looked everything over. The prisoners behind them began slipping treasured items into the rows just inspected. Some men did lose a few items, but the prisoners had learned how to avoid loss as much as possible. The prisoners were allowed to sit by their posses-sions until the officer approached. While being inspected he had to remain at attention and answer any questions asked of him. The inspection went smoothly and we remained in the open. It was great just to be able to stand in the warm sun, stretch and not be afraid of bumping someone. Just to be able to breathe fresh air again was exhilarating.

We all needed a good bath, as we had only saltwater baths at sea, and we were sticky and stinking. A whole case of Lifebouy soap would be needed to remove the B.O. Late in the afternoon it started to rain and everyone stripped down to G-strings and thoroughly washed in the rain. It continued to rain and everyone's gear was getting soaked. The officers asked the Japanese to move us into a building. They agreed and everyone felt better after the rain bath. A binto (lunch box) was issued for the evening rations. It contained steamed rice, a pickled plum, a bit a vege-tables, some kelp (seaweed), and a cup of warm tea topped off a relatively good meal.

At about 2000 hours word was passed to form up into groups and prepare to move out. The rain had slackened as we marched out of the port area. A small detail of about 100 men was left behind. A short distance from the warehouse we came to another long building jutting out into the bay. The Japanese turned us into the building. It was a waiting area for ferry boats. We started loading immediately. The ferry boat whistle sounded and we moved out into the bay. The ferry boat took us across the bay to Shimonoseki, on the southern tip of Honshu. We were unloaded and marched to a nearby railway station. A long line of pas-senger cars were pulled alongside a platform. Thank heavens no box cars. The men were assigned cars in accordance with the Japa-nese plan of distribution. The Japanese transportation officer confirmed with the officers that some would be dropped at var-ious points along the way. The Japanese instructed us that we were not to talk to the Japanese, that the window shades must be down at all times and we were not to leave the cars until told to do so. Loading completed, the train moved out on the main line. The coaches were designed for 80 Japanese, with a benjo uchi in the end. One hundred men were crowded in and some sat in the aisles and some took the seats. The seats were arranged with seats facing each other and were rather narrow for two long legged men. This was better than the conditions on the *Noto Maru* and there was no complaints. We did not know how long we would be on the train but we were moving towards our final destination. Rumors had it that some would be getting off in the morning and others would remain.

Sgt. Kunich, Archie Golson, Haddox and myself, with one other soldier in the aisle, shared two seats. It was comfortable in that we did not have to contend with someone stepping on you and we could sit up with something solid against our back. Our packs were stowed in overhead racks or under the seats. The train rolled on into the night. Some were peeking under the window shades but most were soon sleeping.

Early in the morning we pulled into a station (Hiroshima), and carts came along side of the train loaded with binto boxes with steamed rice, a small piece of dried fish, a dab of vegetable, dikons (pickled radish) and kelp. Warm tea was dispensed from cauldrons on the cart. This was all passed thought the window of the cars, no one was allowed off the train. The officers along with the Japanese transportation officer supervised. Each car was checked for anyone in immediate need of medical treatment.

Another small detail of 100 men was pulled off. We rolled out of the station after changing engines and train crew. We still had no idea of our destination in this land of the cherry blossoms. The excellent breakfast stilled the hunger pains and with everyone comfortable we were ready for another day of travel in the land of the rising sun. The country side was green. All available space was used. Farmers could be seen in the fields. The small villages were tucked into the hills with neat appearing houses. The Japanese were known to be very industrious and hard working. There were no signs of mechanical equipment in the fields. Few people were around the small stations we passed through. The people where we stopped to pick up lunches paid little attention to the strange Americans.

The equipment, cars, road bed and the tracks were relatively well maintained. The national railroad was excellent for the transportation of goods and people. There were no highways and very few autos such as one would expect to see at home. We were evidently on a main line. Automatic switches, signal lights and crossing barricades could be seen. The cars rode smoothly indicating good maintenance of the road bed. A pair of guards occupied seats near the doorway and occasionally walk up and down the aisle. Smoking was permitted, if you had any. The seats had an ashtray on the side near the window. Each time the train slowed and passed through a village or station, everyone tried to peek out and see what was going on. The guards were rather lenient and did not attempt to stop them. They were as curious as we were. Our train traveled on through the country side and passed a panorama of beautiful country side, headed for Tokyo. Lunch was the same as the breakfast meal, except we each received an apple. When was the last time we had an apple to eat? It was delicious.

I sit musing about the last time I had ridden a train. It was June 1939 on the Southern Pacific across west Texas, New Mexico, Arizona, to San Francisco on my way to the Philippines. Riding in a pullman car with meals in the dining car with a sleeping berth to stretch out on at night. I was traveling into the unknown then. Here I am, five years later on the other side of the world, headed for the unknown. Eating from a binto box, sleeping on the floor or a hard seat were no comparison to the Southern Pacific. Will I ever get back home? Here in Nippon the war seems so faraway. We have heard no news and can only hope the war will not last six months more. How many times have we said six months more. Two years and four month as POWs. There will be a time in the future when it will be true. How many of us will see that great day? We still have our faith in God, our country and reasonable good health. With the aid of God and Lady Luck, we will be there at the last roll call. These thoughts rumbled through my head as I lay on the floor. The clicking of the rail joints soon lulled me into that land of sleep.

The Nippon Express with its cargo of slave laborers thundered on through the night. All things considered it had not been a bad trip. We had made good time, there had been no deaths and the men were in good spirits. Under the circumstances we had a lot to be thankful for.

Dawn began to lighten the sky and we could see the passing scenery. The country side was a verdant green. Here and there a field of yellow grain contrasted with the green surroundings. Small garden plots near the quaint houses with shutters closed were visible as we passed. People could be seen at this early hour going about their work. They were walking along the many dikes of their rice fields. They would raise their heads and wave as the train passed, not realizing that the much maligned Americans were aboard. The country side was much like a well manicured golf course. Everything was neat, orderly and with maximum utilization of available space. This country has been at war for over ten years. First in Manchuria, China and then all of the Far East. Man power was short and many of the people were women and children. The younger men were away fighting for the Emperor and the glory of Nippon-Go. The school children were all dressed in a blue uniform with small packs on their way to school.

During the night we had passed through small cities in the heartland of Japan. Large rivers with long trestle bridges and many dikes flashed past like a travel movie scene. The people around the small stations stared at us quizzically as the train slowed to pass through the village. They were probably unaware of the nature of the passengers, the drawn blinds, the green rail traffic lights and the priority travel. Many trains were passed on sidings. There was little evidence of automobiles, only a few trucks and many bicycles. Along the rural roads, the ox drawn honey wagons could be seen, winding their way with an elderly man walking along guiding the beast.

The Japanese method for disposal of night soil is unique. Early in the morning the honey carts make their way into the villages and collect the night soil; from the benjo uchi's at each cottage. The honey collectors move from house to house with a large covered wooden bucket strapped to his back. He stops at each house and bails out the benjo pit and returns to his cart when the bucket is full. By daylight he has finished his rounds and returns to his fields and disposes the night soil as fertilizer. This method has been in use for hundreds of years. It is efficient and a necessity for good crops. Our medics had warned us not to eat any raw vegetables without cooking.

We arrived in a train station about 0600 hours and are met by the usual carts with binto boxes and hot tea. These carts are very similar to the old Railway Express cart that are used on our railways. The Japanese are much better organized in their homeland to care for and feed troop trains such as ours. They have probably had a lot of experience. None of us complain about the quality but some would prefer larger portions. The officers are allowed on the station platforms to insure no one tries to beat the system. This has a two-fold effect as the cars are checked for those needing medical aid and assurance that all are fed. The stops are not lengthy and soon the train is on its way again. We are now on a double track system and see other trains going in the opposite direction. We don't pay much attention as the train leaves, we are too busy digging into the binto boxes. They are about the same and do not last long. Each box has a pair of chop sticks. None of us are very adept at their use, except it prolongs the eating. Most all of the hoarded extra chow has been eaten by now and our appetites are voracious.

We are permitted to smoke and I enjoy my pipe with the hot tea as we rattled on through the land of the rising sun. We are closer to the sea coast now in a largely urban area with many more houses and some factories. The scuttlebutt running through the cars is that soon we will be in Tokyo and that we will drop some cars off. We are down to about 800 men now, having dropped about 200 early in the journey. All are up and talking and joking around after a good nights sleep, either seated upright in the seats or lying on the floor. The word passes back through the cars that we are to gather our gear and be prepared to exit the train at the next station. Everyone starts to try and pack up and get organized at the same time. This results in some jostling and pushing but everyone seems happy to be getting off of the Nippon Express.

The train pulls into a station and draws up to a long platform with tracks on the opposite side. We learn from our guards that this is Shinagawa on the southern edge of Tokyo. The unloading process begins and each car group is to stand by in a group. The Japanese transportation officer and our officers go along to form groups of 100 for each car. A commuter train comes in on the opposite track. The Japanese soldiers with their rifles start shouting at the Japanese civilians to get out and soon have the cars emptied. The order is given for 600 men to board the cars. The balance of about 100 is left standing on the platform. Golson, Haddox, Kunich and I are still together. So far we have not been split up. The Japanese guard shouts "kora, kora" and we are hustled into the empty commuter cars. There are seats around the outside with standing straps. We move out of the station on an electric commuter train which really picks up speed quickly. The men near the windows can see out as there are no blinds to pull. The landscape whisks by in a blur. We are wondering where we are in this land and when will the journey be over. Seems ages since we left Manila, though it was only a couple of weeks.

The commuter train stops at another station on the north side of Tokyo and we are unloaded immediately and loaded into a train on the opposite track. The coaches are about the same as before. Upholstered seats and backs with no padding. With a whistle screaming we leave the Tokyo area. The senior American officer, Captain Samson, and the other officers are conferring with the Japanese officer. We are told that we are to be divided again at the next stop. We relax into our travel lethargy and are busy discussing our trip and impressions of this strange country. Perhaps conditions will be better here in the homeland than they were in the camps in the islands. About an hour out of Tokyo we come to another station and the train stops along another long platform. Two cars are shunted off. We learn that this is Omori and the men in the two cars will be taken to a camp nearby. Captain Samson and a part of the medics are in this group.

The food carts come along and pass out the binto boxes and hot tea. They are about the same as before. Seems this is a standard ration for troop trains. It is not as much as we would like, but it was better than we had been used to. Maybe we will get a Red Cross box when we arrive at our destination. There must be a lot of Red Cross supplies shipped to Japan by the International Red Cross. This is 1944 and they should have a shipping schedule established with a neutral country by now. These and other thoughts pass as we eat and the train pulls out headed north.

We were watching for a glimpse of Mt. Fujiyama. Our high school geographical knowledge of Japan is rather limited. Our concept of the country and its people is based on the experiences in the Philippines, which left us undecided as to what to expect here in the homeland. The train is passing through a panorama of farming. The farmers can be seen plowing with oxen in paddies of water, preparing for planting. This method was not new to those who had to work in the rice paddies at Cabanatuan. Here they have been doing it the simple way for hundreds of years. Another interesting feature is the terracing of the hills. Very efficient use of the water for flooding each terrace. This system of terracing is similar to the northern reaches of the Island of Luzon around Baguio. There the terraces climb the side of the mountains like giant steps to the clouds. This indicates a high level of engineering in a primitive way. They might be illiterate as far as education, but they are practical in their use of the land. These stupendous projects are the work of peasants using only hand tools and hard labor to create these beautiful terraces.

The land begins to show mountains in the distance, dimly silhouetted against the afternoon sun with long slopes fading away in the distance. Truly a beautiful country from a travelog standpoint. The level valleys are abundant in fruit trees, garden plots and rice fields. Several fields have a scrawny straw scarecrow with ragged coats and straw hats, "They even have scarecrows here," Haddox remarked as we pass. The scenery becomes boring and we turned to other pursuits— playing cards, reading, napping and shooting the breeze with our traveling companions. The day goes by and about dark we stop to pick up the evening meal. Our train rolls on into the northern part of Honshu. They will have to send out a search party to find us. Someone came up with the bright idea that our destination is Hokaido, another island at the northern tip of Honshu. "Heaven forbid," was the reply. "I sure hope we get off before then." A storm of ridicule met the rumor monger. "How does he know where Hokaido is? He never got out of Arkansas until the sheriff and the girl's father went after him for a shotgun wedding." Humor is still with us and indicative of high morale as the men talk and kid each other.

Each stop the officers are allowed to check for seriously ill and to walk up and down the cars checking on the men. The Japanese are content with our conduct. We are not harassed by the guards or the civilians in the stations. The detail is now down to 500 men, none are seriously ill and are in good spirits. We have four American officers, Captain E. Pearce Fleming, SAO; Lt. Richard Pullen and medical officers; Major Calvin Jackson; and Lt. John Lamy. This appears to be the makeup of a complete detail. That is good. My friends and I are still together.

The night grows cooler as we continue north. The cars are heated but a blanket helps ward off the chill. The men are quiet and drop off to sleep as the night passes without incident. Tomorrow we should be in our new camp or on a ferry to Hokaido.

We arrive in Sendai, a city on the north east coast of Honshu, early in the morning. Rations are issued and back on the track in short order. Shortly we arrive at another small village, Morokai. Here we are unloaded on to another platform for head count. The tracks on the opposite side appear to be narrow gauge. A string of cars pulled by a steam engine draws alongside and stops. Roll call completed we are instructed to board the narrow gauge cars. They are about the same type; day coaches with wooden seats, 100 men to a car. The Japanese transportation officer is relieved by another officer and a new set of guards. With oriental efficiency we are off again for our final destination. We are tired of the traveling and ready to get into a camp where we can clean up, stretch and walk around a bit. We have been moving steadily since August 27, and it is now the 9th of September, 1944.

The steam engine, with a whistle and hissing of steam, pulls out of Morokai. We can see tall mountains to the west, the direction we are going. The train is moving into the mountainous interior of Honshu. The tracks wind around hills, always climbing and soon pass through a tunnel into a broad valley. The scenery becomes more interesting as we work our way along the edges of the hills. We pass several small villages tucked into the sides of the mountains. The deeper into the mountains we travel, the scenery becomes more beautiful and the fresh smell of pines give us something to remember. Lush fields, quaint houses are clustered along the right-of-way. Some evergreens similar to Douglas fir and pine trees begin to appear. At least we can have a Christmas tree, I thought as the landscape passed in review. As our stream engine rounds the curves we can see the engine drivers, steam from the cylinders and the smoke pouring from the stack. The fireman must have been shoveling the coal to the boiler as we were climbing a fair grade. We can feel the train slowing and the engine straining to maintain speed. Surely but slowly the engine lost out to the grade and we came to a stop with a squealing of the air brakes. The engineer shifts gears and we back down the tracks for several miles until we reached a level stretch. Again we stop and the train crew builds up a head of steam for another run at the grade. With steam up and smoke pouring from the stack, we start again. We watched as the train picks up speed and rushes at the grade. I thought of the old children's story about the little train that said, "I think I can, I think I can." Slowly the engineer begins to win the struggle and we reach the crest. There are only six coaches and this was an indication of the steepness of the grade. The engine begins to pick up speed on the down grade and whizz around the hills. We must be pretty high as we have been climbing steadily from Morokai. We reach a small village and the train comes to a stop. We are to learn its name is Hanawa and we are at the end of the journey. Word has been passed to be ready for off loading and have all gear packed for marching. We start unloading and step onto a cement passenger platform. It feels good to stand up and walk after four days on the Nippon Express. The air is brisk and smells clean and fresh with the scent of pine trees in the air. We stand and suck in the fresh air, stretch our cramped muscles and look the place over. It is a small village and one can see a row of houses along a gravel road. Certainly no bright lights—strictly country. "Probably where the people went to sleep with the chickens and got up with them," someone cracked.

Whatever the Nips had in mind here in this forsaken place would be all right as we were tired of traveling. One consolation was that we would not be in the heavily industrialized section of Japan, and safe from any bombing raids. We were formed into groups for tenko to insure all were present. The Japanese Gunzo barked orders and we moved out. Our officers in front, we marched out of the village into a narrow valley. There were 500 men and four officers. A Japanese officer led the way accompanied by a contingent of guards bringing up the rear. The gravel road steadily climbed as we headed into the narrow valley with a small stream on our left. The guards said this was an ichi ban (#1) camp. "This we shall have to see," remarked Golson. It felt good just to walk and breath the crisp air.

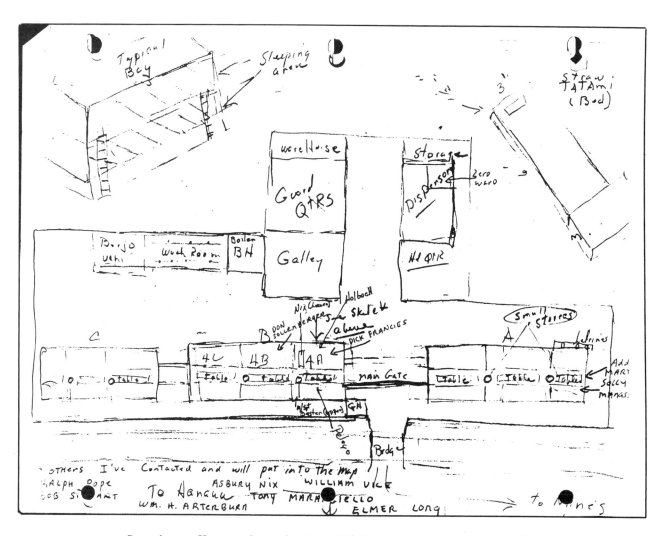

Camp layout, Hanawa, Japan, location of POW work detail. Courtesy Adrian Martin.

CORREGIDOR

OASIS OF HOPE

PART SIX

MITSUBISHI COPPER MINE

Part Six

Mitsubishi Copper Mine

We walked along and rounded a curve and could see some buildings clustered on the far side of the stream. Further ahead were aerial tramways running up the side of the mountain. The grade was steep and the pace brisk, some of the men began to fall back until the column was strung out. With a couple of kora kora and speedo speedo the lagging men caught up. As we approached the buildings on the left, a small foot bridge appeared leading across the stream bed. The buildings were in a long row with a high palisade-type fence and a gate just across the bridge. It looked like something out of a western movie set. We had not seen any Indians and no horses so it must be our stockade. The head of the column swung left onto the bridge and through the open gate. We halted in a clear space between the long barrack-type buildings and other buildings across the quadrangle. The Japanese officer stepped to the center and spoke through an interpreter. "Kioske (Attention). Welcome to Shiragawa and the Mitsubishi Copper Mine. I am Lieutenant Asaka, Japanese Imperial Army." A little speech in Japanese was translated by the interpreter. Boiled down in a nutshell, we were here to stay until the Japanese won the war. We would be expected to obey the established rules and work hard. We were to bow to the guards at all times and obey their instructions. Tenko would be held twice each day. We would be punished for any infractions of the rules and would be treated fairly by the Japanese Imperial Army. As I listened, I thought, "What else is new, we have heard this tripe before." Lieutenant Asaka then turned and walked to his quarters. The senior American officer, Captain E. Pearce Fleming, then stepped up and said, "I was a Battery Commander of the 23rd Field Artillery Battalion (PS). I had been the SAO at Clark Field for 17

months. I ask for your cooperation to make the camp as comfortable as possible in the months to come." We were told to move into the barracks temporarily until permanent details were formed.

Our little group moved into the first barracks nearest the gate. Looking the situation over, we headed for the end next to a dividing wall with a small stove near by. We naively thought that we would be permitted to have a fire in the evening. Dumping our packs on the straw mats, we surveyed our new home.

The buildings were clean and of new construction. A vast difference to the nipa huts at Cabanatuan. The buildings were of lumber, about 150 feet long by 30 feet wide. The space between the sleeping bays had a dirt floor with tables and low wooden benches set into the ground running down the center. The sleeping bays were on two levels along the sides. The lower bays were about 24 inches above the ground and the upper bays were about five feet above with a ladder at each end of the bay. There were small windows along the bays. There were three bays in each barracks. The barracks were connected with a covered walkway between buildings. The stoves were located at the dividing partition of each bay in a space break between tables. There was no insulation on the ceiling or the walls. The bays were covered by a straw mat called a tatami. They were three feet wide, about three inches thick and six feet long, placed side by side. Another mat was placed crosswise at the foot. Each man had three feet wide by nine feet long for living space. A small shelf was attached to the outer wall for personal items. There were four buildings in a long line parallel to the stockade fence.

The benjo uchi was across the compound. It was crude by American standards but functional. A floor of cement with a slot that opened into a cement pit below. Urinals were a sheet metal trough attached to the wall and drained into the pits below. The wash room was a row of cold water faucets connected to the bath house and galley.

The two bath houses with a partition were typical Japanese. A large tub about five feet square and about four feet deep was set in the center with a wooden platform around it. The water was heated from a boiler in the galley. Behind the galley was the Japanese quarters and a storage building. The hospital and dispensary were attached to the camp headquarters across from the galley. The building directly west of the main entrance was divided into several small rooms for the officers. The guard house and the eso, (jail) were attached to the first building east of the entrance way. The entire area was fenced with a gateway on the back side and the front gate. It was well laid out, except for insulation, and would serve the purpose. The approaching of the cold weather would generate some problems in keeping warm. The front of the camp faced north. The barracks would be protected somewhat by the 12-foot fence along the entire north side.

Each individual tatami was equipped with a cloth mattress stuffed with straw, three blankets and a block of wood four inches square and eight inches long to serve as a pillow. We were instructed by the Japanese that we were not to walk on the tatamis with our shoes on. The shoes were to be removed in Japanese fashion and left on the bare ground before stepping onto the straw mat. Two wooden bowls, a small tea cup and a set of Japanese chopsticks were provided for each man. Bill Haddox, Archie Golson, John Kunich and I sat and discussed the layout. The only question was: would we be permitted to have fires in the evening and early mornings and where would we get fuel for the tiny stoves? When this question came up everyone looked at the wooden blocks that were supposed to be pillows. We were certain that we would have cold weather and a lot of snow at this altitude. The open space between the row of buildings was used for the assembly of work groups. The entire camp area was 139 feet by 325 feet.

Our camp was located near the small village of Shiragawa. It was near the larger village of Hanawa, and was listed as Camp No. 6 of the Sendai Military District. This was a copper mining area. Captain Fleming heard that it had been in operation for 2,000 years. Hanawa was 60 miles from the northern tip of Honshu. It was about midway between the Pacific Ocean on the east and the Sea of Japan on the west. The nearest towns of any size was Fataatsui on the east and Kemonsai on the west. The area is rugged and mountainous. Sendai Military District Headquarters was 125 miles to the southeast. The mine was operated by the Mitsubishi Company.

Lt. Asaka had called for a meeting of the officers and the senior NCOs to work out administrative and work details. The first order of business was to get the galley in working order. Sergeant Protz was to be NCO in charge. Several men who had been cooks were chosen for that important detail. This was a choice detail and much sought after by all of us. It had some nice fringe benefits, warm place to work and remaining in camp during the day. Lieutenant Richard Pullen was assigned duty as mess officer. On these men would fall the responsibility of accomplishing miracles in coming up with wholesome food for the 500 men. Their success depended on the **largess** of the Japanese Imperial Army. Here in this far away place, we could not expect to scrounge anything extra and it was too late to plant gardens. Fish, rice, barley, soy beans, mango beans, dried greens, kelp, metsau paste and tea would be the standard rations. Very little meat, if any, could be expected. The men in the galley would have to be innovative, honest and insure that the rations were utilized to the maximum. They were not to take advantage of their position for their own benefit. A fat cook under these conditions was sure to draw fire from the working men.

Another very important detail would be the medical staff. This group was headed by Major Calvin Jackson, MD, assisted by Lieutenant John Lamy, MD and several medical personnel. This group would also be vastly important for the welfare of the men. The remote location of the camp, the severity of the weather and the dangerous conditions associated with mining would present many medical problems. The pitiful small amount of medicines that had accompanied us would be critical to survival and would need augmentation from the Japanese. The medical skills and temperament of the men would determine whether some lived or died. They would have to operate the medical facility under the supervision of a Japanese medical technician.

S/Sgt. Leonard O. Larson, whom I had known before the war, was assigned the job of shoe and clothing repair. Several men were chosen as dog robbers for the Japanese staff. All of these assignments were envied by the men who were unfortunate to be assigned in the mines.

The conference of the officers and key civilian personnel from the mine was to determine the skills needed and job assignments. They required mechanics, electricians, machinists, foundry and saw mill laborers and miners. Screening of the rosters and interviews by mine personnel and officers was accomplished in the first two days. The medical staff was directed to give physical examinations to determine the health and condition of the men.

A detail of men was put to work in the Japanese warehouse to issue winter clothing during the work detail selection. The second day was devoted to issuing clothing. Each man received a pair of canvas shoes, two pairs of thin socks, a pair of thin white cotton gloves, a two-piece work suit, a pull down cap, a pair of short legged pants, a small towel, two G-stings and a cotton shirt with a patch of white cloth for stenciling our number which was used as identification. We also received a very important item, a British long wool overcoat. They had, evidently, come from captured British stocks. However, there were some strings attached to these items. The wool overcoat was to be worn only when going to or returning from the mine. It was not to be worn at work. The canvas shoes were similar to tennis shoes with two exceptions. They did not have laces, but were fastened by a flap that came around the back of the foot and fastened with a metal clip. TGIF, (toes go in first). They were made with the large toe separate from the other toes. This required some getting used to. There were a lot of remarks cast about monkeys climbing trees. I was fortunate that

my feet were too big, I received a pair without the lonesome toe. One advantage in the canvas shoes were they could be dried very easily during lunch break or in the evening. American leather boots or shoes were extremely cold and were difficult to dry quickly. The men had brought very little clothing from the islands to augment the Japanese issue. Usually we wore all the clothes we had in severe weather.

After the detail listings and work assignments, the men were re-distributed in the barracks. I was lucky and did not have to move from my place near the stove. Haddox, Golson, and Kunich moved to another barracks. M/Sgt. Kunich was the NCO in charge of a group of men assigned to work in the mine. He had come from the coal mining region of Pennsylvania. He said, "Hell, I joined the army to get out of the coal mines and now I am back in the hole." M/Sgt. Ivan Buster, USMC was NCO in charge of my section which was primarily mechanics.

One ugly incident arose during the issuing of clothing. One of the men stole a Japanese soldier's jacket. There was a big fuss and everyone was turned out of the barracks in tenko formation. The gunzo, Sgt. Sagai read us the riot act and told us, through the Japanese interpreter, that, "We would remain at attention until the guilty party returned the jacket." The Japanese were furious that anyone would steal from the Imperial Japanese Army. It was a stupid stunt for one of the men to do. He did not consider that he would never be able to wear it or the consequences of his action. We remained at attention under the eye of the guards for about two hours. The guards searched the barracks and other buildings. The jacket was found in one of the latrine pits. Fortunately, the pit was relatively empty and it was fished out. The gunzo huffed and puffed but no one stepped forward for good reason. They had seen what punishment was meted out for stealing from the Imperial Japanese Army at other camps. It was a stalemate and they would have kept us there all night. Captain Fleming and Lt. Asaka worked out a compromise. The **camp** was to return to the barracks and no one was to be punished, if the guilty party would step forward. The burden was on the officers and NCOs to come up with the guilty party or someone to take the blame to avoid punishment of 500 men. A heated discussion of the situation and the possibilty of real serious punishment was considered. All of us were aware of the severe punishment for theft in the islands that usually resulted in torture and even death to the culprit.

The situation was tense and no one had witnessed the theft or at least would not snitch on the guilty man. Finally, one man stepped forward and said he would take the blame. He denied the actual theft but in the interest of the group he would say he "took the jacket and threw it in the benjo pit." The volunteer was PFC Lloyd J. Hill, Army, POW #269. There were some who believed he was guilty and some thought he was foolish to accept the blame. It was never determined if he was or was not the culprit. Lt. Asaka sentenced him to several days in the eso (jail) on reduced rations of water and rice. Fortunately it was not freezing weather. After completion of his sentence, he was put on a camp detail. It appears the Japanese were either unpredictably lenient or they respected Hill's courage in volunteering, not knowing how severe the punishment might be.

Photo of E. Pearce Fleming, Col. Ret. Senior American Officer (Capt.) at Hanawa Prison Camp No. 6 until arrival of Col. Walker. Photo by Adrian Martin.

It is my opinion that the light sentence was directly attributed to Capt. Fleming's insight and knowledge of the Japanese character. He was an astute observer of the Japanese and was able to establish a working relationship, respect and trust that contributed to the wel-

fare of the camp. He was fair, honest, sincere and respected by the men and the Japanese. I, for one, would recommend him for the Legion of Merit, for his example of how an officer should look after the welfare of the men in his command. There were many examples of officers and noncommissioned officers who were woefully inept, selfish, self-effacing, conniving, inconsiderate and failed miserably in their duties. They know who they are and will have to live with themselves.

Each man had been assigned a number to be stenciled on a white patch of cloth and sewn on the left side of his work jacket. This number became your name. The Japanese would always address prisoners by his number. This simplified communication. My number was 97, ku ju nana.

The medics were ordered to have a physical examination of the men to determine their fitness and ability to work. The examinations were conducted by Major Calvin Jackson and Lt. John Lamy supervised by Superior Private Yodo (Cyclops), as we called him. His medical training was extremely limited. Someone reported he had an infected toenail once. His self-importance as a medical technician created a serious situation with our doctors. Both doctors were graduates of medical schools and were very experienced medical men. Cyclops would and often did try to overrule their diagnosis. Occasionally, a doctor from the mine would come for inspection of the dispensary, hospital and treatments. Cyclops was extremely afraid of him.

The examination was conducted by work groups, so the waiting in the cold was minimized. Our group was lined up and deposited our shoes at the door of the dispensary. There was no heat in the building. We were uncomfortable in our stocking feet. Major Jackson was conducting the eye test of reading a standard eye chart. When asked to read the chart, I replied, "I cannot read the chart where you are pointing." Major Jackson worked his pointer up the chart to the big E. I replied. "I can not read the chart, sir." The Major became exasperated and slapped the wall with the pointer. He said, "Can you see the wall?" "Yes sir, I can see the wall," I replied. I was excused. At the time, according to visual standards, I was probably 20 over 400 in the visual acuity test due to optical atrophy.

Major Calvin Jackson was a well qualified physician. It was easy to understand why he was exasperated and humiliated because of the superior attitude of Cyclops, a lowly Japanese medical man with little or no medical training. I am sure that the major felt that Cyclops would not make a pimple on a doctor's behind. Later the major was transferred

Dr. Dan Golenturnik in 1987. The doctor was senior medical officer (Capt.) at Camp No. 6, Hanawa, Japan 1944-45. Photo by Adrian Martin.

to another camp and Captain Dan Golenturnik was sent to Hanawa. Dr. Dan was a superior physician who had to work under awesome limitations and severe restrictions. The eternal shortage of medicines, laboratory equipment, adequate treatment facilities and severe weather were difficult handicaps to overcome. This was further complicated by the fact that only 25 men could be hospitalized and a similar number on quarters. Dr. Dan was able to develop Cyclop's trust and respect and was able to say who would be on quarters or the hospital within the numerical limits. Cyclops probably learned more about medicine from Dr. Dan and Lt. Lamy than he would have in medical school. The medical personnel were dedicated and instrumental in the low death rate of the men. Captain Fleming (Colonel, retired, Columbia S.C.) stated in a taped interview with Adrian Martin (New London WI) in 1987 that "There were eight deaths. One from a mine accident, two from tuberculosis and five from other causes." This was

particularly commendable under the conditions, food quality and quantity, adverse weather conditions, lack of medicine, and susceptibility to disease caused by close association, restriction of access to hospital or quarters, long exposure and residual diseases from the tropics and previous maltreatment for two years.

One of the deaths from tuberculosis was to have a long term effect on me personally. First Sergeant Adrian Martin of the 200th AA Battalion sat in my lap during the voyage of the *Noto Maru* and long train to Hanawa. On return to US control, I was x-rayed and found to have a TB lesion in the left lung.

The medical examinations, the assignment to specific groups and issuing of clothing were completed in the first few days after our arrival. Everything was in order and work was to begin. An American NCO in charge was assigned to each work group. There were ten mine work groups, one special detail of medics, cooks, and orderlies. The officers were not included as workers. Captain Fleming in the referenced taped interview tells of how Lt. Asaka said, "The captain would have to work at the mine." Captain Fleming said in the tape politely but firmly, "That he would not work in the mine. He was not required to work in accordance with the Geneva Convention." The matter was dropped there, though the captain did go to the mine and checked out the working conditions.

My group was Section 2 with M/Sgt. Ivan Buster, Marine Corps, as NCO in charge of 39 men. Among the men in Section 2 were Richard Francies, Burl Cunningham, Rudolph Schuster, Chester Nicholson, Howard Bower, John Hoback, Leslie Canfield, Frank Piburn among others. These were assigned in different areas to the machinery on the outside of the mine. We were assigned to Barracks B. Bay 4A. This was on the left of the main entrance near the guard house and the eso (jail). Our bay was equipped with one small stove for 40 men. All food was served in the bays. Our bay was under the gun, so to speak, as it was the nearest to the guard house and we could expect uninvited guests at any time.

My good friends were assigned to different sections. Archie Golson, 4A, Bill Haddox, 3B, John Kunich, 4A, and Sgt. Adrian Martin, 3A.

Though we were in the same camp, we would not be working together, but could visit in the evening or Sundays. Each group worked in widely separated sections of the mine. Each section had a civilian work honcho, who came each day at morning work call and escorted each group to the place of work. A small contingent of military guards with rifles would accompany us and remain with us all day. They would return to the camp at night as escorts. A tenko would account for the men working and returning in the evening. A bed time tenko was taken after chow and everyone had to be accounted for. Those men on quarters had to be present for the evening tenko. Each morning a report was given to the civilian honchos on the number for work and the number on quarters by group. There was no way one could shirk going to work except to be on quarters by order of the doctor and approved by Cyclops and Lt. Asaka.

The honchos were civilian representatives of the mining company. Most of them were easy to get along with and did not beat or harass the men. Others were mean and brutal during the little time they were in charge. Their sole authority was escorting the working groups to the area of work. A Japanese miner or mechanic would have two or three men to work with him. One honcho (stick man), in particular, carried a loaded walking stick. During the mile and a half walk to the mine we were not supposed to put our hands in our overcoat pockets. We only had a thin pair of cotton gloves to protect us from the severe cold. This particular honcho would come up behind an unsuspecting POW and whack him across the arm with the stick. Once in awhile when our regular honcho, Mr. Watanabe, was absent, our group would catch the Stick Man, his nickname, for escort. He caught me once with my hands in my pockets and almost broke my arm.

The Mitsubishi mine was a typical mine. The main shaft entrance was high up the mountain. The ore would be blasted out in the mine shaft by the miners and loaded into small mine cars. The ore-filled cars would then be pushed out and the contents dumped into large holding bins. The holding bins were just above a row of giant rock crushers set into the mountain. The ore would be dumped into the crushers and then onto conveyor belts that ran to the separators. The fine material would be passed on and mixed with water to form a liquid slurry. The slurry would be pumped into the ball mills to crush it into fine particles. The pulverized slurry would pass through another separator to filter out the copper ore. It was then taken by the overhead tramway. The tramway buckets delivered the ore to the smelters for melting into ingots. Conveyor belts were used to move the material from one process to the other. A conveyor might break down and the crushed rock would pile up at the head of the belt. Shoveling out the crushed rock would have to be done by hand in order to repair the conveyor. The material that had been turned into slurry was handled by large centrifugal pumps. This maze of machinery required constant supervision and maintenance. There were mechanics with POW helpers at various levels to keep the machinery moving.

The men of Section 2 were scattered throughout the machinery area, and usually worked with the same technician (millwright) each day. There were small shacks with a small stove for heat, hot water, locker for stowing the technicians work clothes, and for lunch breaks. The technician usually had two or more POWs that would do the bull work where possible. Nicholson, Francies, Schuster and I generally were assigned to one mechanic named Tanaka. He had served his time in the Japanese Army in Manchuria and was about 45 years old. He was a large man for a Japanese, almost six feet tall, very strong and a compassionate man. Compassionate in that he was considerate of our skinny condition and would do a lot of the heavy work himself. For example, if we had to repair a pump, the impeller housing and impeller were removed. The impeller housing was about three feet in diameter and about eight inches in depth bolted to the pump shaft flange. The impeller housing weighed about 200 pounds. There were no hoists. After first removing the bolts from the intake flange and the outlet pipe, a woven grass rope was put under the housing to form a sling. Two men with a yo-ho pole put through the sling could lift the casting from the pump. Tanaka would often slip the sling towards himself and take most of the weight.

The POW was simply a fulcrum and a steady form at the other end of the yo-ho pole. Tanaka would lower his end of the pole and the POW would bend slightly as Tanaka stood erect so he would be doing the lifting.

Frequently the casting had to be carried a distance and Tanaka would always have the heavy end. The use of a yo-ho pole requires a little getting used to, as it is foreign to our culture and work habits. The muscles in our shoulders were not developed to form a cushion for the pole. We were all skinny and with not much padding. We used our hands to take part of the weight, or our hat for additional padding. We also had to develop a type of shuffling pace and not lock our knees into the full, upright position. Once developed, this shuffling pace made it easier to carry heavy bulky objects with a yo-ho pole.

A yo-ho pole was a piece of pine about six feet in length and about two or three inches in diameter. The yo-ho pole was the main cargo carrier in the Orient. Some were single-man poles with a basket hung on each end. This was the way Orientals moved earth, grain or other commodities. The two-man pole was used for heavy duty work; it was a very efficient cargo mover and employed in many areas of the mine.

The next step was removing the impeller from the tapered and keyed pump shaft, followed by the removal of the backing flange from the shaft housing. The pump shaft housing was about five feet long with a multi-V-belt pulley on the end. Most of our work was in repairing the pumps and the replacement of electric motors. Other work was in the maintenance of the ball mills.

The Japanese were very conservative in maintenance of the equipment. Any cast iron piece that became worn and not usable would be sent to the foundry and melted for recycling. The item would then be sent to the machine shop and machined to standard and returned for use. The impeller and pump housing wore out very quickly due to the abrasive slurry passing through. The pump shaft housing also had to be overhauled frequently. The carrier bearings for the shaft were double roller bearings about eight inches in diameter, fitted into the housing. An unbalanced impeller had an adverse effect on the bearings; it

began vibrating and beat out the bearing seat or the bearing. The pump shaft housing would be disassembled and new bearings installed. If the housing was beat out of round, sheet metal shims would be inserted to seat the bearing. This practice contributed to future failure. If Tanaka did not have the proper open end wrench to fit the nuts or cap screws, he would take a hammer and close or open the wrench jaws. The wrenches were of malleable iron and machined. Another heavy job was the replacement of the electric motors. They had to be removed and sent to the electrical shop for repair. The movement of the motors was by manpower and had to be taken steps at a time. Tanaka would do the same on the yo-ho pole. He was tremendously strong and could lift more with his shoulders than three of the scrawny POWs. Tanaka, to his credit, never lost his temper or struck any of us.

The hardest work was the repair of the ball mills. These are huge cylindrical drums about 30 feet in diameter driven by electric motors with a reduction gear on the motors. The rotating of the drum caused the cast iron balls in the mill to tumble and crush the gravel to a very fine powder. This was the only place where we used an overhead bridge crane.

The interior of the drum was lined with a series of cast iron plates about three inches thick, bolted to the outer drum. During operation the steady tumbling of the mill wore out the cast iron balls and plates. The mill would then be taken off-line for repair. The mill would be rotated and the cast iron balls could be dumped through an access door. The steel plates were secured to the exterior by large cap-screws. The work of removing and replacing the plates was strenuous and slow. Each plate weighed about 85 pounds. All of the plates had to be lowered into the drum, manhandled into place and secured by the cap-screw. The cast iron balls were about four inches in diameter and weighed about eight pounds. After loading a ton or more of them, we felt like we were shot-putters. After the plate installation was completed, the balls dumped at the beginning were sorted and the larger ones were thrown into the drum along with new balls to equal the desired weight. The old plates and scrap bits of the balls were then loaded into a mine car and sent to the foundry for re-casting.

The ball mills were located in a building about 60 feet high and about 300 feet long with no end walls. The cold wind made life miserable. Handling the cast iron plates and steel balls with no gloves was sheer torture. Tanaka, our supervisor, permitted us to have a small fire in a five-gallon bucket. Fuel was scrap lumber and the heavy grease that was scraped off the base for the ring gear and pinion that rotated the drum. It gave off a greasy black smoke, but at least we had some heat. Lunch breaks were great as we could go in the keukai shacks. The Japanese would be there and we could listen to their conversation. We could understand some of their conversation. Once, while working on the mills, I was sent up to operate the electric bridge crane. The lifts were slow and took a lot of time. The cold wind was whistling through the building—it must have been zero degrees. I tried to stand still and draw into my clothes to keep from freezing. I grew warm and drowsy as I stared at the fire below. I suddenly realized that I was at the point of freezing to death. I climbed down and thawed out by the fire bucket. Tanaka looked at me and did not say a word. We preferred this type of work rather than going into the mine. I for one did not want anything to do with the work underground. Of course, we were not asked our preference. According to some friends, who worked underground, they did not have to put up with the cold but were wet from dripping water and puddles in the shaft. I loved to see the sky and be outside instead of hundreds of feet underground. Even on Corregidor, I never waqnted to be in Malinta Tunnel and preferred the outside even though it had its hazards.

The most difficult period of time was from November 1944 to April 1945. We arrived at Hanawa in September when the weather was nice, much like Indian summer at home. It began to snow every day from November through March. The snowfall was about 25 feet. The trail up the mountain was packed by the civilians and Americans. The trail became very slippery at times and some of the men suffered bone-shaking falls. We had to exercise extreme caution so we did not fall and break an arm. If we slipped, the trick was to relax, fall and try not to resist or catch ourselves.

The work days were long and routine. We soon fell into a regular schedule. Washing of clothes was usually done on Sundays. This was sometimes put off because we needed the clothes to keep warm and there was no way to dry them. The small stoves in the bays were almost useless. We could build a small fire after work for about an hour, **if we had any fuel**. The only issue of fuel was a few small briquettes of charcoal. The men would steal coal at the mine and hide it in their mess kits or they would break up wooden forms into small pieces and insert it in their belt. Surprise shakedown inspection by the guards on return to camp caught most of the fuel. What little we were able to smuggle into camp was carefully hoarded. The guards could see the smoke coming from the stoves and knew right away if a fire was being used. The wooden pillows that were issued went into the stoves. Ali Babba and his 40 thieves never had anything on these unfortunate eternally cold bunch of prisoners. Necessity is the mother of invention and we would take risks for a small piece of coal, coke or piece of lumber to feed the stove. This was more important than food. Each man in a group could bring in a sliver of wood or a chunk of coal every day and put it into the hiding place. A fire on Sunday might be possible or on some evenings. Section 2 had a hoard underneath a tatami that was not used. This was so the Japanese could not blame anyone if they found it. Which by the grace of God they never did.

The constant wearing of clothing and lack of hot water for washing created a new problem. The motorized dandruff (body lice) moved in and took over the seams of our clothing. We had no way of controlling these pests except at night before lights out, men would sit and pick lice off and crush them or fry them on the hot stove. The lice-picking was humorous at times. The men would find a nice fat one and say, "Fry you Nip bastard," as they watched him fry on the stove.

Bathing was another problem as we were permitted to bathe once a week. The bath house was attached to the galley. It was a typical Japanese type; a large wooden tub about 25 square feet and about four feet deep, with a wooden platform around the tub. The work groups took turns going in first. The Americans never understood the proper way to use a Japanese tub. They would pile into the tub and soap up in the tub similar to a bathtub at home. By the time the last group went through, it was like soup. The water would not be drained and refilled for the next group. The proper method as practiced by the Japanese was to sit on the wooden platform **outside** of the tub. With a small wooden bucket they would dip out water and soap up with a small hand towel. Wash out the towel, their G-string, shirts, socks or pants and then rinse off good **before** slipping into the tub. Many times the last group would not even go to the bathhouse because the water would be so filthy. They would take sponge baths near the stove. They figured that it would be better to be dirty in your own clothes than to try to get clean in a cesspool. Their turn would come when they would be in the early group.

The Japanese have a fetish for keeping clean. The mining company provided bath houses at the mine. The workers would always take a bath before going home. Amazingly, they would strip down to a G-string and a pair of wooden clogs and walk to the bath house. They carried a small bucket and a small towel wrapped around their head. The weather might be zero, yet after bathing, washing the towel and the G-string, they would walk back to their shack completely nude. How they kept from getting pneumonia was a mystery. Women ran the bathhouse and kept the water hot.

One of the items issued to us during the cold weather was a face mask, much like a surgical mask. The mask was to be worn at all times except in quarters. The mask was about four inches square with two strings attached on each side. The strings were put over the ears and tied. This made it easy to remove or hold in place. The mask covered the nose and mouth. The primary purpose was the control of colds plus it kept the face warm when walking to the mine. The mask served as a dust collector when working under dusty conditions. This was another item that was washed at the time of bathing.

The Japanese issued four cigarettes per day. The Americans would cut them into four pieces. The pieces were smoked with a holder to conserve on every scrap of tobacco. The Japanese smoked a special very thin tobacco that was similar to hair. The tobacco was carried in a small case with a long leather string attached. The string could be looped on the hair pipe and stuck in their belts when not in use. The pipes were about 6 inches long with a metal bit and bowl connected with a piece of bamboo. The smoking procedure was simple and very conservative on tobacco. The Nip would take a small pinch of hair tobacco and roll it into a small ball about the size of a pencil eraser. The ball would be put into the bowl and lit from the stove. After about three puffs, he would knock out the dotal, put in another ball and light the new ball from the dotal. The process was repeated until he was satisfied.

This was another source of tobacco for my Wally Frank pipe. The hair tobacco would get dry and a dust would collect in the pouch. The workman would give me the dust, which I mixed Half & Half with the cigarette tobacco. The mixture helped to make the tobacco last longer. Some of the men acquired a Japanese pipe and used it for a holder. It was also handy to have when one bummed a little tobacco from one of the civilian mine workers.

When cigarettes became scarce, S/Sgt. Archie Golson would come to my barracks and ask if we could light up my pipe for a few drags. He would take a few drags and say, "That will hold me until tomorrow." It was almost like smoking a peace pipe in that it filled a need. There were so many things missing from our life.

When the cold weather became severe there was not much visiting between sections. We usually returned to camp about 6:00 p.m., had our supper meal and climbed into our sacks until tenko. After tenko, back in the sack for the rest of the night. It was too cold to sit up in the cold barracks and talk with anyone. There were very few books and the rumor machine was frozen. News of the war usually came from tags of information from a few of the mine workers or guards. Occasionally we could snitch a Japanese newspaper. Several men could make out Japanese characters. We knew that the Americans were pushing up from the south and that an invasion of France had occurred. By piecing together bits and

118

pieces of information, from here and there, and assuming the opposite from the Japanese propaganda, applying logic and assumptions to the jigsaw, a fair indication of the true status was developed. For example, Saipan, Iwo Jima, Okinawa, Letye and Manila were key indicators. Japanese names and familiar names were excellent clues. When connected with bits of gossip from the Japanese, we could estimate the progress of the war. Japanese actions, expressions, the attitude of the guards and the civilians were indicative clues. This helped greatly to alleviate the uncertainties and gave us motivation to hang on. Six more months and we will be out of this refrigerator called Japan.

During our stay at Hanawa, we were issued Red Cross boxes twice. The first one was the week of Christmas. Red Cross boxes and mail were the biggest boosters of morale. The traders were out in force. Each trying to get something he liked for something he could do without or for jawbone rice rations. It was a free market and it reminded me of trading days on the farm. Each one trying to get the best deal possible without getting taken.

Our third Christmas in captivity was a gala event. The Red Cross boxes were like all the presents from home wrapped in one package. A small evergreen tree was brought in and set up in the bay next to ours. The men made trinkets from aluminum foil, colored paper, tin can covers, and bits of glass for ornaments. It was like home. The Japanese gave us the day off and a Catholic priest from somewhere held mass. Almost all of the 500 men gathered in our barracks for services and the singing of Christmas carols. The cooks had cooked up a little extra and with the Red Cross boxes everyone went to bed with a full stomach, thankful for our lives and praying for the great freedom day to come. Most of the men were thinking of home, our loved ones, and hoped they were well.

Christmas day happened to be our group's turn to bath first. I went to the bath house early, scrubbed out some clothes and myself and then slipped into the hot tub of water to soak. I said to myself, "I am going to stay in this tub of water until they throw me out." I sat there and savored the wonderful hot water and I recalled the words of Robert Service's

Alaskan poem, *The Cremation of Sam McGee*. "Now Sam McGee was from Tennessee, way down near Plum Tree. He could never get warm in the Yukon and asked his friend to cremate him if he died on the trail. His friend agreed and shortly afterwards Sam McGee died. His friend finally found a wrecked barge on Lake LaMarge. 'Ah ha,' he said, 'My crematorium.' He built a hot fire in the old boiler and placed Sam McGee inside and closed the door. He walked away and thought of his friend and their time together. He returned and opened the door. There sat Sam McGee, who said, 'Close the door. I fear you will let in the cold. This is the first time I have been warm since I left Tennessee, down near Plum Tree.' "

The poem described the way I felt sitting in that nice hot tub of water. I remained there for at least two hours. When I crawled out I was as pink as a baby's behind and as weak as a kitten. That was a memorable Christmas. I was warm for the first time in a year.

January of 1945 was a terribly cold month. Many of us came down with colds, flu and pneumonia. I was one of the unfortunate ones. I had gone to work as usual. By noon I was running a high fever and having cold chills. Tanaka, the work honcho, told me to stay in the warming shack until time to return to camp. I went on sick call and told the doctor how I felt. Dr. Golenturnik checked my temperature and listened to my chest. He turned to me and said. "Sergeant, you have double pneumonia. I should put you in the hospital. But if I do that, I will have to put someone out who is as sick as you or worse. However, I will put you on quarters." I told the doctor, "You are the boss." He said he would try and keep me on quarters as long as possible and gave me some pills. I went right to bed after drinking as much hot tea as I could get. The doctor was allowed only 25 men in the hospital at any time. Doctor Dan was a superb doctor and had the health of the men on his shoulders. He was ably assisted by Doctor Lamy and the medics. The next morning the fever was not as high as the day before.

Being on quarters did not excuse you from camp details, only from going to the mine. As a staff sergeant, on quarters, I was assigned to supervising the other men on quarters. The snow removal detail was rotated each hour in removing snow from the compound and dumping it in the ditch in front of the camp. Each hour I had to crawl out of the sack and find the beds of the relief detail to work the next hour. When I had to go to Barracks A, I had to pass in front of the guard house, stop, and render a bow to the representatives of the Japanese Imperial Army.

On one trip I came out befuddled and feverish forgetting the rule to stop and bow. I had enough trouble getting the men out of their sacks. "Kora!" the guard roared at me. I came to a stop and faced the guard house. One of the guards came out and read me the riot act. I said, "I am sorry that I did not bow, I am takuson bioki (very sick)." I was at attention and looking him in the eye. He muttered some more but let me go after I gave the low bow. That was close, I thought to myself, as I went on looking for the man in Barracks A. I didn't forget on the return and gave the bow as I came to the guard house.

Another hour passed in the sack. Wouldn't you know the next time I went out the door and I forgot the damned guard again. "Kora!" I froze and the same guard came out shouting in Japanese. I knew I was in for it but hoped to be able to talk my way out of trouble again. I repeated the same excuse and he started shouting more, as if to say "I have heard that story before." I was looking him in the eye, at attention. He swung with his right hand and slapped me hard. That was not so bad, but I had diarrhea and crapped my pants. I muttered under my breath, "If you slap me again, I will crap my pants for sure and I will not be responsible for my actions." He gave me some more tongue lashing and after a bow, he sent me on my way. Who can say how I would have reacted, in my feverish mind, if he'd hit me again. I was lucky again. January was a bad month, even Captain Fleming had a spell of pneumonia. I returned to work after four days, feeling much better.

Another shipment of Red Cross packages was delivered in early February and placed in the Japanese storeroom. The Japanese would not issue them. Captain Fleming went to Lt. Asaka and asked for the boxes to be issued on a regular basis. Lt. Asaka replied, "We are saving them for a rainy day." Captain Fleming replied, "We have a storm now." Captain Fleming was able to convince him and we received the boxes on a regular schedule.

The days and months dragged on and we kept thinking, six more months and we will be out of here. It is not surprising that men who are eternally hungry, constantly think, talk, dream and fantasize about food. The men would mentally torture themselves and do things out of the ordinary. Our section NCO in charge, M/Sgt. Ivan Buster was an old-time Marine and he fell into this category. He started to collect recipes for all types of meals. Listening to them talk about food, you would think they were all reading menus of restaurants. I would not allow myself to engage in this mental frustration and would leave the area. This usually occurred in the evening or on a Sunday.

We received a contingent of 50 British soldiers and three officers in March. They had been in the Yokohoma area. The allied bombing of the major cities forced the Japanese to disperse some of the camps in that area. They were from the Singapore garrison and had been prisoners since February 1942. They were in reasonably good health. The British soldiers told of the immense flights of American bombers hitting the heart land of Japan.

The three officers moved in with the officers in Barracks A. The doctors moved into a store room in the hospital area in order to make room. Also about this time we received an American officer, Lt. Colonel Arthur J. Walker, a B-24 squadron commander, shot down over Kwajallean in April the previous year. He had been sent to Ofumo for interrogation. Ofumo was where captured pilots and submarine survivors were sent for interrogation by the Kempei-Tai (secret police).

From the accounts of Captain Fleming in a taped interview by Adrian Martin in 1986, Colonel Walker had been through the mill, tortured and mistreated something shameful. He became the senior American officer, but according to Captain Fleming, "Colonel Walker did not want any responsibility for commanding." They agreed that the captain would continue to run things and tell the colonel what he was doing. Evidently this was satisfactory and we still had the captain as an advocate for us. He had a lot of experience and the colonel felt that he should continue in that capacity.

With the coming of spring and the warmer weather, we had a new influx of nuisances to contend with, **fleas!** They were everywhere. They moved into our tatamis and blankets along with the lice. Nights became a nightmare in scratching lice and fleas and trying to kill both before going to bed. Even when walking outside enroute to the latrine or bathhouse, you could feel those monstrous fleas bouncing off your bare legs. The eternal scratching caused ulcerated sores on the lower extremities. We had looked forward to warmer weather but **not** the hordes of fleas and of course the flies came with them.

Spring also was the time to think of gardening and raising vegetables. The Japanese decided that we were to have a garden. On our day off the camp was put on this project. A plot of land behind the camp on a hill was selected and men were put to preparing the ground. A hole was dug about 12 inches deep, and about four feet wide. A detail, in the meantime, was set to work in the camp bailing out the benjo pits with a tin dipper on a stick. The honey wagons had performed this chore during the winter. This was our first experience in this stinking job. One man would bail the liquid out and pour it into a tub made from half of a 50-gallon drum. Two men would then slip a yo-ho pole through a sling and carry the stinking tub up the hill. Another man would dip out a small amount and put it in the freshly dug hole. About six inches of dirt was then shoveled on the honey deposit. The seeds were then dropped in and covered with about an inch of soil. Cpl. Haddox and I were selected to be honey bucket operators. We brought one of the oil drums over by the benjo pit and someone bailed in the mess. When it had about 20 gallons, we shoved our yo-ho pole through the bail. Each one of us turned our backs to the tub of stinking liquid mess. We were like the two mules in the cartoon, each trying to go in opposite directions. We haggled and argued over who would be in front and who would bring up the rear. We were getting nowhere. Finally we agreed that we would rotate the back seat driving. On our first trip up the hill I was the back seat driver. The back seat driver, as we climbed the hill,

had the bucket swing back so that the bucket was almost banging him in the legs, with his head directly over the slopping mess. We made only two trips and then someone else took over the driving. We planted pumpkins and other vegetables.

Summer brought us another experience in Oriental delicacies. On a Sunday we were lined up after tenko for camp details. The Japanese handed out a small square wooden box about six inches square by ten inches, with a small hole in one end. We were to be exterminators of grasshoppers in the fields near camp. It was really a treat to get out in the fields and enjoy the sunshine for a change. We were told on arrival in the field that we were to spread out and catch grasshoppers and put them in the boxes. The one who caught the most would receive an extra cigarette ration. The incentive was enough to encourage us to catch as many as possible. We spent all afternoon and returned to camp with a lot of the pesky critters. I don't recall who caught the most, and the thought never occurred of what would become of the catch. If we had known, we would not have caught so many.

The following morning, to our utter dismay, the cooks had boiled the hoppers in soy sauce and then mixed them in with the morning rice ration. You either ate it, traded, or gave it away. I tried to stomach the damn stuff, but had trouble with the long legs going down, and finally gave it away. The market for rice with sauteed grasshoppers was severely depressed for some reason. That is one Oriental dish this soldier hopes to never see again, much less try to eat.

The practice of trading food was about the only commodity that the prisoners were interested in, either for other food, tobacco, soap or clothing. One individual in a mining section was so addicted to tobacco that he would trade his rice or soup ration for tobacco. The man was so thin and emaciated, the doctors had to step in and have the section NCO supervise each meal to insure that he ate the entire ration and did not trade it off. This helped to put a little weight on him and probably contributed to his making it to freedom. The trading was most prevalent when Red Cross boxes were issued.

Our camp was a cross section of America. The men came from all parts of the country. Each had different values, morals, customs, language accents and attitudes toward his fellow man. Friendship was invaluable in thick or thin. Many men might not have lived through that awful winter without the support and boosting of morale by a comrade. The reverse was true when men became selfish and would steal from friends and fellow workers. We never considered stealing commodities from the Japanese a mortal sin, rather it was a matter of survival. Stealing from one another was counter-productive and a problem. There was no way anything could be locked up or protected when one had to go to the mine.

One case in point was the man who had been put in the eso (jail) for stealing. He was a problem, but cunning and innovative in stealing. While in the eso, he was skinny enough that he could slip through the benjo slot into the pit below. The pit had not been used very much and its contents were frozen. He would lift the outer cover and climb out to the rear of the building. He would slip into the barracks and steal whatever food he could find and return to the eso. He was caught one day and had to do more time in the eso. Captains Fleming and Golenturnik had to intercede with Lt. Asaka to get him released to prevent his dying.

The Japanese are wary of anyone who appears to be on the verge of mental imbalance. One of the men in our section gave the impression of being slightly daffy. He was a sheep herder from Montana and had some habits that were offensive to his comrades. We accepted him with his apparent abnormalities. Considering what some of the prisoners had gone through, it was surprising there were not more. John was caught stealing coal from the galley. The Japanese did not punish him; just said he was sick in the head. He was doing it for the good of the section. John had real long thick black hair. He had the ability to move his scalp back and forth. The evening tenko was always held in the barracks. We would be lined up in double ranks. John would be in the front rank standing at attention. The sergeant of the guard would stare at John as he twitched his scalp back and forth. The guard would look at John and shake his head and say, "Takuson baka. Takuson Baka." (very crazy). John could get away with some things that others would never try.

Summer in the mountains of northern Japan was a delight and we began to look at the brighter side of life. We stopped to sniff the flowers so to speak. The walk to the mine was enjoyable without the cold weather and the heavy overcoats. The clean clear air of the mountains was invigorating. The appearance of green trees and flowers, and the sights and sounds of the Japanese people gave a breath of life to our monastic existence. The progress of the war rumors were good. The new awareness of another life and the eternal hope for freedom gave us a feeling that 1945 was the year. Our white knight would come charging over the mountains and liberate the world, at least our world.

The walk became more interesting. Japanese children dressed in blue and white uniforms walking along in groups. Their faces beaming, voices singing; their laughter, their youthfulness reminded us that we had brothers, sisters, nieces and nephews at home. We had been away from children for so long that we had forgotten what they were like. The Japanese school system was semi-military. The children seemed to be strictly disciplined and motivated in a national pride sense. What would our younger brothers and sisters be like? Would they recognize their brothers? Or would they ask their mother who this strange skinny guy was in a uniform? There would have to be adjustments and understanding with our family members and they would be shocked at some of our peculiar ways. We were positive that we did not ever want rice or soup again. We had enough of that for the past three years. Just give us meat and potatoes, ham and eggs, steaks, chops and lots of apple pie. We would have difficulty in adjusting to our families and the ways of the people at home.

The scuttlebutt, rumors and bits of information gave us new hope. The allied forces had overrun most of Europe. The Germans were beaten back by Russia in the east and the allies in the west. The Japanese were pushed out of the Philippines and General MacArthur was preparing for the invasion of Japan

122

proper. The air force was making daily raids over Japanese cities.

In June of 1945, Sgt. Adrian Martin passed away from tuberculosis. He had been slowly losing the battle for life. Captain Golenturnik and Captain Fleming tried hard to get him sent to Shinagawa, near Tokyo, for treatment. However, due to the heavy bombing of that area, the Nipponese failed or could not get clearance to send him there. Possibly, he might have been saved. The only treatment at that time was bed rest and prayers. The antibiotics to arrest the progress were not available and probably unknown to the Japanese. Sergeant Martin's body was ordered cremated. A Shinto service was held at the insistence of the Japanese. The officers said the funeral prayers for the Christian service. The body was then sent away and the ashes were returned to the custody of the camp officers. The eight men who died were cremated and their ashes were placed in a small white box and returned to the camp for storage.

During the time we had been in Hanawa, we had never had an air raid or even an alert. We had not missed a day of work because of air activity. We might as well have been at the end of the earth. The British had told us how the Americans had bombed in the Tokyo-Yokohama area. Our remote location was not a suitable target.

The 6th of August 1944 we started for work as usual. We got about half way to the mine and the air raid sounded. This was the first time we had heard the alarm since arriving in Japan. We were immediately sent back to the camp and ordered to stay in the buildings. About 1000, the all clear sounded. We turned out and started to march to the mines again. We did not get out of the gate and we were ordered back. There was no work on the next day. This was the first day we did not work other than a Sunday. Laundry chores, chasing lice and fleas occupied our time. There was much speculation and talk of the abrupt change in the routine. Considerable social intercourse between friends gave us renewed enthusiasm and our morale was high. There had to be something out of the ordinary happening since we were not going to work.

That evening, Lt. Asaka called for Captain Fleming to come over to the office. Captain Fleming in a taped interview in 1985 described the occasion. "I went to the office and after bowing and the usual amenities of a cigarette and hot tea, I noticed the interpreter was there. I knew that this was not just an ordinary conversation. This was serious business. A Japanese newspaper was lying on the table." Lt. Asaka spoke through the interpreter, "Ichi B ni ju ku,(B-29), ichi bakadan, toksan haiti pati," (one B-29, one bomb, many soldiers die). Captain Fleming said, "Lieutenant, that is only Japanese propaganda. There were probably a thousand B-29s that dropped one bomb each." The lieutenant remained puzzled and dubious. I returned to my quarters. I told the other officers what had happened. We had no idea what to make of it. It left us thinking, maybe this is the end of our ordeal!

We returned to work on the 7th of August. However the honchos and workers seemed to be confused and very little work was accomplished during the day. The Japanese were nervous and had lost all inclination for work. One of the guards told us about one B-29, one bomb, and many soldiers being dead in Hiroshima. They were shaking their heads and could not understand how it was possible. They had been fed a steady stream of propaganda about how they were winning the war. We had been able to get some news about the war from some of the guards and workers. When Japanese names of battles and places came up, we were able to detect the propaganda and make reasonable assumptions of the true picture.

The following day after tenko, we were turned out for work. We had not gotten very far and we were turned back. Another air raid alert. We neither heard nor saw any planes. We could see the Japanese guards and honchos were extremely nervous and animatedly talking among themselves and watching the sky. The men were excited but calm and reticent to show their true feelings. Let them sweat. We were glad to see the Nips sweating it out. They had been very cocky for so long. Lt. Pullen said there was a rumor that Germany had surrendered. Was Japan being invaded? What was this story about one B-29, one bomb, 100,000 killed? Our day was coming for sure, maybe not today but soon. Was this the end of the six months? Or was it the beginning of the last six months?

To our amazement we did not go to work the following day. The rice ration was increased and the soup had a little more substance in it. Captain Fleming was again called to report to Lt. Asaka. The Japanese newspaper was spread on the table, the interpreter was there, the cigarette and the tea were served. Lt. Asaka opened the conversation, "They did it again, they bombed Nagasaki!" Captain Fleming had no idea of what was happening and left shortly afterward, leaving a very confused and puzzled Japanese Lieutenant. Captain Fleming discussed the conversation with the officers. Lt. Pullen, a graduate chemical engineer, said, "That's it, it must be an atomic bomb! They split the atom several years ago at Berkeley!"

The following day, Lt. Asaka was summoned to district headquarters at Sendai. He returned on the 15th of August and immediately summoned the American officers. Shortly afterwards we were called out for assembly in the open area of the camp. Even the ambulatory men from the hospital were there. Something big was about to happen. We stood at ease waiting in eager anticipation. Lt. Asaka mounted a box and addressed us in Japanese. The interpreter translated. The lieutenant seemed subdued and spoke as though he was embarrassed and under great emotional strain. He said, "The war is over, Japan has surrendered, you are now free men again." When he finished, he turned to Col. Walker and Captain Fleming and saluted, stepped down and went to his quarters without a word. To a Japanese officer this was one of the most difficult and embarrassing duties he ever had to perform. Lt. Asaka took it as a gentleman, an officer in the Imperial Japanese Army, with complete obedience to the Emperor.

Lt. Col. Walker and Captain Fleming then addressed us. **"The war is over, Japan has surrendered."** Five-hundred-forty-two Americans and British ex-prisoners of war spontaneously broke out in loud cheers. Sheer pandemonium—men were hugging one another, slapping each other on the back, with tears running down their faces and all trying to talk at once. The men were savoring the sweet taste of joyous freedom. The long three years and four months of pent up emotions flowed like honey. How sweet it is! God Bless America!

Lt. Col. Walker called for order. The men relaxed and listened with bright eyes, beaming faces and beating hearts. Captain Fleming said, "Men, the war is over. We are going home. However, our orders from supreme headquarters, Allied forces are to remain here until we are ordered to leave. We are to assume all guard posts with Japanese rifles. We are now subject to military authority and the military code of justice. We are not to leave this camp unless duly authorized. The food rations will be increased and the bathhouse will be open 24 hours a day. There will be no more work at the mine. We are waiting for orders. Relax and enjoy your new freedom. Dismissed."

The entire camp was shouting, talking, congratulating each other. It was like a football game where the home team had just won an upset victory.

We returned to the barracks and began to celebrate, circulate, and find friends in other sections. The camp became a seething mass of men rushing here and there. Each man seemed to pass the guard house on purpose several times. Each would glance at the American guard shack and smile at the **American guards**. No bowing at rigid attention. They seemed to say, "No more slapping, no more beatings, no more humiliation. We are free and are going home."

The cooks started to serve larger meals and put a little more solids in the soup. Captain Fleming in a taped interview, said, "I asked Lt. Asaka for a steer and 500 pounds of vegetables." It was great to feel stuffed. The unlucky ones, who had jawbone rice coming from others went out of business. The lucky ones who owed jawbone rice had their debts cancelled.

The Japanese enlisted men were sent away to somewhere else in the district. The Japanese officers and the non-commissioned officers were to remain and assist the Americans and serve as liaison with the Japanese forces, until orders were received to move out. The Japanese officers and NCOs had not mistreated anyone other than the

STATEMENT

Peace! Peace comes to the world again. It is a great pleasure for me. To say nothing of you, to announce it is for all of you to know The Japanese Empire acknowledged the Terms of the suspention of hostilities given by the American Government. Even though these two Nation do not still reach the best agreement of a truce. As a true friend from now I am going to do my best in the future for the convenience of your own life in this camp because of having been able to get friendly relations between them and also the Japanese Government has declined her own National policy for your Nation. Therefore I hope that you will keep as comfortable a daily life by the orders of your own officers from today while you are staying here. All of you will surely get much gladness in returning to your own country. At the same time one of my wishes for you is this, "your health and happieness calls upon your life hence - forth and they will grow up happier and better by the honour of your country in order to guard your life. I have been endeavouring my ability. Therefore you will please cooperate with me in any way more than usual. I hope I enclose the statement in letting you know now that Peace - Peace already has come.

Translated message given by Lt. Asaka, Japanese Imperial Army announcing the end of the war on 15 August, 1945.

slapping when rules were not followed. None of the men showed any inclination for revenge. The only ones who might have been in danger were a couple of the honchos and some of the guards from the camps in the Philippines. The attitude towards the remaining Japanese attested to their conduct for the past year.

Five days of revelry, happiness, just plain relaxing, bathing, washing clothes and planning for the future were the order of the day. Talking and dreaming of the things we wanted to do when we got home. We were jubilant, ecstatic with happiness. Words cannot describe the luxury of being free. Now the only thing was to be home in the land of the truly free. The only ones who can understand the meaning of the word, are those who have lost, or never had freedom and it is suddenly theirs.

The men were allowed considerable freedom. Walking trips were arranged along with swimming parties in the nearby river. Several men were allowed to go to the village of Hanawa. One group of men arranged to have their photo taken by a local photographer. Lt. Asaka was there and posed with them. The lieutenant paid for the photo and gave each man a copy of the photo.

The supremacy attitude of the Japanese military towards the prisoners of war had been harsh, demanding, cruel, insensitive and had required unquestionable obedience. The prisoners were resentful, depressed, intimidated, helpless and deprived of all human rights. The announcement by the emperor of Japan of the acceptance of the surrender demands was accepted by the people without question or dissent. The supremacy attitude was changed 180 degrees overnight. The Japanese people and the military would bow to the Americans and were completely servile in every respect.

We had been told to mark the barracks with a big "POW" on the roof in order for airplanes to easily locate us. On the 21st of August we saw our first American plane; a navy torpedo bomber which circled the camp and wagged his wings. We could see the two men waving to us. What a sight, six big beautiful planes, real, honest to God, American planes. God, we hadn't seen one since Bataan had fallen on the 9th of April, 1942. The officers had one of the navy signal men fashion a crude signal light from a stove pipe and a shaving mirror for signaling. The signal man sent a message

Fifteen newly liberated Americans enjoy a trip into Japanese village. Lt. Asaka paid for photos for each man. Courtesy of Brownell Cole.

to the plane for medicines. One pilot circled the camp and came in low, flying the long way, parallel to the barracks. The canopy slid open and a note was dropped to us. The note was delivered to the officers. Word was passed for everyone to get in the barracks. They were going to drop rations.

The planes circled around and came in from the west. Slowly he descended and a large package with a small chute hurtled from the underside. A second plane could be seen coming in with more following. Each of the planes dropped their packages in the 350 x 30 foot space between the barracks and the bath house. The leader then circled and dropped another note indicating they would return in about four hours.

The rations dropped by the planes were a new type of ration, K rations, ten in one, enough food for one meal for ten men. The cooks lost no time in breaking out the rations and preparing a meal with **real** meat, butter, cheese and other goodies. We stuffed ourselves to the point of stupefaction. We just laid around and enjoyed the feeling of satisfaction from a swell banquet. The only thing missing was a snifter of brandy and a good cigar. Real coffee and tailor-made American cigarettes were just as good. We were living in high cotton and thoroughly enjoying the long forgotten nice things of life. Even honest-to-goodness toilet paper.

The torpedo bombers returned before dark and dropped two duffle bags of magazines and newspapers. The bags also contained another note. In three days, B-29s would come and drop more rations, medicines and clothing. One of the items in the duffle bags was the *Honolulu Advertiser* dated only three days before. The men sat up late reading aloud every word to those who did not have a magazine or newspaper. It was like a teacher reading an exciting story in school. Everyone hung on each word and commented on various points—who was leading in the pennant races, what was happening in the world news fronts. Many stayed awake until the wee hours of the morning, just to get something they could hold in their hands and read for themselves.

The huge B-29s came in two days later and circled the camp searching for a suitable spot to drop their cargo. They came in from the south, lined up on a long row of rice fields and dropped to about 600 feet. Slowly the huge plane with its bomb bays open approached the drop zone. Huge oblong bundles tumbled out and the parachutes opened. They were multi-colored and beautiful to see. The cargo landed with a spray of mud and grass. We sat on the hill and watched as the others came in and discharged their precious cargo. The B-29s were a fantastic sight. We had never seen such a large aircraft.

After the planes had gone, practically the whole camp made for the fields to gather the harvest. The oblong objects were three 55-gallon oil drums welded together. Some of the parachutes had not opened and the contents spewed out the end from concussion. The barrels were filled with everything that someone thought we would need. Medicine, canned peaches, pears, boxed raisins, pork and beans, sugar, flour, beef stew, chicken, cocoa, chocolate candy bars, chewing gum, canned peanuts, clothing, underwear, socks, shoes, undershirts, toothpaste, soap, razor blades, razors, combs and cigarettes.

It was like walking into a grocery store with an open account. The ruptured drums with their contents burst open was a feast. A one-gallon can of peaches with the syrup blown out with beautiful yellow peach halves waiting to be eaten. The men were making pigs of themselves and would pay the price the next day. The doctors passed the word not to overeat and to take it easy; there would be plenty for all. After the first binge, the men settled down to work. The whole camp turned out. We worked all afternoon lugging the supplies into camp. Even some of the Japanese farmers furnished carts and helped to round up the supplies. The hard day's work was a pleasure.

Details had been formed to receive and sort out the multitude of supplies. The food was carried to the galley, medicines to the medics, clothing was put in the Japanese storeroom. The B-29s returned three days later with more supplies. They must have emptied the quarter masters warehouse somewhere. Our cooks were having a field day. Each meal was better than the last. They continued to serve steamed rice, but soon they could not give it away.

One of the items that we really put to use was powdered DDT. The label said it was an insect repellent. The POWs were filling their stomachs and feeding DDT to the fleas and lice in the tatamis and blankets. Let's share with our bed pals. The rags that we had been wearing for so long were burned and roasted with a lot of our over-friendly lice.

The new freedom from work, the free time and the constant eating were beginning to put some weight on the men. Colonel Walker and Captain Fleming ordered close-order drill during the day to burn up some of the new energy, and give the men some exercise. Our senior non-commissioned officers soon had everyone out in close order drill. We did not take it seriously, but went through the motions.

The rich American food, the laying around talking and thinking of the new life ahead, stirred memories of the charms of the opposite gender. These thoughts had been dormant so long they were almost forgotten. One could say that in the spring a young man's fancy turns to romance. It was not spring, but they had missed several springs. The long forgotten sexual desires began to stir in several of the men. They were worried that three years abstinence had stunted or killed their sexual capability. The story goes that a few found an outlet for their curiosity in the village geisha house.

A Criminal Investigation Team accompanied by a Japanese guide and a Signal Corp's photographer arrived in early September. Their mission was to take pictures of the camp and file a report on the conditions of the camp and the prisoners. They were the first Americans we had seen in the past three years and four months who were not prisoners of war. The men crowded around them like they were from another planet. After completion of their mission, they told us to hang tough and wait for orders to leave the camp.

We became restless and wanted to get out of the camp. No word had come from supreme headquarters except to remain where we were until orders were received. We had relaxed,

Hanawa

Happy liberated ex-prisoners of war in Camp No. 6, Hanawa, Japan, with the first liberating Americans to arrive in camp after the cease fire.

eaten heartily and had new clothing. The fleas and lice had been eliminated and we were growing eager and impatient with the waiting to start the journey home. Captain Fleming and the other officers prevailed on Lt. Asaka to get a train up to the rail head and put the show on the road. A train was lined up on the tracks at Hanawa on September 10th. A feast was prepared for the evening meal. We packed up our new clothes and a few other possessions, dressed up in khaki pants, shirts and shined shoes, cleaned up the barracks and burned the last rags along with any pests that remained. Lt. Asaka, Sgt. Takahashi, Sgt. Sagai and other Japanese NCOs had orders to accompany us to the nearest port.

About 2200 hours, we formed up under our section leaders, and with our officers leading the way, we marched out of Camp Number 6 for the last time. Eight men were assigned to carry the eight small boxes with the cremated remains of our comrades, who had died during our stay in Hanawa. Two men carried a footlocker filled with Japanese yen and medical records.

The yen was the pay of the POWs for their labor at Mitsubishi Mining Company and had been deposited to our account. Colonel Walker and Captain Fleming had gone to the bank and withdrew all the yen. The mine had paid 10 percent to the men each month and the balance due had been deposited in the bank.

Our hearts were light and our faces beamed with joy as we walked down the road in a column of four abreast. A few Japanese civilians watched silently and bowed as we passed. We did not have a band to send us off. Each man's heart was beating out the cadence like a drum for the marching feet. Five-hundred-forty-two exuberant men shed the shackles of gloomy imprisonment and marched into the bright moonlight of freedom, happiness and anticipation. This was the beginning of the long journey home. Each was thankful to God for our survival of the long march through the shadow of death. We had feared no evil and had never lost our hopes and faith in our country, our God and ourselves. We were the fortunate survivors of the ordeal of being a prisoner of war in an Oriental country for three years and four months.

The not so fortunate were the sick, injured or those on the brink of death from disease. They would soon pass on from the residuals of disease, malnutrition and mistreatment, or face a long recovery ordeal. The unfortunate were the legions who lost their lives in the prison camps or the hell ships. At this time we were not aware of the loss of thousands of men who died after our trip on the Noto Maru. We were to learn, during our processing at different points, how fortunate we had been to be shipped on the Noto Maru. Praise be to God and Lady Luck.

A long train with a steam engine was waiting at the Hanawa station. The column of men lined up beside the cars and started boarding. We didn't care if we were crowded or not. A sleeping car was provided for the officers and coach cars for the men. The train was loaded without any tenko. Certainly no one would miss this train! The sick men were put into a separate car with the medics. We were ready for the over night journey to the coast. The engineer blew his whistle and the exuberant group of men settled down contentedly, as we rolled off into the night. Some dropped asleep and others conversed with their seat mates or munched on some goodies. We were going home and we were very happy and thankful to be alive. Prayers were said for the many friends who were not with us. We prayed that they were safe and on their journey to freedom from other camps.

The long night gave us the opportunity to review some of our experiences and to evaluate the consequences on our lives. One of the amazing things that had occurred was the change of attitude of the Japanese civilians and their military forces. Practically overnight the Americans had became guests of the Japanese government. Only days before, we had been the serfs and slaves of the Japanese government.

The Japanese supremacy attitude towards the American prisoners of war, up to the dropping of the atomic bomb, was harsh, suppressive and demanded unquestionable obedience. This attitude caused the Americans to feel resentful, depressed, demoralized and impotent to resist the hopeless existence under the severe conditions of the camps. The announcement by the Japanese Emperor of the surrender terms was accepted by the Jap-

Tables turned at Japanese Prison Camp.

anese people without question or dissent. The difference in attitude was like daylight and dark. The same guards who would have slapped you for not bowing were now bowing to the Americans. They were like gracious hosts and completely servile in all respects.

This was difficult to understand for the Americans. There were instances where derogatory remarks were passed and explicit epithets expressed. However, there were no incidents of suppressed feelings towards any specific Japanese. We were amazed in the Dr. Jeckel and Mr. Hyde change. For the most part, we accepted it without question and without trying for retribution on the Japanese people per se. There were some instances that

we could recall where certain prisoners would have liked to extract revenge on some of the guards. However, the guards were not here in Japan.

There have been many hypothetical theories advanced of how man can endure long periods of starvation, mistreatment, brutality, disease, depression, humiliation, isolation and separation from loved ones. The ordeal which the men, women and even children endured in the internment and prison camps has been chronicled in many publications. Many of our people have forgotten or do not care to read of the unpleasantness of that era. The few movies or television documentaries have gilded the truth in fiction designed for viewer entertainment. A good example was the documentary on the story of the nurses in the Philippines. All the nurses who saw this television documentary were appalled at its duplicity and false impressions.

The question remains. How did these men, women and children survive the terrors of endless incarceration? Many psychiatrists have studied the phenomena and many theoretical conclusions have been published. One psychiatrist at a Veterans Administration hospital attempted to determine why some came home and how they coped with the stress. After many interviews he was asked what his conclusions were. "In a nut shell, they never gave up hope," was his reply.

An article appearing in *Reader's Digest*, *Robin's Readers*, entitled, *Holding on to Hope* is indicative of how the POWs and internees never gave up hope.

Holding On To Hope

Medical studies have proven how **hope** sustains many human beings and allows them to incur incredible pain and punishment. The dictionary defines **hope** as a confidant expectation. So it is not just wishful thinking or blind optimism, but a real gut level belief that the situation will get better and eventually pass into history.

A lesson in **hope** can be learned from the experiences of 20,000 American soldiers held captive by the Japanese during World War II. These men had to live under terrible conditions and endure inhumane treatment. Some died, while others lived to return home. There was not a great deal of difference in the physical stamina in those who lived and those who died.

The survivors, however, confidently expected to be released sometime in the future. They talked about the home they would have, of the jobs they would choose and even described the type of person they would like to marry. They drew pictures on the prison walls to illustrate their dreams. Some even found ways to study the subjects relative to the kind of career they would pursue. The doctors who were taken captive even formed medical societies.

It is this kind of hope which keeps us pushing ahead, learning new skills, going after another job or recovering from a serious illness. It is this kind of **hope** that makes us try a different road if the one we are on is leading nowhere. It is also the kind of **hope** that sustains us when we are told there is no **hope**. Because no matter what our ears hear, what really matters is the **hope** that is in our hearts.

CORREGIDOR

OASIS OF HOPE

PART SEVEN

THE FREEDOM TRAIN

Part Seven

The Journey To Freedom

Early in the morning of the 10th of September, we pulled into the station at Sedai. We were switched on to the tracks leading to Shinagawa, a sea port on the coast, where there were American ships in the harbor. A short ride up the line, the train pulled in to the port area on a siding and stopped. Everyone was crowded up to the windows, each wide-eyed and looking for signs of the American forces.

The order was passed to unload and form up on the pier. American military police were standing along the side of the train. An American officer, who seemed to be in charge, discussed the procedure with our officers. Off loading and the waiting in ranks was a pleasure. Our eyes were on everything about us. American military police were most interesting. Different uniforms, weapons, vehicles and the ships in the harbor were from another world. The word was passed to stand by, loading on landing barges would start shortly.

The Japanese military personnel were marched away by the military police for detention and investigation. We were standing, awaiting orders, when someone said, "Look there is our flag." The 1,084 eyes swung to view our American flag, There were tears of joy in those 1,084 eyes, our hearts were pounding and we were choked with emotion as we gazed at our symbol of **Freedom**, of **America**. Captain Fleming, in a taped interview with Adrian Martin in 1985, was telling of this precious moment. His voice began to crack and his words were, "I still choke up with emotion at the thought of that moment of seeing our flag, even after 40 years have passed."

We glanced around us while we waited for the word to board a boat. The hustle and bustle of the American military getting the loading preparations on what, when, where and how we were to be processed. Moored to the dock was a dark gray vessel with its flag flying in the morning sun. It was a strange looking craft. Certainly we had never seen anything like it. It was about a hundred feet long with an open waist, a ramp like device at the bow and the bridge set back near the stern. We were frankly curious and asked an American what type of vessel it was? He replied, "That is a landing ship-tank (LST). It is used for amphibious landings over the beach." We were very much impressed. Looking out in the harbor, we could see a large ship with a huge Red Cross painted on its side. Someone asked, "What ship is that?" A sailor replied, "That is the hospital ship, *Relief*." Again our thoughts turned back to the prison ship, *Noto Maru*, which had no Red Cross markings.

The men were all goggle-eyed and watched in amazement: the new equipment, the nonchalance of the few Japanese in the dock area, and the businesslike manner of handling our group by the Americans. Only a few weeks ago no one in their wildest notions would have guessed that here, in Northern Japan, the two countries were working in the interest of the American ex-prisoners. The Emperor must have a powerful influence on the Japanese people. They were very cooperative, courteous, bowing every time an officer approached.

The loading process began about 1000 hours. We started loading into the waist of the LST. The entire 492 Americans and 50 British soldiers were standing in the waist. The LST slipped its moorings and pulled out from the pier, headed for the hospital ship, *Relief*.

Speculation ran rife, we are going home on a hospital ship! Boy, this is beyond belief, that we could be so lucky. We would have been glad to leave on anything that was headed for home.

The LST eased up on the starboard side of the *Relief* and a gang plank was lowered. We began to pass through a section in the forward part. A naval officer with a loud speaker called "Attention on deck. All prisoners of war who are ambulatory and are able to proceed without medical care will form on the right. Those who are sick and in need of immediate medical care will step forward. Those on stretchers and unable to walk will be taken to the sick bay."

We assembled as ordered and a navy medical men told us, "You are to go through an open door and remove all of your clothing, including your packs and duffle bags. Any personal gear was to be placed in a bag that is to be handed to you as you pass through the door."

The men began moving towards the passage way and could be seen stripping down to their birthday suits. A medical officer was supervising and looking the men over for possible treatment. After undressing and putting our personal possessions in a blue bag, under the watchful eye of a navy petty officer, we stepped into a delousing shower and on the opposite side were issued new clothing. Another ship was on the portside. It was a ship that was new to us—an attack transport. Boy, this navy has everything, we thought as we stepped on deck and were sent below to what would be our quarters for the trip to utopia.

We didn't give a damn where it was going, we were there for the ride and could care less. Comfortable bunks, warm quarters, plenty of water for showers and the navy was supposed to feed good. Hell man, we are on our way home, I'll ride anything and not complain!

The processing through the hospital ship was soon completed and our transport pulled away with its cargo of happy ex-prisoners of war. There are not enough words to express our feelings as the ship eased out of the harbor and headed on a southerly course. Going on deck as the ship was getting underway, Kunich, Haddox, Golson and I wandered around the deck and watched the Japanese mainland disappear in the mist. We were like four men on a luxury liner on a cruise to paradise. The only thing missing were American **round eyes**. We stood on deck and pinched ourselves to see if it was real. What a sensational feeling, we were under way on a United States Navy ship with the national colors waving proudly from her stern. My mind

flicked back to the last time I had gazed on a scene like this. It was as we were steaming out of San Francisco on the *USAT Meigs* in July 1939. I had taken a photo of the San Francisco Bay Bridge with the flag in the foreground. Will I be able to sail under the bridge again on my return? I could tell my grandchildren how I came full circle.

The ships bells were sounding the time and we made for the galley. Chow down, the galley was ready to give us our first meal at sea. We piled in and grabbed a tray, silverware and a china cup and went through the line cafeteria style. No more beat up army mess gear or quan buckets, real tables and stools with white salt, black pepper and beautiful white sugar. I was afraid I took more than I could eat, but managed to stow it away slowly. A big mug of navy java and a pipe loaded with Half & Half topped off a perfect lunch. Everyone was talking to the crew members and to friends. The galley was a bedlam of men talking about everything. I just sat and savored the excitement of the moment.

The afternoon passed slowly and we relaxed and enjoyed everything in sight. The captain announced the galley would be open to anyone and the smoking lamp was lit. The four of us headed down and ordered a big bowl of ice cream, cookies and coffee. This was the dream life as we sat in the galley and filled up on the best tasting ice cream in the world. We had dreamed about all of the goodies for so long, that we had almost forgotten what it would taste like. We made our way back to the quarters for a nap or to read some of the magazines the crew had provided.

We had a lot of reading to catch up on, I was able to read *Time, Newsweek* and *Life*. My eyes had not improved but was able to look at the pictures and headlines and a few of the interesting articles. The men were talking to the crew and hearing about the war and how it had been with them the past three years. Each was learning from the other and sharing information. We were so starved for news of home and the new world.

Our ship steamed on through the night and I went to bed in a nice clean bunk with no bed bugs, fleas or lice to disturb me. I felt content with a full stomach, no serious illnesses and only impaired vision, that hopefully, would improve with proper diet and vitamins. I fell asleep to the throbbing of the ships propeller shaft with a prayer of thankfulness that I was one of the lucky ones.

The ships bells signaled the hour and the mess call was piped through the loud speakers. I was on deck and headed for the galley at 0600 hours. It was a great feeling to pass through the chow line and load up with a plate of fried eggs, bacon and pancakes with real butter and syrup. A couple of cups of steaming hot coffee and a Camel cigarette and I was as happy as a bug in a rug. Haddox and I wandered out on deck and enjoyed the fresh air and the warm rays of the sun. We were coming in close to the mainland and could see the outline of the coast. The people there must be feeling better now that the air raids had stopped and they could begin to rebuild their homes and lives. The scuttlebutt was that our ship was headed for Yokohoma and soon we were in the harbor and easing into a pier. We could see the effects of the bombings. Many areas were completely burned out. The pier we were docking at seemed to be in fair shape. The roof was intact and we could see into the immense pier the many Americans waiting to process us.

The processing began immediately after docking. Everything was orderly and the interviewers were lined up at desks. Each desk was marked with a letter of the alphabet. We were instructed to line up alphabetically at a desk. I made my way over to the desk with the letter N and waited my turn. I waited patiently until I was asked to be seated for an interview. Name, rank, serial number, unit, home of record, next of kin, date captured, camp assignments during captivity, and other pertinent information. I was handed a form to complete for a radiogram to be sent to the next of kin, notifying them I had returned to American control and would be returning to the states in the near future.

After initial processing, the next station was an officer who was interested in developing information in regards to knowledge of specific instances of torture, beatings and circumstances of the incident. Having no knowledge of any serious incidents, I was asked one question that startled me. The officer asked, "Do you know Sergeant John David Provoo?" I replied, "Yes, he had been in Camp Number 9 on Corregidor, from May 1942 until he had been shipped out in late 1942." The officer then asked, "Do you have knowledge of his conduct during that time?" I then said, "He had not associated with the 500 Americans and had worked in the Japanese kitchen. And he conducted Buddhist rites on the upper veranda each morning and evening." He wrote down my name, rank and service number and then excused me.

After completion of the processing, we were allowed to go over to the Red Cross reception area for refreshments and a chance to see a real honest to goodness **round eyes**. **Round eyes** was an expression in the Philippines by soldiers for a white woman. Slant eyes was used as a slang word for an Oriental woman. We had not seen any white women since before the war unless we had an occasion to be in one of the hospitals on Bataan or Corregidor. The Red Cross girls were friendly and a little curious about these strange men whom they had heard of only through the news. We were as interesting to them as they were to us. It was like sweet music to hear their laughter and voices. We were also interested in where their homes were. It was easy to determine those from the south by their accents. What a time we were having just listening to an American woman after almost six years. It made me think of the girls I left behind in Texas.

Captain Fleming had the problem of what to do with the yen he had collected from the bank in Hanawa. This money had been the wages paid by Mitsubishi to the prisoners of war for their labor. The officers discussed what should be done with the money. It was concluded that it had very little dollar value and the decision was made to give it to the American Red Cross through the authorities in charge of the processing.

The officers also had the dilemma of what to do with the eight white boxes containing the ashes of the eight deceased men. The boxes were turned over to the American officials for return to the next of kin in the United States. Unfortunately and with normal foul up the boxes were put into a warehouse in Yokohoma.

Adrian Martin, New London Wisconsin, is

a nephew of First Sergeant Adrian Martin of the 200th AA Battalion. In researching material for a book on his uncle, he learned that the cremated remains were found in a warehouse in Yokohoma. The *Chicago Tribune* in October of 1945 had an article on this apparent foul-up. Adrian's book, *Brothers From Bataan* has been completed and is available at most book stores.

After processing and social chats with the Red Cross canteen girls, we returned to the ship and found we had picked up additional passengers. A group of Dutch prisoners of war, captured in the Dutch East Indies, were to continue the journey south. Scuttlebutt had it that we were going to Manila. Holy Mackerel! Back to where we started from. We had a screening by medical personnel and were found to be in good enough shape to travel by surface transportation. A few had been pulled out for aerial evacuation.

Our ship sailed late in the evening for the Philippine islands. A dramatic difference in our living conditions on our trip north on the *Noto Maru*. We were all in better health, had gained weight, and most important we were not packed like a bunch of sardines into a stinking filthy hold. We had hot water for bathing and flush toilets and could remain on deck as long as we liked and visit the galley at any time. Lots of hot coffee and plenty of tobacco, when the smoking lamp was lit. This was a wonderful way to travel, almost like a cruise ship except without the parties and refreshments.

The Dutch ex-prisoners of war were extremely happy about going home. However, they were greatly concerned with the conditions they would find in the home islands. Many of them had families, some of whom had been put into internment camps in the Dutch Indies. They were overwhelmed at issues of clothing and some were extremely greedy. They could come into the galley at meal times or anytime they wanted and eat all they could hold. That was to be expected after almost four years as Japanese prisoners of war. However, they would empty all the condiments into bags and carry them back to their quarters. They were regular pack rats. The navy finally got tired of that and only gave them what they could put on their mess

gear. The condiments were put out of reach of the pack rats. One Dutch soldier, when he boarded the ship in Yokohoma, had three duffle bags crammed with clothes and shoes. I have often wondered how he carried it all and if he ever got home with all that loot.

Our ship had swung out into the channel and soon we could only see the silhouetted Japanese mainland. There was little to be seen so we made our way down to the galley and waited for the evening chow call. There was so much to talk about with the sailors and our friends. The tales of the sailors were very interesting. Several of them had been in the western Pacific for several years and had been aboard ships during the invasions of Okinawa, Luzon and Leyte. We sat enthralled when they talked about the hundreds of ships that made the invasion of Okinawa. Their stories of the kamikasi planes were almost unbelievable. We realized that the Japanese were capable of such sacrifices, as volunteers they were willing to die for the Emperor. Japanese soldiers had told us how they were considered dead when they left Japan. The only honorable way to return was either victorious or in a little white box. This was known as the warrior code of the Samurai.

The evening meal and the conversation had gone by swiftly and we decided to go on deck and enjoy the sea breezes before turning in. We had heard scuttle butt that it would be about a six or seven day trip from Yokohoma to Manila. Just to be able to be on deck and see the stars overhead and feel the powerful engines purring along through the night was a delight in itself. We were thoroughly enthralled with our new freedoms and the realization that we had survived. The sensation of not having to face the uncertain days in the mines, the eternal fight for poor food, no medical supplies, cold quarters with vermin and the fear of severe illness were now in the past. We had much time to make up for the past three and one-half years.

The days passed rapidly and we just relaxed as if we were on a luxury cruise. Movies, cribbage, reading, daydreaming and meal time with walks on deck and watching the ship's crew go about their work occupied our time. We were looking forward to our arrival in Manila Bay and the Philippines. The sight of them would bring back many poignant memories of happier days and of sorrowful memories of our many friends who had not been so fortunate to have survived.

The great day, September 18, 1945, was here. We would be passing into Manila Bay about 1000 hours. The ex-prisoners hurriedly finished off a grand navy breakfast and headed for a spot on deck. We were anxious to see the Bataan Pennisula and Corregidor as the ship made her way into Boca Chica Channel. The Spanish referred to the channel as Boca Chica (Little Mouth) and the U.S. had always referred to it as the North Channel. Land ahoy! Port quarter was heard as Bataan began to appear in the morning light. The men became animated, pointing and shouting to their friends as we neared the channel and could see the barrio Mariveles on our left. Sailors from the USS Canopus were straining their eyes to see if they could spot their ship where it had been scuttled in Mariveles Harbor in April of 1942. Other men were staring at the dark jungle and mountains of Bataan and recalling the horrors of the siege of Bataan and the horrendous death march to Camp O'Donnell. Many of then had started the long march from Mariveles. I was high enough to see both sides of the channel and my memories flashed back to Bataan and to Corregidor. It was incredible, but the fact was that all of us had managed to survive and be able to relive those months of toil, sweat, hunger, sickness and the horrors of war.

Slowly, our cruise ship made its way past these two historic points with forward lookouts posted, searching for drifting mines. Corregidor was like a ravaged maiden, who had suffered the humiliation of invasion, defeat and surrender, twice in the past three and a half years. Now she was lying there, in the tropical sun, recovering her dignity as she proudly covered the scars and shame with new foliage, waiting for the future. Would she ever serve as a formidable fortress again or lapse into obsolescences and history as the silent victim of technology. Perhaps she would become a national park, a national shrine to those valiant men who had known her in her glory. A place that the veterans could return in their golden years and tell their grandchildren about?

With memories flashing past, our ship entered Manila Bay. A little over a year ago I had sailed for Japan down in the hold of the Noto Maru. Now I was on deck and could see the bay in its entirety. It looked like we were passing through a swamp where drowned trees stuck up out of the water. No, it was not trees, it was ship masts. There seemed to be hundreds of them. One of the sailors explained that the navy carrier planes had caught many ships in the harbor and sunk them. Literally the bay was like a forest of telephones poles set on small islands.

I recalled how Admiral George Dewey had sailed into Manila Bay and caught the Spanish Fleet off shore from Cavite. When the smoke cleared the Spanish ships were beached or sunk off the Manila shoreline. Two of the ships hulk's were still visible along Dewey Boulevard before the war. The sight of so many ships resting on the bottom was impressive and one that cheered our hearts. From all accounts of the men who had carried the battle from Australia, General MacArthur had indeed kept his promise: "I shall return."

There was much evidence of the terrific pounding by American navy aerial attacks on the port area and the harbor. Our Assault Transport pulled into Pier 7 and preparations were made for us to debark. I stood there on deck and reflected on our return to Manila at the same pier that we had left from only a year ago in August. It struck me as ironic. What a difference in our situation from poverty to riches in a year.

Waiting on the street outside of the roofless pier was a long stream of military vehicles. We filed off the ship and boarded the trucks. They pulled away from the port area. The surrounding area was drastically changed, many buildings were burnt or destroyed by the fighting for the city. The Filipinos appeared to have improved dramatically since we had marched down to the pier in 1944. In every direction there were American army vehicles dashing about. There appeared to be many more Filipinos about and they were moving hurriedly in their new freedom. Our convoy swung on to Rizal Avenue and headed towards the Luneta, passing the Manila Hotel and the Army-Navy Club and on to Dewey Boulevard and then F.B. Harrisoo Boulevard.

138

The area did not look as it had in the past. Many of the beautiful palm trees along the side of the road had been blasted out during the recapture of Manila. We were like a bunch of tourists as we eagerly pointed out various sights, landmarks and places of interest. We passed the road to Nichol's Field on the road to Pasay and turned off.

We had arrived at our destination, 29th Replacement Depot, a city of pyramidal tents in long orderly rows. A flagpole standing tall with an American flag flying in the breeze greeted us. Praise God, the United States and the thousands of service men who had fought their way through the South Pacific. General MacArthur had returned in strength and style. We unloaded and fell into ranks. A burly, tough-looking first sergeant stepped forward and gave us our instructions for billets, chow call and the rules of the command. One of the most important announcements was: "All officers and enlisted men will be able to draw a partial pay in the morning. Pass policy will be lenient pending shipping orders for the States. You are to pick out an empty tent, stow your gear and relax until chow call."

Everyone was shouting and whooping after dismissal. **Pay day!** How long had it been since we had heard that expression? Most of us had not drawn any pay since the first of December, 1941. Sergeants Kunich, Golson, Haddox and I, found an empty tent nearby and hastily stowed our gear and discussed what we would like to do. Could we go into Manila? How does one get into town? What would we find there? Were there any night clubs open? How great it would be to walk in and order a beer or a highball? How much were they going to allow on partial pay? How long would we be here in tent city? After much conjecture and discussion we decided to play it cool and wait. We had waited a long time and a little more waiting would not hurt. Supper time was called by bugle, "Come and get your chow, boys, come and get your chow." The old familiar tune was music to our ears. We had not heard that bugle call in a long time.

Chow was served on trays as none of us had kept our mess kits when we left Hanawa. We did not want to ever eat from a mess kit again or at least for a while. We lingered in the area

and enjoyed a couple cups of coffee and talked to a few of the men who had accumulated enough points to be eligible for rotation back to the states. There were stories of the many island battles during the sweep up from the south. Some of the places we had heard of through the rumors and occasionally from Nips. It would be interesting to know if the dates of the rumors coincided with the actual events. We also learned about the terrific battles waged for Leyte, Corregidor, Manila and Luzon. We were surprised to hear that Manila had been the site of a fanatic Japanese struggle to hold onto the Philippines.

We stuck around camp for the rest of the day and enjoyed ourselves with regular meals, sorting out our new uniforms, polishing shoes and brass. Now we began to feel like soldiers again. Letters could be written and mailed. The Red Cross canteen was nearby and more women to talk and joke with. A sight that also intrigued us was the WACs (Women's Army Corps), women soldiers. What had this army come to with women soldiers?

Tomorrow would be the big day, the day of the eagle, **pay day**. We had said good-bye in Yokohoma to our many friends from the navy and marine corps. They had been split up and were being processed through naval channels.

We were roused out of the sack at first call. After morning chores and donning clean uniforms—complete with new chevrons, insignia, polished shoes and brass—we proceeded to the chow tent and ate a hearty army breakfast, S.O.S. (creamed beef on toast), pancakes and fruit with lots of coffee. I stoked up my Wally Frank pipe and enjoyed a bowl of Half & Half. Wally had been a steady friend and was a little worse for wear and tear in the past three years. Strong as a draft horse and smelly as a stable, it had been my security blanket when times looked bleak and clouds of despair hovered overhead.

Somehow I would find a little tobacco for a few drags, and the clouds would disappear and I would look to a brighter tomorrow. I must have been like one of the Chinese opium smokers, floating in never-never land in complete abandon and disregarding the oppression of dismal and pervasive conditions of prison camp life.

At about 1000 hours a call came over the

loudspeakers, "**Pay formation!** Assembly in the company street." That was not difficult, we were waiting in eager anticipation of **pay** and a **pass**. The first sergeant stepped out and called for attention and proceeded to give us a warning about the dangers of Manila. No. 1: Do not buy any liquor, beer or other spirits from native venders. No. 2: Native-brewed spirits were known to cause blindness, retching and possible death. No. 3: Houses of prostitution were dangerous, both from a V.D. standpoint and a possibility of being given knockout drops, or slugged and robbed by bugaos (pimps). No 4: Remain with a buddy and do not go wondering off alone.

Hell, Manila had not changed much since we left in December of 1941, were my thoughts, as the sergeant outlined the pitfalls of the Pearl of the Orient. Our observation of Manila, as we traveled along the streets to the replacement depot, confirmed the reports of severe damage. The veterans of the battle for Manila had told us of the fierce house-to-house fighting and the suicidal defense by Japanese Imperial Marines and Naval forces.

After the lecture by the first sergeant, we lined up for pay call. The enlisted men were paid $300, NCOs and officers $600 in occupation script on account. This would be adequate for the time we were to be in Manila. None of the men had been paid since November 1941. We had no knowledge that our pay records had been sent by submarine to the United States by the finance office just before the fall of Corregidor. Final settlement would be made on arrival in the United States. The many changes in the pay structure during the time of incarceration had to be factored in the final settlement. Each man had been advanced one grade on return to U.S. control except master sergeants and colonels. They were made permanent grades.

Filled with the feeling of affluence and a pass, Haddox and I hitched a ride into Manila. Riding along in a jeep, we made our way into Manila and decided to start our tour of the area we had known before the war. The jeep dropped us off at the Luneta.

The normal sidewalk venders were scattered along the wide streets selling everything imaginable—balutes, GI clothing, native cookies, fruits, sweets, tobacco, and shoe shines. Hordes of children were hustling for cigarettes, chocolate, and gum. Evidently the new Americans had been generous as they were prone to be with children. There were bugaos by the dozens, even small boys hustling for their sisters, "Hey Joe, you like nice girl? My sister very nice, I know, I try myself." The term "Joe" had not changed as all the natives had called Americans "Joe" before the war. Everything was prefaced by "Joe."

Waving the hustlers away, we continued walking towards the port area, marveling at the number of sunken Japanese ships visible from the beach. The navy must have had a field day in sinking so many in the harbor. We could also see many U.S. Navy ships anchored in the bay. It was reminiscent of long ago when the puny Asiatic fleet was in port except for the number of ships.

The damage to the city was tremendous and thousands of the civilians had died. They had been trapped in tight spots between the opposing forces. The Filipinos who had fled the city had returned and were trying to put their homes in order or to rebuild new ones. The reconstruction of the homes was not as difficult as if it had been a western city. Many of the homes were of bamboo with thatched roofs and walls made from Nipa palm trees, without indoor plumbing or water. Water was drawn from a nearby central water faucet for cooking. Bathing was done at the faucet along with the washing. Cooking was done on a small clay slab with an open flame.

The better developed areas had sewers and water as the style of a western home. The majority of the homes were occupied by the lower class families. A small bahay (house) might be occupied by as many as 10 to 15 people—mothers, fathers, kids and relatives. Sleeping arrangements were banigs (straw mats) spread on the bamboo slats. The Filipinos would be able to exist, but labor income would have to feed the group. If a family group was fortunate to have one or two employed, this was their way of life. The girls who went into prostitution were generally supporting a family group.

We continued our walk around the walled city and could see the terrific damage that had occurred. The entire Intramuros, (walled city) had been the scene of intense fighting. The

Japanese had holed up in the fortress-like Intramuros and had to be dug out house by house. The book, *Retaking of the Philippines* by William B. Breuer, gives a picture of the horrors of the battle for Manila. We were appalled at the damage. We passed the Rizal Stadium which was another Japanese strong point. The legislative building had been cut in half by direct artillery fire and collapsed into a pile of rubble.

The fighting in Manila had occurred in January and February, 1945. Now in late September some evidence of rebuilding was apparent. The streets were open and rubble was being removed. The Philippine government would need massive aid and take years to recover from the terrible carnage and horrors of war.

The journey around the city was depressing and our sympathy for the Filipino people was uppermost in our minds on our return to the replacement depot. The comparison between 1940 and 1945 was drastic and almost unbelievable. We had known the city when it was a beautiful soldier's paradise.

We made it back in time to catch the evening meal. We did not desire to eat in any of the local cantinas or cafes. One never knew what might be edible or if it was even clean. One thing that was noticeable was that inflation had set in. A shoe shine by one of the hundreds of hustling boys had gone from 30 centavos to two pesos. A bottle of sarsaparilla was two pesos and Coca Cola was five pesos.

After chow we showered and cleaned up for a trip to see the night spots that we had noticed in the afternoon. Haddox, Golson, and I headed for a relatively clean looking place on F.B Harrison Boulevard near the Luneta. Patio lanterns were burning brightly and the place was crawling with GIs. A Filipino band was blaring out with some of the popular music. Most of the tunes we were not familiar with and a few were from pre-war days in Manila.

We were escorted to a table near the entrance and a waitress came to take our order. The problem was what to order and after considerable discussion with the waitress, we decided that we would buy a bottle instead of trusting the bar liquor. We asked for a pre-war sealed bottle of whiskey. Four Roses was available, guaranteed to be pure pre-war vintage, $45 or 90 pesos, plus mix and ice. We settled on that and a bottle was brought out by the waitress. A very close inspection of the seal was made before we said okay. Glasses, mix and ice were then brought out for another two pesos each.

Relaxing in our chairs and sipping our drinks, we watched the crowded dance floor and the "cheery boys." Cheery boys was a term used by the Filipina women for an American who was new to the Philippines. The soldiers were having a good time and a few of them departed with girls on their arms. The Americans had been in the fighting for Manila and some had moved on to Okinawa. Most of these men were service troops; some had enough points to return to the states and were having a bang-up time before they left. The three of us were leery of hitting the Roses too fast, as we did not know how it would affect us. It was about five miles to camp and we did not want to get so tipsy that we could not make it back to camp. Just to sit and listen to the music, sip a drink, light up a cigarette and eye the sultry dalagas was plenty of excitement for us. Finally we had enough and headed for the street to catch a vehicle going east to the camp. It had started to rain and we were soaking wet by the time a truck came along and gave us a lift. The night life in Manila had a lot more American customers and they were spending money like it grew on trees. We were ready for the sack. Don't be piggish and try to do everything in one night. Take it easy, Rome was not built in a day.

Reveille at 0600 hours brought us from a sound sleep and we headed for the showers. A simple thing like a hot shower and plenty of soap works wonders, a luxury we could now enjoy to our heart's content. Chow call sounded by the time we had dressed and we headed for another luxurious breakfast of S.O.S, a couple of cackle berries and good coffee. This was living, as we listened to some of the men complain about having S.O.S. again. Hell man, this meal is fit for a king. First a visit with the Round Eyes,(Red Cross girls), then I picked up a couple of donuts, a deck of cards and some paperbacks to read. Let's get this show on the road, we are ready and waiting. I thought, "There you go getting all sweated up and nothing to do but wait."

We had been alerted for shipment. After ten days of lounging and getting fat, we were eager to get started on the last leg of our journey.

A long line of trucks pulled in and lined up on the company street. Everyone piled their bags on board and climbed into the back. There must be 500 men or more, I thought, as I looked down the long line swinging out the main gate onto the road to Manila. It had stopped raining and the canvas covers were rolled up on the side. Everyone was turned looking out,watching and waving to the Filipinos as we moved along. Farewell Manila, we are going home. The old refrain came to mind:

So long boys, it's been nice to know you,
But I got to get rolling along.

Our truck convoy swung down to the waterfront and we could see the beautiful Manila Hotel on our left. The penthouse area at the top appeared to be blackened from fire during the struggle for the hotel during the recapture of Manila. General MacArthur had lived there before the war. Now he was in Tokyo as the Supreme Commander. Things had changed in many ways and we had been a part of it.

A large ship was tied up to the east side of Pier Seven and other ship's masts could be seen on the opposite side. The convoy swung into the cavernous-like roofless pier and we began to unload from the trucks. Looking up at the huge ship from the pier we could see some of the ship's officers looking down. The *S.S. Klipfontain* flying the colors of the Netherlands. Holy mackerel! This is all right —a luxury liner for the trip to Utopia. I would rather travel this way than to have been evacuated by air. Good food, clean bunks, salt air, stroll the decks like the big shots. Who could ask for anything more.

We started boarding and made our way forward to the area assigned the ex-prisoners of war. The returning high point veterans were assigned the after-section. Our four-man cabins were on the third deck. The cabins were tight but we had been in tighter cabins on the *Noto Maru.* Flush toilets and wash basins were unheard of luxuries. No human carpet to walk over, no stinking benjo bucket, plenty of fresh air and water. **No** sweating out air or submarine attacks. This would be the voyage to paradise and the real life of the American dream.

We had our health, our lives, our memories and in spite of efforts otherwise, we had endured and now we were going **home**! Glory Hallelujah. Praise the Lord and let's go on deck, the ship's whistle is blowing.

We made our way on deck and worked into a spot where we could see the dock and the crowd waving good-bye. An army band was lined up and playing "The Stars and Stripes Forever," "God Bless America" and "Bon Voyage." There were many women and children standing at the railing waving handkerchiefs and scarves. Must be first class passengers. This could be an interesting trip. The *S. S. Klipfontain* slipped her moorings and backed away from Pier Seven. The music, waving of hands and the excitement cast a euphoric spell on us. Our emotions ran wild inside our hearts. We were ecstatic and beaming with happiness. We are on our way. Someone pinch me, see if it is true, we are going home!

From our spot on deck, we could see the Pearl of the Orient. Mabuhay gallant Filipinos, you have your freedom, independence and now you have your own government. We wish you the best and may you have a happy and prosperous future. Mabuhay! Mabuhay! The ship began to swing and the panorama passed before our eyes as though we were panning a camera—Manila Hotel, the Luneta, Dewey Boulevard, the Army and Navy Club as the broad reaches of Manila Bay passed slowly. We could see the masts of many sunken ships sitting on the bottom of the bay. Scuttlebutt had it that there were 80 ships sunk in the bay.

Our navy must have had another Manila Bay victory, like Admiral Dewey on the day after he had sunk the Spanish Fleet in Manila Bay. Ships beached and sunk as far as the eye could see. The quiet order, "You may fire when ready, Mr. Gridley," must have been on the minds of the navy pilots as they attacked and sunk the Japanese ships.

We turned our heads south and strained to see the outline of Corregidor and Bataan. Eagerly we watched as we approached the Boca Chica Channel separating Bataan from Corregidor. Memories and emotions hit me, like the staccato notes of a drum. The small jungle covered island, looking so peaceful and innocent in the afternoon sun. Bataan off to the right, the mountains in the silhouette of the beautiful Princess Mariveles, sleeping where she could see her lover El Fraile (The Priest), Corregidor (the corrector or magistrate), her beautiful Caballo (horse) and her plodding Carabao. The old Filipino legend of the beautiful Princess Mariveles and the death of all who had helped her in her marriage to the priest. Banished from her home province by the angry people, they attempted to swim the channel and met their eternal death. Now perhaps the princess could tend the valiant ghosts of those who had fallen in these two beautiful serene tropical paradises.

Intense emotions cascaded like water through my mind as these scenes passed, of things not forgotten but still fresh and vivid; of the screams of the bombs, the incessant shelling, the smell of death, the bodies now buried in unmarked graves, the swarms of flies, the stench of the open latrines, the eternal thirst and hunger, the myriad of comrades in arms and friends who were among the dead and the living.

The contrast of memories of all that was good and the evil. The many hours of camaraderie, the fragrance of the gardenias, the old Spanish cannon, the fabulous sunsets, the quiet of the tropical nights, the soft call of the gekko lizards, with the entire sky illuminated by the stars, was like comparing black and white.

Bataan? Corregidor? Would they be forgotten by our children and grandchildren? Would history remember the sacrifices of the legions of Filipinos and Americans who fought and died here in two successive clashes of national ideologies. Such beautiful places, yet important to both antagonists. What were the lofty principles? Was freedom and independence important to the Filipinos? Yes, they had fought and died, though ill-equipped and untrained, with hope, fierce national pride and trust that the United States and General MacArthur would return. May the ghosts of Bataan and Corregidor haunt the future leaders of our country to never again sacrifice our young men and women by isolationism, negativism and an ostrich approach to the dangers of the world. Our freedom and the freedom of the world are at stake.

The ship broke her way through a slight swell and we were out into the China Sea headed in a south-easterly direction. On our right one could see the vague outline of the Island of Mindoro. A sparsely settled island and the home of the ill-tempered tamarao, a small wild water buffalo with short horns, that was without fear of man or beast. Our route would be through the Verde Straits into the Sibuyon Sea, Masbate Island and the Visayan Island group lying to the north of Minadanao and then to pass through the San Bernardino Straits. The passage would take us over the Minadanao Deep, the deepest water in the Pacific.

A call for volunteers to work in the first class galley was piped over the loudspeaker. Haddox and I had the same thought, chow, as we made for the spot indicated. Several others with the same idea beat us and were waiting. We lined up and a sergeant stepped out of a cabin and started taking the first ones in line. The last man was the one in front of me. "There goes our chance at a nice job," we said. We asked the sergeant if he had any other jobs. He replied, "Yes, I need two volunteers to work in the first class wardroom."

"We'll take it, what do we have to do?"

The sergeant said, "All you have to do is clean, sweep and make the beds." We volunteered on the spot.

After getting our instructions as to time and place, we headed for mess call. We were told that due to the number of troops and first class passengers there would be only two meals a day during the voyage. That was no problem, we had been there before. We didn't have to report for wardroom duty until the next morning so we relaxed and picked up some of the magazines and began to occupy the time.

Early the next morning after breakfast, we headed for our new duty station. We would rather be doing something than to lay around and get bored. We had no idea who the ward room occupants would be, but knocked on the door and a woman opened it. She asked us our business. We replied, "We are assigned to clean up the wardroom." She seemed surprised and invited us to come in. The room had about 12 doubled-decked bunks with innerspring mattresses. We introduced ourselves and she reciprocated by introducing us to the occupants.

Most of the group of women and children had been internees in Santa Tomas. Two were Filipino women married to servicemen and shipped to the states. One of the Filipinos had married an officer and was going to Madison, Wisconsin. The other had been married before the war and her husband had died in prison camp. She was going to New York to meet his family. One lady was a missionary, who had been captured in Borneo. She had gone to the Dutch East Indies with her newlywed husband as missionaries. They were stationed in the interior of Borneo, Dutch East Indies, when the war started. When they came down from the interior they were interned and shipped to the Philippines. Her husband had died in Santa Tomas and she was returning to her home in Iowa. The women and children were not well dressed. Their clothing was scrounged up by the Red Cross. They were probably hard up for cash and would have to start from scratch on arrival home.

We listened to them as we went about our chores. We were nervous as a long-tailed cat in a room full of rocking chairs and a little bashful. We had not spoken to a caucasian woman for years except the Red Cross workers we had met in Yokohoma and Manila. Their experiences paralleled ours and we felt sorry for them. We soon gained our confidence and enjoyed talking with them. One of them asked if we were hungry? She was going to the first class dining room and would bring us some rolls, milk and fruit. They were not on the two meals a day routine. This became the pattern for the voyage. We enjoyed being able to visit with them and listen to their trials and tribulations in the internment camp. Their experiences were not too much difference from ours. The main difference was that most of them did not have to work at manual labor except housekeeping chores associated with the welfare of the camp and working in the community gardens. Several of the internees have written excellent books on the two main internee camps, Santa Tomas and Los Banos, that are worthy of reading.

Our journey across the wide Pacific was one of languorous beauty and luxurious enjoy-

ment of the transition into the heady realities of freedom. No tenko, no koras, no slapping, no fear of being beaten for trivial cause, no slaving away in dark deep mines, no bowing to an arrogant guard, no more hunger, no deep longing for home; just euphoric happiness and sublime peace. Soon it would be back into the business of becoming a whole person again. Time for love of country, work, family, marriage and the pursuit of happiness.

Haddox, Golson and I shared in the goodies the ladies brought back and passed the time reading, walking the deck and staying away from the poker and crap sessions. The voyage was uneventful and enjoyable. We had heard that we would probably dock in San Francisco —the land of the Golden Gate and the gateway to a new life.

About six days out, our ship received a change of orders. We were to dock in Seattle. Our date of arrival in San Francisco would have been on Navy Day. San Francisco Bay was filled with naval vessels home from the war. The captain altered course for Puget Sound. Any old place was fine with us and no one complained a bit. There might have been a few who were disappointed but all were anxious to make port.

Our changed destination would put us into Seattle on Halloween Eve. The day before docking, the women of the wardroom held a small party for Haddox and myself. They had taken up a donation from the women and presented us with a beautiful cake, coffee and a small token gift. Bill and I were embarrassed at their generosity and thoughtfulness. We expressed our appreciation to them and wished each a very happy, healthy future. They were a real nice bunch of people and now they too, could start to rebuild their lives.

The good ship *S.S. Klipfontain* pulled into Puget Sound with the decks swarming with eager ex-prisoners of war, ex-internees and high point veterans. Everyone was esthetically happy and filled with emotion as we passed through the beautiful waters of the Puget Sound. Fantastic scenery, homes along the island hills, huge shipyards, heavy maritime activity and at last a long pier jutting out into the harbor. Tugs took us under tow and pushed the ship gently into the pier. A cheer

144

went up when the first hawser was secured to the dock.

Home Sweet Home, Be It Ever So Humble, There's No Place Like Home! Those words so beautifully expressed our feelings as we watched the preparations for debarking. Our gear was packed and we were ready for the next phase of coming home. An army band was drawn up on the pier and the music was sweet to the ear. Hundreds of well wishers festooned the dock with colorful clothing, frantically waving and shouting. Hopefully some knew their men were aboard but who cared. They were enthusiastically welcoming us home. Seattle was beautiful, friendly and was doing her part to make us welcome to the United States of America. We loved it and reciprocated by waving, throwing kisses and shouting to all.

The gang planks was attached and the first class passengers began to disembark, followed by veterans and ex-prisoners of war. A long line of buses was waiting. We climbed aboard with our duffle bags. Our destination was Madigan General Hospital at Fort Lewis. The high point men were to go to the reception center for processing and discharge. We rode along with mouths open in awe at the many sights of the town and countryside. Traffic lights at intersections, hundreds of automobiles everywhere. When would we get to buy a car and go where we wanted to? The bus driver told us they were expensive, 1940 vintage or earlier, and hard to get. Tires and gasoline had been rationed and many tires were poor quality retreads. Shortly, the bus slowed and entered the spacious grounds of Madigan General Hospital. We were greeted by the hospital staff and immediately admitted as patients. Turn in your baggage and uniform and don hospital pajamas and robe was the order. We were impressed with their organization and efficiency. After a good hot shower and dressed in our hospital clothes we headed for the hospital mess. **Wow!** A meal, fit for a king. Anything they served was fit for a king. No complaints from us. The mess hall was filled with men dressed in hospital clothing. After a good lunch, we headed back to the ward via the hospital exchange. Our purchases were candy bars, gum, toothpaste, soap, a magazine or two and a malted milk in the snack bar. We were like kids turned loose in a candy store.

Orientation was ordered for all ex-POWs. We would be here only a few days and then transferred to a hospital near our home for further medical checkups and treatment before discharge. Pay accounts would be settled there. Passes would be authorized to most. Uniforms would be returned after pass approval. All patients were to remain on the hospital grounds unless on pass. After this we returned to our ward and applied for a pass. We relaxed and enjoyed the company of the nurse's aides and attendants. We were adjusting to feminine companionship. Maybe we could ask them for a date? I must be getting back to normal—the desire to be close and smell the fragrance of perfume and hear the laughter of women. We would tell tall tales and they would express awe or amazement. The story of why the monkeys have no tale in Zamboango or why the carabao has no hair in Mindanao would leave them looking incredulous and suspicious of our stories and our sanity. Stories about eating dogs, cats, monkeys, snakes, lizards and other weird things. They were almost ready to call the men in the white coats. However, they soon caught on that we were giving them a line of baloney.

After evening chow we picked up our passes and uniforms and prepared for our first night on the town. Bus service was available and we caught one for the bright lights. It was a grand and glorious feeling to be able to go where and when we wanted. We asked a couple of soldiers where the action was and when to get off the bus.

We dropped off and began to walk along and look at the stores and all the good things to see. One item of great interest was a wristwatch. None of us had one and we determined that would be first priority when we had a pay settlement. We eased into a bar, surveyed the crowd and ordered drinks. We sat there listening and looking at the many men and women, their clothes, mannerisms and dancing. It was like a real live show to us. We were starved for female companionship but bashful and reluctant to show our ignorance of so many things, including dancing. One tune on the juke box caught our ear, "Cool Water." It was a song that had meaning to us.

We finished our drinks and moved on down the street to another bar. It was so crowded that we could not find a seat. We stood at the bar and ordered a drink. The bartender refused to sell us a drink, explaining that Washington state law forbids serving alcoholic beverages to anyone standing. We had to be sitting. Simple enough, but to us it was a bit ridiculous. We finally spotted a chair and one of us sat down and called the waitress for service. She would not bring us three drinks because two were still standing. By this time we were getting a little piqued. Sgt. Golson sat in the one chair and had Haddox and I sit on his knees. The waitress gave us a hard time but finally she did bring us three beers with an admonishment to be sure to stay sitting. A short time later more chairs became available. We started to walk across the floor, carrying our beers. The bartender let out a roar like a marine drill sergeant, "Sit down with those beers." Again we learned that Washington law prohibits a patron from moving around with a drink in his hand. The waitress came over and carried our beers over to the new table. We thought this a strange country and it's going to take time for us to adjust. After all, we had been out of the states for over six years. We soon moved on and caught our bus back to the hospital. A little wiser and a bit tipsy but not obnoxious as others on the bus. We made our way to our ward and turned in for a good night's sleep in a nice clean bed. Tomorrow would be a new day to learn more about the real world.

Returning to the ward after a good breakfast, I was shocked, dismayed and angry to discover my old reliable Wally Frank pipe had been thrown out by some over-zealous ward attendant. There was no use to fret, but something precious to me was summarily thrown away. Wally had been my security blanket, one that I could trust to bring solace and contentment when times were rough and the clouds of depression seemed the darkest. Farewell, old friend, at least you are free in the land of the free. Though you may be in some garbage dump or possibly cremated, I shall never forget our many pleasant hours together.

Orders came in, transferring us to a hospital near our home. Golson was going to Ala-

bama, Haddox and I were to go to Birmingham General Hospital in Van Nuys, California. Bill and I heard of a medic who was going there and he had a car. He agreed to let us ride with him and share the expenses.

We left the next day, traveling in a 1940 Ford V8. We left our many friends and comrades in arms with best wishes and a happy future until we meet again. Our driver knew the way and we were soon on U.S. Highway 101 through the beautiful country of Washington, Oregon and California. Our greatest companion was the car radio which broadcast "Cool Water" almost every hour, and the singing commercials were very hilarious. Our trip was interesting and we just sat back and enjoyed the panorama unfolding through the windshield.

Two days later we arrived at Birmingham General Hospital in Van Nuys, California. We checked in at the headquarters and reported to our assigned ward. We were called back to the front office and told we were on 10 days

Rangers Raid Cabanatuan Camp. General Douglas MacArthur's rangers made a daring raid on the Cabanatuan prison camp on January 30 and liberated many Americans right from under the noses of the Japanese. Here, MacArthur talks to an old friend, Col. A.C. Oliver, who was among those liberated.

146

leave and free to go home, but must return to the hospital for a complete medical checkup and final processing for discharge. Hoorah hippety-high-ho, it's off to home we go. We hastily sorted our duffle bag and made for the train station. We caught a Southern Pacific sleeper and were traveling in style. We passed through San Bernadino where my oldest sister was living. Her husband had just arrived home from the European theater. I was relaxing into the comfortable seats when it dawned on me that I was retracing the route I had traveled in May of 1939 on my way to a tropical paradise in the Philippines. The journey that had turned into an odyssey of hell and uncertainty of whether my comrades and I would ever come full circle. I fell asleep to the clicking of the rails, satisfied that I had been one of the very fortunate ones to return to a country blessed by the Constitution, the Bill of Rights and the wonderful people of a free country. Thank God, may our country never be weak and let our young men and women endure the humiliation of defeat and imprisonment and be sacrificed by our failure to be prepared. Peace through strength must be our watch word.

God Bless America, Land That I Love. Stand Beside Her and Guide Her, Through The Night With A Light From Above.

From The Mountains, To The Prairies, To The Oceans White With Foam. God Bless America, My Home Sweet Home. God Bless America, My Home Sweet Home!

CORREGIDOR

OASIS OF HOPE

PART EIGHT

THE UNFORTUNATE

Torpedoed By Wahoo, Nittsu Maru *dives to floor of Yellow Sea.*
Shallow, treacherous, the Yellow was dangerous sea for subs.
Wahoo *made it dangerous for marus.*
Courtesy of U.S. Submarine Operations in World War II.
By Theodore Roscoe. Photo Courtesy of Harry Alvey.

Part Eight
The Unfortunate

The Americans who were caught up in the raging tropical typhoon of war in the islands were from all walks of life; civilians, missionaries, Army, Navy, Army Air Force, Merchant Marine, construction workers and National Guard from every state in the Union. Most of the military were volunteers augmented by the federalized National Guard units who arrived late in 1941. Many civilians who were living in the Philippines volunteered and joined the armed forces or worked as civilian volunteers. They all suffered the same fate as the military. The Allied civilians and American civilian men, women and children, who remained in Manila after General MacArthur declared Manila an open city, were also rounded up and interned in Santa Tomas University and Los Banos Agriculture campus. Many of them were very wealthy business men and generally from the international community.

The major difference between an internee and a prisoner of war was the POWs were looked on as slave labor. The internees were not required to work except in the maintenance of the camp, gardening, repair and launder of clothing and in the camp kitchen. None of the civilian internees were subject to shipment to Japan. On the other hand, the civilians who were caught up in the battle areas on Bataan and Corregidor received the same treatment as military prisoners. They were shipped to various work camps and later shipped to Japan, Formosa, Korea, and Manchuria. In the eyes of the captors there was no distinction of status.

Shortly, after the capture of Corregidor and the shipment of the men from the Rock to the main camps on Luzon, prisoners of war were dispersed to various areas for work details. The transfer from Camp O'Donnell death camp to Cabanatuan consolidated all the Americans in one camp. The Filipinos were kept at Camp O'Donnell for rehabilitation and incorporation into the grand plan of the Co-Prosperity Sphere. Many were released on furlough. Others were put into labor groups. Some effort was made to draft Filipinos as auxiliary for policing the islands. However, the Filipinos did not take the bait. A puppet government was established as an example of the benevolence of the Japanese. None of these efforts resulted in Filipinos being allowed normal freedoms. Everything was rationed, money was occupational script, farm products were confiscated to feed the occupation army and employment was almost nil. Many Filipinos who had worked for foreign companies and the American military were left without jobs.

The main staples, rice and sugar, were confiscated for the Japanese Army and were in short supply. The Filipinos changed their dietary habits from necessity and ate more vegetables, camotes, soybeans and other substitutes. A thriving black market sprang up for many commodities with inflated prices. The civilian Filipino populace endured many hardships. Transportation was reduced by rationing of fuel. Inter-province travel was restricted by check points at which searches and confiscation of private property occurred. Other arbitrary rules were implemented. The local railroad was controlled and equipment was not maintained. Reliance on carabao carts and horse drawn carotellas was used for transporting commodities to market. Motor buses were converted to burn charcoal for fuel.

The attitude of the Filipinos towards the Americans was one of compassion and sympathy. Many Filipinos engaged in underground activities in attempting to alleviate the medical and food shortages in the prison camps. The Japanese were very harsh in the treatment of Filipinos who tried to help the prisoners. Many were sent to Fort Santiago and tortured, imprisoned and executed by the Kempei Tai (secret police). The Filipinos were in no better position than the internees or prisoners of war. In fact they suffered as much or more during the occupation.

The prisoner of war story has been told in a number of books and articles published in the intervening years. It is a story that has largely been forgotten and lost in the passage of time. However, it is a story that should be brought to light. From the past we can learn much for the future and avoid such calamitous debacles in succeeding generations.

The following part tells the story of some of the unfortunate prisoners and examines the reasoning and logic of the Japanese treatment of prisoners of war. During the years of active duty and after retirement, I have pursued my hobby of reading many books on World War II, particularly about the war in the South Pacific. Many questions came to mind and the answers were vague and uncertain. Part of the answers came in the many books written by individuals that only covered their personal experiences. I was deeply interested in what happened to so many friends and comrades in arms. What was meant by humane treatment of prisoners of war? Was it a matter of interpretation or was it a matter of national policy? Who was responsible for the policies, implementation of and supervision of the Japanese prisoner of war camps? Was the treatment of the prisoners of war in the Pacific different than the treatment of Allied prisoners in the European area, or later in Korea or Vietnam? Were the principal culprits brought to justice? The Nuremberg trials and the fate of the Nazi hierarchy was well publicized. The Japanese War Crimes Trials were not well publicized and few people know of the outcome of those trials.

Most of the countries of Europe signed and ratified the Geneva Convention which established the rules for treatment of prisoners of war. Japan signed the covenant, but the Japanese government did not ratify it. The military cliche were opposed because it was in direct conflict with the Samurai code of the warrior. To surrender was a dishonor and the Samurai warrior would prefer to die in honor on the field of battle. Shinto funeral rites were routinely held for the young men who were called into service. A funeral before the fact. It was assumed by the Japanese that they would not come back alive.

However, when the atomic bomb was dropped on Hiroshima and Nagasaki, the Emperor overruled the military and surrendered the entire country. The Japanese people accepted his order without question. The search for the truth and the responsible persons who committed war crimes against the Allied prisoners of war began immediately after the occupation. The search for creditable evidence, documents and witnesses resulted in the International War Crimes Tribunal and subsequent trials of the principal architects or those who grossly violated the accepted rules for the care and treatment of prisoners of war. Suspected individuals were incarcerated in Tokyo's Sugami Prison pending investigation and trial. Many ex-prisoners of war were called to testify. Captain (Major) E. Pearce Fleming, our commander in Hanawa, was a witness in the trials of Lt. Asaka and the noncommissioned officers of the camp.

The best account of these trials came from an excellent book entitled *The Other Nuremberg, The Untold Story of the Tokyo War Crimes Trials* by Arnold C. Brackman. The following excerpts are quoted as a demonstration and understanding of the diabolic brutalization of human beings by a supposedly civilized country. The overview of the prosecutor's evidence presented and its relation to the treatment of civilians and military prisoners leads one through a dark tunnel not unlike Dante's *Inferno*.

On the eastern front it is estimated that the Germans took 5.5 million Soviet prisoners of whom at least 3.5 million were dead by mid-1944. Being more sensitive to the fate of their own countrymen, however, most military and citizens of the United States and the United Kingdom had a very different picture. Of 235,474 U.S. and U.K. prisoners reported captured by Germany and Italy combined, only 4 percent (9,348) died in the hands of the captors: whereas 27 percent (35,756) of Japan's Anglo-American POWs, of a total of 132,134, did not survive.

The International Military Tribunal during the War Crimes Trials in Tokyo developed testimony in an effort by the prosecutor to determine who was responsible for policy and treatment of the prisoners of war.

In this period of the trials, the American chaplain at Sugamo Prison, Captain Francis C. Scott left for home. In a farewell interview with *Stars and Stripes*, a U.S. Army sanctioned newspaper, he revealed that he had "interviewed many of the convicted Japanese POW Camp commandants as to their reasons for the barbaric treatment of prisoners." In the end Captain Scott put together a composite explanation. "They had a belief that any enemy of the Emperor could not be right. So the more brutally they treated the prisoners, the more loyal to the Emperor they were being." The chaplain ascribed this to Japanese education, training and conditioning. In literature and in history this has a familiar ring. That in *War and Peace*, Tolstoy describes one of Napoleon's aides as unable to express devotion to his monarch except by cruelty.

The Other Nuremberg, The Untold Story of The Tokyo War Crimes Trials presents some of the testimony by ex-prisoners of war.

The most memorable atrocity of the Japanese occupation of the Philippines was the Bataan Death March in April of 1942. There 76,000 Americans and Filipinos on Bataan were marched to a prisoner of war camp at (infamous) Camp O'Donnell near Capas Luzon. Over 10,000 men died on the seven day, 120 kilometer march. Some of the survivors were placed on the stand in Tokyo.

Staff Sergeant Samuel B. Moody testified that the only food they received on the march was either thrown to them by the Filipinos or consisted of stalks of sugar cane grabbed along the road. Water came from carabao wallows and ditches. Those who drank from the former usually contracted dysentery. "The men were beaten," Moody recalled. "The men were bayoneted, stabbed, and kicked with hobnailed boots. If any man lagged to the rear, or fell to the side of the road, he was bayoneted or beaten."

Another witness, Donald F. Ingle recalled, "That many of the Filipinos who gave us food, did so at the risk of their lives and a lot of the Filipino civilians did lose their lives trying." Ingle said, "Some men were taken out of line and either shot or bayoneted." At the end of cross examination the defense counsel said, "You sound bitter about all of this." Ingle appeared to count to ten and replied, "Well there are several thousand buddies that aren't here today, if it weren't for that (Bataan Death March). Use your own judgment . . ."

Describing the conditions at the camp in Davao Mindanao in another now forgotten incident, Lt. Col. Austin J. Montgomery testified to conditions at the Davao penal colony camp in the southern Philippines, where 2,000 prisoners of war were incarcerated. When 10 men escaped, 600 men including Montgomery, were punished by being placed in cages about three feet high by three feet wide and six feet long for two months. Periodically they were beaten or whipped. "Who gave the order of punishment?" asked Pedro Lopez, (Filipino prosecutor). "The commanding officer of the camp, Major Maeda, announced to us that he had received the notification of the punishment to be imposed from higher command . . ."

On Palawan, for example, 150 American POWs, almost double the number massacred at Malmedy, Belgium during the Battle of the Bulge, were slaughtered and forgotten. But their deed is indelibly implanted in the transcript of the International Military Tribunal, Far East, (IMTFE). On December 14, 1944, the Japanese claimed the Americans were going to bomb Puerto Princesa POW camp on Palawan and ordered all Americans into tunnels that served as air raid shelters. Then the Japanese soldiers flipped a lighted torch into the tunnel and followed it with several buckets of gasoline. The gasoline exploded and set the occupants afire. "As screaming men ran from the shelter," said an eyewitness report based on three survivors, "They were mowed down by machine

152

guns and rifle fire." Realizing they were trapped, several ran to the Japanese and asked to be shot in the head, but the Japanese laughingly shot or bayoneted them in the stomach.

At another camp, among the horrors witnessed by Col. Guy H. Stubbs ". . . where five Filipinos were thrown into a latrine and burned alive; a Filipino was spread eagled on the ground and both legs were dislocated; a Filipino who had dysentery was made to eat everything he had eliminated . . ."

Colonel Franklin M. Filiman described the terrible beatings he had received in a Japanese torture chamber, "a bare room with no chairs or table." He testified that he had "witnessed over 100 other beatings. Usually the victim was beaten unconscious and then awakened by a bucket of cold water and then kicked unconscious again. I was told by the captain in charge, when I protested the beatings of different individuals," Colonel Filiman said "that he had orders from his superiors to punish. Who were the superiors? In every occasion the only words used were the High Command . . ."

Each day of the trials more survivors testified in regards to the **brutal . . . bestial . . . barbaric . . . evil . . . crazed . . . inhumane . . . lost to all sense of humanity . . . depraved** or similar words were used by the media of both sides to describe the actions of the opposite side.

It is evident that the acts of violence disregarded the safety and welfare of the prisoners and was of secondary importance to the Japanese military from the top down to the lowly private. The history of the Japanese conquest in Manchuria, China and Korea prior to the outbreak of World War II is an excellent indication of the Japanese military modus operandi. The wanton disregard for the people of China during the capture and rape of Nanking is well recorded but long forgotten. The same military leaders were involved in that mass atrocity as those who perpetrated the atrocities on the Allied prisoners of war and the civilians of the occupied countries in the Pacific. Quoting Brackman in

The Other Nuremburg, The Untold Story of Tokyo War Crimes Trials:

Other than Bataan the world does not remember nor does it care about the other great massacres that took place in the Philippine Islands, Dutch East Indies, Malaysia, French Indo-China, Siam and Burma during the conquest and occupation. There are hundreds of instances both in Japan and the areas of Japanese Army and Navy operations that were brought out into the light. Many if not all were woven into the prosecution's presentation during the Tokyo War Crimes trials.

During this phase (prosecution's presentation) of the case, one day's horrors were transcended by the horrors of the day before. The Americans at the trial found it hard to reconcile the evidence in the courtroom with the evidence outside. After all, we now lived among the Japanese and found most of them decent and likable. How could they and their government have behaved like the monsters depicted in the testimony? We found part of the answer in the prosecution's evidence. A Japanese soldier's diary entry of December 9, 1944, "Taking advantage of the darkness, we went out to kill natives (Filipinos). It was hard for me to kill them as they seemed to be good people. The frightful cries of the women and children were horrible. I myself . . . killed several persons. Another soldier told me how he watched his comrades torture Filipino prisoners. It is pitiful, and I couldn't watch. They also shot them and speared them with bamboo spears." The most pregnant word here is **they.** A Japanese soldier described his comrades in arms as strangers.

Few people today really know the true story of those forgotten military and civilians who endured the awesome treatment in widely diversified places in the Far East. The gross and wanton disregard of all human rights is epitomized by the treatment of thousands in the construction of the Siam-Burma Railroad.

The evidence presented by the prosecution council at this stage describes horrors beyond human conception. The testimony on the Siam-Burma Railroad as depicted in *The Other*

Nuremberg, The Untold Story of Tokyo War Crimes Trials:

In mid-December 1946, the pivotal interest at the trial was on the cruelties the Japanese had meted out to prisoners of war and Asian slave laborers. By all accounts the worst POW and forced-labor camps during World War II was along a 258-mile railroad track running through the almost impenetrable jungles of Thailand and Burma. The infamous Siam-Burma Death Railway was built by Allied prisoners of war and Asian slave laborers during 1942-43 under conditions so vile that 27 percent of the POWs and more than half of the Asian laborers perished. The Allied prisoners laboring on the railway numbered around 50,000; a mix of Australians, Dutch, English and Americans who had been taken prisoner in Malaya, Singapore and Indonesia and shipped to the site like cattle. The number of "labor levies"—largely Indonesian, Burmese, Malayans, Chinese and Indians—will never be known, but the figure may have been as many as 250,000 men with a scattering of women and children. Using spades, baskets and picks, the prisoners and coolies were forced to move three million cubic yards of earth and 250,000 million cubic yards of rock along the route . . . that Tokyo had ordered the construction of the railway and among those in the dock who had authorized the use of prisoners as laborers is in violation of the Hague and Geneva Conventions were Generals Hedeki Tojo and Heitaro Kimura . . . these Japanese Major Generals were identified as the commanders under whom the actual building of the railway had taken place. They had commanded two regiments of troops and auxiliary units, including Korean Guard units. With literally thousands of troops, guards, prisoners and slave laborers involved and the thousands of tons of material and shipping of supplies to the construction site, the project could not be kept a secret.

Despite the generally accepted conventions of war governing prisoners, the Japanese did employ POWs on war related projects and some 60,000 to 70,000 Allied captives—mostly Australians, British, Dutch and Indian—were eventually put to work alongside native laborers on the Siam-Burma Railway. Early in 1945 reports, that later proved quite accurate, reached the west that some 15,000 of these prisoners had died.

The Americans who worked on the Siam-Burma Railroad were captured in the Dutch East Indies. They were the 131st Field Artillery Battalion (The Lost Battalion), survivors of the *U.S.S. Houston* and other ships sunk in the battles off the Dutch East Indies. Many were stranded seamen, airman, and civilians swept up in the early days of the war. One survivor of the cruiser *U.S.S. Houston,* in H. Robert Charles's book *The Last Man Out,* presents a gripping account of the sinking of the *U.S.S. Houston* and the subsequent imprisonment of the survivors and their incredulous inhumane treatment on the Siam-Burma railroad paralleled the treatment of the other Allied prisoners.

The Japanese atrocities in China paled by comparison with those at the construction site . . . Dr. C.B.B. Richards, a British Army officer and survivor testified about a camp where the Japanese Commander's policy had been, "No work, no food." The commandant cured the ill by sending them to the hospital to die. "I can imagine nothing more appalling than the conditions under which these men lived and died." Dr. Richards testified. "It was in effect a living morgue." As for the camp itself Richards said, "Troops were billeted in huts which had been evacuated the previous day on account of cholera deaths . . . coolies walked through huts, spat, defecated and vomited everywhere . . . . Work days varied between 12 and 20 hours with no days off, depending on the monsoon rains . . . ." Hundreds of pages of testimony on the Siam-Burma Death Railway sickened the tribunal in the depth of brutality by the Japanese.

The War Diaries of Weary Dunlop, Java and the Thailand, and Burma Railroad, by E.E. Dunlop, an Australian surgeon, is an excellent document from a medical viewpoint

154

of the frustration and utter hopelessness of the unhealthy conditions and the total disregard of basic human needs in a hostile environment. This is a classic example of the diabolical savagery inflicted on these unfortunate human beings, during the construction of a railway, under conditions so primitive that it is a miracle that any survived such cruelties. It is particularly interesting to the student of history and how mankind adapts to harsh conditions. How the strong survive and the weak fall by the wayside as unworthy of any humane consideration. Brackman wrote in *The Other Nuremberg, The Untold Story of Tokyo War Crimes Trials*:

The prisoners who worked on the Siam-Burma railway were the lucky ones—at least they had survived the journey from their place of capture to the construction sight. Except for a few who made the journey by rail from Singapore, a large percentage traveled by ship and are not included in the deaths on the railway . . . All the Asian coolies were shipped by boat.

The untold story as far as the loss of British, Australian and Dutch prisoners of war on sea journeys is unknown in American literature. It is conceivable that Allied submarines and aircraft did intercept transports moving slaves in the waters off the occupied countries. There were many of those on ships that were sunk or damaged. Some of the ships made it into Manila and discharged some prisoners. How many were left aboard these ships to suffer and die on the long voyages?

The ships that transported Americans to Japan in 1942 and 1943 were not in as much danger as during the latter part of 1944. By this time the campaign had progressed to the point that the American subs and planes were out in force. The noose had been drawn tightly and Japan was being slowly strangled. The steady march of the Allies up the chain of islands towards the Philippines was rolling like a steamroller.

The Satanic Hell-Ships

The mass movement of prisoners and coolie laborers was another element in the War Crimes trial that revealed the fate of thousands of American slaves (POWs) in the Great-

er East Asia Co-Prosperity Sphere. The Japanese military leaders became obsessed with moving as many prisoners as possible to the home islands to supplement their labor force. The orders to ship POWs came from the highest level of command. The implementation of those orders resulted in junior officers being placed in total charge of the hapless POWs. The ships were a responsibility of the Navy for movement. The care and conditions of the prisoners was an Army function. This system was inflexible and the captains of the ship had no authority in how it was accomplished. The **overzealous, inflexible** regimented junior officers were incapable of reasonable care and feeding, but were more interested in accomplishing the task assigned to them. A junior officer who tried to obtain better conditions was subject to severe punishment. It was unheard of for them to consider POWs as anything but animals.

The exact number of American prisoners of war, who were moved to Japan in the last six months of the war, is not known. Other Allied POWs were treated the same as the Americans. Several hell-ships put into Manila and discharged British, Australian and Dutch prisoners that were too sick to travel or were survivors of a tragic sinking. They had been en route for long periods of time. The ships' captains were trying to get their ships home safely. The suffering of the human cargo was harsh and inhumane in all of its aspects. How many Allied prisoners died and were buried at sea is not apparent in books published on the subject in the United States. It is possible to determine the Americans who died or were lost at sea to some degree. The sinking of unmarked ships by submarine and aircraft accounted for many tragic deaths. Deaths as a result of conditions of health, movement and burial at sea were recorded. The Japanese reported to the International Red Cross the arrival in Japan by name. The American Army office of the Provost Marshal received these reports. However those who died at sea or were lost by sinking of the ships were not reported. These lists are a matter of record in the National Archives. U.S. Navy warrant officers and clerks were used for the record-keeping of the movement of prisoners. Some are legible and some are of poor quality and difficult to read.

The best picture can be obtained by reading the accounts of the survivors and testimony of witnesses at the War Crimes trials by the International Tribunal.

Quoting Brackman from *The Other Nuremberg, The Untold Story of the Tokyo War Crimes Trials*:

The **hell-ships** for want of a better term plied sea routes from points of capture to Formosa, Korea, Manchuria and Japan . . . The conditions aboard the ships were uniformly the same. The prisoners and the coolies were forced below decks, kept short on water and rations, provided with virtually no sanitation facilities, and beaten mercilessly. Many of the ships were not cleaned after the previous cargo had been unloaded. Dirty, filthy holds had carried horses on the outbound trip. Prisoners were crowded into these stinking holds with no place to lay but in the offal. The time of a journey varied from a few days to 30 or more days.

The prosecution produced 20 sworn affidavits and put several of the survivors of the other **hell-ships'** voyages on the witness stand. . . . The first affidavit set the tone; 1,200 American prisoners confined in the hold of the *Tottori Maru*, left on 8 October 1942, bound from Manila to Japan. A stop was made in Takao, Formosa and Kobe, Japan. Fifty percent debarked in Japan and the balance went to Mukden, Manchuria, arriving on 11 November 1942. The men were packed so closely together that only two-thirds could lie down at one time. Although many of the prisoners had already contracted dysentery from rotten rations, they were provided with only six latrines. Many of them had to sleep in their own excrement.

The policy of harsh treatment (in the movements of prisoners), the prosecution charged, was deliberate and was carried out on instructions from the Japanese Navy General Staff . . . The **hell-ships** bore no marks distinguishing them from regular transports, and they were armed with anti-aircraft and other weapons . . . They were attacked by Allied aircraft and submarines,

and many of the POWs, civilian internees and coolie laborers drowned. One witness, the survivor of such an attack, painted a picture of the sea journey in terms that rivaled Dante's *Inferno*. His voyage had been on a 5,000-ton cargo ship carrying 1,650 European war prisoners (mostly Dutch), 600 Indonesian prisoners (mostly Ambonese) and 5,500 forced laborers (Javanese) from Java on 14 September 1944. (Total on transport 7,750.) The prisoners were crowded into the ships holds . . . "We were beaten into the hold . . . crowded together standing up, since lying or even sitting down was impossible. Off of Sumatra's west coast in the Indian Ocean, the ship was torpedoed and sank in 20 minutes. Prisoners who survived the initial explosion and floundered in the water tried to grab the edge of a Japanese lifeboat, but instead of taking them in, their hands were chopped off or their head was split with a large axe," the witness said. A Japanese corvette soon picked up survivors . . . 276 Europeans, 312 Ambonese, and 300 Javanese (total survivors, 888). The 888 survivors were confined in a Japanese prison camp on Sumatra. "When we came into the jail, the lavatories were full. We had to relieve ourselves on the floor," he said. "The smell was penetrating and nauseating."

Regular Japanese Army troop ships were also used to transport war prisoners, the International Military Tribunal (IMT) evidence showed. On one occasion the *Nagata Maru* departed Manila on 7 November 1942 and carried 1,659 prisoners and 2,000 Japanese troops. Captain Edward N. Nell, Army Medical officer testified, "The prisoners were bottled up below decks. The latrines were on the deck above, but the men with bowel disorders were unable to get on deck. For three days there were no emergency sanitary facilities below deck." At Moji, Japan (25 November 1942) the surviving were off loaded. Seven men died en route and 150 were left in Moji. They were never heard of again, according to the Provost Marshal office. The debarked prisoners were compelled to line up on the dock naked, in full view of the public for rectal examinations, Captain Nell testified.

On all of these hell-ships, beatings were common place . . . prisoners died and were thrown overboard like garbage. For discipline purpose, beheadings were on deck and the severed heads and torsos were flipped overboard . . . in tropical waters, these vessels were followed by scavengers . . . sharks. In ports, the bodies were piled up on deck to await burial at sea. On a hell ship running from Ambon to Java, along the equator, the stench of corpses piled up on Indonesian docks all along the way was revolting.

Early in the war on October 1, 1942 the *Lisbon Maru* sailed from Hong Kong with 1,815 prisoners and 2,000 Japanese soldiers. At sea, two men who had died of diphtheria were not removed from the holds where the prisoners were confined. The *Lisbon Maru* was torpedoed and settled with her stern caught on a sand bar. When the prisoners broke out of the holds, they were picked off by rifles as they emerged from below. A handful of survivors reached an island nearby, where the Chinese treated us with kindness and gave us food and clothing from their meager supplies. Japanese landing parties soon approached and recaptured them. They were taken to Shanghai where they were confined in Bridgehouse, a notorious Kempe Tai prison.

Evidence was introduced by the prosecution that clearly linked the War Ministry officers with the commanders in the field. Much of the evidence was destroyed prior to the surrender of Japan. However, one document recovered laid the frame work for this determination. Another interesting aspect was that General Hideko Tojo had ordered "that all prisoners of war were to engage in forced labor." This was a decision by the War Ministry in 1942.

There were many incidents involving movements of prisoners of war from the Philippines in which many thousands of men were lost. The *Shinyo Maru* sailed from Zamboanga, Mindanao on 3 September 1944, with 736 POWs. It was torpedoed by the *USS Paddle* off Samar and only 86 survived. These men were a part of the Devao Prison Camp and had been shipped from Luzon in 1942.

Evidence was also tendered that Tokyo planned to execute all prisoners—more than 300,000—in the event of an Allied invasion of Japan. Repeatedly during the trial, camp survivors testified that camp commanders told them that they would be killed if Japan was invaded. No documents were introduced to support these charges, supposition was that the secret directive for the disposal of the POWs had been destroyed in the pyres ignited after Japan surrendered. However, as the prosecutor's case drew to a close, after months of investigation and testimony, the prosecutor introduced a War Ministry Directive dated 17 March 1945, and stamped "Army Secret No. 2257" in which the Vice Minister of War sitting in Tokyo notified commanders, "As the war situation has become very critical, I have been ordered to notify you not to make any blunders in the treatment of prisoners of war based on the attached outline for the disposal of prisoners of war according to the change of situation when the havocs of war make themselves felt in our Imperial homeland and Manchuria." The outline appeared to be a brilliant exercise in double indenter. The outline did not order the murder of prisoners but, it "recommended that in the event of an invasion of Japan, the prisoners be set free." In the light of the Japanese treatment of Allied prisoners during the war, it is fair to interpret this suggestion to mean "free from earthly concerns."

The War Crimes' trials of the military leaders in Japan took the spotlight in the news media and caught the fancy of the people at home. Some of the major trials were held in the Philippines. Generals Yamashita and Homma and other lesser individuals resulted in various sentences ranging from death on the gallows to imprisonment for varying numbers of years. The lower rank individuals were in most cases tried and convicted for specific crimes. One of the cases involved the Japanese officer and guards who were responsible for the hell-ship, *Oryoku Maru*. Lt. Toshino, Mr. Wada the hunchbacked interpreter from Davao and the guards during the last weeks of 1944.

An examination of the various books pub-

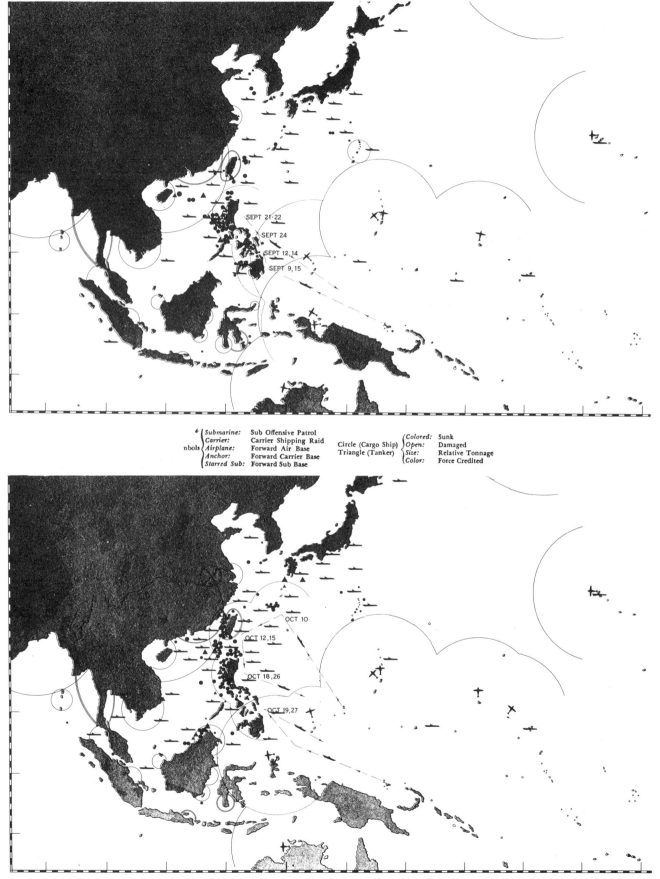

nbols	*Submarine:*	Sub Offensive Patrol			*Colored:*	Sunk
	Carrier:	Carrier Shipping Raid	Circle (Cargo Ship)		*Open:*	Damaged
	Airplane:	Forward Air Base	Triangle (Tanker)		*Size:*	Relative Tonnage
	Anchor:	Forward Carrier Base			*Color:*	Force Credited
	Starred Sub:	Forward Sub Base				

Submarine dispersion maps for September and October, 1944.
Courtesy of U.S. Submarine Operations in World War II.
by Theodore Roscoe

lished in the United States by some of the survivors of the horrible conditions on the transports moving prisoners of war to Japan, is chilling and illustrates the blatant disregard towards shipments through waters fraught with the possibility of sudden death.

The disposition of submarines and the superiority in the air raises a question. How did the fortunate slip through and the unfortunate die at sea? The disposition of the submarines in the last five months of 1944 reveals the perils of a voyage on a Japanese ship under the supervision of the Japanese. Thousands of men were lost at sea during this critical period by the sheer stupidity and insensitive decision to remove all prisoners of war to Japan regardless of the submarine and air menace.

The United States Submarine Operations in World War II by Theodore Roscoe, U.S. Naval Institute, gives detailed descriptions of operations during these critical months. A chart showing the disposition of submarines in the waters from Luzon to Japan show how effective these ships of the silent service were in their operations.

The Unfortunate

Many excellent books have been written by survivors of the atrocious journeys in filthy, decrepit, unmarked ships through submarine infested waters of the Philippines, Formosa and the home waters around Japan. However, the voyage of the *Oryoko Maru* was not interdicted by submarines but by aircraft of Task Force 38, deployed around the Philippines and Formosa. The story of this ill-fated ship is one of the most harrowing voyages endured by the unfortunate prisoners of war. Their protracted exposure to the specter of imminent death for forty-seven days is a shocking picture of death and the survival of very few. The ships that proceeded the *Oryoku Maru* in the summer and fall of 1944 in the waters around the Philippines and Formosa were prime targets for air and submarines. Some were fortunate enough to slip through the gauntlet and others were not so fortunate. Those that were sunk by submarine were more fortunate in one respect. Their death was quick and merciful. The prisoners on the *Oryoku Maru* were exposed twice and had two

ships sunk from under them. They were unfortunate because of the terrible suffering and anguish they suffered for 47 days on two subsequent ships.

The Japanese frenzied efforts to ship all prisoners of war from the Philippines and Southeast Asia culminated in one of the worst examples of man's cruelty to man. Total wanton disregard by the officer in charge, Lt. Toshino, Imperial Japanese Army on the *Oryoko Maru* unquestionably contributed to many deaths and showed absolutely no compassion for the pitiable wretches crammed into the holds.

American Prisoners of War were not the only ones to be swept up in the last half of 1944. The British, Australians and the Dutch were rounded up and shipped like cattle. Several ships made it into Manila and some sick and disabled were off loaded and sent to Bilibid. The stories from these unfortunate men paralleled the horrors of the Americans. Long voyages, in extremely overcrowded holds, little food or water, tropical heat, suffocation, shooting, filthy holds with little or no sanitation facilities, dysentery, malaria and emaciated bodies, contributed to the misery and ultimate death of hundreds en route. The ever present possibility of being sunk at sea by submarines or aircraft attacks in port as well as at sea were ignored by the Japanese. The distribution of the American submarines in the fall of 1944 or the frequent aircraft bombings illustrate the potential death trap that the transports faced on the voyage to Japan. (See map, Distribution of Submarines, September and October 1944.)

Many of the men would have accepted death by Allied forces as a welcome relief from the diabolical conditions aboard these **hellships**. There were occasions when the men actually cheered the Navy planes when they bombed the slave ships. The powerful American invasion forces were already preparing for the landing at Leyte. The entire area from the Philippines to Japan was blockaded by air and sea. The Japanese were determined to prevent recovery of the prisoners in the islands regardless of the dangers. The Japanese headquarters believed the loss of prisoners would be embarrassing to the Japanese government. Slave labor was urgently needed in Japan. The stories of these atrocities would not be known until after the war. Some of the story of the *Shinyo Maru* sinking off Mindanao in September, 1944, has been told by rescued survivors and published by the few escapees who evaded recapture. (See list of ships sunk in appendix.)

Luzon had been raked by scores of Navy planes as they roamed at will over the islands. Airfields and shipping facilities as well as shipping were prime targets. Manila had been raided several times and many ships had been sunk in Manila Bay. The probability of the American planes interdicting ships was recognized by the senior American prisoner officers. Attempts to persuade the Japanese, that it would be suicidal under such conditions to safely move the prisoners. It was pointed out that this was a violation of the Rules of Land Warfare and the Geneva Convention. The pleas fell on deaf ears. The orders from Tokyo were law and no lower ranking Japanese Army official could or would deviate from those orders regardless of the conditions.

The fateful voyage of the final shipment of prisoners of war from the Philippines is the epitome of the worst sea voyage of American and Allied prisoners of war. It began in the early dawn hours of 13 December 1944. The last meal was served in Bilibid. The 1,619 prisoners were the sweepings of homesteaders in Cabanatuan and Bilibid. There were 1,035 officers below the grade of colonel, 599 enlisted men, 47 civilians and 37 British soldiers were consigned to an ominous fate. Approximately 500 disabled prisoners and a few medics were left to attend the seriously ill and disabled men at each of the two camps, Cabanatuan and Bilibid. The draft had been waiting in Bilibid since late October. The majority of the medics from both camps, including the Navy Medical Detachment from Bilibid under Cmdr. Thomas H. Hayes, were included in the final draft. The men marched to Pier Seven and arrived about 1100. The pier had been severely damaged by the air raids of the last month. Two fire-gutted ships were on the opposite side. Over 60 ships sunk or heavily damaged could be seen in Manila Bay.

The ship lying at the pier was the *Oryoku Maru*, a 15,000-ton passenger-cargo type transport built in 1937. The 2,000 Japanese wounded and disabled military, stranded Merchant Marine seaman from the many ships sunk in Manila Bay, and some women and children returning to Japan were loaded first. They were quartered in the upper passenger cabins. No Red Cross markings were visible to indicate presence of prisoners of war. The ship was equipped with anti-aircraft weapons mounted on the deck. The hot afternoon sun beat down on the *Oryoku Maru* as the prisoners began to board ship about 1500. The guard detail was commanded by Lt. Junsbuto Toshino and a Mr. Shunusuki Wada, Interpreter Sgt. Major Sukeyosa Tanoue, Pvt. Jiro Ueda, Sgt. of the Guard, Sho Hattori, Lance Corporal Kasutano Aihara (known as Air Raid) and several guards all of whom had been at the Davao penal colony and Cabanatuan. Their reputations were vile and vicious. Lt. Toshino, after loading and during the voyage rarely appeared and delegated authority to Mr. Wada.

The prisoners were divided into three groups: Cmdr. Warner Portz USN as OIC with 830 men in aft hold (No. 5) with an eight-foot by 29-inch hatch opening for air and light, Lt. Col. Curtis Beecher, 4th. Marine Regiment with 600 men crammed into No. 1 forward cargo hold 60' x 100' x 9' Cmdr. Thomas H. Hayes, USN, two chaplains with 186 men, mostly medics and seven men who arrived from Fort McKinley went into No. 2 forward hold. Bags of grain were packed around three sides of No. 2 hold, which reduced space. Each of the rest of the holds had a horizontal wooden platform triple-decked four feet above each platform around sides and bulkheads as sleeping platforms for troops.

The prisoners were shoved, beaten with bamboo sticks and jammed like loading cattle, until there was no room to sit down. The men were so crowded that it was impossible to lie down on the platforms. Lt. John M. Wright Jr., Army, estimated there were about four square feet per man. Loading in this manner was common practise in rail cars or ships. There was no concern for ventilation or distribution of water and food, sanitation facilities were grossly inadequate and inaccessible to those suffering from dysentery. The only visible latrines were on the deck above. No. 2

160

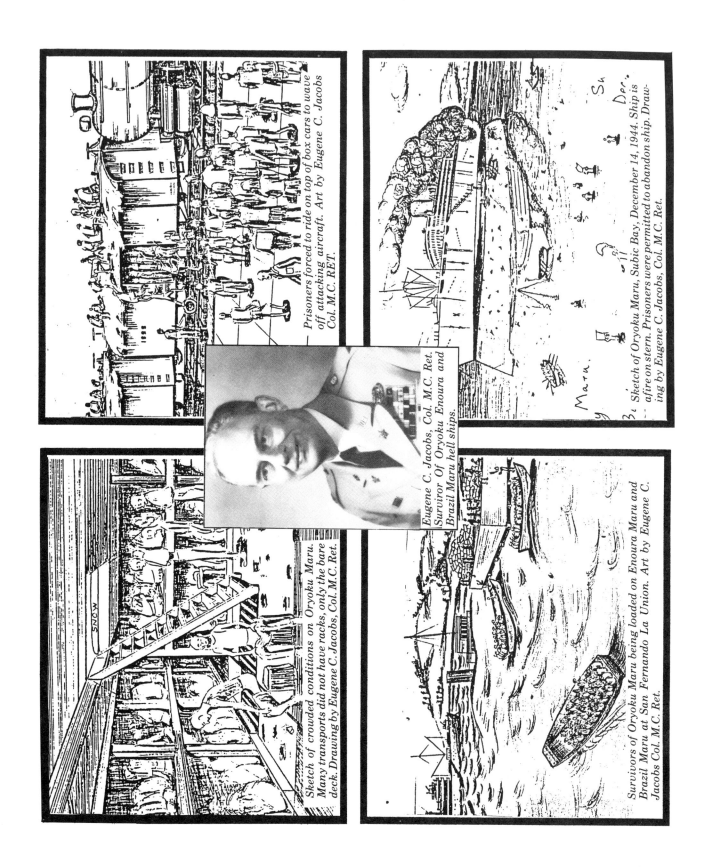

Prisoners forced to ride on top of box cars to wave off attacking aircraft. Art by Eugene C. Jacobs Col. M.C. RET.

Sketch of Oryoku Maru, Subic Bay, December 14, 1944. Ship is afire on stern. Prisoners were permitted to abandon ship. Drawing by Eugene C. Jacobs, Col. M.C. Ret.

Sketch of crowded conditions on Oryoku Maru. Many transports did not have racks, only the bare deck. Drawing by Eugene C. Jacobs, Col. M.C. Ret.

Eugene C. Jacobs, Col. M.C. Ret. Survivor Of Oryoku Enoura and Brazil Maru hell ships.

Survivors of Oryoku Maru being loaded on Enoura Maru and Brazil Maru at San Fernando La Union. Art by Eugene C. Jacobs Col. M.C. Ret.

hold was equipped with air conditioning for horses. The deck had not been cleaned and horse manure covered the deck. Lt. Toshino was asked to allow air conditioning but refused to operate the air conditioner. Temperatures rapidly rose to 100-120 degrees. The men began to remove clothing in the tightly packed holds and attempted to find space to sit or lie down and stow their packs. The wooden platforms served to increase net space but no one could stand up in the confined area. The only area for standing was in the center of the hatch and this was packed. Only one vertical steel ladder led to the hatch combing about 20 feet above. The hold served as a box and simplified control of the prisoners by the guards. An emergency would doom the men to a horrible death as there was no exit except the ladder.

The *Oryoku Maru* moved outside the break water and dropped anchor shortly after loading of the human cargo. Hot steaming rice and seaweed soup were sent into the holds. Distribution was extremely difficult because of the crowding. Several four-gallon buckets of water and warm tea were issued after the rations. Several of the wooden buckets were kept for use as emergency benjos (toilets). The buckets soon overflowed on to the steel deck and fouled the surrounding area. The malodorous miasmic smell permeated the atmosphere causing nausea and more ranting and raving. The Japanese would not allow the buckets to be hoisted on deck for dumping.

Soon after moving out beyond the break water, the prisoners began a steady chant for more ventilation and water for the parched throats of the prisoners. Men under the shelves and in the far corners of the hold began to suffocate and were passed over head to the center of the hatch for revival. The men in Hold No. 2 were more fortunate in that they had slightly more room, though crowded.

Lieutenant Toshino delegated responsibility to Mr. Wada and did not approach the crowded holds. The hunched-back interpreter Mr. Wada refused to provide more water and threatened to close the hatches, if the noise continued. The noise became louder. Mr. Wada ordered the hatches closed. The temperature rose to 120 degrees and everything was in complete darkness. The officers called for quiet and urged the men to be calm and not burn up oxygen in useless shouting, and conserve body energy by not moving around, pushing and shoving. The chaplains urged the men to pray and the words of *The Lord's Prayer* could be heard in the darkness. The cool night breezes brought some relief from the oppressive heat. In one hold, two officers climbed the ladder and shoved the hatch covers aside to provide air. It became as black as a dungeon as night descended on the crowded holds. The prisoners became panic-stricken, pandemonium and chaos increased as men struggled to find space to lie, or stand. The prisoners were fighting, shouting, screaming, pushing, shoving and cursing in the frightening darkness.

The devil himself could not have devised a more diabolical scenario. The devil in charge, Lt. Toshino and the satanic, hunch-backed Mr. Wada were the directors in an inhumane and cruel travesty of horror below decks. The entire scene rivaled anything known to man. It was a Machciavellian scenario of Dante's *Inferno* in a "Danse Macabre" setting. The allegorical satanic figure of death inviting the men to dance with him to the death, replete with vampires sucking blood from the dead and the living, maniacal madness and even brutal murder. The madness continued through the night. The exhausted, hungry and thirsty men slowly settled into an uneasy quiet as the ship began to get under way again in the early morning hours.

The *Oryoku Maru* was sailing along the Bataan coast about 0300 on 14 December, 1944 with four ships in convoy. The sane prisoners hoped the movement of the ship would alleviate the hot humid conditions in the holds. Early dawn filtered some light into the holds and the dead, mangled and maimed corpses could be seen in the eerie light. This night of horror was only the first act of this diabolical voyage of death.

At dawn the guards could be seen peering into the seething maelstrom of human misery, laughing at their pitiable plight. Buckets of rice and seaweed soup with warm tea boosted the spirits of the dejected and miserable prisoners. The shouting, pushing and shoving ceased as each one hungrily watched the distribution. The laborious process of distri-

162

bution of equal portions to the men began. The group leaders supervised with each man closely watching to insure no one got more than the other. The exhausted men began to settle down when the second act of this horrible voyage began to unfold.

Screaming in from the east, harbingers of doom descended on the luckless *Oryoku Maru* and her human cargo of unfortunate prisoners of war. Near the entrance to Subic Bay a flight of 12 Navy dive bombers led by Cmdr. R.E. Reira from the *USS Hornet* had spotted the ship and swung in for the attack. Bombs were dropped on the first pass straddling the ship. One bomb blew away the stern and damaged the steering assembly of the ship. Cmdr. Reira broke off the attack and went on his original mission after radioing Task Force 38. The disabled ship could not maneuver and was a sitting duck.

Aerial photo of Oryoku Maru *on fire in Subic Bay. U.S. Navy photo.*

About two hours later a flight of 12 fighter-bombers roared in for the kill with bombs and machine guns blazing, strafing the ship. The roar of the powerful engines, the AA guns on the decks, chattering of the guns, screaming of the bombs and the heavy explosions along side put new fears into the hopelessly trapped prisoners. An officer stood on the ladder and in a calm and matter of fact way, gave a detailed description as the fighter-bombers circled and came in for a second pass on the doomed *Oryoku Maru*. The frightened prison-

ers could only pray that a bomb would not fall into the hatch. More near misses tore a hole in the side of the forward hold providing fresh air and wounding several of the sweating prisoners.

Even though the prisoners were in mortal danger, they cheered as the strafing continued and the Japanese in the cabins above were terror stricken. The prisoners were happy to see the Japanese receive what they had been wanting to do for two and a half years. The upper cabins on the passenger deck were a frightful mess of dead and dying Japanese.

Colonel Jack Schwartz and other doctors were summoned by Lt. Toshino to treat some of the Japanese passengers with very little medical supplies. Little could be done for them or the prisoners. Col. Schwartz described the chaotic condition on deck with the Japanese dead stacked in one lounge and the severely wounded in another lounge.

The bombing and strafing had damaged the ship's steering. Captain Shinn Kajiyama worked his disabled ship in close to the Olaogapo shore and grounded it. During the night the surviving Japanese passengers were evacuated leaving only the guards, some ship's crew and the prisoners aboard. The prisoners spent another night of abject terror, hungry and thirsty, without any treatment of the wounded. The Americans were told they would be taken off the ship as soon as guards could be arranged on shore. Another long night without food, water or treatment for the wounded and sick added to the misery of the entombed men. The navy planes returned the following day, 15 December, to polish off the stricken ship. A bomb exploded on the stern raining shrapnel into hold No. 5. Heavy beams crashed into the hold killing the trapped men. Coal dust exploded and caught fire. A mad dash was made to get out. Shots were fired into the hold killing Captain Ted Parker.

The Japanese opened hatch No. 5 and dozens of bodies were passed up on deck. One lifeboat was provided for seriously wounded (Americans) and eight guards. The boat was attacked by planes and six guards were killed, one on the right of a prisoner in the stern and one on the left of the prisoner.

One lifeboat was lowered with Lt. Toshino

in full dress uniform and the interpreter, Wada. Captain Kajiyama remained on board. By noon most captives had left the ship. Many of the men could not swim and clung to pieces of wreckage or were aided by their comrades. The planes refrained from strafing the prisoners in the water. It appeared that the planes noted the white bodies and wagged their wings to signify recognition. The *Oryoku Maru*, afire and drifting sank in Subic Bay shortly afterwards.

The captives who made shore were contained behind the sea wall for two hours in blazing afternoon sun. A few guards survived and Japanese Marines took charge of guarding POWs. Over 250 POWs died on ship or drowned, The survivors who made shore were marched barefooted with very little clothing 500 yards to a tennis court. The seriously wounded and sick were not permitted to lag and were beaten into line. The senior officers attempted to bring chaos into some order. The prisoners were divided into groups of 52 men, each group allocated space four feet by fifty feet. A referee stand was placed in the center of the tennis court for a command post. Lt. Col. Beecher and Maj. Ridgely, Adjutant, assumed charge. This was the first time an accurate count of the survivors could be made. A sick bay 15-feet wide near the base line served as a hospital. Medics Webb, Barrett, and Col. Schwartz tended the seriously ill and wounded as best they could. Sunstroke, dehydration and no food or water contributed to the agony and misery. Water from one spigot served long lines, most men were without containers. The hot sun bore down on the almost naked bodies and bare heads. The night became cold and the suffering was intense. The last meal was breakfast on 14 December. Much food could be seen nearby, but it belonged to the Japanese Navy. Wada explained that aboard ship the Navy was responsible, but on shore the Japanese Army was responsible and the Japanese Navy would not cooperate.

The second day began with two tablespoons of dry rice served each man. Cooking facilities were nearby but the men were denied use to cook the rice. The third and fourth day, the Nips were persuaded to allow 25 of the sickest men to be moved to shade, but were returned at night. Two spoons of dry rice were the menu for the day. The fifth day some clothing was issued though already the prisoners were rapidly being broiled alive. Aircraft appeared daily over the tennis court as low as 500 feet, strafing military positions, signalling recognition to the POWs by wagging their wings. After almost two weeks of unmitigated hell on earth, on the 20 December, 16 trucks arrived. One half (650) of the POWS crammed into the trucks for the sixty-mile ride to San Fernando Pampango provincial jail. The following day the balance of the survivors were brought to San Fernando Pampango and lodged in a theater. Again the treatment was brutal; water was scarce and dry rice was the only food. Finally, for the first time in over two weeks, a ration of steamed rice was furnished.

The Japanese officer, Lt. Toshino, told the Americans to "select the men who were unable to travel and they will be shipped back to Bilibid." The selected 15 men were loaded onto trucks and taken to a nearby area and executed by beheading and bayoneting. The order for this was allegedly brought to San Fernando by another Japanese officer from Manila. Again there was no intent or attempt to send the men back to Cabanatuan or Bilibid.

On December 24, the two groups from the jail and the theater were brought out and marched to the railway station. They were jammed into the cars so tightly that there was only room to stand. Some men were put on top as protection from aerial attacks. After 22 hours, the train deposited them in San Fernando La Union on Lingayan Gulf. The prisoners were moved into a school yard and Tenko (roll call) was held. The school building was set up as a sick bay and the rest of the men found places to lie down outside for the first time in 25 hours. Water details were formed and a ration of cooked rice was served.

The nights were very cold with little or no covering. No additional clothing had been provided. Only the clothing on their backs or from the dead was available. Early on Christmas morning the group was formed up and marched about two miles to the beach area. Another meal of rice was served. Groups of 100 men were allowed to go in the water for the first bath since leaving the *Oryoku Maru*.

The third act of this incredibly diabolical scenario was about to begin. The men were marched to a pier jutting out into the bay and loaded into landing barges. Those who could not climb down into the barges were shoved off the pier. The barges then moved out into the harbor to a small freighter, the 6,000-ton *Enoura Maru*. Loading was difficult as the men were so weak they could not climb up the rope ladders on the side of the ship. The ship's captain and the guards were screaming speedo, speedo. All eyes were turned aloft looking for aircraft. Unfortunately, none appeared to sink the ships, and the loading continued. About 1,073 men boarded the freighter *Enoura Maru*. Two hundred-forty men were waved off to another ship nearby, a 3,000-ton freighter, the *Brazil Maru*. The ships immediately set sail in a nine-ship convoy and left Lingayan Gulf.

Discipline broke down and the officers were trying to bring control with some semblance of order. They were on two decks with the sick bay on the upper deck with about 100 men and the balance in the lower level deep in the bowels of the ship. Commander Bridgett, by unorthodox methods, prevailed upon the men for order and they finally settled in with a lot of gripes. Conditions were bad enough, that without some discipline and control it would only get worse.

The holds were filthy with horse manure and no latrines. Five-gallon buckets were provided. Most of the men had dysentery or diarrhea and the buckets soon filled. The Japanese would not let the prisoners haul them up on deck. The filth flowed into the bilges and a heavy noxious odor fouled the air. By 29 December, the situation had deteriorated to a point that the filthy conditions threatened everyone. The filthy method of dumping the rice on a piece of canvas, so the bucket could be sent back up for more rice, was resorted to from necessity. A wild melee broke out at serving time. Fights and near riots spilled some food and water. Most of the men had no containers to put the rice in and had to grab their portion in their dirty hands. Conditions were so appalling that everyone was dejected, dehydrated, demoralized and filthy dirty. They were rapidly losing all hope of ever getting out of the living hell.

The Japanese ships were extremely cautious and only sailed in daylight hours at about 10 knots and pulled into small bays at night. The depressed, bedraggled, starved and thirsty prisoners had hopes that this was the end of the horrifying journey on January 1, when the ships pulled into Takao, Formosa. Alas, their hopes were dashed as the ship remained in the harbor without unloading a soul. On the sixth of January the remaining prisoners from the *Brazil Maru* were transferred to the *Enoura Maru*. Approximately 1,350 wretched men were crammed into one hold on two levels. The crowding on both levels was atrocious. Very little food or water was issued. Water, even in port, was rationed by the spoonful. The night of the seventh was a veritable hell, as men went insane fighting for space to stand, sit or lay down on the cold deck. The following morning the corpses were piled on the hatch cover. Early on the morning of the eighth of January 600 men were transferred to a forward hatch, relieving some of the crowding.

On the ninth of January, those welcome harbingers of doom, American dive bombers roared in to demolish shipping in the harbor at Takao. The harbor was crowded with many ships and one of those unfortunate ships was the *Enoura Maru*. The prisoners were resigned to their fate by now and relished the idea of death. Anything would have been preferable to the living hell of the past month. They even cheered when they heard the roar of the dive bombers in the hope that the Japanese would give up trying to get them to Japan and leave them in Formosa. One of the flights zeroed in on the hapless *Enoura Maru* and placed two bombs squarely on the ship. A third hit the bridge and engine room. The poor souls who had been transferred to the forward hold were hit dead center by a bomb, killing or wounding almost all of the 600 men.

The dead were stacked on the hatch cover and the severely wounded were treated as best as possible by the few who were able to move. The Japanese refused for four days to remove the dead. Finally a detail from the other hold was sent into the hold to load out the mangled corpses of their comrades. Cargo nets were rigged and the bodies stacked like bags of grain and hoisted up and dumped like dead fish from a fisherman net. A detail on the barge below tried to place the bodies in a row, but were hurried by the Japanese. The macabre job was soon finished and the barge was moved up an estuary. The corpses were dragged across a cement dock on to a sandy area. The task of removing the dead continued for three days. Lt. John M. Wright Jr., in his book, *Captured On Corregidor*, gave a very vivid description of the gruesome work of moving over 300 decomposed corpses from the stricken ship.

Late on the evening of the thirteenth of January, the approximate 900 remaining prisoners were transferred to the smaller *Brazil Maru*. About 150 of these prisoners were severely wounded or sick. The movement of the severely wounded resulted in another 12 deaths from shock and pain. The center of the hatch was covered with wounded and sick who had little chance to survive. The best description would be the **ZERO** ward at Camp O'Donnell, where the hopeless terminal cases were moved to die.

The curtain had been opened on the fourth act of this drama of death and tragedy. The wretched prisoners were to endure more unbelievable suffering and death. In all the annals of marine history, even in the days of the slave traffic in the 1800's, is there recorded such wanton disregard of human life, than that described by the few survivors of this deliberate and malicious horror imposed by the warped minds of Lt. Toshino and Mr. Wada.

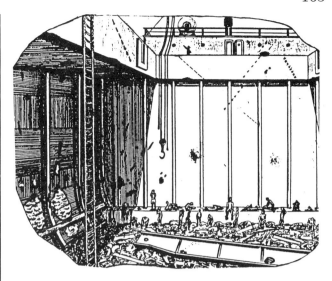

Four days after the bombing (conditions of Enoura Maru*) bodies had not been removed and no treatment for the wounded. Drawing by Eugene C. Jacobs, Col. M.C. Ret.*

The *Brazil Maru* with Captain Kajiyama from the *Oryoku Maru* sailed from Takao on the morning of the fourteenth of January, 1945 in convoy with several other ships and destroyer escorts. Thirty prisoners died the first day and night with an average per day of about 20 rising to 30 in the later part of the journey. The nights grew colder as the ship traveled north. The prisoners had little more clothing than when they had jumped overboard from the *Oryoku Maru*. The dead or dying were robbed of their few clothes by the desperate and nearly frozen living prisoners. No water was issued for the first two days and later only a spoonful twice a day. This was unpalatable and brackish. Water was available for the guards to bathe and ran freely from a tap in view of some of the prisoners. The guards knew how desperate the men were and traded water for whatever of value the men might have after almost 38 months in prison camp and the sinking of two ships. The Japanese were greedy and took advantage of the thirsty, hungry and sick prisoners.

The extreme changes in temperature, men dying of heat exhaustion and suffocation in the tropics, then freezing temperatures off the coast of China, contributed to the misery and death of many more men. The Japanese refused to close the ventilators and stop the cold air from entering the hold. After the second day some of the men found their way into the lower hold which was loaded with

Appalling conditions in the hold of the Enoura Maru *after bombing in the harbor at Takao, Formosa. Courtesy of Eugene C. Jacobs, Col. M.C. Ret.*

sugar. The men had been threatened by Mr. Wada that they would be shot if they stole sugar from the hold below. Death was preferable to the prolonged suffering and the sugar probably saved some lives. It was soon discovered that moderate caloric intake was required rather than the gorging and resultant diarrhea.

The prisoners began to wonder how long the *Brazil Maru* could elude the cordon of submarines around the home islands. They began to pray for a clean hit that would end the misery and suffering. The *Brazil Maru* had sailed slowly along the China coast and provided aid by towing two vessels that were disabled. This action further prolonged the agony and the voyage. When the *Brazil Maru* was off the entrance to Shanghai, Captain Kajiyama, who had been the skipper of the *Oryoku Maru*, tried to persuade Lt. Toshino to drop the prisoners there. Lt. Toshino refused and stated that, "The prisoners were being treated according to international law and that they would be taken to Japan as ordered." This was a situation whereby, the junior officer would not exercise any common sense and insisted on absolute obedience of orders.

The callous guards would quickly look down in the stinking hold every evening to see how many bodies were laid out for burial. The guard would call for a burial detail to hoist the bodies on deck. The few men strong enough to work on the detail were given a little extra rice. Burial services were not permitted on deck and had to be done in the hold. The corpses were wrapped in rice sacks or straw matting and dumped in the sea like garbage. As the ship neared Japan, burials at sea were discontinued. The bodies were stacked on the hatch cover in the center of the hold. The *Brazil Maru* made port at Moji, Japan on the twenty-eighth of January, 1945, after 47 days of unmitigated hell and death for the prisoners crammed into the hold. With below absolute minimum of food or water and grossly inadequate clothing or medical care it was a miracle that any survived. The voyage of death had ended. The original 1,626 prisoners had dwindled to less than 400 starved, emaciated, living skeletons. Over 50 skeletons were stacked on the hatch cover. On the twenty-ninth of January, an inspection party came aboard and looked into the foul-smelling armpit of death that was the hold. They hastily drew back for a breath of fresh air. The weakened, living half-naked skeletons were ordered on deck for the usual glass rod rectal examination for amoebic dysentery. It is interesting to note that this procedure never seemed to identify those with amoebic dysentery. Standing in the freezing cold only added to the indignity and misery of the ridiculous procedure. On the thirty-first of January, 1945 the survivors were issued nothing for breakfast and were ordered up on deck. They were stripped of the rags without a bath and issued new clothing, wool pants, long underwear, shirt and a cotton jacket. After dressing they were moved to a cold and drafty unheated warehouse near the dock. The men found water in fire barrels and drank the foul water, which was intended for fire protection. Late in the afternoon after 24 hours without food, the cold rice which had been cooked on the ship was issued. The group was rearranged and 116 severely sick and wounded men were transferred to the hospital at Moji, 100 officers were to go to Fukuoka Camp No. 3, another group, mostly enlisted men, was sent to Fukuoka Camp No. 17, the third group of 130 officers and 33 medical corpsmen was sent to Fukuoka Camp No. 1. Lt. John M. Wright in his book, *Captured On Corregidor*, writes of the arrival at Fukuoka Camp No. 1, "We were greeted by a detail of medics headed by Sergeant John McIntyre, a medic, whom I had known in Cabanatuan in 1943. We were immediately issued American and British overcoats and crowded around fires which the men had set before our arrival." Trucks were used to transport the men to the camp. In the words of Lt. Wright, "I doubt that there were 10 percent of the men, able to walk from the trucks to the barracks. Many American enlisted men and civilians who had been imprisoned there turned out to greet us and help the weaker ones stumble to the quarters. Some of the worst cases had to be carried. One of the living skeletons, Lt. Cecil C. LeBrin, crawled on his hands and knees to the barracks."

The tragedy of this voyage was not only the suffering but in the extremely high number of deaths, 84 percent, 1,405 died on the voyage or within six months; 16 percent, 216, were still alive by V.J. Day.

The tragic journey of death, despair, torturous living hell, starvation, thirst, filth, disease, and two ships bombed from under them,- had ended after 47 days. Of the 1,626 prisoners, only a little over one percent (216) would be alive at the end of the war. Those that survived to return home faced many months of recuperation in military hospitals. Some of these unfortunate men recovered and returned to active duty. Lt. Colonel Howard K. Johnson rose to the rank of Lt. General and Army Chief of Staff. Lt. John M. Wright Jr. rose to Lt. General, and later attained success in the Boy Scouts of America as national director. Major John N. Shanks, T.C., (Lt. Col.) and Col. Eugene C. Jacobs, Medical Corps also returned and continued in the service. Many have written eloquently of their experiences and have published books about the *Oryoku Maru* Cruise of Death.

The total encirclement of the vaunted Japanese Co-Prosperity Sphere by the American-forces created a gauntlet of submarines and air cover around the home islands. The probability of a ship getting through unscathed was nearly impossible. Every sea route to Japan from the Orient was patrolled by wolf packs of submarines. The skippers of these underseas warships were daring, aggressive and audacious in action. Men of the submarine service were in extreme danger each time they attacked a convoy. At times they would be able to sink all or most of the vessels and were in turn attacked by Japanese escort ships. The skippers would head for the deep and ride out the searching sonar and inevitable depth charges. Rarely was it possible for them to search for survivors.

The responsible perpetrators of this tragedy were tried by The International War Crimes Tribunal and received varying sentences; Toshino, Junsaburo Lt. Japanese Army Officer in charge of draft shipment, formerly at Davao, vile reputation; Japanese Officer in charge of 1626 prisoners of war on the *Oryoku Maru*, *Brazil Maru* and *Enoura Maru*. Tried by International Military Tribunal, sentenced to death by hanging.

Wada, Shunusuke, interpreter, haunch-backed dwarf, *Davao*, and *Oryoku Maru*, sentenced to life imprisonment by the International Tribunal.

Shinn Kajiyama, Captain of *Oryoku Maru*, later of *Brazil Maru*, acquitted, attempted to help POWs, but Lt. Tushino refused to agree.

Other guards were sentenced to lesser terms. Guards were mostly Formosan, commanded by Kazutatane Aihara, Lance Corporal, (nickname Air Raid) at Cabanatuan. Later, all were released effective about 1956.

The Tragic Voyage of the *Oryoku Maru*
Summary
Breakdown of the personnel by grade 1,035 Officers, 47 Civilians, 37 British, 500 Enlisted

Lieutenant Colonels	92	Lieutenants, Navy	36
Commanders	5	Ensigns, Navy	31
Majors	170	Warrant Officers	14
Lt. Commanders	14	Noncoms all serv.	357
Captains	261	Enlisted Men	180
LT.'s AR. MAR.	400	Civilians	47
Lieutenants J.G.	12	(Men from FT Mck.7)	
	954		662

There were instances where attempts were successful in rescuing prisoners of war from the water after a convoy had been attacked. This was the exception rather than the rule.

Miraculous Rescue At Sea

An epic sea rescue of some of the survivors of an attack was carried out in February of 1945. This daring rescue of Allied prisoners of war survivors is described by Theodore Roscoe, in *United States Submarine Operations in World War Two*. "In the early part of 1944 the Japanese at Singapore were cheering the completion of a railroad through the jungles of Thailand which had been built by British, Australian, Dutch, American and native slave labor. This iron trail had cost 22,000 lives of the slaves and prisoners. Abject brutality, merciless floggings, and finger snap medical care, starvation and slow death were normal. The survivors of the railroad detail and the barbarous railroading worked on docks in Singapore from March through September, while the Japanese waited for shipment. Ships to transport them to Japan were delayed by the submarine menace. The prisoners were to become slaves in the Emperors factories and mines.

On the sixth of September, 1944, a convoy of six ships and five escorts sailed from Singapore for Japan. Crammed aboard the *Rakuyo Maru* were 1,350 British and Australian captives. Some 750 of their fellow prisoners were stuffed like cattle into the hold of another ship, *Kachidoki Maru*, formerly the American Lines President Harrison. The other four ships in the convoy were a heavily laden transport, a freighter loaded with rice and rubber, the other two were oil tankers. Several days after sailing, the convoy was joined by three passenger cargo ships and two escorts from the Philippines.

The night of 12 September, 1944, the convoy was sailing on a northward course in three columns, three ships to a column. The *DD Shikinami* was leading the center column, with three small escorts on each flank.

This was the convoy that fell prey to the torpedoes of *Ben's Busters*, (a wolf pack of three subs), *USS Growler*, *USS Pampanito* and *USS Sea Lion II*. Between 0100 and 0130 on the twelfth of September, all three of the subs made radar contact with the convoy about 290 miles off Hainan Island. The submarines went into action.

At 0155 *USS Growler* attacked from the convoy's starboard side and put a torpedo in *Hirado*, leading escort vessel on the starboard bow. This craft, a frigate, blew up amidships and burst into flames and sank in a few minutes. The sky began to flash, reflecting gunfire from the other escorts. The *Growler* withdrew and started an end run around for a second attack. At 0324 hours the *USS Sea Lion II* drove in for an attack on the starboard. In two minutes time, *Sea Lion* slammed two torpedoes into the passenger-cargo *Nankai Maru* in the center of the formation. Another torpedo into a transport leading the right column, and two more in the *Rakuyo Maru*. The Japanese on the *Rayuko Maru* began immediately to abandon ship. The unfortunate (1,350) prisoners were left to fend for themselves. Somehow the prisoners got free and into the water.

At 0650, the *USS Growler*, attacked and sank the destroyer *Shikinami*. The *Nankai Maru* went down an hour later and the *Rakuyo Maru* sank late in the afternoon.

During the day, most of the Japanese survivors were picked up by escorts, while the prisoners in the water were held at bay by rifles and pistols. By nightfall, they were desperately swimming or clinging to mats or wreckage. Nearly all were smeared from head to foot by the crude oil on the surface of the water. After sundown the prospect of survival seemed slim indeed. But these castaways were to have an unexpected deliverance.

Throughout the day *USS Pampanito* had tracked the convoy, but had been unable to attack, because *Growler* and *Sea Lion* were attacking and the convoy had changed course towards Hong Kong. But *Pampanito* hung on doggedly as her Captain P.E. Summers directed the chase. At 2210 hours, the submarine was in position for a surface attack. The *Pampanito* fired nine torpedoes at the remaining four merchant ships. Seven torpedoes hit home. One salvo sank the tanker *Zuiho Maru*, another sank the 10,500-ton passenger-cargo *Kachidoki Maru* (formerly *USS President Harrison*). Now more than 700 prisoners of war struggled desperately as *Pampanito* evaded the escorts and cleared the vicinity. The submarine was unaware, as well as *Growler* and *Sea Lion*, that Allies were in dire need of help. (*USS Harrison* had been trapped in Shanghai at the outbreak of war.)

On 14 September, *Growler* departed the area. *Pampanito* and *Sea Lion* remained on station. On the afternoon of 15 September, *USS Pampanito* passing through the waters where she had made her attack, discovered a crude raft loaded with men. Captain Summers summed up the situation and *Pampanito* immediately began picking up men as fast as she could locate them.

The Patrol Report tells the dramatic story, "As the men were hauled aboard, we stripped them and removed most of the heavy coating of oil and muck. We cleared the after torpedo room and passed them below as quickly as possible. We gave each man a piece of cloth moistened with water to suck on. All of them were dehydrated and exhausted after three days in the water and three years of imprisonment. Many had lashed themselves to the makeshift raft, which was slick with the heavy oil, and some had life belts. All showed signs of beriberi, pellagra, exposure, salt-water sores, ringworms and ulcerated legs and malaria. All were very thin from under-nourishment. Some were in very bad shape, but with the excitement of rescue and as they came alongside with cheers for the Yanks and many a curse for the Nips."

"It was quite a struggle to keep them on the raft as we lifted them off one by one. They could not manage to secure a line to the raft and men went over the side to do the job. The survivors came tumbling aboard and then collapsed with strength almost gone. A pitiful sight that none of us will ever forget. All hands turned to with a will and the men were cared for as rapidly as possible."

At 1710 hours, 15 September, *Papanito* sent a message to the *Sea Lion* asking for help. From that hour on, the two submarines raced the approaching darkness. *Sea Lion* gave a hand and the two submarines combed the area picking up survivors. By 2000 hour no more men could be safely accommodated on the overcrowded submarines. The submarines raced for Saipan. Cmdr. Reich expressed the submariners feelings as he wrote, "It was heartbreaking to leave so many dying men behind." *USS Pampanito* had rescued 73 men and *USS Sea Lion* had picked up 54.

As soon as ComSubPac received the word, they ordered *USS Barb* and *USS Queenfish*, then patrolling in the Luzon Straits, to the rescue area to search for survivors. By the afternoon of 17 September, these submarines were combing the waters where the human derelicts had last been seen. *USS Barb* had sunk an escort carrier the day before. The commander was always ready for this type of assignment. "I received orders from ComSo-WestPac to proceed to the survivor area. I heartily agreed. As an afterthought—after seeing the pitiful plight of the 34 men we rescued, I can say that I would forego the opportunity of attacking a Japanese task force to rescue one survivor." There is little room for sentiment in marine warfare, but, the measure of saving one Allied life against sinking one Japanese ship needs no explanation here, once experienced. "Rescue teams of expert swimmers, hauling out, strippers and delivery parties were immediately organized. *USS Barb* and *USS Queenfish* ran a race

against the threat of enemy attack, heavy seas and winds that were whipping up to typhoon velocity. Incredibly, survivors were found."

A glance at the submarine dispersion maps for September and October 1944, indicates the decimation of the Japanese merchant marine. The tremendous losses reveal the desperation of the Japanese to run convoys with critical materials and risk the loss of critical Japanese merchant crews and ships as well as the human cargo of slave labor. The wanton and inhumane disregard of the provisions of the Geneva Convention by long exposure as potential targets and of the prisoners to horrible deaths in unmarked ships without any means of survival if attacked by either submarines or aircraft, is of importance. These facts should be written clearly in history as the depths of man's inhumanity to his fellow man.

The question arises of what practical labor contributions could be extorted from these slaves after three years of deprivation, disease, starvation, totally inadequate medical care and brutal treatment? At this point in time the Japanese military clique should have accepted the fact that they were losing the war. Even if the Japanese intelligence did not know the precise location of the attackers, a simple chart of the losses would have alerted them to the impossible task of running the gauntlet of doom.

Parallels may be found in the dark dusty tomes of history that are filed away in libraries around the world. The majority of which have not been read or studied by the following generations. The mass extermination of the Jews, the disappearance of millions of prisoners of war into obscurity, the mass murder of the Polish Army Officers Corps and other notable incidents of the period are still not understood or discounted as false.

There are many former military men who still have not been able to cast aside the horrors of imprisonment and suffer from flashbacks, weird dreams and inability to forget their traumatic experiences. There are others who returned from the horrors of the prison camps and have been able to look ahead and remember the past but not to allow it to affect their lives. I have been extremely fortunate in many ways, to be able to reflect on the experiences of others and my own experiences in prison camp, but, not to the extent of letting it interfere with my life in this land of the free. Writing this book has not affected me in recalling or researching other books on the three and one-half years as a prisoner of war of my comrades or myself.

The fortunes of war affect many of our men who are swept into the catalyst. Some of the men measured up as leaders and others failed miserably in their duty to their country and the men under their control. The ordeal of the *Oryoku Maru* was a test of the character and strength of the prisoners. The abysmal depths of humiliation, depravity, starvation, lack of water and brutal mental and physical treatment by the diabolical Lt. Toshino. and Mr. Wada brought out the elements of good leadership expected of our officers and service men. Others failed to measure up and fell back on selfishness, self-pity and self-destruction.

Those who survived this horrendous voyage of death and returned to a normal life are to be commended and worthy of the highest regard. Those who failed and managed to survive will pay the price of their perfidy. Many of our servicemen have fallen into the curse of post-traumatic stress and use its thesis as a crutch for not being able to forget their bad experiences. Many of the ex-prisoners have put those experiences behind them and made the most of their hard-won freedoms. Some have not been able to do so and suffer from the memories of imprisonment. Many will not eat rice in any form. Many will not drive Japanese-made automobiles or own Japanese-made television sets. Most of the prisoners that have attended the national conventions of either American Defenders of Bataan and Corregidor or The American Ex-Prisoners of War, find old friends and talk freely about their experiences. A few will not have anything to do with anything relating to their prison camp experiences. They would rather just forget the horrors. It is too bad that some are this way as there is a certain positive benefit in visiting with old comrades in arms.

An article appearing in *Reader's Digest*, by Lewis Thomas, M.D. is interesting. "The only question I am inclined to turn aside as impossible to respond to, happens to be the one most raised these days, not just by my biologist friends but by everyone: the question about stress, how to avoid stress, prevent stress, allay stress.

"I refuse to have anything to do with this matter, having made up my mind, from everything I have heard or read about it in recent years, what people mean by stress is simply the condition of being human, and I will not recommend any meddling with that by medicine or any other profession."

Perhaps the ending should be a prayer that those who suffered the indignity and suffering of imprisonment under grossly horrible conditions should be remembered by all and particularly by our succeeding generations. It is too easy for historians and educators to cram the experiences and ordeals of these gallant men into a nutshell summation. This prayer is for the thousands who are among the soldiers, sailors, marines and civilians who died in the belief of DUTY, HONOR and COUNTRY. "Please Lord teach us to laugh again, but God don't ever let us forget that we tried."

No Army Has Ever Done So Much With So Little.

—General of the Army
Douglas MacArthur

The story of the tragic voyage of the *Oryoku Maru* was compiled from the stories told by Lt. Gen. John M. Wright, Lt. Col. Eugene C. Jacobs, Lt. Col. Manny Lawton, Lt. Col. Charles M. Brown and Maj. E. Bartlett Kerr from the following referenced publications. The repeating of their experiences are for the purpose of depicting the fickle winds of fate and the smiles of Lady Luck and the desires of someone higher than mortal man.

There are several conflicting points as to the facts. The late loading of seven men from Fort McKinley which increased the number of POWs from 1,619 to 1,626. Second point was a difference of opinion existing as to which of the two ships, *Enoura Maru* and the *Brazil Maru* made the final voyage from Takao, Formosa. The majority believe the final ship was the *Brazil Maru*.

The entire listing of the 1,619 (1,626) prisoners of war may be found in Manny Lawton's book. There is a question as to the total number of prisoners on the shipping roster. Colonel Eugene C. Jacobs in *Blood Brothers*, indicates there were seven prisoners from Fort McKinley who were brought to the pier prior to embarkation. This would make the total on the shipping list 1,626.

References:
Some Survived by Manny Lawton.
Captured On Corregidor, Diary of An American POW in World War II by John M. Wright Jr., Lt. Gen. Ret.
Blood Brothers by Eugene C. Jacobs, Col. Ret.
Bilibid Diary, The Secret Notebook of Commander Thomas Hayes.
POW, Philippines 1942-1944 edited by A.B. Feuer.
The Japanese Story, American Ex-Prisoners of War, Pamphlet #10, edited by Stanley Sommers, National American Ex-Prisoners of War. MedSearch Committee.
Surrender and Survival, Experiences of American POWs In The Pacific, 1942-1945, E. Bartlett Kerr.
The Oryoko Maru *Story,* Lt. Col. Charles M. Brown, AUS Ret.

CORREGIDOR

OASIS OF HOPE

EPILOGUE

"THOSE WHO HAVE LONG ENJOYED SUCH PRIVILEGES AS WE ENJOY, FORGET IN TIME, THAT MEN HAVE DIED TO WIN THEM."

FRANKLIN D. ROOSEVELT

Epilogue

Upon returning to Birmingham General Hospital on a weekend, I met up with Ernest Haddox and Walter Lee White of Phoenix, Arizona. We had a good time going into Oxnard and visiting some of the nice bars. We were feeling our way back into America's mainstream. Girl watching was a tremendous feeling. We had not seen so many round eyes in the past five years. It was nice to sit in a comfortable lounge, talk and dance with some of the girls and listen to the jukebox or a piano player. All of the popular songs were new to us. We were emotionally starved for music, movies, and the better things of life, W.W.S. (wine, women and song). We were tasting the sweetness of freedom which had been a part of our hopes and dreams for so long. We were allowed a pass every night and really lived it up.

Christmas 1945 was a great time. Turkey and all the trimmings, pumpkin and mince meat pies. Oh, such a feast, we tried to make up for the past four Christmases. The United Service Organization (USO) put on a beautiful show with Bob Hope and other great stars. **What** a holiday season.

Medical processing started as soon as we had returned from leave. I received the news after I returned from X-ray. My X-ray showed a calcified tubercular lesion in the left lung. The treatment was complete isolation and bed rest. Haddox and White sailed through with flying colors. I was immediately slammed into isolation, private room with bath. This was quite a shock to me, as I felt like a million dollars and was thanking my lucky stars for having returned from prison camp in good shape. Now I was unable to engage in our favorite pastime of girl watching and visiting with the other patients. I had gained weight and felt in tip top shape except for vision problems. The doctors had put me on a high vitamin diet with the hope of improving eyesight and gave me glasses. In isolation I started to read everything I could get from the library in the way of books, magazines and articles on the war. There was so much in Europe and the Pacific that we knew very little about.

The big day came when the finance department had determined our back pay and we were paid for four years or more. **Wow**, we were loaded. I lay on my bed and looked at those five big numbers on my check and mused what I would do with so much money. The medics would not let me out of my room to go to the PX or a bank. Finally, I prevailed and they took me to the bank and PX in a wheelchair to deposit the money and shop in the PX. I had to wear a face mask and could not go in the snack bar. I desperately wanted to buy a Bulova watch. Such a luxury as looking at a watch to determine time was almost indescribable. I kept looking at the time every few moments.

Walter Lee White went out and bought a 1938 Buick convertible and departed for Arizona. Bill Haddox took his discharge and went home to New Mexico. Most of the other friends of those prison days had been sent to hospitals near their home. Now I was alone and confined in the room 24 hours a day. This was confining but I accepted the doctors orders, except for staying in bed all day. He would give me holy hell for even sitting in an easy chair or going to the bathroom. I was supposed to call the nurse for a duck (urinal) or a bed pan. I would have none of that. I felt able to take care of those chores without any help from a nurse.

In early February I was transferred to Moore General Hospital in Swannanoa, North Carolina. The first order of the day on arrival was a sputum test. My test came back positive and I was slammed into a locked ward again. No freedom, but under far better conditions then before. I still felt good and had no other symptoms of the TB. The doctors were interested in where I had contracted the disease. The only person that I could recall that I had ever been in contact with that had TB was First Sergeant Adrian Martin of the 200th CAC on the *Noto Maru*. We had sat in each others laps and shared water, food and space for the trip to Japan. Sgt. Martin died in June of 1945 at Hanawa of TB.

I started to read and take advantage of some of the educational activities available on the ward. I was able to complete my high school equivalence test and received my certificate. I learned many years later that during the time I was at Moore General Hospital, Captain. E. Pearce Fleming was also there in the officer's ward. He had been the senior American officer at Hanawa, Japan the last year. The ward nurse, was Lt. Mary Mekeel from Dixon, Illinois. She introduced me to her friend, a nurse, Lt. Hazel E. Sievwright of Wisconsin.

Enlisted men were not supposed to fraternize with officers. However, there were ways to get around those rules providing both parties were amendable. Cupid prevails in spite of any regulation. We could arrange dates in the hospital area until I was released from isolation.

Each week the patients had to take a sputum test. A poker chip was placed by your name, red for positive and white for negative. I watched as my string lengthened with white chips. My X-rays continued to show no change. We were not restricted to bed during the day and could move about the ward and play cards, read and enjoy the beautiful warm sunshine from the porch of the ward. I began formulating plans for the future. I would propose to that nice nurse and we could start together on the future.

In June 1946 I finally won my freedom and was let out of the restricted ward. I was to be a guinea pig for a medical research team from Colorado. They were conducting a study to determine why more men contacted TB in the rear areas than in the combat arms. The only requirement was that any chest X-rays be sent to them for study and determination of progress.

When young men are well fed and time is heavy on the mind, their thoughts turn to romance. It was only logical and inevitable that cupid would enter the picture. I decided that it was time for me to settle down and take a wife. I popped the question to Lt. Sievwright and at first encountered some resistance. Finally after more persuasion and determination we were married in August of 1946. After returning from leave, my wife received her orders for separation at Fort Sheridan, Illinois. We returned to North Carolina as I had not been discharged from the hospital.

Late in September of 1946 I was called to the front office. A lieutenant colonel had me sit down and went over my medical records and treatment. He said, "We are going to discharge you with a 100 percent medical discharge." My new wife and I had discussed our future and wanted to remain in the service. After all, I was a technical sergeant with seven years and four months on one enlistment. Much to the surprise of the medical officer I replied, "Colonel, I do not want to be discharged with a 100 percent disability, I would like to reenlist."

The colonel asked, "Are you sure?"

"Yes Sir," I replied.

Shaking his head he said he would pass the word on to the front office. He remarked, "Most of the men cannot wait to be discharged and would have ran out the door, shouting with joy and you want to reenlist."

I received orders for separation and reenlistment and was ordered to Fort Bragg, North Carolina for assignment. Reporting to Fort Bragg, I reenlisted in the Air Force and was ordered to Hamilton Field California with a 90 day delay en route. We arrived in California and I reported for duty on 7 January 1947. Hamilton Field was a choice assignment and we were able to find quarters in Vallejo, California. Choosing the Air Force for a ground pounder was a mistake. There were hundreds of master sergeants (officers were permitted to enlist in Grade E-7), if they desired to remain in the service. The old British marching song came to mind, "There will be no promotions this side of the ocean, so cheer up my lads, bless them all."

The Army announced a new program for warrant officers and I applied and took the test as a heavy equipment maintenance officer. The world tension began to tighten and the National Air Defenses was being reorganized to intercept bombers from over the Arctic. Hamilton Field personnel were divided into two groups of equal size. In some manner the decision was made that one group would be shipped to Moses Lake Air Force Base in Washington. Again Lady Luck smiled on me and I was a part of the 325th Fighter Wing, with Black Widow night fighter and transferred to Moses Lake, Washington. (Now Larson AFB.)

During my time at Hamilton Field one of the first ex-prisoners of war I encountered was Cpl. Lloyd Hill. He was the one who volunteered to take the blame for stealing the Japanese guard's blouse in Hanawa in September of 1944.

The transfer of the 325th Wing to Moses Lake was almost like going back to the days in Hanawa. The base had been a training base for bomber pilots and the only thing going for it was it had two ten-thousand-foot runways. The camp had been closed for a couple of years. The barracks, headquarters, and other buildings were tar paper shacks heated by coal burning space heaters. There was no coal in stock and the base commanding officer had to commandeer a train load in order to get heat in the hospital and barracks. There were no quarters for families on base. Houses or apartments were scarce and prices for any thing off base had skyrocketed.

I had been assigned as the NCO IC of the advance party and arrived there in late October with instructions to get things set up for the arrival of the 325th Motor Vehicle Squadron. Things were in order and the unit arrived on schedule. All the key jobs were assigned and I was left out, much to my dismay. One morning at the central mess, I met another ex-prisoner of war from Hanawa, Technical Sergeant Clayton C. Burns. He was originally Army Air Force and was assigned to Moses Lake on special assignment with Boeing Aviation Company. He was to live, breathe, talk and absorb information from the Boeing technicians working on the XB-47 which was undergoing flight tests at Moses Lake.

The central mess was the only place where all the men of the base met daily. One day one of the men said, "Hey isn't your name Nix? Your name was in the Army Times as being selected for the warrant officer program." I returned to the squadron area and spoke to the squadron commander. He told me that he had known it for two weeks but was waiting for the official orders. I asked for leave to go to Sixth Army Headquarters to determine why I had not received orders. Arriving at Sixth Army Headquarters at Presidio of San Francisco, I received my orders and was processed for appointment to Warrant Officer Junior Grade, Regular Army. The Corps of Engineers was to be the monitor of 4880 MOS (Military Occupational Specialty).

My new career was interesting and a challenge. My first assignment was to a general depot in New Jersey for three years. Next came three years in Austria with an engineer construction battalion and a field maintenance company, two years in the engineer section of another general depot in Stockton California, 14 months in Korea with an engineer depot and then the best assignment, to the Office of the Chief of Engineers in Washington D.C. My final assignment was to Chinon, France with the 528th Heavy Maintenance Company. Retirement came easy after 23 years active duty.

I started researching and talking to many who were ex-prisoners of war both from Europe and the Pacific. The two main organizations that were formed by ex-prisoners of war are: The Defenders of Bataan and Corregidor and The American Ex-Prisoners of War. These two organizations have made it their goal that the sacrifices of the thousands who survived and those who were unfortunate and did not survive shall not be forgotten.

My association with these two groups has stimulated my desire to learn more about what happened to the unfortunate and why. Perhaps I may be able to better understand in my own mind and tell the story as it was from the worm's eye view of one who was more fortunate, but could have very easily been one of the less fortunate or one of the unfortunate. The dark and dismal picture that emerges from the murky past is beyond human com-

178

prehension in this world of today. The story has not been accepted by those who never suffered the loss of their freedom or are not aware of the horrors of being at the mercy of an Oriental captor. As the survivors begin to fade away into history, the true story will die. Even today, there are people who do not believe the horrible things that are recorded and look at one who tries to promote the truth as one who is ready for the men in the white coats.

This story of the past has been written to illustrate how some are fortunate to have survived three years and four months of imprisonment with little lasting effect. Whereas, there are some who still face the trauma of their experiences each day. There are others who have closed their minds to that period of time and do not wish to recall the good with the bad. Either way they have made new beginning for themselves. They have succeeded and pray that never again shall our succeeding generations be sacrificed needlessly. As J.C. Holland once wrote, "God gives every bird its food but does not throw it into their nest." So it is with us, the ex-prisoners of war, we must make it on our own. No one is going to bring it to us.

Note: The Japanese and Filipino words in the narrative are the phonetic sounds and are not necessarily correct spelling.

Appendix 1
Personnel Roster
Port Area Depot
1939-1941

Men stationed in the Port Area were a mixture from various units in the Philippines. They were carried on the roster of the parent unit but were attached for quarters and rations to the Port Area Detachment for duty.

Officers

Name	Rank	Stationed	Current Rank/Status
Byrd, Cornellius Z.	Captain,	Detachment Commander. 1939-40	Died on Oryoku Maru, December 1944
Robbins, Pasha	Captain	Detachment Commander, 1939-41	
*Quinn, Michael A.	Major	Depot Cmdr.	Died in Washington 1987
*Montgomery, Austin J.	Captain	Depot	Survived the Oryoku Maru./Died in 1990

Enlisted Men

Name	Rank	Stationed	Current Rank/Status
Abel, Gilbert A	S/Sgt.	Depot Shop Foreman	Commissioned 2nd. Lt./Died on the Arisan Maru, 24 October 1944
Appleby, John			
Barrone, Sylvestor		USAFFE, Hdqtrs.	
*Becraft, Leroy	PFC	31st Inf. Welder	Retired USAF Master Sergeant/Lives in Manila P.I.
Beyack, Steve		Vet. Corps.	
Combs, Charles		Motor Pool	
Cooper	T/Sgt	Port Area Detachment	F/Sgt./Died on the Arisan Maru, 24 Oct. 1944
Cox, Hershel B.		Depot Supply	Died on the Arisan Maru
*Delapp, George H.		VET. Corps	Lives in Kansas City, MO.
Emanual, James		USAFFE Hdqtrs. G-2.	Lives in Golden, CO.
Fogel, Eddie	PVT.	Fort Mills, Corregidor	
*Golson, Archie M.	S/Sgt.	Depot Shop Clerk	Whereabouts unknown
*Haddox, Ernest	PFC	Depot Shop	Died in Albuquerque N.M. 1985
Hawkins, Ralph		USAFFE, G-4	Lives in Cashmere, WA.
Hendrix, James		Shop Clerk,	Discharged, Civilian
Hundley, Henry	PFC	QMC Supply	
Hickman, Richard	PFC	Depot Shop Carpenter	
*Hilton, Chas. M.	PVT.	Service Company, 31st. Inf.	Lives in Ky.
Kuklinski		Vet. Corps	
*Kunich, John	S/Sgt.	Service Company. 31st. Inf.	Died in Ohio, 1987
*Larson, Edward J.	S/Sgt	Welding and Sheet Metal Shop	Lives in Snohomish, WA.
*Larsen, Leonard O.	S/Sgt	Supply	Survivor
Lilley, William		Depot Motor Pool	
Milliken, Myron	Sgt.	Depot Motor Pool	
Miller, Joe			
*Nix, Asbury L.	S/Sgt.	Depot Shop	Lives in Stevens Point, WI.
Ocedek, John T.	T/Sgt.	Machinist	Died on Arisan Maru, 24 Oct. 1944
Petersen, Lester J.	S/Sgt.	3rd. Pur. Sqdn., Depot Shop Inspector.	Executed at Camp O'Donnell
Puzan,	T/Sgt.	34th Lt. Maint. Co (PS)	
Price, John	CPL.	Supply	Died on Arisan Maru, 24 Oct, 1944
Reynolds, Ralph	S/Sgt.	Welder	Died on Bataan
*Rust, William	PFC	Motor Pool	Lives in Illinois
Schwartz, Abraham	S/Sgt	Supply	Died (Major) on Oryoku Maru
*Shanks, John N.	M/Sgt.	Depot Shop NCO 1C,	(Major) survived the Oryoku Maru, last heard of in Berlin Germany 1949
Standridge, William	Sgt.	Welder	Died on Arisan Maru
*Teske, Clyde	S/Sgt.	PX Manager	Died in San Antonio, Circa 1988
Timm, Thomas			

Appendix 1 (continued)

Troy, Wm. G.		31st Inf. Det./USAFFE Hdqtrs.G-3	Falls Church, Va.
Vansall, David		Army Air Corps	
Verdugo, Joe			
Watson, Donald		Veterinary Corps	
Watson, Hadley			
Wesley, Scott			
*Wheeler, Tony	Cpl.	Depot Motor Pool	Died in Colorado
*White, Walter Lee	PVT	Welder	Lives in Arizona
Woods, R.G.			
Worthington	PFC	Veterinary Corps.	

*Names are those known to have returned to the United States. There may be others who were assigned in the Port Area who returned or died in prison camp.

This list was compiled by Asbury L. Nix during interviews of various men over the years. The Port Area Detachment was made up of men attached from other units. They worked in various sections, finance, headquarters, veterinary corps, quartermaster, signal engineers and transportation.

Appendix 2
Order of Battle
Harbor Defenses, Manila and Subic Bay
Headquarters, Fort Mills
Corregidor, P.I.

			Enlisted		
Unit	Commander	Officers	Men	PS	Total
Hqtr, Hqtr, HDMSB	M. Gen. Geo. F. Moore	335	3,318	1,572	5,225
Hqtr, Hqtr Btry		42	326	70	438
59 CAC	Col. Paul Bumker	55	1,237		1,303
60 CAC (AA)	Col. Theo. Chase	72	1,693		1,765
91 CAC	Col. Joseph Rohn	49	27	761	837
92 CAC	Col. Octave DeCorre	45		627	672
U.S.Army Mine Planter	Harrison	4	8	34	46
Station Hospital		50		110	160
Chem. Warfare		3	1		4
		659	6,636	3,144	10,439

Attached Units

4th Marine Regt.	1st BN	2nd BN	3rd BN	4th BN	Res BN	Total
Col. Samuel Howard, Regt. Cmdr.						
USMC	360	331	577	6	188	1,440
USN	125	170	210	286	50	841
USA	312	117	173	11	2	615
Philippine Navy		29	11		4	44
Philippine Air Force	224	206	201		89	720
Philippine Army	22	46	80			148
Constabulary	2	12	5			19
Philippine Scouts	33	13	18			64
	1,078	924	1,275	303	311	3,891

Total Strength——14,250

Other small support detachments were moved to Corregidor in late December from Manila, including USAFFE Headquarters. These units are not counted above. Escapees from Bataan were put into the line outfits listed above.

Note: 4th Marine Regiment Strength at time of arrival in Philipines—44 officers, 728 enlisted men.

Appendix 3
Main Armament
Harbor Defenses Manila and Subic Bay

Corregidor, Fort Mills

	Batteries	Calibre	No. of Guns
2	Geary & Way	12-inch mortars, 1890 & 1908	12
3	Cheney, Crocket & Wheeler	12-inch rifles, disappearing	6
2	Hearn, Smith	12-inch barbette, 360 degrees	2
1	Grubbs	10 guns, disappearing	2
1	RR Mtd. RJ 43	8-inch guns	1
2	Ramsey, Morrison	6-inch guns	5
8	Mobile Field Artillery	155 MM GPF	19
4	James, Maxwell Keyes	3-inch guns	10
23	Batteries		Total 57

El Frle, Fort Drum

2	Marshall & Williams	14-inch, Turreted	4
2	Roberts & McCrea	6-inch	4
1	Hoyle	3-inch	1
5			9

Caballo, Fort Hughes

1	(2 pits) Craighill	12-inch mortars, model 1912	4
2	Gillispie & Woodruff	14-inch, disappearing	2
1	Leach	6-inch disappearing	1
1	Fuger	3-inch	2
5			10

Carabao, Fort Frank

1	Koehler (2 pits)	12-inch mortars, model 1908	8
2	Greer & Crofton	14-inch disappearing	2
3			10
36	Batteries		Total 83

Notes:
1. Most of the 12 & 14 disappearing rifles could not fire on Bataan.
2. The lower turret of Fort Drum could not fire 360 degrees.
3. The mortars on Fort Frank were out of range of Bataan.

Appendix 4
Corregidor, POW Camp No 9
1942-1944

Listing of Personnel

Source, Cable Tokyo, via Geneva to Wash. D.C. Provost Marshal Office, *National Archives*

Technical Sergeants

1. Alford, W.G. — 192 TK. BN.
2. Anderson, L.D. — 5 ABG
3. Beardon E.N. — 12 M.P.
4. Beason, Benj. F. — FIN.
5. Burdwell, R.B. — VMF
6. Bone, R.G. — 19 B.G.
7. Bradford, J.A. — 19 B.G.
8. Brasington, Theo. — DEML
9. Burkett, Albert — Ukn.

Staff Sergeants

10. Anderson, F.A. — Corr.
11. Bailey, Kenneth W. — Med.
12. Barber, A. L. — Corr.
13. Barden, Donald — Ukn.
14. Biddison, WM. T. — 48 M. SQ.
15. Bishop, E. W. — 19 B.G.
16. Boyd, Jack G. — Ukn. —Hanawa 64
17. Braga, G. F. — Corr.
18. Brooks, C.L. — Med.
19. Brooks, R.M. — 19 B.G.
20. Brookshire, O.R. — 19 B.G.
21. Bryant Harold. E. — 8 M. SQ. —Hanawa 94
22. Burcan, C.E. — Ukn.
23. Campbell, J.A. — 19 B.G.
24. Carmichael, J.W. — 19 B.G.
25. Cauvel, Chester M. — HQ. VMF
26. Chavez, R.E — Med.
27. Chism, F.J. — 24 PUR.
28. Cornell, W.P. — 200 CAC
29. Cother, H.E. — 91 B.G.
30. Courts, R.D. — 27 B.G.
31. Cox, H. K. — Unk.
32. Crebill, W.C. — 440 Ord.
33. Danenza, V.A. — Med.
34. Darling, WM. F — HQ. VMF
35. Darey, C.E. — 19 B.G.
36. Diches, D.D. — AAF
37. Doss, L.G. — 24 Pur.
38. Dunagan, Thos. — Ukn.
39. Dzimba, P. — AAF
40. Estes, Clarence A. — Ukn.
41. Francis, Richard. E. — 228 —Sig. Richard E. Francies same name. Not on Corregidor
42. Flores, Howard — 5 ABG
43. Fergeson, Jack D. — 515 CAC
44. Frederio, Miller — Med.
45. Freeman, Aubrey J. — 28 B.S.
46. Gannon, Harold J. — Corr.
47. Gatewood, R.A. — Med.
48. Gervais, Joseph — Ord.
49. Giardini, Joseph A. — 19 B.G.
50. Gooson, Felix E. — 5 ABG
51. Gordon, Melvin E. — 5 ABG
52. Gourdeau, Henry J. — AAF —Hanawa 114
53. Grove, J.C. — AAF
54. Hannah, Elmer F. — 5 ABG
55. Hanson, J.A. — 19 B.G.
56. Hartson, E.L. — 19 B.G.
57. Henly, W.L. — 19 B.G.

Appendix 4 (continued)

58. Heuston, Wallie	19 B.G.	107. Newtom. C.H.	440 Ord.
59. Hilderbrand, Warren	192 Tk. Bn.	108. Nicely, S.	CAC
60. Hinkil, Wayne P.	27 B.G.	109. Niday, Floyd	Engrs.
61. Holladay, Otha L.	31 Inf.	110. Nix, Asbury L.	QMC —Hanawa 97
62. Hough, Richard R.	19 B.G.		
63. Hruocho, Joseph J.	194 Tk. Bn.	111. Noecilar, C.H.	3rd. Pur.
64. Howell, Elmer	59 CAC	112. Norman, W.E.	19 B.G.
65. Huddle, David D.	Ukn.	113. Olson, E D.	Ukn.
66. Hudson, Jack	Ukn.	114. O'Sullivan, J.V.	Army —Hanawa 99
67. Hull, Wm. O.	Med.		
68. Hutchins, W.W.	AAF	115. Oswell, F.N.	CAC
69. Hunn, Richard	24 Pur.	116. Owens, D.T.	CAC
70. Hutto, Calvin R.	515 CAC	117. Palmer, Vernon	Ukn.
71. Jaeger, Robert C.	440 Ord.	118. Parker, J.A.	14 B.S.
72. Jenkins, Geo. M.	30 BS	119. Parry, E.R.	Ukn.
73. Jerman. Bertram R.	5 B Cmd.	120. Partridge, Walter	19 B.G.
74. Johnson, Edward N.	20 ABG	121. Pegher, H.B.	14 B.S.
75. Johnson, Leonard J.	Mer. Mar.	122. Peterson, R.E.	192 Tk. Bn. —Hanawa 90
76. Jones, Carl R.	19 B.G.		
77. Jones, J.P.	Med.	123. Poncio, J.H.	91 B.G.
78. Jones, R.H.	Deml.	124. Pratt. D.R.	5 Int Cd.
79. Kirk, Harold S.	454 Ord.	125. Prisby, J.L.	Ord.
80. Knapp, Joseph T.	228 Sig.	126. Purvis, H.H.	Ukn.
81. Keaul, J.T.	93 B. Sg.	127. Pyetski, M.H.	AAF
82. Kocsis, Bela	34 Pur.	128. Raab, C.E.	5 ABG
93. Koerner, R.A	Ukn	129. Raach, Lewis E.	60 CAC
84. Kolstead, J.T.	21 Pur.	130. Rabin, F.	Med.
85. Kruchowski, S.J.	803 Engr.	131. Rankin, Leslie C.	21 Purs.
86. Kyllo, C.B.	5 ABG	132. Ransberger, E.H.	5 ABG
87. Lang, O.G.	194 Tk. Bn.	133. Redd, J.J.	5 ABG
89. Langfitt, N. C.	20 ABG	134. Regan, D.C.	4 Material Sqdn.
90. Larson, A.R.	20 M. Sqdn.		
91. Lawrence, M.R.	27 B.G.	135. Reider, Leo	Med.
92. Lewis, William S.	Med.	136. Retterrath, P.N.	A/Co. 803
93. Lowe, Ben	28 M. Sg.	—Engr Bn. Botomside Detail, 18 Months, Operater Generators.	
94. Luther, John P.	192 Tk. Bn.	137. Richards, Chas.	440 Ord.
95. MacCurdy, David J.	Ukn.	138. Riddel, P.E.	19 B.G.
96. Manson, M.A.	Ukn.	139. Rizzo, Joseph	31st Inf.
97. Matuozzi, R.E.	Med.	140. Rose, Lawrence	Ukn.
98. McFadden, Ward E.	19 B.G.	141. Rose, Norman	2 Obs.
99. McQuian, Clarence E.	701 Ord.	142. Roy, W.F.	19 B.G.
100. Meirr, Ed	AAF	143. Sayan, R.D.	29 Ord.
101. Miller, E.Z.	Med.	144. Seres, John	19 B.G.
102. Milton, J.B.	Unk.	145. Satkofsky, Andrew	19 B.G.
103. Morgan, N.E.	QMC	146. Schiinger, Howard	Ukn.
104. Mortimer, G.C.	3 Pur.	147. Schiffner, James F.	200 CAC
105. Myers, C.D.	19 B.G.	148. Shaw, Ted	59 CAC
106. Nangle, J.J.	19 B.G.	149. Shubert, A.A.	Med.
		150. Sheanut, A.C	701 Ord.
		151. Shomo, O.F.	781 Ord.

152. Shearwood, Marvin	803 Eng. —Hanawa 71	
153. Slemmer, V.	CAC	
154. Slinka, Michael	89 QMC	
155. Simer, Z.R.	3rd. Pur.	
156. Six, W.T.	2rd. Pur.	
157. Smith, A.R.	19 B.G.	
158. Smith, H.G.	Hq. 2nd. Corps	
159. Soichitio, R.H.	Ukn.	
160. Sollenberger, Robt.	19 B.G.	
161. Sparks, G.P.	19 B.S.	
162. Stangl, Vincent K.	28 Mat. S.	
163. Strann, Garrett B.	27 B.G.	
164. Straus, A.A.	Ukn.	
164. Sullivan, C.P.	440 Ord.	
166. Swope, W.P.	Ukn.	
167. Talbot, E.I.	2 Obs. Sq.	
168. Tantori. S.J.	4 Mat. Sq.	

169. Thasher, H.R.	19 B.G.
170. Unic. Walter	CAC
171. Walker, C.M. Harbor Defense Manila & Subic Bay	
172. Wallace, N.F.	17 B.S.
173. Walsh, H.R.	Hdqtrs, USFIP
174. Wasato. Mansueto	Ukn.
175. Whatley, J.D.	AAF
176. Williams, Howard M.	Fin. Dept.
177. Wilson, F.E.	17 B.S.
178. Wierlchon, J.J	192 Tk. Bn.
179. York, H.P.	20 ABG
180. Young, A.R.	28 B.S.
181. Zagarri, J.R.	USFIP
182. Zanirato, P.A.	Hdqtrs. USFIP
183. Zincke, H.L.	14 B.S.

NOTES:
Other personnel known to have been on the Rock in the period of May 1942 through 27 June, 1944 were:

2. * Kirkpatrick, Lewis C.	Lt. Col. 59	CAC, Cmdr.	Fort Drum
2. ** Buttner, Lorin R.	Civ.	PNABC Note	
3. Cooper, Robert G.	Capt.	Ukn.	
4. ** Coughlin, John J.	Capt.	Ord	
5. Curret, Fred		USMC	
6. ** Davis, (Jack) Ches.	Civ.	PNABC	
7. ** Dunlap, Kenneth	Civ.	PNABC	
8. Derr, Walter		Ukn.	
9. Goldsmith, Leonard	Lt.	Ukn.	
10. Golson, Archie M.	S/Sgt.	QMC	Hanawa #67
11. Haddox, Ernest C.	Cpl.	QMC	Hanawa #312
12. Hanson, R. W.		Sig I/C	USN
13. ** Haucks, Herman H.	Capt.	CAC	
14. Hewitt, Thomas H.	Capt.	Med	
15. Holmes, James R.	Capt.	Ukn.	
16. Huff, Arthur	Capt.	CAC	
17. ** Kinder, Blackie	Civ.	PNABC	
18. Kunick, John	M/Sgt.	31 Inf.	Hanawa #6
19. Milam, H.H.	Cpl.		
20. Lasch, —-		USMC	
21. Lawler, Robert	Capt.	92nd CAC (PS)	
22. Merkell,	Capt.	Med. Corps	
23. Olsen, L.J.		Rad. Mn. USN	
24. ** Olferioff, Sergio	Civ.	Merchant Marine	
25. Peterson, Arthur	Maj.	60th CAC (AA)	
26. ** Piland, James E.	Civ.	PNABC	

Appendix 4 (continued)

27.	Provoo, John David	Sgt.	Hdqtrs.	

Reported at Karenko Formosa, later shipped to Japan. Tried for Treason, Appeals Court over turned guilty verdict.

28.	Ramsey, Kenneth W.	1st Lt.	60th CAC (AA)	
29. **	Rose, Frank	Civ.	Engr.	
30	Rose, Robert	Civ.	Brother of Frank	
31.	Ryan,	T/Sgt.	USMC	
33 **	Schwab, Lester	Civ.	PNABC	
34.	Sense, George R.	Lt.	92 CAC	*Noto Maru*
35.	Sampson, Henry T.	Lt.	Ukn.	
36.	Stoddard, John D.		Ukn.	Hanawa
37.	Wallach, R.	Sgt.	Ukn.	
38. **	Wiedlich, Charles	Civ.	PNABC	
39.	Wright, John M.	Lt.	92 CAC,	(Lt. Gen. Ret)
40.	Wozniak, L.W.	PFC	QMC	

* Died on Corregidor,   ** Died on Japanese Transport *Arisan Maru* at sea 24 Oct. 1944.

Notes: The final fourteen Americans POW's at Middleside on Corregidor were shipped to Bilibid Prison on June 27, 1944. Only four, Nix, Haddox, Kunich, and Golson are known to have returned to the United States. Asbury L. Nix is the only known survivor, Ernest Haddox died 1985, John Kunich died 1986. The whereabouts of Archie Golson is unknown. He was last known to have been at Carlson AFB. Fort Worth Texas in 1946.

Corregidor
P.O.W. Strength figures 1942-1944
Middleside Detail

Strength 1 June, 1942	250	Shipped Dec-May 43	71
Returned to Corregidor		Died April 1943	1
5 June, 1942	76		—
—		72	
	326	Strength May -June 43	99
Shipped June to Dec 42	135		
	—	Shipped June 43	85
Strength December 42	191	Strength Jun. 43-Jun 44,	14*

* Strength numbers are based on Lt. Gen. John M. Wright's Book, *Captured on Corregidor, A Diary of A POW in WW. II*

Another detail of prisoners were held by the Japanese Navy at Bottomside. They operated the water and electrical service. The Senior American Officer was Major Robert Lathrop. The fate of the final 16 men of this detail has not been resolved. Graves Registration recovered some remains after recapture of Corregidor.

Appendix 5
Hell Ships
July 1942-December 1944

	Date Dep.	Date Arr/ Sunk	No. POWs	No. Died	Destination
Argentina Maru	?/01/42		480		Allied
Nitta Maru	?/01/42		1,235		Allied
Montevideo Maru	2/06/42		1,050		Allied
Natoru Maru	?/07/42		7		Allied
Dai Nichi Maru	?/10/42		1,000		Allied
Lisbon Maru	2/10/42	7/10/42	1,815	845	Allied
Shinsei Maru	?/10/42		840		Allied
King Komg Maru	?/10/42		1,500		Allied
Singapore Maru	?/10/42		1,100	240	Allied
Yoshidi Maru	?/10/42		3,000		Allied
Nagato Maru	7/11/42	25/11/42	1,700	157	Amer. Japan
Umeda Maru	7/11/42	25/11/42	1,400	15	Amer. Japan
Tattori Maru	8/10/42	8/11/42	1,202	11	Amer. Japan, Mukden
Nagata Maru	?/11/42		1,700	140	Allied
Kamakura Maru	?/11/42		2,200		Amer.
UNKNOWN MARU	?/12/42		74		Allied
Mayebashi Maru	?/ ?/42		1,800		Allied
Yinagata Maru	?/ ?/42		1,800		Allied
England Maru	?/ ?/42		1,000		Allied

1943 Shipments

	Date Dep.	Date Arr/ Sunk	No. POWs	No. Died	Destination
Nitimei Maru	?/1/43	13/01/43	1,000	35	Allied
Kuritmata Maru	?/4/43		1,400	1,400	Allied
Koyka Maru	?/4/43		1,500		Allied
Amagi Maru	?/4/43		2,000		Allied
Kurimata Maru	?/4/43		1,500		Allied
Weils Maru	?/5/43		950		Brit.
Thames Maru	?/5/43		2,150	250	Allied
Taga Maru	?/08/43		850	70	Allied
Corral Maru	?/10/43		800		Amer.
Rio De Janeio Maru	?/10/43		200		
Ryuku Maru	?/11/43	17/11/43		41	Allied Torpedo
Suez Maru	?/11/43	29/11/43	1,150	540	Allied Torpedo

1944

	Date Dep.	Date Arr/ Sunk	No. POWs	No. Died	Destination
Tango Maru	16/2/44	25/2/44	3,500	3,000	Allied, Torpedo
Tomohoku Maru	?/6/44	6/6/55	772	559	Allied, Torpedo
Yasha Maru	?/*/44		1,240		Amer.
Canadian Inv.	14/7/44		1,100		Amer. Japan (Mati Mati Maru) 17 days
Nissyo Maru	17/7/44	03/07/44	1,600		Fukuoko 3 & 10
Noto Maru	27/8/44	05/9/44	1,035		Amer. Moji, 500 Hanawa
Kachidoki Maru	06/9/44	13/09/44	750	591	Allied, Singapore

(Former President Lines Harrison) sank September 13, 250 miles off Hanian Island. Mostly British & Australian POWs. 73 picked up by USS Pampanito, 54 by USS Sea Lion, 32 men were picked up by other subs six days later.

	Date Dep.	Date Arr/ Sunk	No. POWs	No. Died	Destination
Rakuyo Maru	06/9/44	12/09/44	1,350	1,350	Sank on

12 Sept. same convoy as Kachidoki Maru, Wolf Pack, Growler, Sea Lion II, Pampanito. Wolf Pack was called Bauers Busters. No known survivors.

	Date Dep.	Date Arr/ Sunk	No. POWs	No. Died	Destination
Shinyo Maru	05/09/44	07/09/44	750	668	Allied Sank near Mindanao
Junyo Maru	12/09/44	19/09/44	6,520	5,640	Allied & Japanese
Hako Maru	*05/10/44	25/10/44	1,100	39	Moji, Japan
Arisan Maru	10/10/44	24/10/44	1,800	1,792	

Sunk about 200 miles off China coast. Five survivors. Sunk approximately 250 miles east of Hong Kong. Five survivors reached safety in China. Several others were picked by Japanese Navy in very poor condition and later died.

	Date Dep.	Date Arr/ Sunk	No. POWs	No. Died	Destination
Oryoku Maru	13/12/44	15/12/44	*1,619	314	Sunk 10,500 ton

Survivors moved to San Fernando by truck

	Date Dep.	Date Arr/ Sunk	No. POWs	No. Died	Destination
Enoura Maru	28/12/44		1,074	34	(97) 7,599 ton.

97 died at Olongapo & San Fernando after Oryoku Maru sank.

	Date Dep.	Date Arr/ Sunk	No. POWs	No. Died	Destination
Brazil Maru	28/12/44	28/12/44	240	**	3,000 ton
Brazil Maru	13/01/45		930	370	After Takao bombing.
	28/01/45				Moji Japan,

525 survivors, 150 died within two weeks after arrival in Moji, Japan. Approximately 200 lived to see the end of the war. The voyage, on three ships was 47 days.**

(All these dates are military style of Day/Month/Year.)

Shipments of American prisoners of war in August-December 1944 = 6,404; 3,873 died en route to Japan, 2,531 **arrived in Japan.** These figures do not include Allied POWs from other parts of the theater for this period, except the two ships from Singapore. This listing includes Allied prisoners from Singapore or Thialand transported during 1942-1944.

Summary:	number shipped	number died en route
1942	26,223	1,402
1943	13,200	1,876
1944	23,136	14,820
total	62,559	18,098

It is readily apparent that the death rate of prisoners of war during ship movement increased each year as the gauntlet of air and sea slowly tightened. 1944 saw a large increase in prisoners lost and in ships sunk.

The Japanese Merchant Fleet at the beginning of the fall of 1944 had been thoroughly blockaded on most maritime routes leading to Japan by air and submarines. The flow of oil and other critical raw materials was under constant attack from every direction. The Japanese Maritime fleet was severely decimated through aggressive actions. United States Navy estimates of the status as reported in *Submarine Operations in World War II, Naval Institute* by Theodore Roscoe, are based on captured enemy records and after action reports as follow:

Fleet Tonnage

1 October	1944	3,474,008	tons
1 November	1944	3,495,820	tons
1 December	1944	2,841,534	tons
1 January	1945	2,786,407	tons

In spite of the enormous losses, the Japanese were desperately determined to ship Allied prisoners of war to Japan. The ships were tramp steamers and not marked in accordance with International Law. The human cargo was left to fend for themselves, in the event the ship was attacked. Very few of these unfortunate prisoners, if any, were picked up by either the Allied subs or the Japanese Naval vessels in the area. There were some instances of rescue as noted when possible.

References
The voyage of the Oryoku, Enoura and Brazil Maru are described by the following:
Bilibid Diary; Secret Diary of Comdr. Thomas Hayes by A.B. Feuer
Captured on Corregidor by John M. Wright Jr., Lt. Gen.
Surrender and Survival by E. Bartlett Kerr
Blood Brothers by Eugene C. Jacobs, Col. Ret.
Some Survived—An Epic Account of Japanese Captivity During World War II by Manny Lawton, published by Algonquin Books

Some of the data on ships being sunk may be found in the book *Submarine Operations In World War II*, Naval Institute, Annapolis MD, by Theodore Roscoe. Other data came from many sources and compiled herein for the purpose of illustration. Transporting prisoners of war through hostile waters in ships that are not marked with international recognition signals is not in conformance with accepted rules of war and the Geneva convention. Many more deaths can be attributed to poor health conditions due to prison camp conditions and the health of individuals at the time of shipment.

Appendix 6
Noto Maru
Shipping List—27 August 1944
Company One

#	Name	Rank	H#	A	#	Name	Rank	H#	A
1.	Samson, Charles	Capt.		A	43.	Cape, Jack	Cpl.	H174	
2.	Kirk, David	1st. Lt.			44.	Carlson, William	Cpl.	H171	
3.	Kipps, Harold	WOJG			45.	Chambers, Robert	Cpl.	H172	
4.	Crane, Stanley	M/Sgt.	H4		46.	DeBoer, Arlen	Cpl.	H173	
5.	Flowers, Howard B.	1/Sgt.	H25	A	47.	Erickson, Jack	Cpl.	H174	
6.	Maeder, Leroy	Pvt.	H371		48.	Felty, George	Cpl.	H175	
7.	Hustad, Loyal	1st/Sgt.		A	49.	Jacques, Ralph	Cpl.	H176	
8.	Willbourn, Lacewell	T/Sgt.			50.	Knapp, Vernon R.	Cpl.	H177	
9.	Abramowitz, John	S/Sgt.	H62		51.	Markland, Herbert	Cpl.	H178	
10.	Ammons, Cecil	S/Sgt.	H63		52.	Mohr, Arthur	Cpl.	H179	A
11.	Boyd, Jack	S/Sgt.	H64		53.	Moore, Carl	Cpl.		
12.	Derryberry, Sam	S/Sgt.	H69		54.	Morten, Carrel	Cpl.		
13.	Duino, Anthony	M/Sgt.	H66		55.	Seems, Felix	Cpl.	H181	A
14.	*Golsan, Archie M.*	S/Sgt.	H67		56.	Stablinski, Tony	Cpl.	H282	
15.	Howard, Walter	S/Sgt.	H68		57.	Shelton, John			
16.	Jensen, Gordon	S/Sgt.	H69	A	58.	Sollenberger, Don			
17.	Otis, Fred				59.	Stewart, Robt. J.	Cpl.	H185	
18.	Sanders, Harry	S/Sgt.	H70		60.	Alred, John	PFC	H372	
19.	Shearwood, Marvin	S/Sgt.	H71		61.	Bain, Francis	PFC	H373	
20.	Tribby, James	S/Sgt.	H72		62.	Baldwin, Richard	PFC	H374	
21.	Benedict, James	S/Sgt.	H73		63.	Ballow, John	PFC	H375	
22.	Cahill, Paul	S/Sgt.	H74		64.	Bean, Roy	PFC	H376	
23.	Christianson, Harold	Sgt.	H75		65.	Bowers, Elmer	PFC	H377	
24.	Litch, Thomas	Sgt.	H76		66.	Brooks, Seymour	PFC	H378	
25.	Matthews, Thomas	Sgt.	H77	A	67.	Clemmer, George	PFC	H379	
26.	Mooney, Percy	Sgt.	H78	A	68.	*Cole, Brownell*	PFC	H380	
27.	Moore, Delbart	Sgt.	H79	A	69.	Coleman, Goff	PFC	H381	
28.	Moravee, Earl	Sgt.	H80	A	70.	Cusano, Louis	PFC	H382	
29.	Murphy, James T.	Cpl.	H193	A	71.	Demers, Raymond	PFC	H383	
30.	*Nickolson, Chester*	Sgt.	H82	A	72.	Floyd, Lee	PFC		
31.	*Pelayo, Lee*	Sgt.	H83	A	73.	Foster, Malcolm	PFC	H384	
32.	Rosenfelt, Gustave	Sgt.	H84	A	74.	Frazier, Clyde L.	PFC	H385	
33.	Rutledge, Robert	Sgt.	H85		75.	Gemtry, Adrian	PFC	H386	
34.	Slownick, John	Sgt.	H86		76.	Ghillardi, Werner	PFC	H387	
35.	Sotak, George	Sgt.	H87		77.	Greenlee, Leslie	PFC		
36.	Stublefield, Lawrence	Sgt.	H88		78.	Guiterrez, Eddie	PFC	H388	
37.	Tolendo, Mitchell	Sgt.	H89		79.	Harrison, Ferrill	PFC	H389	
38.	Urbam, Anton	Sgt.	H90		80.	Henry, John	PFC	H390	
39.	Vanish, George		H91		81.	Higdon, Patrick	PFC	H391	
40.	Winters, Clyde	Sgt.	H92		82.	Horn, Vance	PFC		
41.	Bodine, Ken	Cpl.	H168		83.	Hughes, Archie	PFC	H392	
42.	Canfield, Leslie	Cpl.	H169		84.	Holbert, Lyle G.	PFC	H393	

Company One (continued)

85.	Inman, Henry	Pvt.		
86.	Fox, Andre	Pvt.		
87.	Lawler, Jay	Pvt.	H395	
88.	Lerrit, Walter	Pvt.		
89.	Lewis, Robert	Pvt.		
90.	Liskowski, Henry	Pvt.		
91.	Marlangelle, Tom	PFC	H398	
92.	Mazer, Maurice	PFC	H399	
93.	McClure, Murrell			
94.	McFarley, Albert E.	PFC	H400	
95.	McDill, Thomas	PFC	H401	
96.	McTigue, James	PFC	H402	
97.	Miller, Paul			
98.	Neece, Henry	PFC	H404	
99.	Parks, Wilson	PFC	H405	
100.	Pennington, Wilson	PFC	H406	
101.	Quintana, Aurrelo	Pvt.	H284	
102.	Ring, Gay R.	PFC	H407	
103.	Roth, Albert	PFC	H408	
104.	Sequin, Clarence	PFC	H409	
105.	Shaw, Carl	PFC	H410	
106.	Simonds, Glen			
107.	Sisneros, Angelno	Pvt.	H411	
198.	Taves, Harold	PFC	H412	
109.	Thurston, Eugene	PFC	H413	
110.	Webb, George	PFC	H414	A
111.	Wheeler, William	PFC	H415	
112.	Whitman, James	PFC		
113.	Wuhrmann, Carl	PFC	H417	
114.	Yohn, Leonard	PFC	H418	
115.	Alton, Gordon	Pvt.	H419	
116.	Adair, Don	Pvt.	H420	
117.	Arnold, John			
118.	Atterburn, Willie	Pvt.	H421	
119.	Avery, Harrison	Pvt.	H422	
120.	Barker, Matthew	Pvt.	H423	
121.	Bartley, Millege	Pvt.	H424	
122.	Bayhart, J.H.	PFC	H425	
123.	Beach, Amos	Pvt.	H426	
124.	Brundage, Jack*	Pvt.	H427	
125.	Bustmante, Nestor	Pvt.	H428	
126.	Butler, John	Pvt.	H429	
127.	Burks, Chester	Pvt.	H430	
128.	Calvits, Ken*	Pvt.	H431	
129.	Carner, J.D.			
130.	Clifton, William	Pvt.	H432	
131.	Moritz, Emil	Pvt.	H456	
132.	Cox, Eugene			
133.	Crown, John		H433	
134.	*Cunningham, Earl*	Pvt.	H434	
135.	Curtis, Bill	Pvt.	H435	
136.	Dehr, Burt	Pvt.	H436	
137.	Dickson, Adolph	Pvt.	H437	
138.	Dilells, Joseph			
139.	Donalson, Ronald.			
140.	Edmunds, William			
141.	Elder, Warren			
142.	Emerick, John*	Pvt.	H438	
143.	Fennel, Bernard	Pvt.	H439	
144.	Fleming, Earnest	Pvt.		
145.	Garcia, Ben	Pvt.	H440	
146.	Ford, Norman	Pvt.	H481	
147.	Gilbert, Robert	Pvt.	H482	
148.	Gray, Lonnie			
149.	Gundrun, Howard			
150.	Harris, Clay	Pvt.	H443	
151.	Harris, W.L.	Pvt.	H444	
152.	Haywood, John	Pvt.	H445	
153.	Heinz, Leon	Pvt.	H446	
154.	Hietnen, Wayne	Pvt.	H447	
155.	Holl, Edward			
156.	*Hoback, John*	Pvt.	H448	
157.	Howard, Frederick	Pvt.		
158.	Inme, Vicent	Pvt.	H449	
159.	Jones, Jack	Pvt.	H451	
160.	Jones, John H.	Pvt.	H450	
161.	Kean, Leon	Pvt.		
162.	Keesley, Raymond	Pvt.	H452	
163.	Kimball, David	Pvt.	H453	
164.	Lopes, Alfonso	Pvt.	H454	
165.	Kiser, John	Pvt.	H455	
166.	Knowles, Jasper	Pvt.	H456	
167.	Lane, Harold			
168.	Lane, Jesse	Pvt.	H457	
169.	Lee, Walter	PFC	H226	
170.	Lindermuth, Paul			
171.	Link, Herman			
172.	Lopez, Albino	Pvt.	H459	A
173.	Manzanares, Ben	PFC	H460	A
174.	Martin, Wiley	Pvt.	H461	A

Company One (continued)

175.	McGraw, A.C.			189.	Phillips, Earl	Pvt.	
176.	Merritt, Joe	Pvt.	H462	190.	Pine, Edward	Pvt.	H469
177.	Miller, Arthur	Pvt.	H463	191.	Poltz, Joseph	Pvt.	
178.	Moore, William			192.	Preston, Homer	Pvt.	H470
179.	Morris, Burl			193.	Rankin, Roy		
180.	Muller, George			194.	Reisher, George	Pvt.	H471
181.	Murray, James			195.	Richeson, Forest		H472
182.	Nelson, John	Pvt.	H464	196.	Ring, Robert V.	Pvt.	H473
183.	Olson, Noel	Pvt.	H465	197.	Robertson, Samuel		H475
184.	Pierce, Harley	Pvt.	H466	198.	Rogers, Marion		
185.	Peltier, Disiree	Pvt.	H467	199.	Roehm, Robert		
186.	Penerberry, Dwight			200.	Rye, Jay		
187.	Perez, Joe			201.	Saddler, Campbell		H475
188.	Fowler, Brian			202.	Sanford, Paul	Pvt.	H476

Company No. Two

No.	Name	Rank	Code	A/N
203.	Perkins, Peter	1st. Lt.		A
204.	*Kunich, John*	M/Sgt.	H6	A
205.	Adkins, Wm	T/Sgt.		A
206.	Bowman, Donald	T/Sgt.	H27	A
207.	Caster, Chas.	T/Sgt.	H26	A
208.	*Hamburger, Emanual*	F.Sgt.	H39	A
209.	LeBeau, Alfred	T/Sgt.	H30	A
210.	*Martin, Adrian R.*	F/Sgt.	H31	A
211.	Mathieson, James	F/Sgt.		A
212.	*Pope, Ralph*	T/Sgt.	H32	A
213.	Scruggs, James	F/Sgt.	H33	A
214.	Berry, Cecil A.	S/Sgt.	H93	A
215.	Bryant, Harold	S/Sgt.	H94	A
216.	Gartman, Curtis	AMM 2	H136	N
217.	Davis, Kenneth	S/Sgt.	H95	A
218.	*Francies, Richard*	S/Sgt.	H96	A
219.	*Nix, Asbury L.*	S/Sgt.	H97	A
220.	O'Sullivan, James	S/Sgt.	H99	A
221.	Peterson, Robert E.	S/Sgt.	H98	A
222.	*Britain, Lewis*	Sgt.		A
223.	*Burns, Clayton*	Sgt.	H100	A
224.	Carle, John	Sgt.	H101	A
225.	Coker, Lawrence	Sgt.		A
226.	Crowe, Malcolm	M/Sgt.	H102	A
227.	Emery, Shelby	Sgt.	H193	A
228.	Fields, Colby	Sgt.	H104	A
229.	Howard, John	Sgt.	H105	A
230.	Howell, Pat	Sgt.	H106	A
231.	Leyba, Max	Sgt.	H107	A
232.	Likeday, Vincent	Sgt.		A
233.	Macy, Francis	Sgt.		A
234.	Marcom, Sidney L.	Sgt.	H108	A
235.	Price, Stanton	Sgt.	H109	A
236.	Summons, David	Sgt.	H110	A
237.	Adams, Jesse	Cpl.	H186	A
238.	Ballou, William	Cpl.	H187	A
239.	Brian, Phillip	Cpl.	H188	A
230.	Casanove, Stanley	Cpl.	H189	A
241.	Craigle, Ben	Cpl.	H190	A
242.	Deal, Volney	Cpl.		A
243.	Karr, Austin	Cpl.	H191	A
244.	Mills, James	Cpl.	H192	A
245.	Murphy, John	Cpl.	H193	A
246.	Powell, Joseph A.	Cpl.	H194	A
247.	Reen, Vernon C.	Cpl.	H195	A
248.	*Silverstien, Louis*	Cpl.	H196	A
249.	Barkhart, E.R.	PFC		A
250.	Bolt, Charles	PFC	H304	A
251.	Borruano, Angelo	PFC	H305	A
252.	Box, Claude W.	PFC	H306	A
253.	Carr, Leslie J.	PFC	H307	A
254.	Coffin, Clifton	PFC		A
255.	Diaz, Panlo A.	PFC	H308	A
256.	Drake, James		H309	A
257.	Farmer, James	PFC	H310	A
258.	Flowers, James	PFC	H311	A
259.	*Haddox, Earnest*	PFC	H312	A
260.	Hilton, Gordon K.	PFC	H313	A
261.	Jacques, Joseph	Cpl.	H176	A
262.	Jones, Elven	Cpl.		A
263.	Lambathas, Stephen	Cpl.		A
264.	O'Conner, Richard D.	Cpl.	H314	A
265.	*Piburn, Frank*	PFC	H315	A
266.	Prewitt, Granville*	PFC	H316	A
267.	Schott, Edward	PFC	H317	A
268.	*Schuster, Rudolph*	PFC	H318	A
269.	Wilkeson, Edward	PFC	H319	A
270.	Bain, Charles	Pvt.	H320	A
271.	Barnes, Gordon	Pvt.	H321	A
272.	Begley, Charles	Pvt.	H322	A
273.	Bower, Howard F.	Pvt.	H323	A
274.	Browder, Leonard	Pvt.	H324	A
275.	Brown, James R.	Pvt.	H325	A
276.	Carter, Howard R.	Pvt.	H326	A
277.	Free, Edward	Pvt.		A
278.	Harris, Carl	Pvt.		A
279.	Holder, Don H.	Pvt.	H327	A
280.	Kimball, Ray W.	Pvt.	H328	A
281.	Lemanski, John S.	Pvt.	H329	A
282.	Lowhead, Roger R.	Pvt.	H330	A
283.	Mines, James	Pvt.	H331	A
284.	Morris, Lee	Pvt.	H332	A
285.	Nelms, John	Pvt.		A
286.	Oakes, Donald	Pvt.	H333	A

Company Two (continued)

287.	Ortez, Cruz	Pvt.	H334	A	329.	Jarrett, J.T.	CMS	H12	N
288.	Paras, Ted T.	Pvt.	H335	A	330.	Stocks, Wm. S.	CWT	H13	N
289.	Quinn, Joe	Pvt.		A	331.	Zorzanello, B.G.	CEM	H14	N
290.	Prehm Ernest	Pvt.	H336	A	332.	Cobb, George	SC1	H35	N
291.	Purcell, Wm. W.	Pvt.	H337	A	333.	Darneal, Dillard	MM1	H36	N
292.	Samsen, Walter	Pvt.	H338	A	334.	Dudley, Noble	MM1	H37	N
293.	Schuette, Walter	Pvt.	H339	A	335.	Feher, Arthur	MM1	H38	N
294.	Tripp, Phil B.	Pvt.	H340	A	336.	Gray, James	MM1	H39	N
295.	Self, William	Pvt.	H341	A	337.	Hallman, Leonard	RM2	H40	N
296.	Sharp, Jason (Jack)	Pvt.	H342	A	338.	Johnson, Earl	RM2	H41	N
297.	Sheldon, George	Pvt.		A	339.	Mann, Phillip L.	BM1	H42	N
298.	Sills, Robert	Pvt.	H343	A	340.	Marigiotte, Frank	Y1	H43	N
299.	Skowomski, Taduaz	Pvt.		A	341.	McCarthy, James	BM2	H44	N
300.	Smith, George J.	Pvt.	H344	A	342.	McCullough, Geo.	GM1	H45	N
301.	Smith, Gilmore W		H345	A	343.	Montgomery, Robert	RM1	H46	N
302.	Spencer, John		H346	A	344.	Muenich, Gustav J.	RM1	H47	N
303.	Stefanski, Walter		H347	A	345.	Parrish, Al	MM1	H48	N
304.	Stengler, Albert		H348	A	346.	Rector, Earl	BM1	H49	N
305.	Stone, Ken	Pvt.	H349	A	347.	Sauers, Virgil	BM1	H50	N
306.	Strickland, Lacy	Pvt.	H350	A	348.	*Sheats, Robert*	EM1	H51	N
307.	Thorneberry, Raphael	Pvt.	H351	A	349.	Tinen, Herman	EM1		N
308.	Taylor, Ernest	Pvt.	H352	A	350.	Galbary, Ted J.	CM2	H137	N
309.	Taylor, Richard	Pvt.	H353	A	351.	Gale, Thomas	EM2	H138	N
310.	Torres, Joseph	Pvt.	H354	A	352.	Kenny, John	RM2	H139	N
311.	Trains, Michael	Pvt.	H355	A	353.	Town, Paul	QM2		N
312.	Tucker, Francis	Pvt.	H356	A	354.	Wheat, Patrick	WT	H140	N
313.	Turner, Pat	Pvt.	H357	A	355.	Carter, Walter	SM2	H141	N
314.	Underwood, Ray	Pvt.	H358	A	356.	Chandler, Arthur	GM3H	H142	N
315.	Urban, Chas.	Pvt.	H359	A	357.	Fisher, Howard Cox		H143	N
316.	Van Akman, Wm.	Pvt.	H360	A	358.	Gmeiner, Ken	EM3	H144	N
317.	Van Lier, Lawrence	Pvt.	H361	A	359.	Hawkes, Warren	CM3	H145	N
318.	Vaughn, Jimmy	Pvt.	H362	A	360.	Hoggard, Pritchard	CW	H146	N
319.	Strahl, Robert E.	CY	H9	N	361.	McDuffie, Wm	CM3	H147	N
320.	Waldrop, Leon	CY	H363	A	362.	Nelson, Clarence	EM3N	H148	M
321.	Wallace, Lewis	CY	H364	A	363.	Shawhan, Wm.	FC3	H149	N
322.	Watkins, Fred	CY	H365	A	364.	White, Harold	EM3	H150	N
323.	Webber, Clarence	CY	H366	A	365.	Hahn, Dale	SM1	H498	N
324.	Wichard, Lafayette	CY	H367	A	366.	Johnson, Robert	SM1	H499	N
325.	Wills, Alexander	CY	H368	A	367.	Lanbasio, James	SM1	H500	N
326.	Young, George	CY	H369	A	368.	O'Mears, Albert	Pvt.	H370	A
327.	Dix, Lee	CCs	H10	N	369.	Vondette, Robert	SM1	H497	N
328.	Gullickson, Arthur	CEM	H11	N	370.	Kirchgesner, P.	FM2	H495	N

Company Two (continued)

#	Name	Rank	Code	M/N
371.	McClean, Thomas	Sea		N
372.	*Buster, Ivan*	M/Sgt.	H7	M
373.	Jackson, Chas.	S/Maj.	H22	M
374.	Martin, Keith M.	S/Sgt.		M
375.	White, Ed	T/Sgt.	H61	M
376.	Protz, Al	S/Sgt.	H111	M
377.	Schlatter, Wilfred	Sgt	H112	M
378.	Allen, Stanley	Cpl.	H197	M
379.	Davenport, Jame	Cpl.	H198	M
380.	McDonald, Alvin F.	Cpl.	H199	M
381.	Mensching, Wilfrd	L/Cpl.		M
382.	Nikkelson, Melvin	Cpl.	H200	M
383.	Newman, Junior	Cpl.	H201	M
384.	Riddle, Merril	Cpl.	H202	M
285.	Rundle, Clayton	Cpl.	H203	M
386.	Sinders, John	Cpl.	H204	M
387.	Abrahams, F.	PFC	H481	M
388.	Arney, Billy	PFC	H482	M
389.	Best, John A.	PFC	H483	M
390.	Faulkner, James	PFC	H484	M
391.	Fish, Jack	PFC	H485	M
392.	Helfing, William	PFC		M
393.	Hunt, Arthur	PFC		M
394.	Jenson, Francis	PFC	H486	M
395.	Schroeder, Robert	PFC		M
396.	Jones, Arthur	PFC	H487	M
397.	Kindle, Julius	PFC	H488	M
398.	Meyers, Delmar	PFC	H489	M
399.	Saefke, J.R.	PFC	H490	M
400.	Vardeman, Wm. H.	PFC	H491	M
401.	Wegner, Frank	PFC		M
402.	Watson, Richard	PFC	H492	
403.	Werner, Joseph	PFC	H493	M

Company Three

404.	*Sense, George*	1st Lt.	A	447.	Showalter, Robert	Sgt.	
405.	Aidet, Chas.	WOJG	N	448.	Stephens, Lee	Sgt.	
406.	Drakke, Hampton	M/Sgt.	A	449.	Thames, Robert	Sgt.	
407.	Milkey, Lloyd	M/Sgt.	A	450.	Trujillo, Paul	Sgt.	
408.	Arundell, Alvin	F/Sgt.	A	451.	Whiteman, Rufus	Sgt.	
409.	Neverson, Phillip	Pvt.	A	452.	Whitavage, Geo.	Sgt.	
410.	Norris, George	T/Sgt.	A	453.	Berghower, Harold	Cpl.	
411.	Randolph, James	T/Sgt.	A	454.	Mrenner, Norman	Cpl.	
412.	Shirk, George	F/Sgt.	A	455.	Calderone, Thomas	Cpl.	
413.	Smith, William	T/Sgt.	A	456.	Carter, Richard	Cpl.	
414.	Wright, Edward	T/Sgt.		457.	Cobb, John	Cpl.	
415.	Coleman, Elbert	S/Sgt.		458.	Day, Ken	Cpl.	
416.	Dixson, Gifford	S/Sgt.		459.	Dotson, Alonzo	Cpl.	
417.	Dunsworth, Robert	S/Sgt.		460.	Dye, Joseph	Cpl.	
418.	Dyches, Dale	S/Sgt.		461.	Faulkner, James	Cpl.	
419.	Hicks, W.	S/Sgt.		462.	Fuentes, John	Cpl.	
420.	York, Wm.	PFC		463.	Hale, Nelson	Cpl.	
421.	Krowl, John	S/Sgt.		464.	Hansen, John	Cpl.	
422.	Leckey, Lloyd	S/Sgt.		465.	Houser, Wilbur	Cpl.	
423.	McFadden, Ward	S/Sgt.		466.	Kellene, Wm.	Cpl.	
424.	Ready, Mike	PFC		467.	Lee, Clifton	Cpl.	
425.	Stein, John	PFC		468.	McCombs, Earl	Cpl.	
426.	Wallace, Malcolm	S/Sgt.		469.	McDonough, E.	Cpl.	
427.	Weaver, Milton	S/Sgt.		470.	Melnick, Fred	Cpl.	
428.	Womack, Paul	S/Sgt.		471.	Shimko, Frank	Cpl.	
429.	Adams, Edgaar	Sgt.		472.	Silva, Vincent	Cpl.	
430.	Boyer, Robert	Sgt.		473.	Smith, Dewey	Cpl.	
431.	Dahm, Richard	Sgt.		474.	Stone, Claude	Cpl.	
432.	Dixon, George	Sgt.		475.	Sturt, Harold	Cpl.	
433.	Domreschs, Ed	Sgt.		476.	Swann, Alton	Cpl.	
434.	Goodnight, Hulan	Sgt.		477.	Thompson, Thomas	Cpl.	
435.	Green, George	Sgt.		478.	Wents, Ken	Cpl.	
436.	Hess, Walter	Sgt.		479.	West, Clarence	Cpl.	
437.	Hobbs, John	Sgt.		480.	Anderson, Donald	PFC	
438.	Holmes, Howard	Sgt.		481.	Ante, Chas.	PFC	
439.	LeBeau, Bernard	Sgt.		482.	Ashcraft, Chas.	PFC	
440.	Lloyd, Dewey	Sgt.		483.	Barnett, Chas.	PFC	
441.	Lujack, Johnny	Sgt.		484.	Beard, Robert	PFC	
442.	Miller, Marvin	Sgt.		485.	Blackwood, John	PFC	
443.	Nord, George	Sgt.		486.	Bollinger, Fred	PFC	
444.	Parents, James	Sgt.		487.	Bray, Rex	PFC	
445.	Parish, Phil	Sgt.		488.	Brown, Chas.	PFC	
446.	Roeske, Clarence	Sgt.		489.	Chambers, John	PFC	

Company Three (continued)

#	Name	Rank	Code	
490.	Cole, Jack	PFC		
491.	Collins, James	PFC		
492.	Davidson, Gibson	PFC		
493.	Dempsey, John M.	PFC		
494.	Edwards, Bill	PFC		
495.	Eresh, Peter	PFC		
496.	Fullerton, Fred	PFC		
497.	Gallegos, Miguel	PFC		
498.	Vetter, Phil	PFC		
499.	Gooddiffe, Chas.	PFC		
500.	Graham, Francis	PFC		
501.	Grossman, Joseph	PFC		
502.	Harless, Everett	PFC		
503.	Haynie, Hoyt	PFC	H262	
504.	Herring, Louis	PFC		
505.	Hostom, James	PFC		
506.	Golt, James	PFC		
507.	Howard, George	PFC		
508.	Johnson, Otha	PFC		
509.	Kilby, Bill	PFC		
510.	Kincaid, David	PFC		
511.	Klien, Bert	PFC		
512.	Tumala, Reino	PFC		
513.	Lacy, Lester	PFC		
514.	Lafitte, William	PFC		
515.	Lane, Frank	PFC		
516.	Lawson, John	PFC		
517.	Lear, Victor	PFC		
518.	Marlton, Curtis	PFC		
519.	McCanis, Herbert	PFC		
520.	McCaugherty, M.	PFC		
521.	McDaniel, Delbert	PFC		
522.	McClain, Armand	PFC		
523.	Moore, Donald	PFC		
524.	Oakes, Luther	PFC		
525.	Peschel, Richard	PFC		
526.	Paparo, Francis	PFC		
527.	Ray, Clarence	PFC		
528.	Shelton, Lee	Gen.		
529.	Shorthill, Ellis	PFC		
530.	Smith, Hubert	PFC		
531.	Sokolik, Francis	PFC		
532.	Sorenson, Alfred	PFC		
533.	Spaulding, Don	PFC		
534.	Stemeler, Joe	PFC		
535.	Stevens, Robert	PFC		
536.	Strong, Dale	PFC		
537.	Thompson, John	PFC		
538.	Tomcavage, Alfred	PFC		
539.	Treida, Frank	PFC		
540.	Valecic, Bernie	PFC		
541.	Vercher, Lee	PFC		
542.	Armijo, Pete	Pvt.		
543.	Berman, Jan	Pvt.		
544.	Boyle, Ralph	Pvt.		
545.	Cabeza, John	Pvt.		
546.	Caudill, Glen	Pvt.		
547.	Cardenas, Elroy P.	Pvt.		
548.	Chavez, Clovis	Pvt.		
549.	Chesebrough, John	Pvt.		
550.	Connor, John	Pvt.		
551.	Craig, Vernon	Pvt.		
552.	Crookshank, James	Pvt.		
553.	Crookshank, Sherman	Pvt.		
554.	Culliman, Ralph	Pvt.		
555.	De Luna, Juan			
556.	DuPont, Raymond	Pvt.		
557.	Duran, Joe	Pvt.		
558.	Emkin, Roy	Pvt.		
559.	Endres, Robert	Pvt.		
560.	Felts, Dwight	Pvt.	H63	A
561.	Ferratti, David	Pvt.	H224	A
562.	Forsythe, Don	Pvt.	H265	A
563.	Friediu, Louis	Pvt.	H266	A
564.	Knappenberger, V.	Pvt.		
565.	Goodman, Phillip	Pvt.	H267	A
566.	Griffin, Thomas	Pvt.	H268	A
567.	Hill, Lloyd	Pvt.	269	A
568.	Hill, Algen	Pvt.	H270	A
569.	James, Tony	Pvt.	H271	A
570.	Kelley, Gail	Pvt.	H272	A
571.	Knight, James	Pvt.	H273	A
572.	Krinock, Joseph	Pvt.	H274	A
573.	St. John, Walter	Pvt.	H480	M
574.	Lambo, Jerry	Pvt.	H275	A
575.	Little, Cecil	Pvt.	H276	A

Company Three (continued)

#	Name	Rank	Code	
576.	Marcella, Vincent	Pvt.	H277	A
577.	Martinez, Ralph	Pvt.	H278	A
578.	Morris, Gordon	Pvt.	H279	A
579.	Osborn, David	Pvt.		
580.	Overly, George	Pvt.	H280	A
581.	Ororoxy, Julius	Pvt.	H281	A
582.	Padget, John	Pvt.	H282	A
563.	Pearson, Sedric	Pvt.	H283	A
584.	Quintana, Patrico	Pvt.	H284	A
585.	Ross, Edward	Pvt.	H285	A
586.	Schmidt, Carlos	Pvt.	H286	A
587.	Seagent, Edward	Pvt.	H287	A
588.	Schuman, Al M.	Pvt.	H288	A
589.	Speckens, James	Pvt.	H289	A
590.	Spencer, Alden	Pvt.	H290	A
591.	Stanley, Harold G.	Pvt.	H291	A
592.	Staudenraus, Ger.	Pvt.	H292	A
593.	Stewart, Charlie	Pvt.	H293	A
594.	Stroudt, Dan	Pvt.	H294	A
595.	Suskie, John	Pvt.	H295	A
596.	Taylor, Howard	Pvt.		
597.	Torres, Miguel	Pvt.	H296	A
598.	Trones, Arthur	Pvt.	H297	A
599.	Vidaurri, Miguel	Pvt.	H298	A
600.	Virgil, Atonio	Pvt.	H299	A
601.	Walton, Ray	Pvt.	H300	A
602.	White, Wilton	Pvt.	H301	A
603.	Willis, Grover	Pvt.	H302	
604.	Zack, Barney	Pvt.	H303	A

Company Four

605.	*Flemming, E.P.*	Capt	H1	A	654.	Anderson, Arthur	Cpl.		
606.	Andrews, Wm.	T/Sgt.			655.	Chato, Melvin	Cpl.		
607.	Beardon, Frank	T/Sgt.			656.	Coleman, Phillip	Cpl.		
608.	McGuire, Wilson	F/Sgt.			657.	Fontana, Francis	Cpl.		
609.	Minnis, Frank	F/Sgt.			658.	Garner, Nathan	Cpl.		
610.	Gutturrez, Joe B.	F/Sgt.		A	659.	Gilcrease, Art	Cpl.	H206	A
611.	Spooner, Harold	F/Sgt.			660.	Joder, Richard	Cpl.		
612.	Waltmen, Melvin	T/Sgt.			661.	Love, Johnny	Cpl.	H207	A
613.	Burgan, Chas.	S/Sgt.			662.	Moore, Ralph	Cpl.		
614.	Canfield, Edward	S/Sgt.	H113	A	663.	Payne, Gaylord	Cpl.	H209	A
615.	Clark, Horace	S/Sgt.			664.	Rossotto, J. R.	Cpl.	H209	A
616.	Elkins, Lawrence	S/Sgt.		A	665.	Sanchez, Gregorio	Cpl.		
617.	Gourdeau, Henry	S/Sgt.	H114	A	666.	Schoonover, Ken	Cpl.	H210	A
618.	Hinkle, Wayne	S/Sgt.		A	667.	Smith, Fred	Cpl.		
619.	Johnson, Edward C.	RM1	H41	N	668.	Stoddard, John	Cpl.	H211	A
620.	Langfelt, Wm.	RM1		A	669.	Williams, Robert	Cpl.		
621.	Larson, Alf.	RM1		A	670.	Angus, Richard	PFC		
622.	Morgan, Bill	RM1			671.	Ball, Ivan	PFC		
623.	Pope, Bryan	RM1		A	672.	Brown, Douglas	PFC	H223	
624.	Smith, Harold G.	RM1			673.	Brown, Joseph	PFC	H222	A
625.	Unic, Walter	RM1			674.	Brown, Mavis	PFC		
626.	Van Hook, David	RM1	H117	A	675.	Coucet, Dennis	PFC		
627.	Watts, Thomas	RM1			676.	Ferrari, Dominico	PFC	H224	A
628.	Apel, Rudie	Sgt.			677.	Goldstein, Frank	PFC	H225	A
629.	Baxter, William	Sgt.	H118	A	678.	Hoggaboom, Larry	PFC		
630.	Beasely, Leon D.	Sgt.	H119	A	679.	Hutchins, Roland	PFC		
631.	Byers, Lloyd	Sgt.	H120	A	680.	Larchmiller, Burk	PFC		
632.	Campbell, John	Sgt.			681.	Lee, Willis	PFC	H226	A
633.	Cook, Ted	Sgt.			682.	McClanhan, Chas.	PFC		
634.	Davis, Thomas G.	Sgt.	H121	A	683.	Moody, Harold	PFC	G227	A
635.	Fensmore, Raymond	Sgt.			684.	Morehead, James	PFC	H228	A
636.	Fines, Roy	Sgt.			685.	Platt, Earl	PFC		
637.	House, Roy	Sgt.			686.	Rathjen, Reuben	PFC		
638.	Hutchibson, Woodrow	Sgt.	H122	A	687.	Romero, Sam	PFC		
630.	Jones, James	Sgt.			688.	Torma, Solbe	PFC		
640.	*Larson, Leonard O.*	Sgt.	H123	A	689.	Trout, Hobart	PFC	H230	A
641.	Lawhorn, George	Sgt.			690.	Vandal, David	PFC	H231	A
642.	Leach, Albert	Sgt.			691.	Whittinghill, Harry	PFC	H232	A
643.	Lorenzen, Norman	Sgt.			692.	Wilcoxson, Elmer	PFC	H233	A
644.	Maxwell, Albert	Sgt.			693.	Wisneski, John	PFC	H234	A
645.	Moskalick, Peter	Sgt.	H124	A	694.	Wood, Everett	PFC	H235	A
646.	Noffsker, W.A.	Sgt.	H125	A	695.	Wood, John	PFC	H236	A
647.	Sachwald, Louis	Sgt.			696.	Zwelser, Rolans	PFC		
648.	Shadoan, John	Sgt.			697.	Alt, Russell	Pvt.		
649.	Smith, Joseph	Sgt.			698.	Daniels, Clarence	Pvt.		A
650.	Swearengen, Jack	Sgt.			699.	Boyd, George H.	Pvt.	H237	A
651.	Webb, Don	Sgt.			700.	Brown, Chas.	Pvt.		
652.	Williams, Chas.	Sgt.			701.	Thomas, Charlie	Pvt.	H238	A
653.	Alhstedt, Harold	Cpl.			702.	Lehner, James	Pvt.	H239	A

Company Four (continued)

#	Name	Rank	H	
703.	Cogair, Dana	Pvt.		
704.	Collier, James	Pvt.		
705.	Deans, Walter	Pvt.		
706.	Dickson, Chas.	Pvt.	H240	A
707.	Mroz, Stanley	TM2	H151	N
708.	East, Franklin	Pvt.		A
709.	Foster, Henry	Pvt.		
710.	Franzwa, Arthur	Pvt.		
711.	*Galloway, AL.*	Pvt.	H241	A
712.	Gollasch, Joseph	Pvt.		
713.	Grego, Jose	Pvt.		
714.	Havilland, Wm.	Pvt.		
715.	Hester, Wynton	Pvt.		
716.	Hornback, Everett	Pvt.		
717.	Irvin, Chester	Pvt.		
718.	Kemp, Willie	Pvt.		
719.	Kirk, David	Pvt.		
720.	Knight, Robert	Pvt.		
721.	Larkin, Russel	Pvt.	H245	A
722.	Mackey, Oscar	Pvt.		
723.	Maurino, Tone	Pvt.	H246	A
724.	McCormick, James	Pvt.		
725.	Mikita, Thomas	Pvt.	H247	A
726.	Miller, Merle	Pvt.		
727.	Nez, Sam	Pvt.		
728.	O'Brien, Bernard	Pvt.		
729.	Preston, Edwin	Pvt.		
730.	Pruss, Harry	Pvt.		
731.	Renfro, Aubrey	Pvt.		
732.	Roberts, Keyton	Pvt.		
733.	Rodriguez, John	Pvt.		
734.	Rose, James	Pvt.	H248	A
735.	Salcedo, Tony	Pvt.		
736.	Schooley, Albert	Pvt.	H249	A
737.	Secrist, James	Pvt.		
738.	Sherwood, Virgil	Pvt.	H250	A
739.	Siple, James	Pvt.		
740.	Stewart, Thomas G.	Pvt.	H251	A
741.	Surcek, Joe	Pvt.		
742.	Vice, William	Pvt.	H252	A
743.	Wade, Floyd	Pvt.		
744.	Warnick, Jack	Pvt.	H253	A
745.	White, Herbert	Pvt.		
746.	Wolf, Clyde	Pvt.		
747.	Workman, Franklin	Pvt.		
748.	Wright, Marvin	Pvt.	H255	A
749.	Zimpe, Francis	Pvt.		
750.	Banbary, Archie M.	CBM	H15	N
751.	Mereshal, Robt.	CBM		N
752.	Markwell, Norman	CBN		N
753.	Morrison, George	CBM		N
754.	Wesley, Thomas	CBN		N
755.	Wilson, Robt.	CB1		N
756.	Bordwell, James	SK1	H53	N
757.	Dennis, Francis	TM1		N
758.	Gorman, Martin	CM1	H54	N
759.	Lafferty, John	MM1		
760.	Milikin, Emerson	TM1	H155	N
761.	Newmann, Herbert	MM1	N	
762.	North, Sylvestor	TM1	H56	N
763.	Peda, Charles	SC1		N
764.	Ritter, Wm.	BM1	H47	N
765.	Ryan, John	SF1		N
766.	Wiley, Abdrew	AMM1		N
767.	Byran, Alton	GM2		
768.	Hanson, Russell	SM2		N
769.	Howton, John	BM2		N
770.	McConn, Donald	AERM		N
771.	Wilson, Alfred	BM2		N
772.	Rinker, Lynn	CTM	H17	N
773.	Devoss, Wilson	SC3	H155	N
774.	Frazee, Russell	MM3		N
775.	Garsa, Frederick	TM3		N
776.	Gearhart, Harold	MM2		N
777.	Goudge, Alfred	GM3	H157	N
778.	Hoffman, Raymond	RM3		N
779.	Hooten, James	SK3		N
780.	Hooten, Wm.	SK3		N
781.	Michels, Glen	EM3		N
782.	Roach, Homer	COX	H159	N
783.	Casey, Leo	FM1	H494	N
784.	Bjork, Clarence	M/Sgt.	H23	M
785.	Schilling, Floyd	F/Sgt.		M
786.	Harril, Claude	Sgt.		M
787.	Vardin, Wm.	Pl/Sg	H164	M
788.	Gasper, Tony	Sgt.		M
789.	Graham, Paul	Sgt.		M
790.	Kill, Ollie	Sgt.		M
791.	Long, Elmer E.	Sgt.	H166	M
792.	Murphy, Frank	Sgt.		M
793.	Provencher, Ray	Sgt.		M
794.	Anderson, Lloyd	F.Clk.		M
795.	Bass, George	Cpl.	H213	M
796.	Dillman, Frank	Cpl.	H214	M
797.	Hooker, Francis	Cpl.	H215	M
798.	Horvath, Chas.	Cpl.	H216	M
799.	Howard, Ray	Cpl.		M
800.	Jansen, Shirk	Cpl.		M
801.	Johanson, Carl	Cpl.		M
802.	Parker, Gerald	Cpl.		M
803.	Patterson, Chas.	Cpl.	H217	M
804.	Pickett, Albert	Cpl.		M
805.	Anderson, Earl	Civ.		A

Company Five

No.	Name	Rank	Code	Col
806.	Pullen, Richard	1st. Lt.	H4	
807.	Bryan, Doughty	M/Sgt.		A
808.	Thomas, Elmer	PFC		A
809.	Kulas, Harry	1/Sgt.		A
810.	Rosenburg, Louis	1/Sgt.		A
811.	Annss, Joe	S/Sgt.		A
812.	Dolde, Wilson	S/Sgt.		A
813.	Emmanuel, James	S/Sgt.	H130	A
814.	Manasse, Solly	S/Sgt.	H131	A
815.	Stein, Chas.	S/Sgt.	H132	A
816.	Alcorn, Ed.	Sgt.	H133	A
817.	Baits, Bill	Sgt.	H134	A
818.	Bartle, Edsel	Sgt.		A
819.	Baskin, John	Sgt.		A
820.	Bogie, Thomas	Sgt.		A
821.	Copeland, James	Sgt.		A
822.	Cummins, Gerren	Sgt.		A
823.	Daum, Daino	Sgt.		A
824.	Gregory, Jack	Sgt.		A
825.	Harrell, Thomas	Sgt.		A
826.	Horn, Robert	Sgt.		A
827.	Hryn, John	Sgt.		A
828.	Houston, Lowe	Sgt.		A
829.	Piercy, Issac	Sgt.		A
830.	Rayburn, Brada	Sgt.		A
831.	Reveglia, Armanso	Sgt.		A
832.	Shannon, Homer	Sgt.		A
833.	Simpson, Orval	Sgt.		A
834.	Tonndreal, Alphonse	Sgt.		
835.	Uphoff, Milton	Sgt.		A
836.	Wheatley, Vernon	Sgt.		A
837.	Ziellnski, Ed.	Sgt.		A
838.	Barnum, Chas.	Cpl.		A
839.	Bussell, Rohden	Cpl.		A
840.	Comancho, Arturo	Cpl.		A
841.	Chavez, Ciprano	Cpl.		A
842.	Ciborek, Adam	Cpl.		A
843.	Davis, James	Cpl.		A
844.	Escalante, Arel	Cpl.		A
845.	Howel, Lawrence	Cpl.		A
846.	Johnson, Herbert	Cpl.		A
847.	Johnson, Terrel	Cpl.		A
848.	Korpal, Leonard	Cpl.		A
849.	Mithallpoulousm Geo.	Cpl.		A
850.	Ohmvedt, Clifford	Cpl.		A
851.	Perrette, John	Cpl.		A
852.	Twigg, Wm	Cpl.		A
853.	Vistula, Lee	Cpl.		A
854.	Angert, Alfred	PFC		A
855.	Baker, Howard	PFC		A
856.	Black, Wm.	PFC		A
857.	Bowman, Lawrence	PFC		A
858.	Cook, Alfred	PFC		A
859.	Jax, Cooper	PFC		A
860.	Earing, Dave	PFC		A
861.	Edwards, Kames	PFC		A
862.	Fort, Stanley	PFC		A
863.	Gilliespie, Laurel	PFC		A
864.	Gunnup, Wm.	PFC		A
865.	Haynie, Boyd	PFC	H259	A
866.	Hicks, Howard	PFC		A
867.	Hobbs, Homer	PFC		A
868.	Hoffman, Edward	PFC		A
869.	Horten, Floyd	PFC		A
870.	Howard, Raymond	PFC		A
871.	Jakabowski, Paul	PFC		A
872.	Kafer, Otto	PFC		A
873.	Knight, Ray	PFC		A
874.	Kusiak, John	PFC		A
875.	Mallkowski, Francis	PFC		A
876.	Martinez, George	PFC		A
877.	McGee, Thomas	PFC		A
878.	McHenry, Wayne	PFC		A
879.	Milsap, Eliza	PFC		A
880.	Moore, Alvert	PFC		A
881.	Plymale, Vecil	PFC		A
882.	Pope, Edgar	PFC		A
883.	Petris, John	PFC		A
884.	Scott, George	PFC		A
885.	Semenchick, Joseph	PFC		A
886.	Shuford, James	PFC		A
887.	Stanbaugh, Melvin	PFC		A
888.	Stanley, Andrew	PFC		A
889.	Tyrell, Edward	PFC		A
890.	Wagner, Lee	PFC		A
891.	White, Gordon	PFC		A
892.	Whitecotton, N.	PFC		A
893.	Williams, George	PFC		A
894.	Williamson, Lee	PFC		A
895.	DeBauche, August	Pvt.		A
896.	Adamson, Floyd	Pvt.		A
897.	Aragon, James	Pvt.		A
898.	Atwood, Walter	Pvt.		A
899.	Baker, Raymond	Pvt.		A
900.	Barton, Robert	Pvt.		A
901.	Blackman, Joseph	Pvt.		A
902.	Calvin, Chauncey	Pvt.		A
903.	Carabine, Donald	Pvt.		A
904.	Chism, Aubrey	Pvt.		A
905.	Chovan, Edward	Pvt.		A
906.	Coats, Claude	Pvt.		A
907.	Coxey, Eugene	Pvt.		A

Company Five (continued)

No.	Name	Rank			No.	Name	Rank		
908.	Davis, Francis	Pvt.		A	958.	Turner, Gerald	Sgt.		M
909.	Meyer, Floyd J.	Pvt.		A	959.	Butler, Edmund	Cpl.		M
910.	Pickett, Leonard	CRM		M	960.	Meyers, Malvin	Cpl.		M
911.	Garola, Donald	Pvt.		M	961.	Pepitone, Vito	Cpl.	H218	M
912.	Carona, Ramon	Pvt.			962.	Ray, John	Cpl.	H219	
913.	Himes, Glen	Pvt.			963.	Richter, Adolph	Cpl.		M
914.	Holman, George	Pvt.			964.	Russel, Wm.	Cpl.		M
915.	Hopkins, Wallace	Pvt.			965.	Smith, Raymond	Cpl.		M
916.	Hutson, John	Pvt.			966.	Strickland, Ken	MMN		N
917.	Joplin, Ray	Pvt.			967.	McClung, William	MMN		M
918.	Lawrence, Wayne	Pvt.			968.	Vinson, Benjamin	PFC		M
919.	Leavins, Ivy	Pvt.			969.	Amirant, Raymond	PFC		M
920.	Lloyd, Ralph	Pvt.			970.	Baker, Roger	PFC		M
921.	Macey, David	Pvt.			971.	Corley, John	PFC		M
922.	Martin, Lawrence	Pvt.			972.	Coulson, Dale	PFC		M
923.	McClammans, Landys	Pvt.			973.	Craig, Thomas	PFC		M
924.	McGuinness, Roy	Pvt.			974.	Etters, Frank	PFC		M
925.	Nodenley, Stanley	Pvt.			975.	Fisher, Culver	PFC		M
926.	Paiden, George	Pvt.			976.	Fisher, George	PFC		M
927.	Phillips, Chas.	Pvt.			977.	Gilbertson, Homer	PFC		M
928.	Pote, Ralph	Pvt.			978.	Handy, Thornton	PFC		M
929.	Ryan, Mike	Pvt.			979.	Hawthrone, Walter	PFC		M
930.	Satoyo, Stanley	Pvt.			980.	Hosler, James	PFC		M
931.	Shaffer, Ralph	Pvt.			981.	Jorgeson, Warren	PFC		M
932.	Torvillo, Ralph	Pvt.			982.	LaFluer, George	PFC		M
933.	Young, Cyrus	Pvt.			983.	Lang, William	PFC		M
934.	Hirschberg, Harold	Pvt.			984.	Latham, John	PFC		M
935.	Hurtt, Thomas	SSM	H18	N	985.	Lee, Charles	PFC		M
936.	Johnson, Arnold	CSK	H19	N	986.	Matheney, Wilford	PFC		M
937.	Lietz, Ted	CYM	H20	N	987.	Ratliff, Owen	PFC	H479	M
938.	Orcutt, Lyle	Cmm	H21	N	988.	Ruzek, Lester	PFC		M
939.	Conn, Floyd	BM2	H58	N	989.	Saulter, Alfred	PFC		M
940.	Gustafson, W.	PRTR1	H59	N	990.	Scott, Chas.	PFC		M
941.	Pasino, John	CM1		N	991.	Scott, Irvin	PFC		M
942.	Yurshak, Stephen	CM1		N	992.	Smith, George T.	PFC	H345	M
943.	Washburn, Roy	WT1	H68	N	993.	Vidal, Donald	PFC		M
944.	Andrews, Alvin	MM2		N	994.	Wells, Verdie	PFC		M
945.	Blair, Rollie	CM2		N	995.	Haynes, James	PFC		M
946.	Burton, Robert	MM	H39	N	996.	Anderson, Garland	Civ.		A
947.	King, Clifton	SC2		N	997.	Anhorn, Fred	Civ.		A
948.	Kirby, Jack	GM2	H161	N	998.	Chung, Alfred	Civ.	A	A
949.	Stone Wendell*	Y2	H162	N	999.	Cook, George	Civ.		
950.	Welch, Robert	BM2		N	1000.	Davis, Edward	Civ.		
951.	Benson, James	BM1		N	1001.	Forth, Courtney	Civ.		
952.	Lowdy, Chas.	COX		N	1002.	Ing, Alvin	Civ.		
953.	Loring, Lance	CM3		N	1003.	Lake, Harold	Civ.		
954.	Pruitt, Chas	CM3		N	1004.	Smith, Frank	Civ.		
955.	Linton, Herbert	F1		N	1005.	Nerisaar, Rein	Estonia		
956.	Duncan, Louis	Sgt.		M	1006.	Starshuag, Olaf	Norway		
957.	Ditzel, Dan	Sgt.		M					

Medical Detachment, *Noto Maru*

1007.	Artman, Ralph	Maj.		A	1022.	Rifkin, Morris	PFC	A
1008.	*Jackson, Calvin*	Maj.	H4	A	1023.	Roberts, Norman	PFC	A
1009.	Bernstein, Max	Capt.		A	1024.	Wilkens, Joseph	PFC	A
1010.	D'Amato, Adanto	Capt.		A	1025.	Young, Horace	PFC	A
1011.	*Golenternik, Dan*	Capt.	4A	H	1026.	Dugan, James	Pvt.	A
1012.	*Lamy, John*	Lt.	3A	H	1027.	Lense, Wilbur	Pvt.	A
1013.	Hunt, Hugh	Sgt.		A	1028.	Morgan, Ira	Pvt.	A
1014.	Long, Leslie	Sgt.		A	1029.	Norquist, Ernest	Pvt.	A
1915.	Mayer, Frank	Sgt.	H220	A	1030.	Smith, Charlie	Pvt.	A
1016.	Warnock, Robert	Cpl.	H221	A	1031.	Sorochtey, Chas.	Pvt.	A
1017.	Adams, Robert	PFC		A	1032.	Wolt, Lawrence	Pvt.	A
1018.	Hervat, John	PFC		A	1033.	Braun, Fr. Albert	Maj.	Chap.
1019.	O'Keefe, James	PFC	H261	A	1034.	Naumann, Herman	Fr.	Chap.
1020.	Porche, Clyde	PFC		A	1035.	Boyce, James	Sgt.	Intp.
1021.	Ricks, Donovan	PFC		A				

* Major Jackson, assigned originally to Hanawa was replaced by Dr. Dan Golenternik at Hanawa

Cruise Of The *Noto Maru*, Medical Detachment
27 August, 1944—5 September, 1944

The men on the passenger list of the *Noto Maru* came from several camps:
Bilibid—135   Cabanatuan—465   Clark Field—135   Murphy—135   Cabanatuan—185

The following listed men were replaced on the shipping list prior to departure;

1.	Muellet, Chas	Capt.		420.	Holladay, Otha	S/Sft	
2.	Farlet, Phillip	Lt.		424.	Schla——, Albert		
6.	Harman, Phil	T/Sgt.		512.	Knighton, Harold	PFC	
116.	Anderson, Willard	T/Sgt.		513.	Lackey, Marvin	PFC	
131.	Cochran, Henry	Pvt.		565.	Garleb, Wm.	PFC	
146.	Grachino, Martin	Pvt.		574.	Knasha——, Joseph	PFC	
164.	King, Don	Pvt.		610.	Smith, Joe	PFC	
188.	Petrosius, Joseph	Pvt.		698.	Black, James	PFC	
205.	Bennett, Chas.	2 Lt.		702.	Evereat, Reginald	PFC	
216.	Cooney, Floyd	S/Sgt.		707.	Dequette, Anthony	Pvt.	
269.	Pettis, Chas.	S/Sgt.		772.	Delsinger, Geo.	COX	N
294.	Scawright, Chas.	S/Sgt.		780.	Kana——, John	Pvt.	
319.	Vidal, Ben	S/Sgt.		786.	Nolan, Emmett	Pvt.	
368.	Lathern, David	S/Sgt.		895.	Woodsen, James	PFC	
404.	Beard, Wm.	S/Sgt.		909.	Flippen, Roy	Pvt.	
409.	Lossett, Eugene	T/Sgt.		910.	Gastclur, Al		

The number to the left of the names listed above are the replacements for the name appearing on the sailing list with the same numbers. The numbers followed by H are the numbers assigned at Hanawa.

Credit to Adrian Martin, New London, WI, and F. (Acey) Rudkin.

Appendix 7
Work Details
Camp No. 9, Habawa, Japan
September 1944-September 1945
Headquarters Detail

1.	Fleming, E. Pearce	Capt.	H1	A	4.	Pullen, Robert	1st Lt.		A
2.	Jackson, Calvin	Maj. MC	H2 #	A	5.	Lyman, John	1st. Lt.	MC	A
3.	Walker, Arthur H.	Lt. Col.	H5	AF	6.	Golenternik, Dan	Capt.	MC	A

#Transferred to Tokyo, A-Army, N-Navy, M-Marines, C-Civilan, *Deceased ★Other Camps

Section 1, Special Detail—25

1.	Bearden, Frank	T/Sgt.	34		13.	McConn, Donald	Avn 2	154	N
2.	Brown, Douglas	Pvt.	223		14.	Miliken, Emerson	TM	155	N
3.	Chandler, Anthony	GM3	142	N	15.	O'Keefe, James	S/Sgt.	111	
4.	Conn, Floyd	BM1	158	N	16.	Protz, Albert	PFC	261	
5.	Hill, Lloyd	Pvt.	369		17.	Rundle, Clayton	Cpl.	203	A
6.	Howton, John	BM2	135	N	18.	Stewart, Thomas G.	PVT	251	
7.	Hunt, Hugh	Sgt.	123	A	19.	Van Hook, David	S/Sgt.	117	A
8.	Hurtt, Thomas	Csm	18	N	20.	Vice, William	Pvt.	252	
9.	Larsen, Leonard	M/Sgt.	123		21.	Warnock, Robert	Cpl.	221	
10.	Lietz, Theodore	C4	20	N	22.	Washburn, Roy	WT 1	60	N
11.	Mann, Phillip	BM1	142		23.	Whittinghill, Harry	PFC	232	
12.	Mayer, Frank	CPL	220		24.	Williamson, Lee	PFC	258	
					25.	Wills, Grover E.	Pvt.	302	

Section 2—40

1.	Adams, Jesse	Cpl.	186	A	23.	Morton, D.E.	Cpl.	180	A
2.	Andrews, Alvin	S/Sgt.	73	A	24.	Murphy, James	Sgt.	81	A
3.	Andrews, W.W.	MM 2	159	N	25.	Nelson, Clarence	EM3	140	N
4.	Benedict, James	S/SS	73	A	26.	Nelson, John	Pvt.	464	A
5.	Buster, Ivan	M/Sgt.	7	M	27.	Nicholson, Chester	Sgt.	82	A
6.	Bower, Harold	Pvt.	323	A	28.	Nix, Asbury L.	S/Sgt.	97	A
7.	Canfield, Leslie	Cpl.	169	A	29.	Oakes, Donald	Pvt.	333	A
8.	Carter, Walter	SM	314	N	30.	Piburn, Frank	PFC	315	A
9.	Cobb, George	SC	135	N	31.	Price, Stanton	Sgt.	109	A
10.	Creagle, Ben	Cpl.	190	A	32.	Rosenfelt, Gustave C.	Sgt.	84	A
11.	Cunningham, Burl	Pvt.	34	A	33.	Schuster. Rudolph	PFC	318	A
12.	Davenport, Jesse	Cpl.	198	A	34.	Shawkan, Wm.	EM2	149	N
13.	Dickson, Chas.	Pvt.	240	A	35.	Stein, Chas.	S/Sgt.	132	A
14.	Dix, Lee	CAS	10	N	36.	Stocks, Wm.	CWT	13	N
15.	Feher, Arthur	MM	138	N	37.	Trout, Hobart	PFC	229	A
16.	Fields, Colby	Sgt.	104	A	38.	Walton, Roy	Pvt.	300	A
17.	Francies, Rich. E.	S/Sgt.	96	A	39.	Webb, George	PFC	414	A
18.	Ghilardi, Werner	PFC	387	A	40.	White, Harold	EM3	150	N
19.	Hoback, John	Pvt.	448	A					
20.	Holder, Daniel	Pvt.	327	A					
21.	Horvath, Chas.	Cpl.	216	A					
22.	Lane, Jesse	Pvt.	457	A					

Section 3 A—33

#	Name	Rank	No.	
1.	Banbury, Archie M.	S/Sgt.	15	A
2.	Berry, Cecil	Pvt.	430	
3.	Bjork, Clarence	M/Sgt.	23	
4.	Bodine, Kenneth	Cpl.	168	
5.	Bowman, Donald	T/Sgt.	27	
6.	Cahill, Paul	S/Sgt.	74	A
7.	Cape, Jack	Cpl.	174	A
8.	Caster, Charles	T/Sgt.	28	
9.	Duino, Anthony	M/Sgt.	66	A
10.	Fredieu, Louis	PFC	266	
11.	Galbary, Theodore	CM3	137	N
12.	Gale, Thomas	EM2	138	N
13.	Gilbert, Robert	Pvt.	482	
14.	Gilcrease, Arthur	Cpl.	206	A
15.	Hallman, Leonard	RM1	40	N
16.	Hamburger, Emanuel	F/Sgt.	29	A
17.	Huston, Royal	F/Sgt.	24	A
18.	Johnson, Earl	S/Sgt.	116	
19.	Lacewell, W.	T/Sgt.	26	
20.	Loring, Lance	CM3	163	N
21.	Manasse, Solly	S/Sgt.	131	A
22.	Marchal, Robert	CBM	16	N
23.	Martin, Adrian*	1st Sgt.	31	A
24.	Martin, M. Keith	S/Sgt.	167	A
25.	McDuffie, William	CM3	147	N
26.	Parks, Wilson	PFC	405	
27.	Payne, Grayford	Cpl.	209	A
28.	Ritter, William	TJ1	57	N
29.	Roach, Homer	COX	159	N
30.	Roth, Albert	PFC	408	
31.	Sherwood, Marvin	S/Sgt.	71	
32.	Stewart, Bob	CPL	185	A
33.	Underwood, R.C. *	Pvt.	358	

Section 3 B—49

#	Name	Rank	No.	
1.	Begley, Carl	Pvt.	322	
2.	Brian, Fowler	CBM	8	N
3.	Burns, Crayton	S/Sgt.	100	A
4.	Butler, John	Pvt.	429	
5.	Carlson, William	Cpl.	171	A
6.	Cusano, Louis	PFC	382	
7.	Dolne, Wilson	S/Sgt.	128	
8.	Dudley, Noble	MM1	37	N
9.	Flowers, Moble	F/Sgt.	5	A
10.	Gmiemer, Kenney	EM3	144	N
11.	Gourdeau, Henry	S/Sgt.	114	A
12.	Gray, James	RM1	39	N
13.	Gustafson, Wilbert	PR1	59	N
14.	Haddox, Ernest	PFC	312	A
15.	Harris, Clay T.	Pvt.	443	
16.	Harris, William	Pvt.	444	
17.	Hawkes, Warren	EM2	145	N
18.	Jackson, Charles R.	M/Sgt.	22	
19.	James, Tony	Pvt.	271	
20.	Jarrett, Jesse	CMS	12	N
21.	Kenny, John	TM2	139	N
22.	Lawler, Jay	PFC	395	
23.	Leritte, Anthony	PFC	396	
24.	Long, Elmer E.	Sgt.	166	
25.	Marcello, Vincent	Pvt.	277	
29.	Marcom, S.L.	S/Sgt.	108	
26.	McCarthy, James	BM1	44	N
27.	Moritz, Emil	PFC	496	
28.	Morris, Gordon	Pvt.	279	
30.	O'Sullivan, J.N.	S/Sgt.	99	
31.	Orcutt, Lyle	CMM	21	
32.	Pierce, Harley	Pvt.	468	
33.	Pope, Ralph	T/Sgt.	32	A
34.	Preston, Homer	Pvt.	470	
35.	Rector, Emil	BM1	49	N
36.	Riddle, Merril	Cpl.	202	M
37.	Rinker, Lynn	CTM	17	N
38.	Scruggs, James	1st Sgt.	33	
39.	Speckens, James	Pvt.	289	
40.	Taylor, Richard (D)	Pvt.	353	
41.	Thomas, Elmer	PFC	256	
42.	Ilken Herman I.	BM	52	N
43.	Traino, Carl.	Pvt.	35	
44.	Tribby, James	S/Sgt.	72	A
45.	Urban, Charles	Pvt.	359	A
46.	Van Lieke, Larry	PFC	361	
47.	Wheat, Patrick	TM2	140	N
48.	Wright, Marvin	Pvt.	255	
49.	Zarzanello, Oscar	CEM	14	N

Section 3 C

#	Name	Rank	No.	
1.	Ammons, Cecil	Cpl.	62	A
2.	Burk, John	Pvt.	430	
3.	Guitterrez, Eddie	PFC	388	
4.	Staudenraus, Gerald	Pvt.	292	

Section 4 A—63

1.	Allen, Stanley	Cpl.	197		33.	Love, John E.	CPL	207	
2.	Arney, Billie	Pvt.	482		34.	Mazer, Maurice	PFC	399	
3.	Bayhart, Joseph	PFC	25		35.	McCullough. Geo.	GM	145	
4.	Beasley, John	Sgt.	119		36.	McDaniel, Alvue	Fld Ck	199	
5.	Bordwell, James	SM1	53	N	37.	Meyers, Delmar	PFC	489	
6.	Bryan, Alton	GN 3	152	N	38.	Miller, Arthur	Pvt.	463	
7.	Bryant, Harold	S/Sgt.	94	A	39.	Moore, Delbert	Sgt.	79	
8.	Byers, Lloyd	Sgt.	120		40.	Mashalick, Peter	Sgt.	124	
9.	Canfield, Edward	S/Sgt.	113	A	41.	Murphy, John	Cpl	193	A
10.	Christianson, H.	Sgt.	75		42.	Neece, Harry	PFC	404	
11.	Crane, Stanley	M/Sgt.	4		43.	Newnan, Junior	Cpl.	291	A
12.	Crowe, Malcolm	Sgt.	102	A	44.	North, Sylvestor	TM	156	N
13.	Curtis, William	Pvt.	435		45.	Parrish, Albert	BM1	48	
14.	DeVoss, Wilson	SC3	155	N	46.	Pine, Edward	Pvt.	469	
15.	Derryberry, Sam	S/Sgt.	69	A	47.	Richeson, Walter	Pvt.	472	
16.	Dilman, Frank	Cpl.	214		48.	Robertson, Sam	Pvt.	474	
17.	Enbry, Shelby	Sgt.	103		49.	Romero, Sam	PFC	229	A
18.	Felty, George	CO1	175	N	50.	Rossotto, James	Cpl.	209	A
19.	Gartman, Curtis	AMM2	136	N	51.	Ruitledge, Robert	Sgt.	65	A
20.	Garza, Frederick	TM3	156	N	52.	Sauers, Virgil	BM1	59	N
21.	Golsan, Arthur M.	S/Sgt	67	A	53.	Schlatter, Widfred	Sgt.	112	A
22.	Goudge, Alfred I.	GM3	157	N	54.	Sheats, Robert	BM1	51	N
23.	Hoggard, Prichard	CWT	146	N	55.	Slabinski, Anthony	Cpl.	282	
24.	Harrel, Claude	S/Sgt.	165	A	56.	Slownick, John	Sgt.	86	A
25.	Haynie, Boyd B.	PFC	259		57.	Sotak, George	Sgt.	86	A
26.	Haynie, Hoyt B.	PFC	262		58.	Stoddard, John	CPL	211	A
27.	Hietanen, Weiro P.	PFC	447		59.	Strahl, John	CY	9	N
28.	Howell, Pat	Sgt.	106		60.	Stubblefield, L.	Sgt.	88	A
29.	Hutchinson, W.	Sgt.	122	A	61.	Urban, Tony	Sgt.	90	A
30.	Jensen, Gordon	S/Sgt.	69	A	62.	Vanish, George	Sgt.	91	A
31.	Kunich, John	M/Sgt.	6	A	63.	Winters, Clyde	Sgt.	92	A
32.	Little, C.H.	Pvt.	276						

Section 4 C—60

1.	Aldred, John	PFC	372		32.	Ray, John	Fld. Ck.	219	M
2.	Anderson, Lloyd	Fld. Ck.	212	M	33.	Ross, Edward	Pvt.	235	
3.	Bain, Charles	Pvt.	320		34.	Saddler, Campbell	Pvt.	471	475
4.	Baldwin, Richard	PFC	375		35.	Schmidt, Carlos A.	Pvt.	286	
5.	Brown, James	Pvt.	325		36.	Schodley, Albert	Pvt.	249	
6.	Carr, Leslie	Pvt.	307		37.	Schoonover, Kenneth	Cpl.	210	
7.	Clemmer, George	PFC	379		38.	Schuette, Walter	Pvt.	339	
8.	Clifton, William	Pvt.	432		39.	Sequin, Clarence	PFC	409	
9.	Demers, Raymond	PFC	383		40.	Sherwood, Virgil	Pvt.	250	A
10.	Farmer, James	Pvt.	310		41.	Sills, R.B.	Pvt.	343	
11.	Ferratti, David	PFC	224		42	Silvertein, Louis	Cpl.	196	A
12.	Flowers, James A	Pvt.	311		43.	Stanley, Henry G.	Pvt.	291	
13.	Forsythe, Don	PFC	265		44.	Stefanski, Walter	Pvt.	347	
14.	Foster, Malcolm	PFC	384		45.	Stewart, Charles	Pvt.	293	
15.	Galloway, Alfred	Pvt.	241	A	46.	St. John, Walter	PFC	480	
16.	Goodman, Phillip	PFC	267		47.	Suskie, John	Pvt.	295	
17.	Gorman, Martin	CM1	54	N	48.	Taylor, Ernest	Pvt.	352	
18.	Griffin, Thomas	PFC	268		49.	Tucker, Francis	Pvt.	356	
19.	Hester, Wynton	Pvt.	243		50.	Trones, Arthur	Pvt.	297270	
21.	Howard, Walter	S/Sgt.	68		52.	Vandel, David	PEC	231	
22.	Hughes, Archie	PFC	392		53.	Vigil, Antonio	Pvt.	299	
23.	Irvin, Chesley	Pvt.	246		54.	Wallace, Lewis	Pvt.	364	
24.	Kelley, Gail	Pvt.	272		55.	Warnick, Jack	Pvt.	253	
25.	Knight, James	Pvt.	273		56.	Wilcoxson, Elmer	PFC	233	
26.	Krinoch, Joseph	Pvt.	274		57.	Willis, G.E.	Pvt.	302	
27.	Larkin, Russell	Pvt.	245		58.	Wilkeson, Edward	PFC	319	
28.	Maurino, Tony	Pvt.	246		59.	Williamson, Chas.	Pvt.	258	
29.	McDill, Thomas	PFC	401		60.	Willis, Alex.	Pvt.	368	
30.	O'Meara, Albert	Pvt.	370						
31.	Morris, Lee M.	Pvt.	332						

Section 4 D—59

1.	Boyd, Jack*	S/Sgt.	64	A
2.	Bolt, Charles	Pvt.	304	
3.	Bowers, Elmer E.	PFC	377	
4.	Brundage, Jack	Pvt.	427	
5.	Box, Claude	Pvt.	306	
6.	Carle, John	Sgt.	101	
7.	Charles, Thomas	Pvt.	238	
8.	Cole, Brownell	PFC	380	
9.	Davis, Kenneth	S/Sgt.	95	
10.	Drake, James	Pvt.	309	
11.	Fennel, Bernard	Pvt.	439	
12.	Ford, Norman	Pvt.	481	
13.	Gentry, Adrian	PFC	386	
14.	Higdon, Patrick	PFC	391	
15.	Hilton, Gordon	PFC	313	
16.	Hobert, Lyle	Pvt.	393	
17.	Jacques, Ralph	Cpl.	176	
18.	Jeffre, Andre	PFC	394	
19.	Johnston, Robert	S1	494	N
20.	Jones, Jack	Pvt.	451	
21.	Jones, John	Pvt.	450	
22.	Lewis, Robert	PFC	397	
23.	Lowhead, Roger	Pvt.	330	
24.	Lopez. A.	Pvt.	459	
25.	Martin, Wiley	Pvt.	461	
26.	Martinez, Ralph	Pvt.	278	
27.	McFarley, Albert	PFC	400	
28.	Mines. Roger	Pvt.	3931	
29.	Mohr, Arthur	Cpl.	177	A
30.	Mooney, Perry	Sgt.	78	A
31.	O'Conner, Raymond	PFC	314	
32.	Overly, George	Pvt.	280	
33.	Padget, John	Pvt.	282	
34.	Paras, Theodore	Pvt.	335	
35.	Patterson, Chas.	Cpl.	217	
36.	Pearson, Sedric	PVT	283	
37.	Prehm, Ernest	Pvt.	336	
38.	Prewitt, Granville*	PFC	316	
38.	Samson, Walter	Pvt.	338	
40.	Seargeant, Edward	Pvt.	287	
41.	Sharp, Jason	Pvt.	342	
42.	Shaw, Carl	PFC	410	
43.	Schott, Edward	PFC	317	
44.	Sisneros, Angelo	PFC	411	
45.	Smith, G.W. *	Pvt.	345	
46.	Snellen, John	Cpl.	183	A
47.	Spencer, John C.	Pvt.	346	
48.	Strictland, Lacy	Pvt.	350	
49.	Thornberry, R.	Pvt.	351	
50.	Torres, Miguel	Pvt.	296	
51.	Van Almen, Wm.	Pvt.	360	
52.	Vaughn, Jimmy	Pvt.	362	
53.	Vidaurri, Manuel	Pvt.	298	
54.	Watkins, Fred	Pvt.	365	
55.	Webber, Clarence	Pvt.	366	
56.	Wheeler, Wm.	PFC	415	
57.	Wichard, Lafayette	Pvt.	367	
58.	Witham, James	PFC	416	
59.	Young, George	Pvt.	369	

Section 4 E—31

1.	Bain, Francis	PFC	373	
2.	Barnes, Gordon	Pvt.	321	
3.	Ballow, John	PFC	375	
4.	Bean, Roy	PFC	376	
5.	Brools, Seymour	PFC	378	
6.	Brown, Mavis	PFC	222	A
7.	Browder, Leonard	Pvt.	324	
8.	Cook, Alfred	PFC	260	
9.	Coleman, Gorff	PFC	381	
10.	Dugan, J.J.	Pvt.	477	
11.	Davis, Thomas	Sgt.	121	A
12.	Diaz, Pablo	Pvt.	308	
13.	Fish, Jack	PFC	485	
14.	Fontana, Francis	Cpl.	205	A
15.	Karr, Austin	Cpl.	191	A
16.	Kimball, Raymond	Pvt.	328	
17.	Lee, Walter	PFC	226	
18.	Lehner, James	PFC	239	
19.	Leyba, Max	Sgt.	107	
20.	McTigue, James	PFC	402	
21.	Meador, Lloyd	Pvt.	371	
22.	Mooney, Perry C.	Pvt.	78	
23.	Purcell, William	Pvt.	337	
24.	Ring, Gay	PFC	407	
25.	Spencer, Aldon	Pvt.	290	
26.	Stengler, Albert	Pvt.	348	
27.	Stoudt, Dan	Pvt.	294	
28.	Taves, Harold	PFC	412	
29.	Watson, Richard	PFC	492	
30.	White, Wilton,	Pvt.	301	
31.	Zack, Barney	Pvt.	303	

Section 4 F—36

1.	Adair, Don	Pvt.	420		19.	Howard, John	Sgt.	10	
2.	Avery, Harrison	Pvt.	422		20.	Jensen, Francis	PFC	486	
3.	Barker, Matthew	Pvt.	423		21.	Keesly, Robert A.	Pvt.	452	
4.	Best, John	Pvt.	483		22.	Kimball, David	Pvt.	453	
5.	Bustamente, Nestor	Pvt.	420		23.	Kirby, Jack	QM 2	161	N
6.	Casey, Leo	FM1	494	N	24.	Knowles, Jasper	Pvt.	456	
7.	Calvit, Kenneth	Pvt.	431		25.	Muenich, John	RM1	147	N
8.	Crown, John	Pvt.	433		26.	Lambo, Jerry	Pvt.	275	
9.	Darnell, Dilliard	MM1	136	N	27.	LeBeau, Alfred	T/Sgt.	30	
10.	Dehr, Bert	Pvt.	436		28.	Olson, Noel	Pvt.	465	
11.	Dickson, Asolp D.	Pvt.	437		29.	Pelayo, Leo	Sgt.	83	A
12.	Emerick, John	Pvt.	438		30.	Phillips, Henry	Pvt.	468	
13.	Emanuel, James	S/Sgt.	130	A	31.	Sanders, Harry	S/Sgt.	70	
14.	Faulkner, James	PFC	484		32.	Sanford, Paul	Pvt.	476	
15.	Fisher, Howard	COX	143	N	33.	Saefke, J.J.	PFC	490	
16.	Garcia, Ben	Pvt.	440		34.	Thurston, Gene	PFC	413	
17.	Haywood, John	Pvt.	445		35.	Valden, William	Plt. Sgt.	164	
18.	Heinz, Leon	Pvt.	446		36.	Yohn, Leonard	PFC	418	

Section 4 G—25

1.	Abramowicz, John	S/Sgt.	62	A	14.	Mroz, Stanley	TM3	151	
2.	Atterburn, Wm.	Pvt.	421		15.	Pennington, Wayne	PFC	406	
3.	Bartley, Milledge	Pvt.	424		16.	Peltier, Desire	Pvt.	467	
4.	Kindle, Julius	Pvt.	488	M	17.	Quintana, Patrick	Pvt.	284	
5.	Kirhgesner, Peter	FM2	495	N	18.	Reed, Vernon	Cpl.	195	
6.	Lambasio, Jenro	SM1	500		19.	Reisher, George	Pvt.	471	
7.	Lemarski, John E.	Pvt.	329		20.	Soltenberger, Don	Cpl.	184	A
8.	Litch, Thomas	Sgt.	76		21.	Summons, David	Sgt.	110	
9.	Lopez, A.A.	Pvt.	454		22.	Tolendo, Mitch	Sgt.	89	A
10.	Margiotto, Frank	Y1	43	N	23.	Tripp, Phillip	Pvt.	340	
11.	Marangiella, Tony	PFC	398		23.	Vondette, Robert	S1	497	
12.	Matthews, Thomas	Sgt.	77		25.	White, Edward	T/Sgt.	61	A
13.	Merritt, Joe	Pvt.	462						

Work Group Undetermined

1.	Frazier, Clifton L.	PFC	385	Hospital
2.	Henry, J.H.	PFC	390	
3.	Jones, Arthur W.	PFC	487	M
4.	Montgomery, R.	RM	46	
5.	Moravee E.	Sgt.	80	Sick in hospital
6.	Newman, J.H.	Cpl.	201	
7.	Ratliffe, O.R.	PFC	478	M
8.	Stone, K.	Pvt.	349	
9.	Wood, C.C.	Pvt.	254	
10.	Ring, Robert V.	Pvt.	473	Died, Hanawa, 10 November, 1944
11.	Smith, Gilmore W.	Pvt.	345	Died, Hanawa, 9 December, 1944
12.	Underwood, Ray C.	Pvt.	358	Died, Hanawa, 3A, 5 February, 1945
13.	Werner, Joseph	F/Pvt.	493	Died, Hanawa, Accident, March, 1945
14.	Haviland, Wm.	Pvt.	242	Died, Hanawa, 4B, 31 May, 1945
15.	Knowles, Jasper	Pvt.	456	Died, Hanawa, 4F, 8 July, 1945
16.	Martin, Adrian	F/Sgt.	31	Died, Hanawa, 3A, 8 June, 1945
17.	Miller, Paul		403	Died, Hanawa, 24 October, 1944
18.	Spotte, I.C.	Capt.	503	USA, Arrived March, 1945

British Army personnel in Camp No 6, Hanawa at time of liberation.

Thompson, R.H.	Lt.	Aust, Jones, C.		Crabes, D.		Salmon, D.	
Appleyard, J.	Brit.	Lawson, T.	SC	Crapper, A		Schoales, C.	Eire
Armstrong, J.	Brit.	Legge, B.		Eagle, Robert	Brit. Capt.	Shenton, H.	SC
Barker, F.	Brit.	McLachland, F.		Deakins, S.		Stoker, B.	
Bates, J.		McVey, T.	SC	Evitts, J.		Thomas, V.	
Begg, E.		Mills, E.	SC	Freeman, F.		Tuton, C.	
Bell, R.		O'Rourke, C.	SC	Fergus, A.	SC	Wedge, A.	
Bicket, G.		Reid, W.	SC	Farren, J	SC	Willoughy, W.C.	Brit
Brown, E.		Reid. W.	SA	Gibson, J.	SC.	Wilson, J.	SC
Campbell, A.	SC	Rudkin, F.		Gibson, W.		Woolford, G.	
Campbell, J.		Richards, H.		Grantham, G		Worboys, R.	
Cleary, F.	SC	Roberts, H.		Harvie, C.		Henderson, J.	SC
Cook, J.	SC	Russell, C.	SC	Hubbold, E.	Iliffe, E		

SC—Scotland, Aust.—Australian, SA—South Africa, Eire,—Ireland

These prisoners arrived in Hanawa in the spring of 1945 from other camps in the heart of Japan, which were in emminemt danger from the extensive bombing by B-29's.

List of Illustrations, Sketches & Maps

Map of Philippine Islands, 1935 xi
Map of Fort Santiago, Intramuros (Walled City) xii
Legend for Fort Santiago Map xiii
Map of Manila, 1935 xiv
Map of Philippines and Surrounding Area xvi
USAT Republic, USAT Grant and USAT Meigs... xviii
USAT Grant Departing Manila, P.I. xix
Mount Mayan Volcano xx
Terraced Rice Paddies North of Baguio xx
Volcano Crater................................ xxi
Guadalupe Ruins xxi
Mountain Tribes Barrio (Village) xxii
Rice Paddies in the Mountains of Luzon xxii
Fort Santiago, Main Gate, Walled City xxiii
Plaque at Fort Santiago xxiii
Bamboo Organ at Las Pinas xxiv
A Native Hut of the Mountainous Tribes xxiv
Rural Scene xxv
Escolta Shopping Center xxv
Caraamato Near San Augustin Church xxv
Spanish Sentry Tower xxv
Tropical Sunset, Manila, P.I. xxv
Entry Port, Walled City xxv
Dewey Boulevard xxvi
American YMCA in Intramuros xxvi
Army-Navy Club on Manila Bay xxvii
Inter-Island Boats, Manila, P.I. xxvii
0-46 Douglas Observation Aircraft xxviii
Pan American Clipper xxviii
Army Depot Port Area xxix
Aerial View of Fort Santiago xxix
Bureau of Posts, Manila, P.I. xxx
Manila Hotel xxx
Tagaytay Ridge and Lake Taal 1
Map of Bataan 3
Map of Corregidor Island 4
USS Canopus, with Submarines in Manila Bay 5
4th Marine Regiment moving into field............ 5
31st Infantry, the Polar Bears 5
Map of Malinta Hill Tunnel 6
USAT Republic under Golden Gate Bridge 7
Aerial View of Corregidor...................... 7
Small Boats Docked at Corregidor............... 8
Philippine Rail Car, Electric Trolley 8
Lt. Col. John N. Shanks 10
Finance Lateral, Malinta Tunnel 12

Battery Crocket, 12-inch Disappearing Gun 14
Battery Way, 12-inch Mortar 14
Typical Squad Room 15
5th CAC Regiment 15
Anti-aircraft Sound Detector 15
Anti-aircraft Guns 15
Fort Drum Gun Deck 16
Fort Drum in Action........................... 17
Troops Training 18
Six-inch Disappearing Guns 18
Coastal Defense Guns 18
Lt. General Homma, Commander................. 20
Malinta Tunnel Men Meet their Captors........... 24
Battery Way, Fort Mills, Corregidor.............. 25
Station Hospital, Fort Mills 27
Special Orders #23, Hdqtrs., Philippine Dept....... 36
Battery Geary, 12-inch Mortar Barrel 56
Mile-long Army Barracks 59
Battery Hearn, Fort Mills, P.I. 62
Antique Spanish Cannon 63
How Old Are You? 65
Boy—Am I Tired! 65
Prison Camp 71
Filipino Humor 74, 75
Transportation 76
Yo-ho Pole 76
Common Sights in Manila 76
Crowded Streetcars 77
Bilibid Prison, Main Gate 78
Central Guard Tower 78
Aerial View of Bilibid Prison.................... 78
Example of Administration in Bilibid Prison........ 81
Thatched Roof Chapel 87
Camp Layout, Hanawa, Japan 105
E. Pearce Fleming, Col. Ret. 112
Dr. Dan Golenturnik 113
End of War Statement 124
Liberty Pass at War's End 125
Liberation Day, Hanawa, Japan 127
Tables Turned at Prison Camp................ 129
General MacArthur 145
Nittsu Maru 147
Submarine Dispersion Maps.................. 157
Sketches by Col. M.C. Eugene Jacobs, Ret....... 160
Aerial View of Oryoku Maru 162
Enoura Maru Death Trap..................... 165

Index

A

Aihara, Kasutano Lance Corp. (Air Raid) 159, 167
Aihara, Kazutatane 167
Ames, Godfrey R. Capt. 13
Artman, Ralph Maj. 99
Asaka, Lt. 110, 111, 113, 114, 119, 121, 122, 123, 125, 128, 150
Ashton, Paul Dr. 82

B

Barrett 163
Becraft, LeRoy 32
Beecher, Lt. Col. 159, 163
Bell, Don xvii
Bernstien, Max Capt. 99
Birneson, Emily 87
Blouse, Max 82
Boudreau, Napolean 16
Bower, Howard 113
Brackman, Arnold C. 150, 152, 154, 155
Braly, William C. Col. 22, 54, 56, 58, 85
Breuer, William B. 140
Bridgett, Cmdr. 164
Brown, Charles M. Lt. Col. 170
Bunker, Paul Col. 25,51
Burns, Clayton C. Tech. Sgt. 177
Buster, Ivan M/Sgt. 111, 113, 119
Buttner, Richard (Lorin) 58, 64, 67, 68, 70

C

Canfield, Leslie 113
Charles, H. Robert 153
Churchill, Winston Sir 58
Cooper, Robert G. Capt. 35
Coughlin, John J. Capt. 35, 54, 58, 61, 62, 69, 75, 85
Cunningham, Burl 113

D

Danjo, Sup. Pvt. 44, 61, 63, 64, 68
Davis, Chester (Jack) 58, 64, 67
Dewey, Admiral xv, 53, 137, 141
Dobervich, Mike Lt. 19, 79
Dunlop, Kenneth 58, 63, 67
Dunlop, E.E. 153

F

Fetter, A.B. 79
Filiman, Franklin M. Col. 152
Flanagan, E.M. Lt. Gen. 54, 55, 69
Fleming, E. Pearce Capt. 95, 99, 104, 109, 110, 111, 112, 113, 119, 121, 122, 123, 127, 128, 133, 135, 150, 176
Francies, Richard 113, 114

G

Goldsmith, Leonard E. Lt. 40, 43, 47, 48
Golenturnik, Dan Dr. Capt. 82, 95, 97, 99, 113, 118, 121, 122
Golson, Archie S/Sgt. 10, 30, 40, 51, 55, 58, 68, 74, 80, 83, 96, 101, 103, 105, 110, 111, 113, 117, 134, 138, 140, 143, 145
Gridley, Mr. 141

H

Haddox, Ernest S. Cpl. 10, 30, 40, 43, 44, 45, 50, 52, 55, 58, 67, 70, 74, 83, 94, 96, 101, 103, 110, 111, 113, 120, 134, 135, 138, 139, 140, 142, 143, 145, 175
Harrison, G.G. Cmdr. 80, 86
Hattori, Sho Sgt. of the Guard 159
Haucks, Herman Capt. 16, 35
Hayes, Thomas Cmdr. 75, 77, 82, 159, 171
Hewlett, Thomas H. Dr. Capt. 35, 39, 40, 46, 53, 81
Hill, Lloyd J. PFC 112
Hill, Lloyd Cpl. 177
Hilton, Charles M. Cpl. 10, 12, 13, 30
Hoback, John 113
Holland, J.C. 178
Homma, Gen. 20, 156
Hope, Bob 175

I

Ingle, Donald F. 151

J

Jackson, Calvin Dr. Maj. 95, 99, 104, 110, 112, 113
Jacobs, Eugene C. Col. 167, 170, 171
Johnson, Howard K. Lt. Col. 167

K

Kajiyama, Shinn Capt. 162, 163, 165, 166, 167
Karnow, Stanley xvi
Kerr, E. Barlett Maj. 170, 171
Kimura, Heitaro 153
Kinder, Burl B. (Blacky) 48, 49, 58
King, Gen. 79
Kingman, John M. Lt. 17
Kipling, Rudyard 23
Kirkpatrick, Lewis M. Col. 17
Kirkpatrick, Lewis S. Lt. Col. 25, 34, 40, 53, 56,
Kisi, Pvt. 64, 68, 69
Kunich, John M/Sgt. 32, 35, 40, 42, 43, 44, 45, 55, 58, 63, 67, 68, 74, 75, 83, 93, 96, 101, 103, 110, 111, 113, 134, 138

L

Lamy, John Dr. Lt. 95, 99, 110, 112, 113, 118
Larson, Leonard O. S/Sgt. 111
Larson, Edward J. (Swede) Sgt. 10, 13, 14, 19, 23, 37, 79
Lathrop, Robert Maj. 54, 55
Lawton, Manny Lt. Col. 170
LeBrin, Cecil C. Lt. 166
Lee, Robert E. Gen. 33
Lopez, Pedro 151
Lyman, John Lt. 104

M

MacArthur, Douglas Lt. Gen. xvii, xix, 11, 42, 66, 121, 137, 138, 141, 142, 170
Maeda, Maj. 151
Martin, Adrian F/Sgt. 94, 96, 113, 119, 122, 133, 136, 176
Martin, Adrian (nephew) 36, 81, 135
Massello, William (Wild Bill) Capt. 20, 22, 25

McGee, Sam 118
McGrew, Al C. 21
McIntyre, John Sgt. 166
Meese, Bill 82
Mekeel, Mary Lt. 176
Montgomery, Austin J. Lt. Col. 151
Moody, Samuel B. S/Sgt. 151
Moore, Thomas H. Maj. Gen. 25
Morris, Eric 20

N

Napoleon, Lt. Col. 47
Nell, Edward N. Capt. 155
Nicely, Floyd 47
Nicholson, Chester 113, 114
Nix, Asbury L. S/Sgt. 36, 58, 81
Norquist, Ernest 99

O

Olferioff, Sergio 58, 61, 62, 64, 67, 68

P

Parker, Ted Capt. 162
Perkins, Peter Lt. 93, 95
Petersen, Lester J. Lt. 19, 79
Piburn, Frank 113
Piland, James 58, 67
Portz, Warner Cmdr. 159
Protz, Sgt. 110
Provoo, John David 40, 41, 135
Pullen, Richard Lt. 95, 104, 110, 122, 123

Q

Quezon, Manual 11

R

Reich, Cmdr. 169
Reira, R.E. Cmdr. 162
Reynolds, Ralph S/Sgt. 10
Richards, C.B.B. Dr. 153
Ridgely, Adjutant, Maj. 163
Robbins, Pasha Capt. 9
Roosevelt, Franklin D. 12, 65
Roscoe, Theodore 158, 184, 167
Rose, Robert (Bob) (Snuffy) 48, 58, 61, 66, 67, 68, 70
Rose, Frank 48, 58, 61, 67

S

Sagai, Sgt. 111, 128
Samson, Charles Capt. 95, 99, 103
Sayre, Mr. 11
Schuster, Rudolph 113, 114
Schwab, Lester 58, 63, 64, 65, 66, 67
Schwartz, Jack Col. 162, 163
Scott, Francis C. Capt. 151
Sense, George B. Lt. 35, 86, 95, 96
Service, Robert 118
Shanks, John N. Maj. 10, 12, 14, 22, 32, 96, 167
Sheats, R.D. B.M. 1st/Cl 80
Sievwright, Hazel E. Lt. 176
Southerland, Maj. Gen. 42
Standridge, William (Stan) Sgt. 10, 12, 13, 30
Star, Warren Capt. 13
Stickney, Henry Col. 54
Stubbs, Guy H. Col. 152
Summers, R.E. Capt. 168

T

Takahashi, Sgt. 128
Tanaka 114, 115, 116, 118
Tanoue, Sukeyosa Sgt. Maj. 159
Thomas, Lewis M.D. 170
Tojo, Hedeki 153, 156
Tokashige, Lt. 40, 43, 44, 55, 57, 61, 62, 64, 66, 67, 68
Tolstoy 151
Toshino, Junsaburo Lt. 156, 158, 159, 161, 162, 163, 165, 166, 167, 170

U

Ueda, Jiro Pvt. 159

W

Wada, Shunusuki 156, 159, 161, 165, 166, 167, 170
Wainwright, Jonathan M. Gen. xix, 19, 23, 33, 49, 85
Waldron, Ben D. 87
Walker, Arthur J. Lt. Col. 119, 123, 127, 128
Watanabe, Mr. 114
Webb 163
White, Petty Officer 42
White, Elmer (Ed) J. SF/2nd 16, 49, 50, 52, 58, 80, 175
White, Walter Lee 175
Wiedlich, Charles 48, 58
Wozniak, Larry C. S/Sgt. 56
Wright, John M. Jr. Lt. Gen. 22, 25, 35, 40, 50, 51, 52, 53, 55, 159, 165, 166, 167, 170, 171

Y

Yamashita, Gen. 55, 156
Yodo, (Cyclops) S. Pvt. 112, 113, 114

Bibliography

References: Books, Publications, Pamphlets and Magazines

America's Empire in the Philippines, Stanley Karnow; Random House, Inc.

Apocalypse Undone, Preston John Hubbard; Vanderbilt University, Nashville, TN

A Trial of Generals, Homma Yamashita MacArthur; Lawrence Taylor, Icarus Press, South Bend, IN

American Guerrillas in the Philippines, Ira Wolfert; Kingsport Press, Kingsport, TN

At Dawn We Slept, The Untold Story of Pearl Harbor, Gordon C. Prange; Penquin Books

Bataan and Beyond, Texas A. M. University Press, College Sta. TX 77843

Bataan, Our Last Ditch, John W. Whitman; Hippocrene Books, 171 Madison Ave., New York, NY. 10016

Bilibid Diary, The Secret Notebooks of Commander Thomas Hayes, POW Philippines, 1942-45, A.B.Feuer; The Shoe String Press, Hamden, CN

Blood Brothers, Eugene C. Jacobs; Carlton Press, New York, NY

Brothers from Bataan: POWS 1942-1945, Adrian Martin; Sunflower Press, Manhattan, KS

But Not In Shame, Cabanatuan; Shopolsky Press, W. 22nd St. New York, N.Y. 10011 Out of Print.

Chained Eagle, True Story of Eight and A Half Years Imprisonment in Vietnam, Everret Alvarez and Anthony Pitch.

Corregidor, The End Of The Line, Eric Morris; Stein & Day Publishers

Corregidor, From Paradise To Hell, Waldron/Burneson; Pine Hill Press

Corregidor, The Rock Force Assault, E.M. Flanagan; Presidio Press, 31 Panaron Press, Navato, Ca. 94949

Death March, The Survivors Of Bataan, Donald Knox; Harcourt, Brace, Jovanovich Publishers, New York and London

Delayed Manila. Out of Print.

Deliverance At Los Banos, Anthony Arthur; St. Martins Press, New York, NY

Douglas MacArthur, The Far Eastern General, Michael Schaller, Oxford University Press, NY

Eagle Against The Sun, Richard H. Spector; Free Press, Division of MacMillin Inc., 886 Third Ave. New York, NY 10022

Empire Of The Sun, J. G. Ballard; Pocket Books, 1230 Avenue of Americas, New York, NY 10020

Fall of the Philippines, Barrie Pitt; Ballentine Books, Inc., 101 Fifth Ave., New York, NY 10003

General Wainwright's Story, General Jonathan M. Wainwright; Bantam Books

Give Us This Day, Sidney Stewart; W.W. Nortan & Co, Vail—Ballou Press

Guests of The Emperor; Four Freedoms Press, Freedom Press P.O. Box 325, High Ridge, MO 63049

Hardway Home, Col. William C. Braly; Washington Infantry Press, 1115 17Th. St. Wash. DC

Heroes of Bataan, Marcos Griffin, editor and publisher; 1st Edition. Out of Print.

Heroes Of Bataan, Corregidor and Northern Luzon, 2nd edition, Eva Jane Matson; Yucca Tree Press, Carlsbad, NM

Hirohito, The War Years, Paul Manning; Bantam Books, NY

Hodio, Tales of an American POW, Clarence Nixon Day; ICS Books Inc., Merrillville, IL

Honorable Conquerors. Out of Print.

I Saw the Fall of the Philippines, Carlos P. Romulo; Doubleday, Doran & Co.

Last Man Out, H. Robert Charles; Eakin Press, P.O. Box 23069, Austin, TX 78735.

The Life of a POW under the Japanese in Caricature, Malcolm V. Fortier, Colonel, U.S. Army

Long Road Home. Out of Print.

MacArthur, Illustrated History of W.W.II, S. L. Mayer; Ballantine Books

Never Say Die, Jack Hawkins; USAF. Out of Print.

90 Days of Rice. Out of Print.

Nothing But Praise, Henry G. Lee; Murray & Gee, Culver City, CA

Occupation, A Searing Novel of Post War Japan, John Toland; Mandarin Books, P.O. Box 11, Falmouth Cornwall, TR109 England

O'Donnell, Andersonville of the Pacific. Out of Print.

Philippine Expeditionary Force. Out of Print.

Prisoner of War, Collection of Prisoner of War Drawings, Ben Steele; Eastern Montana College, Billings, MN

Retaking The Philippines, Wm. B. Breur; St. Martins Press

Return to Freedom, British, State Mutual Book, 521 Fifth Ave., 17th Floor, New York, NY 10175

Return to Freedom, Col. Sam Grashio, USAF Ret.; printed in OK. Out of Print.

Some Survived, Mannie Lawton; Algonquin Books of Chapel Hill, NC

Soldier Of Bataan, Phil S. Brain, Jr.; Rotary Club of Minneapolis, 625 Second Ave. South #925, Minneapolis, MN 55402

Soldiers Of God, Christopher Crossin, collaboration with Major General Wm R. Arnold; E. P. Dutton & Company, New York, NY (Part Two, *Religion Behind Japanese Barbed Wire*)

Soochow and The Fourth Marines, Wm. R. Evans; Atwood Publishing Co., Rogue River, OR

Surrender and Survival, The Experiences of American P.O.Ws in the Pacific, 1941-1945, E. Bartlett Kerr; Wm. Morrow & Co. Inc.

Survival Amidst the Ashes. Out of Print.

Tell MacArthur to Wait, Ralph R. Hibbs, M.D.; Carlton Press. New York, NY

The Japanese Story; American Ex-Prisoners of War, Packet No.10, Stanley Sommers; MedSearch Chairman, Marshfield, WI

The Naked Flag Pole, Richard C. Mallonee; Presidio Press, P O Box 1535, San Raefel, CA 94902

The Other Nuremberg, The Untold Story of the Tokyo War Crimes Trials, Arnold C. Brackman; Publisher William Morrow, New York, NY. Permissions Department, William Morrow and Company Inc., 105 Madison Ave., New York, NY 10016

United States Submarine Operations in World War II, Theodore Roscoe; U.S. Naval Institute, Annapolis MD

War Diaries of Weary Dunlop, E.E. Dunlop; Nelson Publishers, 480 La Trobe St., Melbourne, Victoria 3000

War Without Mercy, Race and Power in the Pacific, John W. Dower; Partheon Books, New York, NY

We All Returned, Video Tape, Department of Defense, Audio/Visual.

We Remember Bataan and Corregidor, Mairano Villarin; Gateway Press Inc. 1001 N. Calvert St., Baltimore, MD. 21292